D0772590

Socio-Economic Results of Land Reform in Taiwan

Socio-Economic Results of Land Reform in Taiwan

Martin M. C. Yang

楊懋春

East-West Center Press   Honolulu

Books in English by Martin M. C. Yang

A Chinese Village: Taitou, Shantung (New York, 1945)

Socio-Economic Results of Land Reform in Taiwan (Honolulu, 1970)

Other publications in Chinese

PREFACE

In order to have the reader informed from the very beginning of the purposes of making this study, of the objectives it tries to achieve, and of the fact that it will not be simply another routine report on a land reform, I wish to make statements as to why this study was undertaken, why there was a need for land reform in Taiwan, the reasons and objectives of this land reform, and the policies and methods applied in the implementation of this particular land reform.

There have been numerous studies already made on land reform in various countries during the last couple of decades. In the same period of time, a large number of works on relationships between land reform and community development have also been produced. In regard to the land reform in Taiwan, Republic of China, again, there are quite a few treatises written both in Chinese and in foreign languages. Some are books; others are monographs. It is fairly safe to say that people who are interested in knowing the facts and stories of land reform in any of the countries must have already become acquainted with some of the literature on this topic. Or, if one has just started to have such an interest, he can surely find enormous quantities of materials to read.

Then what is the need for this study? Would it not be just another addition to a list which is already too long? To answer this question, or to discharge this worry, this writer is not going to say that he will make a study on this subject better than any of those already in existence. He does feel, however, that most of the reports written about the land reform in Taiwan have the shortcoming of either being superficial and seeing only the outward results, or of overpraising the merits of this land reform. For it seems to me that most of the studies or reports on Taiwan's land reform either include only the reduction of the farm rental rates, the redistribution of the landownership, the assistance to the building up of owner-farmer families, and the eagerness of the small cultivators toward these agrarian changes, or make claim that practically all the social, economic, and political improvements or progresses which took place in Taiwan in the last decade can be directly attributed to the results of the land reform. Within the literature there are, inevitably, materials put out by governmental, or semi-governmental, agencies which appear to contain some degree of overpraise, or some degree of propaganda. Because of such overpraise and propaganda, some of the leaders and statesmen of other countries who have come to see Taiwan's land reform and have read its reports are suspicious of the results of this undertaking. They have raised the question as to how true things are as stated in those reports. To be fair, none of those writings has purportedly been made for undue propaganda purposes. The fact is that the authors of these reports have only been conscious of the successes and the immediate results of the land reform, which can be readily seen, but somehow they failed to mention things unachieved and problems unsolved, and they seemed incapable of observing subtle consequences of the land reform movement.

This writer believes that in talking about the results of any land reform, especially the one so thoroughly undertaken in Taiwan, one's observations should not, and must not, be limited to immediate and obvious accomplishments, such as the practice of 37.5% farm rent limitation, the transfer of landownership from a small number of landlords to a great number of tenant-cultivators, the increase in the number of owner-farmers, and the elimination of the evil practices in the traditional farm tenancy. For it is very likely that the land reform has had more profound and far-reaching effects on the people's daily life and on the nation's economy. In other words, it seems very possible that the completion of this land reform might have caused numerous socio-economic changes in Taiwan. To this writer, it is important to explore these likelihoods and possibilities. On the other hand, the observations should not be gross exaggerations giving credit to the land reform for all kinds of improvements. It cannot be too extravagant to say that inasmuch as the traditional land tenure and the oppressive farm tenancy had been the chief evils accountable for the poverty and stagnation of Taiwan's rural life, and, to a great extent, for the scarcity of the province's whole economy, the reform or elimination of these evils should be the solution to all the relevant problems. Therefore, land reform deserves a claim on every one of the economic progresses seen in Taiwan in the past decade or so.

None of these two observations is acceptable. The first one is too shallow, whereas, the second one is too complementary. After enumerating the immediate accomplishments of land reform and also citing those things which have failed to take place, I would then like to go further to see if the agricultural improvements, if the improvements in the rural people's living conditions, if the raising of cultural levels, and if a number of other socio-economic changes which have occurred in Taiwan since 1954 could have any relationship to the completion of the land reform. In other words, I think it important to determine if land reform in Taiwan has given rise to any significant socio-economic change in that society.

Up to this point, it should be clear that what this writer wants to do is to make a study of Taiwan's land reform which will, on the one hand, probe to see whether or not it has had a deeper effect than the reduction of farm rental rates, the transfer of landownership from landlord to tenant-cultivator, and the increase in number of owner-farmers and, on the other hand, give a fair and objective evaluation of land reform's influence on the solution of various kinds of problems in Taiwan as well as its incompetence in satisfying that nation's other needs. If these aims can somehow be reached successfully, then this study would have to be different from those which are now in existence, and it should be more useful to those countries which now, or in the near future, may be contemplating some kind of land reform. It may also be a legitimate wish that a study made by people of the academic world using scientific methods as much as possible should be able to reduce some of the suspicions people have had previously toward the results of the land reform in Taiwan.

To be more specific, this study intends to find the answers to questions as follows:

1. Was there a real need for land reform in the Province of Taiwan?

2. What have been the stated and unstated reasons for undertaking such a program at such a time?

3. What have been the specific objectives which the Government and the reformers originally intended to achieve through land reform?

4. What were the principles, policies, methods, and tactics employed in the implementation of the three important programs in the land reform?

5. What problems have been solved and what objectives achieved after the land reform was brought to completion?

6. What problems have not been solved and what objectives not achieved through the land reform?

7. What were the most formidable oppositions and difficulties when the land-reform programs were being carried out?

8. To what extent, if any, has the land reform helped to lift up the farm people's morale?

9. Granted that agriculture in Taiwan has made significant progress in the past ten or fifteen years, what are, if any, the relationships between this progress and the land reform?

10. Granted that important changes have been made in living conditions in recent years, both in general and in particular, what are, if any, the relationships between these changes and the land reform?

11. Granted that there has been manifest advancement in the farm people's cultural levels, what are, if any, the relationships between such advancement and the land reform?

12. Granted that there have been obvious changes in the rural people's community participation, in what ways can these changes be attributed to the completion of the land reform?

13. What are the land-reform program's effects, if any, on Taiwan's agricultural economy?

14. Have the results of the land reform created new problems for the rural people and for the nation's economy which the reformers had not originally seen or anticipated?

It is obvious that every one of these questions has significance in relation to the true meaning and importance of the land reform to the farm people's well-being as well as to the whole nation's development. Only the factual answers to these questions can lead people to make a sound evaluation of the successes and failures of Taiwan's land reform and can give reasonable and practical advice to those who wish to undertake a similar program.

It is advisable to classify the fourteen questions into two groups. Questions numbers 1 to 7, inclusive, form the first group, while the other seven questions make up the second group. It shall be so arranged that answers to the first four questions are given in Chapter One, and answers to the other three questions in the first group in Chapter Two, where a review of the content of the three important land-reform programs and the experience of their implementation shall be discussed. Answers to the questions in the second group will be the core of this study and, therefore, they shall constitute the main body of this treatise. Each of these seven questions shall be the title of a particular chapter. Information and materials which make up the answers to the first group of questions are available in official documents, in the various land laws and laws concerning the land reform, and in literature written about policies, principles, and methods for dealing with the land-tenure and farm-tenancy problems in various periods of the past. Information and materials necessary to answer the questions in the second group were completely lacking. Therefore, they had to be collected by the researchers themselves. If the reader wishes to know in what ways and by what methods such materials and information have been searched and collected, Chapter Three will be devoted to a statement of methods employed to collect and analyze the necessary lacking information and materials.

August, 1967

CONTENTS

Preface   v

1. Introduction   3

      I.   Need for Land Reform 3
      II. Reasons for Land Reform 11
      III. Objectives of Land Reform 17
      IV. Policies and Methods in Land Reform 21

2. Land Reform Programs   38

      I.   The Three Programs 38
      II. Implementation of the Three Programs 49
      III. Objectives Achieved 81

3. Plan of Study   86

      I.   Scope 86
      II. Methods 92

4. Land Reform and Morale   132

      I.   Emotional Response: A Precondition
            toward Acceptance 133
      II.   Former Tenant-Farmers 136
      III. Present Tenant-Farmers 143
      IV.   Original Owner-Farmers 146
      V.   Farm Laborers 151
      VI.   Landlords 154
      VII. Non-farm People 159
      VIII. Conclusion 163

5. Land Reform and Agricultural Improvement   168

      I.   Recent Agricultural Improvements in Taiwan 169
      II. Agricultural Progress Made by the Former-tenant
           Farm Households 196
      III. Agricultural Improvements by Other Farm Households 211
      IV. Non-farm People's Observations 223
      V.   Conclusion 225

6. Change of Occupation of the Landlords   230

    I.   The Government's Way of Inducing the Landlords
       to Change Occupation 230
    II. The Landlords' Own Efforts toward
       Change of Occupation 239
    III. Difficulties in Change of Occupation 245
    IV. Other Observations 249
    V.   Conclusion 256

7. Land Reform and Farm Living Conditions (Part I)   261

    I.   Changes Over-all 262
    II. Changes in Specific Areas 276

8. Land Reform and Farm Living Conditions (Part II)   313

    III. Relationship between Land Reform
       and Changed Farm Conditions 336
    IV. Conclusion 350

9. Community Participation After Land Reform   351

    I.   Community Participation as Viewed
       by Farm People 353
    II. Education as a Precondition
       for Positive Community Participation 370
    III. Educational and Social Activities 388
    IV. Participation in Farmers' Associations 406
    V.   Land Reform and Community Participation 411

10. Social Structure and Social Relations After Land Reform   419

    I.   Traditional Social Structure 420
    II. Changes in Social Structure 445

11. Changes in Power Structure and Leadership
    in Rural Communities   472

    I.   Traditional Power Structure 473
    II. Traditional Community Leadership 476
    III. Changes in Power Structure 480

12. Land Reform and Modernization of Rural Life   507

    I.   A Recapitulation 507
    II. Modernization 510
    III. Dynamics of Modernization 515
    IV. Characteristics of the New Farmers 521
    V.   Other Factors for Modernization 528
    VI. Modernization of Agriculture 533

    Bibliography   551

Socio-Economic Results of Land Reform in Taiwan

Chapter One

INTRODUCTION

I. Need for Land Reform

II. Reasons for Land Reform

III. Objectives of Land Reform

IV. Policies and Methods in Land Reform

I. Need for Land Reform

Although China as a whole had never been a country of universal
landlordism and predominant tenancy, it was nevertheless a fact that
in many parts or regions of the Chinese mainland rights in land tenure
had at one time or another gone from bad to worse; that ownership of
considerable amounts of good farm land was concentrated in the hands
of a small number of big, medium, and minor landlords; and that large
numbers of the people who actually cultivated the land had not owned
it. In these parts of China there grew up a thoroughly undesirable
farm-tenancy system. Under this system great masses of farm tenants
remained always poor, and average rates of farm rent had been as high
as 50 per cent, or even more.[1] Most of the landlords, especially those
who lived far away from the countryside, that is, the absentee landlords,

led a life of extravagance and wasting, whereas the great numbers of tenant-cultivators had to toil extremely hard day and night, yet make at best a subsistence living. With such a land tenure of this kind of farm tenancy, the inevitable outcome was a society consisting of a small, extravagant ruling class and great masses of poor, ignorant, exhausted and apathetic peasants. The cultural level of such peasants was low but their temper could be easily aroused and exploded into agrarian uprising. Methods in agriculture in such districts were as a whole backward, and, therefore, the farm production was generally meager in relation to the land's potential productivity. The national economy, basing itself on such an agricultural foundation, could only be poor and stagnant. Of such nature were the old social and economic conditions in many rural districts of China. These conditions had simply been taken for granted by both landlords and peasants. Statesmen and civic leaders did no serious or comprehensive complaining about them.

This attitude of indifference was, however, no longer the role among the new generations when the present century started. People of the new ages were informed of the forward steps being made in every aspect of life in the advanced countries. They acquired the conviction that Chinese farmers too must have the opportunity of improving themselves, their children, and their means of livelihood before they could achieve a decent living and become a productive farm population. As a first step toward improving their economic conditions, the farmers must have modern and progressive methods of agriculture. A modern and progressive agriculture can be developed only under a sound system of land tenure, and this means farmers who own their farms and have a high morale. To achieve these conditions land-reform programs were essential and urgent. The rates of farm rent must be first among readjustments, so that the tenant-farmers should have fair shares in the things they produced, and by thus having a sense of social and economic justice being restored to them, their morale should be raised. When, and only when, these things happened would the agriculture be improved and economic conditions bettered. Next, the land-tenure system must be corrected so that the people who actually cultivate the land may own it. In the holding or not holding of landownership lie the differences between a decent, creative, self-respecting farm population and a peasantry plagued by economic and cultural poverty.

It was under the pressure of these considerations and convictions that various kinds of land-reform programs had in recent decades been formulated, experimented, and to a limited extent put into practice in a number of localities on the mainland of China. But owing to the strong opposition of the feudalistic tradition and to the disturbances created by the Chinese communists, none of the efforts had met with any degree of success.

In the Province of Taiwan the history of land tenure had been as bad as any, and the farm rental rates were almost uniformly higher than those prevailing in its counterparts on the Chinese mainland. The system in Taiwan had come about over more than three centuries of historical development. In the Dutch administration (1624-1661) all fields reclaimed[2] and cultivated were known as "Crown Lands" and might not be privately owned. All cultivators of Crown Lands were tenants of the Government and had to pay heavy annual tribute, including farm rent, taxes, and interest on Dutch investments. During the 30-odd years of Dutch rule, ownership of all land was vested in the hands of the rulers, and the position of the cultivators was somewhat similar to that of serfs. This period saw the rise of the reclamation-tenacy system based on exploitation.

Cheng Cheng-kung, a general loyal to the disintegrating Ming Dynasty, who is better known to Westerners as Koxinga, began his 22-year administration of Taiwan by driving out the Dutch in 1661. In dealing with the land problem, Cheng adopted the ancient Chinese practice of military colonization. He divided tilled and reclaimable lands into three kinds. The first was known as "government land." Its cultivator bore the title of "government tenant." Government tenants were obliged to pay the same amount of rent and taxes as they had done under the previous regime. Then there was the category called "officer's land," reclaimed and cultivated by tenants under contractual obligations but belonging to members of the Imperial household, civil and military officers, or influential individuals. The tenant-cultivators of "officer's land " paid rent to lessors who, in turn, paid taxes to the Government. Lastly, there was the "barracks land," allotted to soldiers for reclamation and cultivation.

When the Government of Ch'ing Dynasty extended its control over Taiwan in 1683, it immediately introduced the private ownership of land by converting all cultivated land into private property. Further, any person might apply for the reclamation and cultivation of uncultivated land, of which he would enjoy the ownership after he had duly carried out the obligations of a reclaimer-cultivator. This was a great reform

and brought about many changes in the complex relations between reclaimer
and tenant. But a continuing impairment and source of abuses stemmed
from the Government's failure to safeguard sufficiently the interests of
the actual tillers. There had been few peasant properietors among those
who undertook to reclaim land in the two centuries before 1886.
Practically all those reclaimers were simply financial promoters who
furnished the capital necessary for each enterprise. Few of the ordinary
immigrants from the mainland had the financial resources to undertake
reclamation by themselves. The so-called "reclaimers" or "reclaiming
chiefs," the financiers, after having obtained governmental permission
to reclaim certain tracts of land, would proceed to enlist the services
of immigrants to do the actual cultivation for them. In this way each
"reclaimer" or "reclaiming chief" would acquire ownership of the land
after it had been cultivated by others, using his financial backing.
Thereafter, he would pay the taxes and collect rents from the cultivators,
who thus became his tenants.

As population kept on increasing and the demand for land became
ever more pressing, most of the tenants were induced to sublease to
others part of the land they had been cultivating, and to collect rent
therefrom for their own benefit. Thus, there arose a hierarchical system
of tenancy. At the top of the hierarchy was the Government exercising
supreme authority and control over all land. Next below the Government
were the "reclaimers" or "reclaiming chiefs," who had now become
landowners; below them were the original tenants, and at the bottom
were the subtenant-cultivators. The rent collected by the landowner
from his tenant was usually a one-tenth or one-ninth part of the farm's

annual products; that collected by the tenant from the subtenant-cultivator was 50 or 60 per cent. Thus, the subtenant-cultivator had to bear very heavy burdens under this hierarchical form of tenancy. Out of this tenancy system there grew an unexpected and unusual phenomenon, in that the landowner's grip on the land was gradually weakened and the power of the tenant became stronger and stronger. In other words, the feudalistic authority of the landowner gave way before the rising economic strength of the tenant, to such degree that the tenant might even turn over his rights to another person without the consent of the landlord. Transfers of rights by both landowner and tenant were frequent and common. Relations between one party and another in connection with land became increasingly complex and the collection of land tax increasingly difficult.

Taiwan was compulsorily given to Japan in 1895 by the Ch'ing Government as a result of the Sino-Japanese war at the end of the 19th century. The Japanese authorities put an end to the confused land situation in 1904 by buying out the rights of the landowner and conferring them on the tenant. In this way the tenant became the rightful owner of the land in place of the original "reclaimer." Thus, the hierarchical tenancy system was wiped out. The rights of the new owner were soon legally recognized and he was officially known as "landlord."

These changes made by the Japanese administration had, however, the effect of benefiting only the original tenant, who was now invested with the full rights of landownership. Nothing was done to better the lot of the actual cultivator who continued to bear the same burden of high rents as of old. Tenancy disputes became more numerous beginning

from 1927. Meantime, there had been a marked tendency for farm rents
to keep on increasing.

At the time when Taiwan was again restored to China, the land-tenure
and farm-tenancy systems on private farms were dominated by many evil
practices such as the following:

1. High rental rates. It was not unusual to find a lease requiring
for the landowner a share of more than 50% of the total harvest. The
most common practice was lease on a 50-50 basis, but a 60% share for
the owner and 40% share for the tenant was not unusual in the more
fertile and more densely populated areas. The greatest demands from the
owner had been occurring in the most fertile area of Taichung and the
most densely populated area of Hsinchu, where he was entitled to 70%
and the tenant only 30% of the total harvest. There were certain cases
providing a share of less than 50% of the crops to the owner. These were
found mostly in the least fertile areas where crops were poor and harvest
uncertain or the land was newly reclaimed.

There were other levies also, an "ironclad rent" and a rent on
by-products. The former was a kind of fixed rent which the tenant
must pay to the owner in spite of any crop failure; it amounted usually
to 60% of the crops. As to by-products, though they were the result
of the additional application of capital and labor on the part of the
tenant, he was required by practice to share them equally with the
landowner or to pay an extra secondary rent, according to the rental rate,
for his main crop. In a number of cases the landowner would require the
tenant to grow fruit trees, bamboos, or lumber for him, and would reap
the full harvest without paying anything to the tenant for the extra

labor involved. Some landowners would ask their tenants to raise chickens and ducks for them without pay.

2. Rent deposits. To guarantee rent payment, the tenant was required to pay a lump sum in advance as deposit which was generally equal to one whole year's rent but sometimes more than twice the annual rent. This practice was more prevalent in Taipei and Hsinchu Hsien and their neighboring districts than elsewhere.

3. Period of lease. It was customary not to fix a definite period of time for a farm lease. In the few cases in which a definite period was fixed, it was likely to be one or two years. In general, however, the landowner could increase the rental rate and the rent deposit or terminate the lease as he pleased.

4. Verbal contracts. Verbal contracts were the general practice. Only one out of ten contracts was written. In practical fact, because of the tenant's inferior social and economic position, a verbal contract could not be enforced and was therefore worthless.

5. Advance payment of rent. Though farm rents were supposed to be paid once every half-year, most landlords demanded and received advance payment. The methods by which the landlord collected farm rent in advance were three: for a two-year lease, the whole amount of the two years' rent would be collected when the lease was agreed upon; if it was agreed to pay the rent one year in advance, the amount of the rent would be collected before harvest time, either in the preceding autumn or in the spring of the current year; if it was agreed to pay the rent in advance for one crop, the rent for the second crop would be collected simultaneously with that for the first crop.

6. <u>Farming-out the farm lands</u>. Some landowners had so much land that they found it impossible to look after it personally. To save trouble, they used the device of farming the land out to an agent who thus became a sort of "sub-landlord" and, by subletting the land, exploited and oppressed the tenants much more severely than even the landlords themselves did.

Needless to say, these practices had made the land-tenure and farm-tenancy system in Taiwan most oppressive. It would be absolutely impossible to develop a modern and progressive agriculture and ensure a thriving rural civilization under these unhealthful conditions.

II. Reasons for Undertaking the Land Reform

An obvious case for undertaking land reform came from the great needs pointed out in the preceding section. The land laws of the Republic of China state that the various governments may "prescribe limits on the maximum area of private land which individuals or corporate bodies may own respectively."[3] The governments "shall formulate measures requiring that all lands in excess of the prescribed limits shall be set apart and sold within a definite period of time,"[4] and "All private lands in excess of the prescribed limits that are not set apart and sold according to the provisions...may be compulsorily purchased by the competent <u>Hsien</u> or Municipal Government according to the provisions of this law."[5] Inasmuch as many of the landlords in Taiwan had an amount of land much in excess of the prescribed limits, and because this condition caused considerable damages to farm production, to the nation's economy, and to the livelihood of the great majority of the people, there was certainly legitimate reason for making changes or corrections. The regulations governing the lease of private farm lands in Taiwan Province state at the very beginning that "In order to improve the land-tenancy system and to stabilize the rural social order in Taiwan Province, these regulations are hereby drawn up to govern the lease of private farmland," and that the amount of farm rent shall not exceed 37.5 per cent of the total annual yield of the main crop.[6] These words are surely clear enough in stating the Government's reasons for readjusting the rate of the farm rent and limiting it. Improving the land-tenancy system was, however, a direct reason, and stabilizing the rural social order was an indirect reason. At the time when the farm rent-limitation program was undertaken, the second reason was of more urgent importance than the first one. But, realization of the second was dependent on realization of the first. The most prominent founder and leader of Kuomintang and also founder of the Republic of China, Dr. Sun Yat-sen, conceived the "land-to-the-tiller" ideal, and this ideal has guided the land policy of the Central Government under the Kuomintang rule for many years. The Chinese National Government might also have declared that the reason for undertaking this land reform, especially in regard to the "land-to-the-tiller" program, was to put Dr. Sun Yat-sen's teaching into practice and certainly the time was ripe to do so.

What has been said in the foregoing could be considered the stated, or open, reasons. There was another reason which was more important but somehow not openly stated. And this came from

the Government's, or to be more exact, the Kuomintang Party's
efforts to combat the Chinese communists' intrigue of using the
illness of the land-tenure and farm-tenancy system to instigate
agrarian uprisings. As has been pointed out previously, in many parts
of the Chinese mainland there was great need for land reform to get
rid of oppressive practices in the farm-tenancy system and to
readjust the distribution of landownership. But, owing to the fact
that practically any kind of land reform intended to benefit the
great masses of farm-cultivators had to be in diametrical conflict
with the interests of the landlords, the enforcement of such a
program always met formidable opposition. Because of the strong
opposition, both the national and the local governments in the
various provinces undertook the task half-heartedly. The result
was that not one of the land-reform attempts on the China mainland
had achieved any degree of success.

The Chinese communists took the matter differently. The difference
was not that the communists had genuine concern with the peasant-
farmer's lot, but that they made to their advantage a great use of the
fact that China urgently needed land reform. They used it to feed their
propaganda machine, to spread hatred among tenants against landowners,
and, finally, to foment peasant uprisings against the Government. Basing
their drive on the peasants' fervent desire for a bearable farm-rental
rate and for the right of landownership, the Chinese communists
used every kind of trick and disguise to proclaim themselves agrarian
reformers and ready to undertake a most complete land reform beginning
with eliminating all the evil practices in China's farm-tenancy

system and then giving the poor peasants all the land they should want as soon as communists captured the whole political power through the cooperation and support of the peasants. The communists' propaganda and disguise were extremely successful. They won the direct and indirect support of the general populace, including a considerable part of the intellectuals who might have been expected to discern such deceits, and they took the whole country except the Province of Taiwan.

While the communists were making one great leap after another by capitalizing on the need for land reform, the ruling party (Kuomintang) began to be terribly alarmed. Out of this belated sense of danger, they came to the realization that they had done too little about checking exploitation and improving economic conditions for the tenant-cultivator and the small owner-farmer through farm-rent reduction and redistribution of landownership. When finally they tried to launch such rent-reduction programs as those started in the provinces of Kwangtung, Hupeh, Hunay, and Chekiang in the mid-1920's and then in 1940's, and such land-to-the-tiller programs as those undertaken in Peipei, Szechuan Province, in the Huanghui Dam District, Kansu Province, and in Lungyen, Fukien Province, with the idea of reversing the deterioration of the political situation, it was already too late. The Kuomintang regime had to give up all hopes and retreat to Taiwan. Thus came about the loss of the Chinese mainland to the communists which was so great a tragedy to both Kuomintang and the whole nation of China.

As described previously, the need for land reform in Taiwan was just as urgent as it was on the mainland. If nothing were done in

regard to the high farm rent and the oppressive land-tenure system,
or if something were to be done only half-heartedly, the communists
could just as easily use the situation to grab this last foothold into
their holdings. Fortunately, a much-reduced Kuomintang group under
the leadership of Chiang Kai-shek and Chen cheng, together with a
small number of refugee scholars, administrators, business executives,
civic leaders, and military heads, made up their minds to stay in
Taiwan and hold it as a last fortress. They had set up a reform
committee to revitalize themselves individually and as a group.
Numerous "mainland recovering" and national rebuilding programs were
contemplated and discussed. One of the most important of these programs
was land reform. As the memory of their saddest defeat on the mainland was still fresh, the plan of undertaking a program of land reform
was solemn and determined, and it was also intelligent. Intelligent
because it had this threefold purpose:

> Real and thorough elimination of the evils in the tenancy
> system so that the cultivators got their fair share of their
> production and could own the land they tilled;
>
> The improvement and modernization of Taiwan's agriculture,
> farm and living conditions through removal of those adverse
> social and economic factors related to land tenure so to
> deprive the communists of making use of them for political
> advantage;
>
> Demonstration to the world of an effective program in land
> reform and the good fruits to be enjoyed therefrom.

It would show the people on the Chinese mainland, as well as the
peoples of other countries, what a difference existed between the land
reform enforced by the communists on the China mainland and the reforms
taken in Taiwan. Mainland reform was carried out entirely with brutal

force, a task filled with hatred, sadism, killing and destruction,
whereas, on Taiwan the program was approached in a democratic and
rational way. It was undertaken with reason, sympathy, persuasion,
fair play, and a constructive objective. What has been done in Taiwan
toward the solution of the land problem should prove to the world
that land reform in its greatest advantages and fullest meaning can
be carried out with altogether peaceful and democratic measures.
This is the essence of what might be called the political reason for
the undertaking of the Taiwan land reform.

Taiwan is a relatively small province of China. It is an
island about 100 miles off the southeast coast of the China mainland.
Any kind of social and economic reform, or reconstruction program,
undertaken here can be, to a great extent, free from interference or
influence from other parts of the country. Also, in comparison with
many parts of the Chinese mainland, there were here more favorable
conditions for the implementation of such a program. Specifically,
the people as a whole had more knowledge, were more enlightened, had
better transportation and communication facilities available; their
community units were largely organized and functioning; there were
higher administrative structures also functioning, and they were endowed
with moderately good leadership. Furthermore, the United States, not
wishing to see the last part of China be devoured by the communists
or become disintegrated, was ready to extend through such agencies
as the China-United States Joint Commission of Rural Reconstruction
and the AID her technical and financial assistance, as much as China
might need. Thus, there were present in Taiwan the need, the policy

and legal basis, the freedom of doing things, the favorable conditions,
and the outside help. What needed to be added were the Administration's determination and sincerity in having the tasks carried out.
The Administration understood this. It realized that this time the
opportunity must not slip, if it were to survive at all.

III. Objectives of the Land Reform

In principle, any significant land reform ought to have two sets
of objectives. One set would include the building up of a sound land
tenure in which ownership would be fairly distributed, and, most
especially, it should provide that most of the lands be in the hands of
the actual cultivators; it should set up limits on the rental rates,
whereby both landowner and tenant get their fair shares of what is
produced; it should establish a thorough system of land registration
under which all cultivated and developed lands would be periodically
surveyed and duly and accurately registered, so that no land should be
lost to the Government or incorrectly assessed for taxation purposes;
and it should set forth a just and firm system of land taxation under
which every inch of land in use would be rightfully taxed, so protecting
landowners, while at the same time insuring that the nation will not
suffer significant loss to its revenues. Of these four objectives,
the first two emphasize socio-economic justice and, as a derivative,
the maintenance of social order, while the latter two direct their
attention to an accurate and up-to-date inventory of a country's
useable land and the smooth flow of land revenue to the nation's
treasury.

The second set of objectives of land reform ought to be formulated
in such terms as the most efficient utilization of all the useable and
cultivatable lands for construction and production purposes; the scientific
development of farm land to provide the conditions and means upon which
the highest agricultural production depends; the development of a sound
agriculture in which not only the production per unit of land is high but
that of per unit of man is high too; and the development of a prosperous
rural civilization, wherein both the farm people and the people whose life
is in relation with land would enjoy economic, social, and cultural
prosperity. One may argue that the last objective is too far outside
the perception of the reformers. Superficially, it might be so, but if
one does some deep thinking, one would certainly realize that the ultimate
purpose of any and all rural reconstruction programs, of which land reform
is an important one, must be that the farmers and all other rural people
have a prosperous life. By prosperous life is meant abundant and high-
quality economic materials, rich and meaningful community participation,
high and decent cultural activities and achievements. The ultimate purpose
in undertaking any kind of task is to satisfy man's needs and wishes from
life, individually and in groups. Land reform must in the end be
able to fulfill such an obligation. Otherwise, all its efforts must
be considered wasted. To avoid being accused of being idealistic,
practical rural-reconstruction workers may decline to mention the
development of a prosperous rural civilization as one of the objectives
of land reform. When, however, the final evaluation is to be made,
in regard to the results achieved by the reform, this must be the most
prominent goal its appraisers should look for. And this is the very

purpose for which this study is undertaken. It is true that no kind
of land reform would of itself be able to fulfill such a big purpose.
But in cooperation with other efforts, it ought to be able to play a
prominent role and make great contributions. Many people are acquainted
with the great advances witnessed in Denmark in the last one-and-one-half
centuries. These were accomplished by a great number of efforts and
reform programs, but the Danish land-reform programs certainly played
important roles in the achievements.[7]

From the very early times[8] to the present China has undertaken
numerous land-reform programs. After all the significant ones have
been analyzed, it is discovered that practically all such efforts had
limited their emphases to the objectives in the first set described
in the preceding section. The statesmen who took part in the planning
and carrying out of the land-reform programs gave their attention
mainly to such matters as breaking up the concentration of landownership in the hands of a small number of big landlords and redistributing
it among the small farmers and tenant-cultivators; lowering or limiting
farm rentals; surveying and registering already developed land; reclaiming
of land as yet uncultivated; and assuring the Government's revenue
from land. In a few instances the programs also included the re-
settlement of war-dislodged farmers and the granting to such farmers
of various kinds of agricultural assistance. But these again were in
the final analysis, done for the reason of increasing the land revenue
rather than for the benefits of the farmers.

Dr. Sun Yat-sen established three important ideals in regard
to China's land problem in his "Principle of People's Livelihood."

These ideals are, first, that landownership is to be equally distributed among the citizens; second, that people who actually cultivate the land shall own the land; and, third, that the portion of land price, gained primarily because of the public development of the community, is to be returned to the public. The first two ideals are mainly and directly concerned with farm lands and with an agrarian social justice, whereas, the third is chiefly related to policies and problems of urban land. It is clear that Dr. Sun's concern is with China's traditional land problem. What he had seen and worried about was the concentration of landownership and its consequences: the tenant-cultivators' anxiety over getting, or not getting, a piece of land to cultivate, the high farm-rental rates that burdened the cultivator, and the most miserable conditions of the peasant's everyday life. Because his comprehension was tradition-oriented, his conceptions in regard to measures for dealing with the problems had to be traditional, too. Bound by traditional thinking, Dr. Sun could not visualize any of the objectives outlined in our second set of purposes.

From the middle of the 1920's up to the time the Chinese Communists took over the Chinese mainland, the power and government of China were in the hands of the ruling party of Kuomintang. The Kuomintang has always proclaimed that all its national policies and reconstruction programs are based on the teachings of Dr. Sun Yat-sen's three people's principles: nationalism, democracy, and people's livelihood. Most of the nation's economic policies and programs, especially those which have direct bearing on the people's everyday life, have had their foundations or roots in the principle of people's livelihood. Thus, all the land laws promulgated and land-reform experiments conducted on

the Chinese mainland by the Kuomintang administration had been in

accordance with Dr. Sun's three ideals mentioned in the preceding

paragraph, and this was true of all prior modern-day, land-reform programs

and land-reform laws in Taiwan. This meant that concern had been directed

only to the redistribution of landownership, the limitation of farm-

rental rates, and the principle of land-to-the-tiller as objectives.

There had been no clear and adequate definition of goods for the

development of a modern and highly productive agriculture, the

improvement of the rural people's living conditions, the transformation

of a rural civilization of poor peasantry into a new civilization of

agrarian prosperity. Therefore, it should not be supposed that the

purpose of the present study is to find out whether land reform in

Taiwan has accomplished such far-reaching goals as mentioned herewith,

but rather to see whether it has had some significant, but unforetold,

effects on the farm people's work spirit and work techniques, on their

daily living conditions, on their educational inspirations and cultural

activities, and on their interest in community organization and social

participation. It is acknowledged that such a land reform as the one

performed in Taiwan may not have had these things clearly stated as

official objectives, but they could very likely be among its profound

effects.

IV. Policies and Methods in Land Reform

Policies and methods used in carrying out land-reform programs

can generally be divided according to their nature and spirit into two main types. One type may be called democratic policies and methods, and the second type, authoritarian policies and methods. By democratic is meant chiefly that in making policies, all parties, and every party affected by the programs, are to be treated with fairness, that is, those who give shall receive adequate compensation and those who gain shall pay reasonable prices; programs are to be carried out with persuasion, explanation, and reasoning rather than with compulsion; peacefulness, orderliness, and gradation take the place of violence, confusion, and shocking measures; the central aim is to be the correction of injustices and evil practices, not the avenging of one man's grievance at the expense of another's well-being and life. Policies of an authoritarian nature or spirit are, in all aspects, opposite to these characteristics. There is no place here for their usages, their sheer force, brutal violence, and outright confiscation, their hatred and sadism, nor their underlying motivation, which is to get every profit for the state at the expense of all the people, including the poor peasants, the proletariat.

In its methods, the democratic type of land reform makes use of accurate surveys, registrations, and classifications. It uses careful calculations to decide upon compensations, prices, and other remunerations. Data-recording, record-keeping, filing, checking and rechecking are employed to obtain and keep accurate information. Public announcement, fact-posting, mass communication, circuit-instruction meetings are the measures taken to keep the people informed of the meaning, the significance, and the progression of the different steps in the reform programs. Finally, training, discussion, organization, and conciliation are the techniques for arriving at any agreement, or conclusion, in dealing with problems and disputes which may come up at any time during the implementation of the programs. The authoritarian type of land reform uses almost none of these methods. Its whole task consists of simply taking over property and chasing out people. For purposes of displaying power and creating fear, it employs mass meetings or accusation meetings. The power so displayed and the fear so created serve to suppress any idea or action which could lead to revolt against the so-called land reform.

Policies and methods seen in the land-reform programs performed in Taiwan belonged, by and large, to the democratic type just described in the preceding paragraphs. The basic spirit of the farm rent-limitation program, for instance, was an intention to readjust the rental rates so that both the landlord and his tenant should get their fair shares of the farm products according to what each of them had put into the production. It was an intention to correct an old wrong, not to overturn the table so that the former downtrodden, oppressed one got a chance at reprisal by stepping upon his enemy and making an underdog of him.

The 37.5 per cent limitation figure was a result of careful calculation, which indicated that this percentage is, in general, the fair share to which the landlord is entitled for the use of his land. This measure also had the merit of being easily understood by the farmers and easy to calculate. Briefly, its rationale was this:

At one time, a 25 per cent farm rent reduction plan was advocated. This plan suggested that 25 per cent of the rental was to be taken off from the landlord's 50 per cent share. By so doing, the farm rent paid to the landlord would have been reduced to 37.5 per cent instead of the usual 50 per cent. Thus, a 25 per cent reduction would result in the same payment as would a 37.5 per cent limitation. But the latter was better than the former in that China is a vast country and farm-rental rates were by no means uniform everywhere, so that it would not be entirely fair to require that all farm rents be reduced by 25 per cent, irrespective of local differences. The 37.5 per cent limitation measure was much more equitable. Also, the 37.5 per cent figure was only a ceiling rate. It was not meant that all farm rents were to be fixed at this rate. Those which had been originally lower than 37.5 per cent were to remain unchanged. This was another consideration for the benefit of both tenants and landlords.

It was also provided by law that the meaning of such terms as "the main crop," "the principle product," "the determination of total annual yield" should be lucidly defined and adequately known to all people concerned. According to the law,[9] the standard amount of the total annual yield of the principal product of the main crop must be appraised by the Farm Tenancy Committee of the Village, Township, or District office, and the amount so appraised must be submitted to the Farm Tenancy Committee of the Hsien or City Government for confirmation, and to the Provincial Government for final approval.

The Farm Tenancy committees were composed of representatives of tenants, owner-farmers, landlords, and local administration leaders. All these provisions were designed to emphasize and demonstrate the democratic spirit and policies and the use of scientific methods in arriving at and implementing the 37.5% farm rent limitation program.

These same policies, methods, and spirit prevailed in the land-to-the-tiller program, and were manifested in the particular features characterizing it. According to Dr. Hui-sun Tang,[10] its first particular feature was its consideration for the immediate livelihood and the future development of the landlords after their land had been compulsorily purchased. Policy with respect to landlords was two-fold: on the one hand, all their farm land leased to tenants was to be compulsorily purchased according to law in order to deprive them of any further opportunity to live chiefly on farm rents; on the other hand, they were encouraged to interest themselves in industrial development by converting their farm holdings into industrial holdings and thus increasing their income therefrom. It was with the latter purpose in view that compensations for the purchased land were paid 70 per cent with land bonds in kind and 30 per cent with public enterprise stocks. But as it would be impossible for any landlord to change his occupation overnight, provision was made for the retention of three chia[11] of medium-grade land by individual landlords so that small landlords whose holdings did not exceed the retention limit might have their land exempted from compulsory purchase altogether, and big and medium landlords, whose holdings exceeded the retention limit, might still retain a part of their land and have something to live upon.

In regard to the interests of the tenant-farmer, provisions in the laws enforcing the land-to-the-tiller program were more comprehensive and far reaching. The program not only gave to the tenant-farmer the right of ownership over the land he was tilling, but other forms of assistance were also designed and entered into the rules. For example, the tenant-farmer was allowed to pay for the land resold to him by the Government in installments spread over a period of ten years; the payments he had to make in each of those years would not exceed the burden he had been bearing since the introduction of farm rent reduction in 1949. If his landlord should wish to sell the land he was entitled legally to retain, the tenant would have first priority of purchase and might apply to the Government for loans to pay for the land. It was further provided that until the tenant-farmer had completed purchase of the land he was tilling, he would continue to be protected by the 37.5% per cent farm-lease contract he had signed with the landlord.

After a tenant-farmer had acquired ownership of land, he also acquired the responsibilities that a landowner is bound to have. In fulfilling his new responsibilities, the new landowner might find himself in great need of money. In order to help these farmers keep free from exploitation by the professional money lenders, the Government set up agricultural production funds from which loans at low rates of interest were extended to them, so that they would be able to pay taxes and also buy things needed for the improvement of the land and the operation of the farm business. It is to be expected that after a tenant-farmer has become an owner-farmer, he and his family would be lifted in morale, and, for that reason, might become interested in seeking better ways and better tools for cultivation of the land. To help in this respect, an agricultural-extension education program, including farm information, home-economics instruction and rural-youth work, was made available. All

these considerations for the benefits of the farmer constituted the
second particular feature of the land-to-the-tiller program.

The third particular feature was represented by the peaceful and
orderly procedures by which the land was purchased from the landlord and
resold to the tenant. The land-to-the-tiller program in Taiwan provided
for the resale of the farm land, too, and its continued cultivation by
the present tenant-farmer or farm hand, as the case might be. It did not
try to carve the land into standardized unit farms to be resold to some
arbitrarily chosen farmers, nor did it involve a strictly-equal distribution
of land according to the ratio between the amount of available land and
the number of the population. The methods actually employed did not
require either exchange or subdivision of the land being cultivated by
any tenant-farmer or farm hand, nor any change in his dwelling. There was
not the least disturbance in rural life when the right of ownership
over farm lands under tenancy was transferred from the landlord to the
farmer. That this peaceful transition was possible was due largely to
the experience gained in the sale of public land in the previous years,
in which the same procedure had been followed and found to be convenient
and practical. It was also due to the fact that, as a result of the enforcement of farm rent-reduction measures since 1949, the tenant's rights were
given ample protection and he himself came to be closely attached to the
land he was tilling. Consequently, it was only natural and expedient that
its present tenant-cultivator or farm hand should be the purchaser of the
land compulsorily purchased and resold by the Government.

To sum it up, the land-to-the-tiller program was a means by which
the dogma that one who tills the land should own it was to a great extent

realized. People who designed and built this program did not believe that
the landlord should be deprived of all his land outright without any
compensation, nor be left alone with no provision for his immediate livelih
nor anything for the future. They believed that there must be fairness
and consideration for every party involved in the matter. They further
believed that there must be guaranty that the carrying out of such a
program be peaceful and orderly.

What has been said in the foregoing does not mean that the land reform in Taiwan had been carried through all the way with entirely voluntary
measures. To a certain extent compulsory methods had to be used. This
was especially true in the implementation of the land-to-the-tiller
program whose chief feature was the enforced purchase of farm land from
the landlords and its resale to its current cultivator. The purchase
had been a gigantic and difficult task. Chief reasons for its being
difficult were, first, that a great majority of the landlords and their
families had been making a living principally on the rents from their
farm land. The land had been the chief, sometimes the only, security of
their livelihood. They would not know how to make a living and would not
be able to support themselves if and when one day the land, the source
of farm rent, were gone. Second, up to very recent times the Chinese
people, by and large, still dearly treasured the farm land. They vested
the highest economic and social values and also the most stable values in
the arable land. If the land were gone, gone too would be these values.
Third, in most of the Chinese farm families, land was the property earned
and handed down through the generations. Inheritors ought to, and must,
keep the property intact by all possible means and with the greatest

determination. To have it go out of the family, in whatever manner, would constitute a great shame for the ancestors and a great danger to the continuity of the family line. And fourth, the ownership of land, especially the ownership of a large amount of good farm land, was the most tangible certification of the rights of a man or a family. It was also the most manifest evidence whereby the neighbors, relatives, and friends observed and respected one's rights. Not being familiar with the concepts of Western democracy, or the Bill of Rights, the Chinese people became aware of the infringement of individual rights only when ownership of land was forcibly taken into controversy.

With all these deep-rooted feelings and ideologies attached to the ownership of farm land, it is obvious that a majority of the landlords would not agree to give up their land simply by persuasion, or in an ordinary business deal. If persuasion, or ordinary business deals, cannot do the job, then compulsory methods have to be put in use. But as soon as the idea of using compulsion or force was introduced, people who have faith in democracy and people who have picked up some ideas about freedom and the right to private property immediately raised their voices in protest. These people argued that Taiwan is the bastion of free China, and free China is now forging toward the building of a democracy. Therefore, nothing should be done, and no methods should be used, in contradiction to this young but general trend. Other members in the legislative bodies on both national and provincial levels and numerous civic leaders put forward counter-viewpoints by arguing that what the protesters had said is not true democracy. True democracy is to live and let others live. The extension of this principle leads to the verity that when one makes himself a good living, he should also let others make a good living; and when one makes good opportunities for himself, he should also let others have equally good opportunities. The traditional tenancy system let a comparatively small number of landlords have the best opportunities, the greatest amount of farm land, and the most extravagant life, but left a huge number of tenants, farm hands, and small owner-farmers without land, or with only a little of it. These people have been a long time living in nothing but misery. They have been deprived of all opportunities for development, for fulfilling a life of happiness and decency. This is social, economic, and humanistic injustice. This is not democracy. As long as there exists in a society this kind of landlordism, and its opposite which is a poor peasantry living in an inequitable social and economic system, the country is in danger of stagnancy and revolution, all kinds of upheavals. These leaders even cited President Lincoln's fighting against the southern plantations' ownership of Negro slaves as an example. The plantation had the right to keep their slaves, so far as the private property law is concerned. But Lincoln's use of force to destroy slavery was not considered as destroying democracy. Instead, it was considered necessary to protect the true democracy.

After a number of such arguments and debates, open and secret, the Government finally made the decision to use compulsory methods to force the landlords to give up their surplus land. Hence, when the Government purchased land from a landlord, it was a forced purchase. There were other points, too, on which decisions were arbitrarily made and carried out with authoritarian methods.

The result of this study shows that all but a very few of the
landlords gave cooperation to the Government while the 37.5% farm rent
limitation and the land-to-the-tiller programs were being carried out.
In spite of this fact, people,who for this matter had a grudge against
the Government,made the accusation that the cooperation was extracted
from the landlords by force. If the statement means that in a great
majority of cases the purchasing of the land was compulsory, it is true.
But it is not true if it means that the landlords had really been deadly
opposed to the undertaking. Because if that had been the case, or if the
Government had imagined it could be that way, then it would have had
resorted to all those cruel and abominable measures used by the communists to
enforce their kind of land reform on the Chinese mainland. The conditions
in Taiwan were entirely different from what happened on the mainland.
There was not even one case in which the landlord had to be severely
punished. Not one drop of blood had been shed for this matter. In view
of all these facts, there should be no bias in saying that the cooperation
given by the landlords was to a great extent genuine and voluntary. How
could this have happened? Based on findings of this study, the reasons
are as follows:

First, though the purchasing of land from the landlords was compulsory,
it was not outright confiscation. It was, on the contrary, duly compensated
and carefully calculated and, to a great extent, justified land price and,
besides, a number of other landlord interests were taken into careful
consideration. As has been pointed out previously in this chapter, one of
the important characteristics of the land reform in Taiwan is that it

took into consideration the legitimate rights and interests of every
party concerned, be it the landlord or the tenant. It had even gone
so far as to consider assistances to be given to the landlords for their
future when they entered businesses, or other new ways of life, by fixing
30 per cent of the land compensation in enterprise corporation stocks.
According to this study, it is true that many of the landlords did not
get much benefit from holding the corporation stocks but suffered losses
instead. This was, however, due largely to their own faults. These faults
will be pointed out in the following chapters. It is not right, however,
to let the landlords' own faults nullify merit of the land reform.

Second, the payment of the land price was carefully arranged and
guaranteed. Neither the arrangement nor the guaranty was based on, or
backed by, force but was according to reason and was according to the
particular kind of human relations in a Chinese society.

As the tenant-cultivators who were purchasing the land could not
possibly pay the whole price at one time, after careful calculation, a
division was made into ten large installments, or twenty small installments.
When pursuaded, the landlords were also willing to receive their compensation
accordingly. To some landlords this arrangement might not have been satisfactory; to others, there were advantages. Inasmuch as the land-purchasing
tenants made their payments regularly and on time, the landlords also receive
their portions of compensation on time. In the very few cases in which the
tenants failed to meet their obligation, the landlords received their payment
from the Government as usual. This was the guaranty.

Third, the time was ripe to change the dependence of one's living
on farm rental. As an outmoded feudalistic way of life, it was rapidly

being replaced by developing self-respect through independent careers in modern businesses. Most of the landlords, or their enlightened sons, were aware of this social trend. Many of the big and medium landlords were able to figure out that while industries and businesses were developing and social orders were stable, investment in industries and businesses were more profitable than investment in farm land. Those who were unaware of this trend were in confusion, perplexed, and lost confidence in what to do about the future. Under such circumstances, most of the landlords, who at first felt reluctance or even bitterness in giving up their long-treasured land, soon realized that it might be a good thing, that help had come to aid them in making an important decision in their confusion and darkness. This feeling, or realization, was by no means strong enough to make the landlords give full cooperation in the implementation of the land reform. It did, however, help to prevent the rise of any serious opposition. Furthermore, cooperation or opposition from the landlords depended a great deal on whether or not they could be convinced that there would be no great difficulty in their going into businesses, or other non-farm occupations, and making a satisfactory living after the land was sold. Whether the Government and the society at large was willing to help them make this transition was important to them.

Fourth, in the years between 1949 and 1953, the Chinese communists had taken over the mainland of China and had practiced cruel and inhuman atrocities on all kinds of landlords in order to carry out their particular brand of land reform. They had not only confiscated all the landowners' lands and other properties but had also killed or imprisoned them and some of their relatives. The communists were threatening to take over Taiwan and would do exactly the same things to Taiwan's landlords if they should ever get there. The landlords in Taiwan knew all of these facts. A great number of them had been convinced that if they refused to cooperate with the Government, and in that way give the communists opportunity to come to Taiwan, they would meet the same kind of fate which the landlords on the mainland had met. This fearful possibility made the landlords accept the democratic and fair-play type of land reform.

It is in this writer's knowledge that the Government and civic leaders of many countries today are anxious to see a land reform take place in their own countries but are afraid of strong opposition from their landlords. In view of these analyses, this study is willing to suggest that if the Government and civic leaders of a country are really sincere in their concern with the people's suffering and well-being, and if they have strong faith in the use of democratic measures and procedures in planning and undertaking any socio-economic reform or reconstruction programs, and if they make every possible effort to ensure the landlords a future with hope and a better living, land reform of any kind, or in any degree, can be carried out peacefully and be satisfactory to all parties involved. It is hoped that the information in this study can be a useful reference to these governments and statesmen.

Notes

1
After reading the first draft of this chapter, Dr. A. B. Lewis
wrote a letter (February 21, 1967) to comment on the rental rate. "So
far, the only question that has occurred to me in reading your report is
that of the justification of 37½ per cent of the principal crop as the
rental rate. Presumably this was based on studies of relative contributions of landlords and tenants to the operation of the farm. One study
made by the University of Nanking in 1935-36 is reported in 'Economic
Facts' No. 2, Oct. 1936, a periodical published by the Department of
Agricultural Economics, University of Nanking. The study indicates
landlords earning about 10% per year on their investment, which was the
same as bank interest. This was before rent reduction. Dr. J. L.
Buck's article, 'Fact and Theory about China's Land' in Foreign Affairs
for October 1949 may also be of interest. Figures that he quotes indicate
that rents in China were generally lower than 37½ per cent of <u>total receipts</u>,
even though sometimes they were a higher percentage of the <u>principle crop</u>.

Generally speaking, in the USA, farm share rents are generally 50
per cent of receipts from crops.

In Taiwan now, it seems to be the general practice for tenants who
pay rent at 37½ per cent of the principal crop to consider that they have
an equity in the land. This would lead one to suspect that rent at this
rate does not pay landlord's costs, so the landlord has to hand over part
of his owner's function to the tenant. In this case the tenant automatically

becomes a part-owner of the land which he occupies and has to invest in its maintenance. He therefore charges a price to any tenant who proposes to displace him as a renter. A new renter has to pay rent plus a price to the old tenant. There are no such charges in the USA, that I know of, where rents are determined on an economic basis.

In other words, the burden of proof rests on anyone who claims that 37.5 per cent of the principal crop is an economic rent, and I suspect that this rate was arrived at by considerations but not by economic studies. If the latter, it would be essential, if possible, to show the figures arrived at in the studies.

Of course, as you point out in your report, the justification for the government taking action in this field may not be entirely or directly economic. If people decide for social or political reasons to limit land renting, then one way to do it is by reducing rents, thus making the renting out of land unprofitable. This would cause some land-lords to sell their land-as you report that many did. It would make the renting in of land unusually profitable-but less land would be offered on this basis."

Dr. Lewis is an expert in China's agricultural economics. He once was professor of agricultural economics at the University of Nanking. Now he is an Associate of the Agricultural Development Council in New York. At the moment he is in Taiwan connected with the Agricultural Economics Research Institute of Chunghsing University in the city of Taichung.

[2]After occupying the island, the Dutch authority had various ways to encourage the Chinese people on the opposite mainland to immigrate to Taiwan. In Taiwan they were assisted with farm implements, seeds, draft animals, and money to reclaim the virgin land as much as possible.

All reclaimed lands were "Crown Lands" which could not be owned by
private cultivators. In this sense the cultivators were tenants of
the Dutch authority. For purpose of controlling the people and collecting
land revenue, the households of the cultivators or tenants were organized
into, first, small groups of tens. A strong and capable person was
chosen by the authority from among the members of the group and appointed
as its leader or foreman. Several small groups were combined to form a big
group. The big group had also a head, and he was also selected and
appointed by the authority. The head of the big group was to take orders
from the Dutch authority and to oversee the cultivation of the farm households and to collect the tribunes for the Government.

[3]The Land Law (promulagated by the National Government, June 4,
1930; enforced, March 1, 1936; amended, April 29, 1946) Chapter V, Article 28.

[4]Article 29, first paragraph.

[5]Article 29, second paragraph.

[6]Regulations Governing the Lease of Private Farm Lands in Taiwan
Province (promulagated by Taiwan Provincial Government, April 14, 1949),
Article 1 and Article 2.

[7] Books on Denmark's land reform. See Bibliography.

[8] Shang-yang (or Lord Shang) made a well-known land reform at the
beginning of the Ch'in dynasty 2000 years ago.

[9] Farm Rent Reduction to 37.5 per cent Act, Article 4.

[10] Dr. Hui-sun Tang was one of the important leaders in planning and
implementing Taiwan's land reform; author of Land Reform in Free China;
see Bibliography.

[11] Chia is the name of a farm land unit traditionally used in
Taiwan. It is approximately 0.9699 hectare.

Chapter Two

LAND REFORM PROGRAMS

I.   The Three Programs
     1.   The 37.5% Farm Rent Limitation
     2.   The Sale of Public Farm Land
     3.   The Land-to-the-Tiller

II.   Implementation of the Three Programs

III.   Objectives Achieved

I.   The Three Programs

The widely known land reform conducted in Taiwan Province, Republic of China, during the years from 1949 to 1953, consisted of three chief programs, namely, the 37.5% farm rent limitation program, the public land sales program, and the land-to-the-tiller program. Upon the completion of these three programs, the work of land reconsolidation, the development of hill lands and seashore lands, and the promotion of joint cultivation were started one after another. None of these works has so far been undertaken in any large scale and information about their operation is still limited to a small number of people. For these reasons, these recent efforts shall not be included in the land reform which is to be reviewed here.

1. The 37.5% farm rent limitation program. The farm rent reduction program is better known as the 37.5% farm rent limitation program. Formerly, when the high farm-rent rate and its possible correction were discussed on

the China mainland, it was frequently suggested that a 25 per cent reduction should be a right solution of the problem. Therefore, at that time people were familiar with the term "25 per cent farm rent reduction." When land reform was about to be undertaken in Taiwan, the new concept of "37.5% farm rent limitation" was introduced. In practical terms, the two meant the same. Both consisted essentially in taking 25 per cent off from the farm rent the tenant was obliged to pay to the landlord, which usually was half (50%) of the annual produce. After making this reduction, the tenant would have to pay no more than 37.5% as rent to the landlord. The formula is as follows:

$$\frac{50}{100} - (\frac{50}{100} \times \frac{25}{100}) = \frac{375}{1000} = 37.5\%$$

There is another way of arriving at this 37.5% limitation. It is to earmark, first of all, 25 per cent of the total annual main-crop yield for the tenant-farmer, and then to divide the remaining 75 per cent equally between the landlord and the tenant. In this way, the rent paid by the tenant-farmer would be exactly 37.5 per cent of the total annual main-crop yield.

In this farm rent limitation concept, there was an important point to be remembered and that was that the 37.5 per cent was a ceiling rate, or, in other words, it was the maximum portion of the total annual main-crop yield that the landlord could charge his tenant as farm rent. It was not meant that all farm rents were to be fixed at this rate. Therefore, those farm rents which had been originally lower than the 37.5 percentage were to remain unchanged. All these provisions were designed to have the merit of being easily understood by the farmers and easy to calculate.

In Taiwan, as well as in many parts of the Chinese mainland, the farm rent paid by tenants to landlords was entirely too high and hard on the tenants. A reduction of this amount by 25 per cent would be much more reasonable, and this is the theoretical basis of the 37.5 per cent farm-rent limitation. In spite of the fact that in meaning, as well as in result, the 25 per cent reduction and the 37.5 per cent limitation were the same, the rule actually adopted was the better choice, in view of China's great area and the variations in the farm-rental rates. It would not be entirely fair to require that all farm rents be reduced by 25 per cent, irrespective of local differences.

It would be well to explain here the meaning of some of the terms used in this program. For instance, what was meant by "the main crop," "the principal product," and how was the "total annual yield" to be determined? The main crop was the crop most commonly grown, or it might be a rotation crop periodically grown according to local farming practice. Generally speaking, however, the crops harvested in the summer and autumn seasons were considered to be main crops. In the case of double-crop paddy fields, rice was the main crop; in the case of one-crop paddy fields, rice and sweet potato were the main crops; and in the case of three-year rotation fields, rice, sweet potato, and sugar cane were the main crops. In signing a farm-lease contract, the name of the main crop or crops must be clearly stated in black and white. The principal product was the chief article, or commodity, for which the crop was grown. In regard to the determination of the total annual yield, the rule was laid down in Article 4 of the Farm Rent Reduction to 37.5% Act. According to this Article, the standard amount of the total annual yield of the principal product of the main crop must be appraised by the Farm Tenancy Committee of the Village,

Township, or District Office, and the amount so appraised must be submitted

to the Farm Tenancy Committee of the Hsien or City Government for confir-

mation, and to the Provincial Government for final approval. Such standard

amounts were appraised by the 37.5% rent campaign committees of the

different hsien and cities according to the regulations that were in force

in 1949 when the rent-reduction program was being initiated in Taiwan.

The Farm Rent Limitation to 37.5% Act, which came into force in 1951,

provided that the landlord shall not demand or collect any security deposit

and that all security deposits already collected shall be returned to the

tenant or deducted by installments from the rent payable by the tenant.

All advance payments of farm rent have been strictly forbidden since the

very beginning of the farm rent-reduction program in 1949. The Farm Rent

Limitation to 37.5% Act further provided that anyone who collects rent in

advance, or demands any security deposit, shall be punished with detention or

a fine of $200 or less. Some landlords had tried to make up for their loss,

as a result of the rent reduction, by charging their tenants a rent on the

farmhouse which was purposely built for the use of the tenant and his

family. To correct this abuse, the Farm Rent Limitation to 37.5% Act of

1951 provided that the landlord shall not, under whatever pretext, demand

any charge for the use of his farmhouse by the tenant.

According to the Farm Rent Limitation to 37.5% Act of 1949, a farm-

lease contract in written form must be drawn up and signed. The amount,

kind, quality, and standard of rent payable, date and place of payment,

the period of lease, and other relevant matters were all to be clearly

specified in this written contract, which had to be registered upon the joint application of the landlord and tenant whether it was newly signed, renewed, changed in certain details, or terminated altogether. In regard to the period of a farm-lease contract, the new Act of 1951 provided that it shall not be shorter than six years. This provision put a stop to the abuses the landlords used to inflict on the tenants by not fixing the period of the lease contract, or by making it too short.

There were problems which arose after the 1949 farm rent-reduction program was put in force. First, quite a few of the landlords were successful in taking back the land from the tenants under the pretext that they wanted to cultivate the land themselves. This action not only threatened the tenant's only livelihood but also constituted a serious danger to the successful operation of the program. To deal with this problem, provisions were added to the Farm Rent Limitation to 37.5% Act forbidding the landlords to take back the land for their own use. These provisions made it clear that farm-lease contracts shall not be terminated before the expiration of the period of the contracts; that the landlord shall not take back the leased land for his own cultivation on the expiration of the lease contract, if he is, in fact, unable to cultivate the land himself, or if his total income is already sufficient to support his family, or if his action in taking back the land will deprive the lessee's family of its means of living; that if, on the expiration of the period of the farm-lease contract, the lessee is willing to continue the lease, the contract shall be renewed; and that the landlord shall be punished if he terminates the lease contract in violation of the Act.

Another problem was that some landlords chose in outrage to sell their land rather than have it leased to tenants and thus be under the

influence of the Farm Rent Limitation Act. This situation caused the
Government to take action to protect the tenant's preferential right if
the land were offered for sale or dien.[1] A provision in the Act states
that if farm land is offered for sale or dien, its current tenant shall
have preferential right to accept the offer, and the landlord shall give
him a written notice of the terms of sale or dien. If the tenant makes
no reply to the notice within 15 days, he shall be deemed to have waived
his preferential right. The provision also states that if the landlord
transfers the ownership of the leased land to, or creates a dien over it
in favor of a third party before the expiration of the period of the
lease contract, the contract shall remain valid and binding upon the
transferee or dien-holder, and the transferee or the dien-holder shall,
in conjunction with the tenant, apply for the registration of the said
contract duly revised to include the transferee's name.

To deal with the undesirable practice of "farming out the land" and
subleasing, the Farm Rent Limitation to 37.5% Act provided that the lessee
shall cultivate the leased land himself and shall not sublease the whole
or part of it to another person. If he violated this provision, the lease
contract shall become null and void, and the landlord may take back the
land for his own cultivation or lease it to another person. If such
violation occurred before the enforcement of this Act, the actual cultivator
of the part of the land which had been subleased,and the original lessee
cultivating the other part which had not been subleased,were required
individually and separately to sign new lease contracts with the landlord.

If such violation occurs after the enforcement of this Act, the lessee shall be punished.

In conclusion, the farm rent limitation program had been designed with provisions which would eradicate from the farm tenancy all the extra burdens and ill practices the landlord had traditionally added to the already too heavy farm rent. Thus, the purpose of the program had not been limited to the establishment of a sound and fair farm-rent rate, but was broad enough to include the building up of a clean, free-from-abuses farm-tenancy system, when a farm-tenancy system had been allowed to exist.

2. The public land sales program. At the time when Taiwan was restored to China after World War II, there were 181,490 chia of public farm land. These chia of land had belonged under the Japanese administration to the various levels of Government and to individual Japanese nationals. They were transferred to the Chinese Government with the retrocession of Taiwan to China. Formerly, in order to control the resources of Taiwan and facilitate the immigration of Japanese nationals, the Japanese Government had actively encouraged Japanese nationals, both individuals and organizations, to acquire ownership of land in Taiwan. Up to 1945 Japanese industrial organizations and enterprises such as the various sugar companies and the Taiwan Colonization and Settlement Corporation had already acquired ownership over 121,089 chia of farm land. Individual Japanese nationals had acquired 10,304 chia, and the various levels of government got 50,097 chia. All these lands were taken over by the Chinese Government in 1945 and thus became public property. Hence, the term Public Farm Land.

Under the Japanese administration, most of these public lands were
"farmed" by Japanese veterans, retired officials, industrial companies,
and the local gentry, who subleased them to tenant-farmers to cultivate.
The annual rent which the Japanese Government received from the "farmers-
generals" was approximately 30 per cent of the total annual produce,
although the tenants were often required to pay as much as 55 per cent of
the same to those from whom they had leased the land for cultivation. In
the majority of cases, there were neither written contracts nor a definite
period of time in which the lease was to be in force. Consequently, the
lessor had complete liberty of action if he wanted to increase the rent or
to terminate the lease altogether and turn the land over to a new tenant.
After Taiwan was restored to China, the Chinese Government took immediate
action to correct this situation. For instance, the Office of the High
Commissioner ordered in October, 1946, an urgent investigation of the
matter and the next year promulgated a set of regulations governing the
lease of public lands in Taiwan Province and rules governing the application
of these regulations. The essential points of these regulations were that
all public lands should be leased to cooperative farms, that each cooperative farm was a lessee, that in case any public land was to be leased to
individual farmers, the order of priority would be the present tiller, farm
hand, tenant-farmer, and part-owner-farmer; that the area of public land
to be leased to each farming family was to be limited: from 15 mow^2 to
45 mow of paddy field, or 30 to 75 mow of dry land; that the maximum
rental rate of public lands might not exceed 37.5 per cent of the annual

main-crop yield; and that the period of lease was limited to nine years in the case of cooperative farms and five years in leases to individual farmers The leasing of public farm lands under the new regulations did not, however, produce as good results as were anticipated. In spite of repeated attempts by the Government to correct the various abuses, its efforts were none too successful because of the many unconquerable obstacles. In view of such a situation, it was, therefore, proposed that public lands should be sold to farmers in order to solve the problem once and for all.

In another sense, however, the sale of public farm land to farmers was one step forward in the direction of abolishing the system of land tenancy and realizing the land-to-the-tiller ideal. The initial sale of public farm land, which was effected in 1948, had a double purpose in view: to help establish owner-farmers and to relieve rural unemployment through the reclamation of land. The original plan called for the sale of 10,000 chia of public land to help establish 7,000 families of owner-farmers and, by using the proceeds therefrom, to create employment for 20,000 families to reclaim 120,000 chia of public waste land. Following the success of the farm rent limitation program in 1951, the Taiwan Provincial Government drew up another set of regulations governing the implementation of the projected sale of public farm land. These regulations provided that all the proceeds from the sale of state-owned lands and that part of the proceeds from the sale of province-owned lands which exceeded the amount of the annual rent, should be earmarked as a fund for the establishment of owner-farmers. This event marked the beginning of a new stage, after the implementation of the farm rent limitation program, in land reform in Taiwan.

The public lands to be offered for sale were limited to those that
were state-owned and province-owned. Of these public lands, some were to
be retained for public use and only a part, approximately 100,000 _chia_, were
to be sold to individual farmers. Of the public land retained for public
use, those in use by the Taiwan Sugar Corporation for the growing of sugar
cane accounted for the largest part, and the remainder was kept by various
governmental departments and schools for their own specific uses. The
public farm lands offered for sale were to be sold chiefly to their current
tenant-cultivators. If the current tenant-cultivator did not care to make
the purchase, or if there was adequate reason for the rejection of his
application, the land could then be sold to one of the following kinds of
purchasers according to this order of priority:

    a. some other tenant-cultivators of public land,
    b. farm hands,
    c. tenant-farmers with insufficient land to till,
    d. part-owner-farmers with insufficient land to till,
    e. persons with an interest in the land (like an original
        reclaimer) in need of land to cultivate, and
    f. persons who had newly become farmers by changing their
        occupation.

The amount of public land which any one farming family might be
permitted to purchase was 0.5 to 2 _chia_ of paddy field and 1 to 4 _chia_
of dry land. The amount could vary according to the categories and grades
of the land. The price of public land purchased by farmers was to be paid
in equal installments on an annual basis. The number of such yearly installments was fixed in 1948 to be from 5 to 8. The yearly payments were
to be remitted in equal amounts at two different times every year to
coincide with the harvest seasons. Since the price was expressed in terms
of farm products, all paddy fields purchased had to be paid for with rice

and all dry land purchased had to be paid for with sweet potato. But the Government could not store up sweet potato, so this payment was converted into monetary terms, according to the official market rate for sweet potato.

To summarize the above, the public farm-land sales program was first conceived with the idea of providing a final solution to the public land problem. When the sale was actually readied to take place, the second objective and plan was added to help establish families of owner-farmers and to create employment for still other families through the reclaiming of public waste land. It was not until the program was in successful operation, and had achieved satisfactory results, that people saw that it was a step forward in the direction of abolishing the system of land tenancy and realizing the land-to-the-tiller ideal.

3. <u>The land-to-the-tiller program</u>. Land-to-the-tiller was a direct way through which a tenant-farmer was to be transformed into an owner-farmer. It entailed the compulsory purchase of tenanted, private farm land by the Government and its resale to the actual tiller, that is, the current tenant. The important obstacles were the landowners, or landlords, who owned large amounts of farm land. They themselves actually cultivated none of the land, or cultivated only a part of it. They depended upon rentals of land parcels to those who had no land to cultivate. The people who rented the land for cultivation, the tenants, did not own any part of the land but they performed the actual cultivation of it and paid rent to the people who did own it. This was a farm-tenancy system and many kinds of exploitation and abuses were inflicted by the landlords upon the tenants. To stop the exploitation and to eradicate the abuses, the Government took action to compulsorily purchase

the land that the owner did not actually cultivate or use and resell it
to the tenant, or tenants, who were tilling it. Hence the title, "land-
to-the-tiller program."

II. Implementation of the Three Programs

In the following section there will be a brief account of the implementation of each of the three programs. As mentioned previously, the
sequent order in which each took place, one after another, had the significant
effect of bringing peacefulness and smoothness to the land-reform operation
as a whole. Therefore, our account has to start first with the farm rent
limitation program, then take up the public farm-land sales program, and
then the land-to-the-tiller program.

1. Implementation of the 37.5% farm rent limitation program.

a. Experiment on the China Mainland

This program was actually started on the mainland of China, but it was
only on an experimental basis with limited scope. There was a serious drought
in Hupeh Province in 1940 and 1941 during which the farmers, owing to the
heavy drain of farm rent upon their rice, showed little interest in the
Government's irrigation projects and turned their attention to the planting
of other crops, for which they were paying only a nominal rent, or no rent
at all. To deal with this situation, the Provincial Government of Hupeh
began in 1941 to carry out a farm rent reduction program in the districts
of Enshih, Hsienfeng, Hsuenen, Laifeng, Lichuen, Hofeng, Chienshih, and
Patung, all in western Hupeh, and extended it in the next year to Yunsi,
Chushan, Chunhsien, Fanghsien, Chuhsi, and Yunhsien in northern Hupeh.
The program was officially known as a "25% farm rent reduction," but it

was really one for the enforcement of the "37.5% farm rent limitation."
With the implementation of this program, there was a phenomenal increase
in rice production.

In 1949 the Office of the High Commissioner of Military and Political
Affairs for the Southwest decided to initiate a simplified form of 25%
farm rent reduction in Szechuan, Sikang, Yunnan, and Kweichow provinces
where farm rent had been particularly high. There was to be a uniform
reduction of all existing farm rents by 25 per cent, irrespective of the
original amounts, and a new lease contract was to be signed between the
landlord and his tenant according to this new rental rate. Because of this
requirement, written contracts were signed in cases where there had been
no such contracts before. In implementing this program in Szechuan Province
with the technical and financial assistance of the Joint Commission for
Rural Reconstruction (JCRR), some 144,000 persons had been mobilized and
employed as field workers. It was estimated that approximately 17,500,000
tenant-farmers had benefited by the program.

b. Large Scale Implementation in Taiwan

In Taiwan the implementation of the 37.5% farm rent limitation
program began in April, 1949 and was successfully completed in August the
same year. First, the National Defense Supreme Council announced a resolution
in 1946 that all farm rents payable by tenants should continue to be 37.5
per cent of the total annual main-crop yield. This resolution was duly
handed down to the several provinces for their guidance through an order
of the Executive Yuan, No. Tsung Er 10050, dated March 20, 1947. In
complying with this order, the Taiwan Provincial Government undertook to
implement a 37.5% farm rent limitation program on private, tenanted land in

1949. The limitation of farm rent and the revision of farm lease contracts were completed in the four-month period between April and August, 1949. Beginning with the first harvest season of 1949, over 100,000 landowning families and 300,000 tenant families on private, leased farm land bound themselves to the rights and obligations documented in their new lease contracts.

c. Establishment of Supervisory Agencies

The implementation of the program was completed in three stages. During the first stage, supervisory agencies on the provincial, hsien, city, and township levels were established; field workers were trained; publicity measures were adopted; standard amounts of the total annual yield of the main crop were appraised. A recounting of this stage shows the breadth of its work. The provincial supervisory agency, the provincial Committee for the Supervision of the 37.5% Rent Campaign, was responsible for information, assistance and supervision in the implementation of farm rent limitation. It was composed of 17 members, including the Speaker of the Provincial Assembly, Chief Justice of the Provincial Supreme Court, five members of the Provincial Council, Director of the Provincial Land Bureau, Director of the Provincial Information Office, and eight, prominent civic leaders. The Hsien or City 37.5% Rent Campaign Committee was responsible for information, assistance, and supervision in the implementation of farm-rent limitation, the fixing of the periods of lease, the appraisal of the standard amounts of the total annual main-crop yield, and the concilia-tion of disputes. It had from 21 to 23 members and included the Magistrate, or Mayor, heads of the Land Office, Departments of Civil Affairs, Social Affairs, Agriculture and Forestry, and Police, representatives of interested

organizations and civic bodies, prominent civic leaders, and two representatives from the tenant-farmers, two from owner-farmers, and two from the landlords. The District or Township Subcommittee had from 15 to 17 members, including the Chief of the District of Township Office, principal and teachers
of the Primary School, representatives of interested organizations, prominent civic leaders, and representatives of tenant-farmers, owner-farmers,
and landlords. The Subcommittee's functions were, in most respects, similar
to those of the Hsien or City Committees. All these committees and subcom-
mittees were created in April and May, 1949 and started to function at once.

d. The Training of Workers

The training of staff workers was carried out on four levels: provincia,
hsien and city, district, and township. The training of provincial-level
workers lasted five days. The training emphasized especially an exposition
of regulations and rules governing farm rent limitation, lectures on special
topics, and the discussion of techniques to be used in the enforcement of
the limitation. In the training on lower levels, particular emphasis was
laid on techniques to be used in the enforcement of the program and on
discussions of practical problems and their solution. The training lasted
from one to two days. The total number of staff workers involved was
4,257, of which 85 belonged to the provincial level, 227 to the hsien and
city level, 945 to the district level, and 3,000 to the township level.

e. Appraisement of Total Annual Main-Crop Yield

Because the 37.5% farm rent limitation involved a calculation of annual
yield, it is obvious that the degree of accuracy in this calculation had a
direct bearing on enforcement and, of course, the success of the program
depended upon fair and equitable enforcement. There were three possible

methods for working out an appraisement. The landlord and his tenant could make an appraisal themselves; or, the actual annual harvest could be taken as the standard; or, the Government, or some representative group of land-lords and tenant-farmers, could determine the standard yield per unit of land in each locality. If either the first or second method were used, it would be extremely difficult to harmonize the views of the landlord and the tenant, and the tenant-farmer was certain to be the aggrieved party because of the disparity between their economic and social positions. The third method, however, provided an objective and clear-cut standard which, if accurately calculated, would ensure effective implementation. But this method also had an inherent limitation: it could be successfully employed only in regions where the categories, grades, and areas of land had been duly investigated and surveyed and land rights had subsequently been properly registered. Fortunately, these had been done in Taiwan. There-fore, it was possible to use the third method to do the appraisal.

The appraisal was carried out independently by each hsien and city, and a standard amount was fixed for every grade of paddy field and dry land, in respect to the annual yield of the principal product of its main crop per chia. As both paddy fields and dry lands are divided into 26 grades and the principal product of the main crop may mean either rice, sweet potato, or sugar cane, the final results of appraisal for every hsien and city are embodied in a detailed table showing standard amounts for all grades of land expressed in different farm products.[3] Because the yield from a given grade of land in one hsien or city might differ from the yield of land of the same grade in another hsien or city, on account of numerous natural and human factors, each **hsien** or city was permitted to arrive at its own standard.

f. Revision of Farm-Lease Contract

Revision of the farm-lease contract refers to the signing of a new written contract, in place of the old one which might have been either written or oral, between the landlord and tenant. This was a required step in the procedure of their registration. The landlord and tenant first negotiated and agreed between themselves upon certain terms for the lease, following the provisions of the 37.5% limitation. They then applied togeth for registration of the lease contract in the township office. The form of all farm-lease contracts was prescribed by the Government, and printed copies of the prescribed form were distributed to the landlord and tenant on the payment of a small charge. Every lease contract was signed in triplicate. The landlord and the tenant each kept one copy, and the third remained in the township office.

Lease revisions in the various **hsien** and cities began toward the end of May, 1949, and the whole task was completed in the next month. With the exception of certain small pieces of land used as tea plantations, orchards etc., for which the revisions of leases would be carried out later on, all contracts for private farm land were duly revised in May and June, 1949, fo a total of 377,364.[4]

g. Problems

Despite the revision of so many farm-lease contracts in accordance with the regulations in so short a time, the program was by no means completely or satisfactorily carried out. The field inspection and recheck ing, which followed a year later, discovered a host of problems and dispute which had arisen to put the program in danger. Most problems rose because landlords tried by various schemes to evade the application of the new regulations to their land or began to abuse their tenants in order to make up some of their losses. The most critical problems rose around the termination of leases and tenancy disputes. The termination of any lease was at bottom invariably the result of threats or inducements offered by the landlord. If the practice of terminating leases went on unchecked, it would not only contravene the rent-limitation policy, but would also give rise to a most serious social problem in consequence of the tenant-farmer's loss of livelihood. In the one-and-one-half year period from the beginning of 1950 to the end of June, 1951, there had been 16,349 cases of lease termination and tenancy dispute, and one year later the number had increased to 35,313.

    h. Establishment of the Farm Tenancy Committee

    It was to cope with this serious situation that a system of supervision was introduced in March, 1951, whereby supervisors were sent out to the various regions to offer guidance and assistance and thus possibly forestall disputes. In addition, a Farm Rent Limitation to 37.5% Act was promulgated by a presidential decree and came into force on June 7 the same year. This was the legal foundation on which all farm rent limitation measures rested.

    Most of the essential provisions contained in this act have been mentioned in the preceding section, explaining the meaning and main features of this program. But one provision was added in 1951 and it concerns the establishment of the Farm Tenancy Committees. Though the enforcement of rent limitation depends to a large extent on legal protections and governmental direction and guidance, it can hardly be successful in operation without the active and willing cooperation of·the parties most intimately concerned, and it was because of this that a 37.5% Farm Rent Campaign Committee for each hsien and city was set up when the program was initiated in 1949.

Then, in 1951 the Farm Rent Limitation to 37.5% Act provided also for the creation of a Farm Tenancy Committee in each hsien, city, and township. Landlords, owner-farmers, and tenant-farmers were represented on each of these committees, which came into being in the summer of 1952. They supplanted the original 37.5% Farm Rent Campaign Committees. It is necessary to bear in mind that the members of committees were representative democratically chosen by, and from, the landlords, owner-farmers, and tenant farmers. This was the only way, short of force, to assure their cooperation

The importance of a Farm Tenancy Committee is illustrated well by the functions it performed:

(1) it furnished information, assistance, and supervision to the implementation of farm rent limitation;

(2) it appraised the standard amount of the total annual yield of the principal product of the main crop on farm lands;

(3) it investigated crop failures caused by natural disaster and recommended measures for the reduction or remission of farm rent;

(4) it worked out conciliations of disputes over the lease of farm lands; and

(5) it investigated, or advised, on matters concerning farm rent limitation when referred to it by the several levels of government.

2. Implementation of the public farm land sales program. The procedure to be followed in the sale of public farm land consisted of several steps: field investigation of the land to be offered for sale;

public announcement of the sales offered and the purchase applications; screening of purchase applications; issuance of purchase certificates and land-ownership certificates.

a. Investigation of Public Lands for Sale

Field investigation of the public land to be offered meant an on-the-spot check of each plot of land and of each of its present cultivators. The principal items to be investigated included:

(1) particulars, such as a description of the particular points of the land;

(2) efficiency of land utilization;

(3) cultivator, whether lessee or farmhand, his name and address;

(4) other available labor force, and description of the area of cultivation.

In undertaking the field investigation, the various hsien and city governments took pains to select only the best qualified staff who, after a short course of training, went out into the townships where, in cooperation with township personnel, they formed themselves into small groups and assigned each group to work in a particular locality. Armed with all necessary maps and records, these groups checked over each plot of public farm land and the farm family cultivating it. It was due partly to the thoroughness of this field investigation that the successive sales of public farm land in Taiwan could be smoothly and successfully carried out.

b. Public Announcement of the Sale

When, after a field investigation, the hsien or city government decided to offer certain public lands for sale to farmers, it would draw up a list of such lands for each township showing all particulars of each piece of land, its sales price, and the name and address of its present cultivator.

This data was published by the township office for a period of twenty days prior to the sale.

c. Application for Purchase

Meantime the Government sent a written notice to each cultivator and asked him to apply for the purchase of the public land of which he was lessee. Again, groups of personnel were sent to the townships where the cultivators of those public lands affected by sales program were assembled to present a detailed explanation of the meaning and significance of the sales program, the procedures to be followed in applying for purchase of public lands, and the rights and obligations of the purchaser after purchase. A 15-day period was allowed for filing application for purchase. The applicant was required to obtain for his application the counter-signatures of two guarantors and file it together with all other necessary documentary evidences.

d. Screening and Approval of Application

On the receipt of the application forms, the **hsien** or city government checked them against the list of public lands offered for sale and against the original cadastral maps and files, then submitted them for screening by the **hsien** or city Committee for the Establishment of Owner-Farmers. If, when an application had been screened, the applicant were found to be fully qualified to purchase public land, the **hsien** or city government placed his name on a list of qualified applicants and submitted it to the provincial government for final approval.

When the applications had then been approved by the Provincial Government, the applicants were notified by the **hsien** or city government. Thereupon, the tenant becomes owner-farmer and responsible for the payment

of the land price and the land tax instead of farm rent. On receiving
payment of the first semiannual installment of the purchase price, the
hsien or city government issued to the purchaser a purchase certificate,
which would be exchanged for a landownership certificate after the entire
purchase price had been paid. The issuance of the landownership certificate
marked the completion of this particular public farm-land sale.

e. Public Land Sold

According to the program drawn up by the Taiwan Provincial Government,
the public land administered by the hsien and city governments was to be
the first offered for sale, and next would be that administered by public
enterprise. There were five successive sales from 1948 to 1953. Of the
106,959 chia of public land leased to tenant-farmers, 90,547 chia, or
84.7%, were opened to purchase. However, only 63,000 chia, or 69.5%,
were actually sold and the remaining 27,574 chia, or 30.5%, were struck
off the official list of public land offered for purchase because these
lands were, in one way or another, not suitable for cultivation. The
farming families who purchased public land in these sales reached a
total of 121,953. They accounted for 26.7% of the average number of
farm families of tenant-farmers, part-owner-farmers, and farmhands,
and 17.3% of the average number of all farm families in Taiwan, for
the three-year period 1950-1952.

3. Implementation of the land-to-the-tiller program. The task
of implementing the land-to-the-tiller program was really gigantic--
gigantic because tremendous amounts of preparatory work had to be
done before the purchasing of land from the landlords and its resale
to tenants actually took place, and even while the program was in

motion a number of rechecks and corrections had to be made in order
to prevent serious mistakes and abuses. This program can be described as follows:

a. The Laws

The first step of the preparatory work was the drawing up and
promulgation of laws upon which later actions had their base. Actually,
the land-to-the-tiller program had a legal basis in the old laws as
well, and in the Constitution of the Republic of China. The old Land
Law of June 30, 1930 already implied that people who actually
cultivate the land should own it. The new Land Law, as amended and
promulgated on April 29, 1946, was, however, more explicit on this
particular point. In the Constitution of the Republic of China,
promulgated on January 1, 1947, one of the Articles in the Chapter
on Fundamental National Policies states that "in land distribution
and land replanning, the State shall, as a matter of principle, help
those who need land for their own cultivation to acquire the land,
and shall regulate the appropriate size of land to be so cultivated."
Methods both direct and indirect were devised to help cultivators
acquire the land, as provided in the new Land Law. The principal
provisions, which were indirect in nature, were:

> Article 30. "The ownership of private farm land shall
> be transferred only to such transferees as can cultivate the
> land themselves after the transfer is effected."

> Article 107. "When the lessor offers his farm land for
> sale or _dien_, the lessee shall have preferential right to
> purchase it or accept the _dien_...."

> Article 33. "Any tenant who has cultivated any leased
> land continuously for eight full years may request the competent

hsien or city government to purchase it for him at its statutory
value if the owner of the said land is an absentee landlord,
or if he is not a farmer cultivating his own land."

The main provisions of the new Land Law that had effects were:

Articles 28 and 29. "Provincial Governments or City
Governments under the direct jurisdiction of the Executive
Yuan may, in the light of local conditions..., prescribe limits
on the maximum area of private land..." and "shall require
that all lands in excess of the prescribed limits shall be
set apart and sold within a definite period of time. All
private lands in excess of the prescribed limits that are
not set apart and sold...shall be compulsorily purchased by
the competent hsien or city government...."

Article 34. "Governments of all levels may...make
compulsory purchase of land for the creation of owner-
cultivated farms according to the following order of
precedence....(1) Private uncultivated land; (2) Land
owned by absentee landlords; (3) That part of the land
under tenancy which exceeds the maximum limits prescribed...."

In the years 1947 to 1949 the Executive Yuan of the National Govern-

ment drew up and enacted a set of measures for the Administration of Land

in Areas Recovered from the Chinese Communists. These measures provided

that all farm land in recovered areas was to be compulsorily purchased by

the Government and resold to either the original tenant-cultivator or the

present tiller; but if the original owner of the land was also its farmer,

he might take it back for his own cultivation; if the original owner of

the land was a landlord, he might be allowed to retain a part of it for

his own use. In those disturbing years these measures had been put into

practice in a number of areas for experimentation, for instance, the Peipei

Demonstration Center in Szechuan Province, the Huanghui Dam District in

Kansu Province, and the Experiment at Lungyen of Fukian Province.

When the 37.5% farm rent limitation program in Taiwan had been

successfully carried out in 1949, the Government was surer of itself, the general public had a better understanding and appreciation of the rationale

for changes in existing land tenure, and the tenant-farmers were more

enthusiastic for further reforms. Thus, the way for the enforcement of a

land-to-the-tiller program was paved.

In order to acquire data for the formulation of the land-to-the-

tiller project, the Taiwan Provincial Government undertook a general

landownership classification for the province as a whole with the technical

and financial assistance of JCRR in 1951. On instruction from the Executiv

Yuan in the spring of 1952, the Provincial Government drew up a provisional

set of practical measures for the limitation of private landownership and

worked out a plan for compensation for land to be compulsorily purchased

by the Government. The Land-to-the-Tiller Act was formally promulgated on

January 26, 1953, and the Executive Yuan designated, on January 29, Taiwan

Province as the area for its application. In the meantime, the Kuomintang

Reform Committee passed a resolution stating that "A land-to-the-tiller

program shall be enforced in Taiwan beginning from January 1953; all

Kuomintang members in responsible government positions shall regard this

as the central task for the year; all activities of the Kuomintang shall

be effectively coordinated therewith; and all efforts shall be directed

to the enforcement of this program."

The Land-to-the-Tiller Act was promulgated for the reason that the

earlier Land Law contained only general provisions relating to the estab-

lishment of owner-farmers and, therefore, it was necessary to adapt the

law to local conditions of Taiwan, in order to meet the actual needs of the

time and place. The new act consisted of 36 Articles, divided into five

chapters: General Provisions, Purchase of Farm Land by the Government,

Resale of Farm Land Purchased by the Government, Restrictions and Penalties, and Supplementary Provisions. Simultaneously, there were enacted two other laws of a subsidiary character entitled Regulations Governing the Issuance of Land Bonds in Kind in Taiwan Province, and Regulations Governing the Transfer of Government Enterprises to Private Ownership. After these three laws were finally passed by the Legislative Yuan on January 20, 1953, the Land-to-the-Tiller program's legal base became complete and clear.

The second phase of preparatory work which had to be completed before the purchase and resale of land could be actually carried out included the undertaking of a general landownership identification, the setting up of administrative organs, the selection and training of working staff, the planning of procedures, the investigation of farm land, and the surveying of individual plots cultivated by more than one farmer.

 b. The General Landownership Identification

This work was undertaken by the Taiwan Provincial Government. Included in the task were:

(1) The compilation of land-record cards. Each plot of land was given a separate card with a serial number, or card number. These cards were kept in the land office of the locality where the lands were situated. On the card were these headings: Particulars, Land Use, Ownership, and Other Rights Over Land.

(2) The identification. Landownership identification was determined on the basis of the residence of the landowner. This was the only way to do it, and, fortunately, Taiwan keeps excellent household-land records. The household number, name or number of neighborhood, name or number of hamlet, or section, name of township, and name of hsien, or city, of each assumed landowner had been duly recorded.

Identification work began on the township level. First, all the land-record cards of a township, recording the residences of the individual landowners, were classified and put together. Work then proceeded from the township level, through the hamlet or section level, down to the neighborhood level, until it reached the household in which the landowner had his residence. Thus, the plot of land and its owner were accurately put together. If a person owned a plot of land in one township, but had his residence in another township, whether of the same or a different hsien, or city, his land-record card would be transferred to the land office of the latter for purposes of landownership identification. In this way, all the cards, recording all plots of land belonging to every individual landowner, would be assembled together for ready use.

c. The Setting Up of Administrative Organs

In setting up the administrative frame, the Ministry of the Interior was in charge on the national level, the Land Bureau of the provincial government's Civil Affairs Department held the intermediate responsibility, and the hsien and city governments were in charge on the next level. The Farm Tenancy Committees of the hsien, cities and townships, were assistant agencies. Below the hsien and city level, the local land offices were in charge of technical work, and the township offices were basic executive agencies. The Taiwan Land Bank was the financial agency for the compulsory purchase and resale of land, and for the issuance of land bonds in kind and the payment of principal and interest thereon.

It was also responsible for the transfer of government enterprise stocks to landlords in partial payment for the land purchased from them by the Government. The Taiwan Provincial Food Bureau was the agency for the acceptance and safekeeping of payments in kind made by farmer purchasers. It was also responsible for the issuance of payments in kind in connection with servicing on the land bonds. To give more attention to the whole matter on high levels, the Executive Yuan ordered on May 22, 1953 the creation of a Committee for the Handling of Problems Relating to the Enforcement of the Land-to-the-Tiller Act. This committee was composed of over a dozen members, including Heads of competent ministries, members of the Executive Yuan Council, chairman of the China-United States Joint Commission on Rural Reconstruction, the governor and heads of competent departments and bureaus of the Taiwan Provincial Government, and General Manager of the Taiwan Land Bank, with the Minister of the Interior and the Governor of Taiwan as conveners.

d. Training of Working Staff

The working staff totalled 32,000 people. They were given training courses lasting from 2 to 20 days. The training of officers in charge of the program in the hsien, cities and townships, which lasted for twenty days, was given by the provincial government. The training of field workers employed by the township offices, which lasted for ten days, and of members of hsien and city Farm Tenancy Committees and township officers, which lasted for two days, was given by the hsien and city governments. Training of the township Farm Tenancy Committee members lasted for three days and was given by the township offices. Training of hamlet and section chiefs and officers lasted for two days and was given by field representatives of the township offices. It was a large and elaborate training program.

    e. The Procedure

The procedure for the enforcement of the land-to-the-tiller program was divided into ten main phases and certain sub-processes. They were carried out, step by step, according to a fixed schedule and were expected to be completed by the end of 1953:

(1) Formulation of practical measures;

(2) Training of working staff;

(3) Popular information and education;

(4) Rechecking;

(5) Compilation of lists of land to be compulsorily purchased, retained, or resold to farmer purchasers;

(6) Screening and approval of the lists compiled;

(7) Compulsory purchase of land and its resale to farmer purchasers, including

    (a) public announcement,
    (b) individual notification,
    (c) compensation to landlords and payment of the first installment by farmer purchasers,
    (d) registration of the transfer of landownership,
    (e) issuance of landownership certificates to farmer purchasers;

(8) Checking over of maps and records;

(9) Compilation of statistics;

(10) Critique and appraisal.

    f. Investigation of Farm Lands

The investigation of farm lands included within its scope all private farm lands that were governed by the 27.5% rent lease contracts, as well as

those which were cultivated either by the owners themselves or by farmhands.
All told, 2,020,000-odd plots were investigated, and over 500,000 families
of tenant-farmers, farm hands, and owner-farmers were visited. Such a
comprehensive investigation was necessary, inasmuch as the compulsory
purchase of landlord's land, its resale to its present cultivators, the
retention of part of the cultivator's land by the landlords, or exemption
from compulsory purchase, all served to involve the rights and obligations
of the citizens and the use of farm lands and farmhouses in a vortex of
complicated relationships.

The factors under investigation included all particulars of farm
land, the method of its use, rights and obligations involved, the amount
of annual yield, together with the economic condition of the farm family,
their capacity to undertake farming, and their personal inclination and
wishes concerning the purchase of farm land. Any information which was
originally available in the land cards and records would be checked over
on the spot to see whether the data were correct, or whether there had
been some change in the situation. Any information which was not
originally available in the old files, such as the employment of farmhands and the use of farmhouses, drying grounds, ponds, fruit trees,
bamboo groves, and woods, would now be duly investigated and recorded.
Cases of illegal termination of lease contract, illicit sublease, failure
to sign lease contracts as required by law, and disputes concerning land
rights and tenancy were especially important areas to be investigated.

The investigation proceeded smoothly from the very beginning and
was completed throughout the whole province early in April of 1953. Its
findings were vital data in the making of subsequent decisions.

g. Surveying of Individual Plots of Land

The inspection of individual plots, cultivated by more than one

person, included a survey and physical division of the following kinds

of farm land:

(1) Any plot of land which was in part cultivated by the owner himself and partly
leased to a tenant-farmer would be surveyed and divided into two plots, each of
which would be given a separate serial
number and its area separately computed.

(2) Any plot of land which was leased to
several tenant-farmers would be surveyed
and divided into as many separate plots,
each of which would be given a separate
serial number and its area separately
computed.

(3) Any plot of farm land, part of which had
become non-farm land, would be surveyed
and divided into two separate plots, each
of which would be given a separate serial
number and its area separately computed.
In case a portion of any given plot of
farm land had been washed away, the
remaining portion would be surveyed and
its area computed.

(4) Any plot of land, part of which should
be subject to compulsory purchase by the
Government, would be surveyed and divided
into two plots, each of which would be
given a separate serial number and its
area separately computed.

It must be understood, in this connection, that the survey and division

of individual plots of farm land cultivated by more than one person, as

described, did not mean any further fragmentation of the land. For the

fact is that what is called a "plot" in the land records in Taiwan is

frequently a combination of several pieces which, being cultivated by

several families, can be fairly large over-all and its pieces fairly
numerous. Under such circumstances, any given piece of land that was
cultivated by a given family was an integral unit with definite boundaries.
Consequently, the task of the surveyor was merely to describe the original
plot according to its existing component pieces and usage, and not to
subdivide a small piece into still smaller units.

      h. The Compulsory Purchase of Land

Immediately after the completion of all the preparatory steps reviewed
above, compulsory purchase of farm land began. The task consisted of the
computation and approval of areas to be retained or compulsorily purchased,
the public announcements listing farm land to be compulsorily purchased,
the notification of compulsory purchase and surrender of title deeds, the
identification of the would-be purchasers (the present tenant-cultivators),
the application for purchase of farm land by present tenant-cultivators,
the confirmation of applications for purchase, the public announcement of
the resale of land to purchasers, the notification to purchasers, and the
issuance of landownership certificates. In the following, a brief statement
is made concerning each of these steps:

Computation of areas to be compulsorily purchased, or retained, meant
the consideration of all land of all grades in each landlord's possession and
then calculating them together to determine what part was to be compulsorily
purchased by the Government and what was to be retained by the landlord.
Since compulsory purchase and retention were interrelated or reciprocal,
the area subject to either process had to be determined along with the other.
The computation was made by assembling together all the cards belonging

to the 170,000 lessor families out of the 800,000-odd landowning families, for whom landownership cards had been compiled previously and kept in the 59 local land offices throughout the whole province.

All compulsory purchases of farm land had to be approved by the hsien or city governments. All retentions of farm land by the landlords were considered by the township farm-tenancy committee, and the results of such considerations reported to the hsien or city farm-tenancy committee for confirmation, then submitted to the hsien or city government for approval. As the farm-tenancy committee members were thoroughly familiar with the respective local conditions, had a firm grasp of the basic ideas of the land-to-the-tiller policy, and had had ample experience in helping to enforce the 37.5% farm rent limitation program, they carried out their duties smoothly and speedily.

The lists of farm lands to be compulsorily purchased and those to be retained were publicly announced after approval by the hsien or city government. The lists of the lands for compulsory purchase then were handed down by the hsien or city government to the respective township offices in whose jurisdiction the lands were located, to be publicly announced at the said offices and in the local newspapers. Those lists included the names of landlords, their addresses, particulars of the lands, the purchase price, names of the present cultivators, and other rights existing over the lands. The period of public announcement was 30 days, during which the owner of any given piece of land or any interested party might, if he objected to the inclusion of the said land as erroneous or unjustified, file a request that the error be rectified. The official public announcements began on April 26 and up to May 1 they appeared in all places throughout the province. During this period of public announcement, large numbers of landowners and other interested parties went to examine the lists. Before the expiration of the thirty-day period, the township offices sent our representatives to call on the few landlords who had not appeared and urge them to go and take a look.

Notification of compulsory purchase and surrender of title deeds occurred when the areas of farm land to be compulsorily purchased became definitive; then the different hsien and city governments proceeded to notify the landlords individually and in person by serving each one of them with a duplicate copy of that sheet of the original list on which his name appeared, and to require him to surrender his title deeds and other relevant documents within a certain time limit. More than 90 percent of the required documents were duly surrendered by the landlords within the prescribed time limit. The small number of cases in which neither title deeds nor other relevant documents were surrendered were ascribed, in part, to the loss of the papers, partly to mortgage, partly to the absence of the landlords from the hsien, city or province, and partly to joint ownership. Those documents which had not been duly surrendered within the prescribed time limit were declared to be null and void, according to the provisions of the Land-to-the-Tiller Act. In all other cases, upon the receipt of the summoned documents from the landlords, the hsien and city governments gave each of them a written notice with which he might go to the Land Bank of Taiwan to get the compensation for his land.

i. Resale of Land to Tenants

According to statistics compiled by the provincial Land Bureau in 1952, the total amount of farm land, including both public and private, in the

Province of Taiwan was 854,918 chia. Of this amount, 681,154 chia, or about 80 per cent, were private farm land. Of the private farm land, 255,334 chia, or 37.63 per cent, were private, tenanted farms. Not all private, tenanted farms were subject to the compulsory purchase. There was a big portion which included farms retained by the landlords for their own cultivation and farms which were, for adequate reasons, exempted from the compulsory purchase. The final amount compulsorily purchased was 143,568 chia, or 56.23 per cent; of this, 121,535 chia, or about 85 per cent, were paddy field, and 22,033 chia, a small portion, were dry land. The number of landlord families affected was 106,049 or 40.46 per cent of the total number of owner-farmer families.[5]

Next came resale of the farm land. This phase of the program also included a number of steps. The first step was the identification of the present tenant-cultivators, who were the potential purchasers. They were identified by means of the landownership cards of their landlords, and their identity was rechecked by the investigators making on-the-spot inspections of the farm land. As the landownership cards contained detailed information about each tenant and the area he had leased, they could be relied upon for accurate help. If there should be a termination of lease, a sublease, a death of a tenant, or a failure to sign a 37.5% farm-lease contract, those events would have been investigated and noted down. Thus, both the identity of the present cultivator, to whom the land could be resold by the Government and the area available to him could be ascertained.

Next came the submitting of applications for purchase. Application was to be made within twenty days after the expiration of the period of public announcement. But in order to save time and to make applying convenient

for the tenants, this part of the work was carried out simultaneously with
the on-the-spot inspection. On the Farm Land Check Sheets used by the
investigators in making the investigation, there was a special column under
the heading of "Applicant for the Purchase of the Land." The investigator
would ask the tenant whether he was ready and willing to make the purchase.
If he was ready and willing, he then put his personal seal under the said
column of the Check Sheet.

The application procedure went on smoothly. Most cultivators, on
being approached by the investigators, gladly put their seals on the
Check Sheets. Only a few were reluctant to apply for purchase, either
out of fear of the landlord's influence and prestige or on account of
personal affection for the landlord. But these,too,would eventually be
persuaded by the Government to put in their applications for purchase.
Only a very few cases, in which the tenants knew that the land was too
poor in productivity or had other defects, had refused to the last to
make application. Such exceptional cases were duly reported to the
Provincial Government for approval. The Government kept a record why
these lands were not bought.

As soon as the names of the present cultivators had been ascertained
and a List of Farm Lands to Be Resold to Farmer Purchasers had been compiled,
the said List would be sent over to the township farm-tenancy committees
for rechecking and to the hsien or city farm-tenancy committees for confirmation. By the end of April, 1953, the work of rechecking and confirmation
in the various hsien and cities was completed. This ended the third step.

The fourth step was the public announcement of the resale of farm
land to farmer purchasers. Both the compulsory purchase and the resale

were publicly announced by the hsien or the city government at one time.
The manner and duration of the announcements were identical for both the
purchase and the resale. During the period of public announcement, every
aspirant for the purchase of land would go to examine the list of lands
to see if his own name was there and to scrutinize all particulars of the
land he would be purchasing. There were more requests for correction of
errors from tenant-farmers than from landlords.

The fifth step was notification to farmer purchasers. After the
expiration of the period of public announcement, the various hsien and
city governments sent a duplicate copy of the List of Farm Lands to Be
Resold to Farmer Purchasers to each of the prospective purchasers to
notify him to pay the purchase price at the Land Bank at the appointed
time.

Finally, there came the issuance of landownership certificates. After
the collection of the first installment of the purchase price, the hsien
and city governments began to register changes in land rights and issue
landownership certificates. The new landownership certificate was
identical in shape and size with the ordinary title deed, but a note was
affixed to it stating how the ownership had been acquired and enumerating
the provisions of Article 28 and 30 of the Land-to-the-Tiller Act. As
soon as the entire purchase price had been paid, the Land Bank of Taiwan
put a chop on the certificate stating "the purchase price had been paid
in full."

According to statistics compiled by the Provincial Land Bureau, the
principal results of the program were as follows: 143,568 chia of farm
land compulsorily were purchased by the Government and resold to farmer

purchasers; the land of 106,649 landlord families had been compulsorily purchased by the Government; and 194,823 farming families had purchased the land when it was offered by the Government.[6] Of this number, 133,395 families, or 68 per cent, had purchased all the land (amounting to 101,634 chia, or 71 per cent of all the land offered by the Government for resale) they used to cultivate as tenants or farm hands; 61,428 families, or 32 per cent, had purchased only part of the land they formerly cultivated as tenants or farm hands, and the area thus purchased was 41,934 chia, or 29 per cent, of all the land offered by the Government for resale.

In 1953 there were 28,960 tenant families which purchased directly from landlords 15,646 chia of farm land. By adding 28,960 to 194,823, we find the total number of farming families which acquired the ownership of land in 1953 to be 223,783; and by adding 15,646 to 143,568, we find the total area of farm land acquired by these families to be 159,214 chia. Consequently, the ratio between owner-cultivated and tenanted farm land, with regard to the 681,154 chia of private farm land in Taiwan, underwent a great change. It changed from 61.4:38.6 to 84.8:15.2.

j. Compensation for Landlords

That the landlords from whom the Government had compulsorily purchased the farm land were duly compensated for giving up their land right is one of the important facts whereby the land reform in Taiwan has been able to proclaim its democratic spirit and policies. Therefore, it deserves a separate description.

The price of paddy fields and dry land compulsorily purchased was calculated for the respective land grades at two-and-one-half times the total amount of the annual main-crop yield, as appraised in the respective

hsien and cities at the time when the 37.5% rent limitation program was
being undertaken. The paying of the compensation was entrusted to the
Taiwan Land Bank by the Taiwan Provincial Government. It was paid 70
per cent with land bonds in kind and 30 per cent with government enterprise
stocks. Land bonds were of two kinds: rice bonds and sweet potato bonds.
Compensation for paddy fields was paid with rice bonds and that for dry
land and immovable fixtures with sweet potato bonds. Paddy fields were
classified as double-crop, single-crop, weather-depending, three-year
rotation, and specially-irrigated fields. Because the main crop on double-
crop paddy fields is rice, their purchase price was expressed entirely
in terms of rice; but as the main crops on all other paddy fields are
usually rice and sweet potato, and include even sugar cane in the case of
three-year rotation fields, their purchase price could not be directly
expressed in terms of rice but had to be converted into rice in a round-
about way, according to the relevant provisions of the Regulations Governing
the Implementation of the Land-to-the-Tiller Act in Taiwan. Compensation
for dry land in terms of sweet potato, to be paid with sweet potato bonds,
was a rather simple affair. The standard yields of the annual, main crop
on the various grades of dry land had all been estimated in terms of sweet
potato during the enforcement of the 37.5% farm rent limitation program,
and the same standards could now be used in calculating the price of dry
land. In August, 1953, the Taiwan Land Bank began payments to the landlords.
By the end of June, 1954, approximately 92 per cent of the compensation
due in rice bonds and 88 per cent of the compensation due in sweet potato
bonds had been paid to the landlords, of whom about 85 per cent had gone
to the Taiwan Land Bank to pick up their bonds.

The Taiwan land bonds in kind were issued by the Taiwan Provincial Government on the authorization of the Central Government and bore an interest rate of 4 per cent, per annum. Both principal and interest were to be paid in equal, semiannual installments spread over a period of ten years. In the case of the double-crop paddies, both principal and interest would be paid with rice. But those rice bonds which were issued to compensate for the purchase of single-crop and weather-depending fields would be paid, upon maturity, 50 per cent with rice and 50 per cent with cash, by converting half the amount of rice payable into monetary terms at the current market value of rice. Still other rice bonds, issued for the compensation of the three-year rotation and specially irrigated fields, would be paid entirely with cash by applying the same method of conversion. Similarly, all sweet potato bonds would be paid, entirely with cash, by converting the full amount of sweet potato payable into monetary terms at the current market value of sweet potato.

When part of the compensation to landlords was paid with government enterprise stocks, a temporary certificate issued in the first instance was to be exchanged later on for the stocks. This was necessary because the government enterprise stocks were not yet printed when the Taiwan Land Bank began to pay compensation to landlords in August, 1953. As a makeshift, the temporary certificates, jointly signed by the Ministries of Interior and Economic Affairs and the Taiwan Provincial Government, and specifying the quantities of rice and sweet potato to be paid to the certificate holder, were issued by the Taiwan Land Bank together with the land bonds. When the government enterprise stock certificates were ready on March 1, 1954, the Taiwan Land Bank handed them over to landlords in exchange for the temporary certificates.

Paying the landlords with government enterprise stocks meant that the Government had to sell to private citizens some of the enterprises which it took over from the Japanese after Taiwan was restored to China. Those offered for sale were the Taiwan Cement Corporation, the Taiwan Paper and Pulp Corporation, the Taiwan Agricultural and Forestry Development Corporation, and the Taiwan Industrial and Mining Corporation. The Government established a Re-evaluation Committee, representing most of the concerne parties, to readjust in terms of the New Taiwan Dollar the real value of the four corporations. The total capital value, as finally refixed, was NT$970,000,000. This was divided into 97,000,000 shares. Thus, the face value of each share was NT$10. Of the ninety-seven million shares, 28,244,414 were state-owned and 50,758,003 province-owned, making a total of 79,002,417 shares, or NT$790,024,170 worth of stocks, owned by the state and province. These were to be tender for the payment of 30% of the landlords' compensation In February, 1954, the Taiwan Land Bank announced that within two months holders of the previously-mentioned, temporary certificates might exchange them for regular stocks. Toward the end of May, 1954, when all of the 79,002,417 shares of stocks were hands of the 100,000 landlord families who had sold their land under the land-to-the-tiller program, the ownership of the above mentioned, four corporations was transferred from the Government to the private stockholders.

The question as to how the four corporations would be operated after their transfer to private ownership had been a subject of much discussion and concern. Both the Legislative Yuan and the Taiwan Provincial Assembly recommended continual Government assistance when they approved of the sale of the Government stocks. On October 15, 1954, the Government set up a

Committee to Assist Public Enterprises Transferred to Private Ownership under the Land-to-the-Tiller Program. The Committee drew up a set of Rules governing public assistance to those four corporations. The rules were duly submitted to, and approved by, the Executive Yuan on October 21, 1954. The rules provided that the Ministry of Economic Affairs should be the responsible agency and should be guided by the following principles: The four corporations would be given, in addition to the usual facilities, the same special facilities for short-term loans as are given to public enterprises by the Bank of Taiwan. They would be encouraged to utilize, as far as possible, raw materials and equipment that are procurable on the domestic market and would be assisted by the Government in increasing their production. They may be allotted foreign exchange in amounts necessary for the purchase of raw materials and equipment and for carrying out approved new production projects for which they need imports. The four corporations would be assisted by the Government to carry out all projects for the improvement and expansion of productive installations that had been approved by the Government before the transfer to private ownership. They would be assisted by the Government to market their products, and assisted in other matters relating to business management and future development.

    k. Collection of the Purchase Price from Farmer-Purchasers

The price of farm land offered by the Government for resale was calculated on the same basis as was its price when it was compulsorily purchased from landlords: namely, **two-and-one-half** times the total amount of its annual, main-crop yield for the respective land grades. Beginning from the season in which the land was purchased, the farmer purchaser **would pay the price of the land, plus interest, in equal, semiannual**

installments spread over a period of ten years, either in kind or in land
bonds redeemable in kind. The dates of installment payments were closely
coordinated with the harvesting seasons. Except for the first one, all
installments had to bear an interest of 4 per cent, per annum. In case of
crop failure, a farmer purchaser could be permitted to postpone the payment
of that particular installment of the purchase price, if his request for
delay was approved. But the unpaid installment, or installments, must be
made up, one after another, immediately after the ten-year period was over.

Methods of payment differed with the different categories of land.
Payments were made in cash, calculated in terms of the current value of
sweet potato, in respect to dry land, and the immovable fixtures thereon.
Payments for paddy fields were in rice. In the case of one-crop paddy
fields, and paddy fields depending on weather, the installments due in
years when no rice was planted were paid in cash, calculated in terms of
the current value of rice; in the case of rotation fields, including the
specially irrigated fields, the entire purchase price was paid in cash,
calculated in terms of the current value of rice. Payments in rice were
delivered to the local warehouses designated by the Provincial Food Bureau,
and payments in cash were made at local branches of the Taiwan Land Bank.
It has been reported that at the end of 1964 all payments for land purchases
had been collected in full.

Reasons for taking up so much detail about the implementation of the
land-to-the-tiller program are obvious. It was this program which constituted the main body of the land reform undertaken in Taiwan. Sucess or
failure of the whole effort was chiefly dependent upon the results of this
program. To be successful, tremendous care had to be given to the laying

out of the various steps and the different kinds of work done. Sound policies counted too. But without good procedures and work plans, sound policies could be utterly defeated. The Government and all the responsible personnel in the program were aware of this fact and, therefore, practically every step and every point, which were deemed necessary for assuring smooth operation of the task, had been thoroughly discussed, well prepared, and carefully put into practice. If the implementation of this program had been brought to a satisfactory completion, it had not been so by accident or by luck, but by careful and hard work. People who were responsible for the execution of the program took no chance in allowing any negligence or omission. It is, therefore, suggested, without any self-righteousness, that those countries which are considering a land reform like the land-to-the-tiller program should pay attention to the things that have been devised and performed in Taiwan.

III. Objectives Achieved

After reading the foregoing, one should be able to see that the first set of objectives of the land reform in Taiwan have largely been achieved. The high farm rent was successfully limited to a single, reasonable, and fair-to-everybody rate. The revision and conclusion of 377,364 (one hundred per cent) new, farm-lease contracts, each one completely in accordance with the new rent regulations, wiped out much that was unjust in the farm-tenancy system. The new supervisory agencies and the farm-tenancy committees protected the public and provided solutions to many of the problems and disputes which arose because of the new farm rent limitation regulations. It has been reported that a majority of the landlords were not happy about the reduction or limitation, which was natural; but they raised no active opposition against it.

The objective of helping to build up more owner-farmers has, to a great extent, also been realized. First, the public farm land sales program sold 63,000 _chia_ of farm land to a total of 121,953 farm-tenant families who now became owner-farmers. They represented 26.7 per cent of the average number of farm families of tenant-farmers, part-owner-farmers, and farm hands; and 17.3 per cent of the average number of all farm families in Taiwan for the 1950-1953 three-year period.

Through the land-to-the-tiller program the Government compulsorily bought 143,568 _chia_ of farm land from 106,649 landlord families. Immediately these _chia_ were sold to 194,823 farm-tenant families who thus acquired landownership and became owner-farmers. In 1953, 28,960 tenant families bought directly, that is, not through the land-to-the-tiller program, 15,646 _chia_ of farm land from landlords and so increased further the numbers of tenant families who had become owner-farmers. These direct land transactions might have been an indirect result of the land-to-the-tiller program. It was very possible that some of the landlords sold their land privately to their tenants because they had heard of the land-to-the-tiller program and had thought that they might have to suffer a loss if they waited till the Government came to purchase their land compulsorily. So far as the building up of more owner-farmers is concerned, it makes no difference whether the transaction was accomplished through the good office of the Government or by a direct deal between the landlord and the tenant-cultivator. At the time when the land-to-the-tiller program was about to go into enforcement, there were 681,154 _chia_ of private farm land in Taiwan. The ratio between owner-cultivated and tenanted farm land was 61.4:38.6. When the program was brought to completion in 1954, it changed to 84.8:15.2. This means that at the end of 1954, only 15.2 per cent of the private farm land was still tenanted farm land.[7] And it should be remembered, too, that this 15.2 per cent of farm land was cultivated by tenants who paid now to the landowners as a rent not more than 37.5 per cent of the annual yield of the main crop raised on the land.

Looking at it from another angle, the effort to readjust the distribution of landownership was an effort to realize Dr. Sun Yat-sen's ideal that one who cultivates the land shall also own it. And the successful implementation of the land-to-the-tiller program brought, also, the realization of Dr. Sun Yat-sen's land-reform objective.

As has been repeatedly indicated, successful implementation of the three programs demanded extensive and exhaustive surveying, identification, and registration of both public and private farm lands. There is no doubt that Taiwan now possesses a most clear, inclusive, systematic, and reliable cadastral system. If the designers and executives of Taiwan's land-reform programs had as one of their objectives the establishment of a cadastral system, or the refining of the existing one, they certainly realized it to the full. Under such a cadastral system no farm land in production can possibly be hidden or lost to the Government. Together with its repeated appraisments of productivity, in terms of annual-crop yields, the Government in Taiwan has the essential, and very efficient, farm land taxation system which allows revenues from land resources to be collected fairly and fully. This is another of the first set of objectives to have been achieved through the land-reform programs.

In summary, it is quite fair to say that the land reform in Taiwan had made some people unhappy, especially among the big landlords. Generally, however, or as far as the fulfillment of its immediate purposes was concerned, it was a great success. Although its social and political stability and the relatively prosperous economy now being enjoyed by the people in Taiwan can be attributed to a number of factors, the completion of the land reform is certainly one of them. As for the question of whether or not the land reform has created new problems, and whether or not, or to what extent, it has fulfilled objectives of the second set, answers are to be found in later chapters.

Notes

[1]Dien means that a landowner surrenders the right of using a piece of land, together with the title deed, to another person from whom a certain amount of money is borrowed. The term of the deal can be a number of years. Within the term, the person who has acquired the right can use the land for farming purposes, or rent it to someone else to farm and keep the title deed. When the term is about to expire, the original owner must come to redeem the land by paying back the borrowed money. If he fails to do so, the dien holder can keep the land as purchased, unless another term of dien is arranged in advance.

[2]Mow is a farm-land unit term used on the mainland of China. The size of a mow varies from place to place. In official documents, it is the official mow. One official mow is about one-sixth of an acre. In

the eastern part of Shantung Province, the local people's _mow_ was one-third of an acre.

[3]See Table 4 showing the standard amounts in Taiwan catties of the total annual main-crop yield per _chia_ on the twenty-six grades of private paddy field in the various _hsien_ and cities, Taiwan Province; table 5 shows the same on dry land. Hui-sun Tang, Land Reform in Free China, Appendix 1, pp. 290-91.

[4]_Ibid._, Appendix 1, Table 3, p. 289.

[5]_Ibid._, Appendix 1, Tables 1, 3, and 7.

[6]_Ibid._, Appendix 1, Table 7.

[7]These lands were retained by the owners according to regulations in the Land-to-the-Tiller Act. But because they were rented to tenants for cultivation, the owners were allowed to take them back, as long as the tenants had to depend for their living on the land, or the owners had other ways to earn a living. Later on, when some of the owners had become business men, or other job-holders, in the cities or towns, they voluntarily sold the land to the tenants.

Chapter Three

PLAN OF STUDY

```
┌─────────────────────────────────────────────┐
│                                             │
│    I.  Scope                                │
│                                             │
│   II.  Methods                              │
│        1.  Interviews:  Samplings           │
│            from Ten Categories              │
│        2.  Use of Existing Literature       │
│        3.  Use of Case Studies              │
│                                             │
│                                             │
└─────────────────────────────────────────────┘
```

No study of human behavior will yield any informative and meaningful results if it has not been carefully and intelligently planned. Our study is expected to be a significant one, and it is expected, therefore, to bring forth important and dependable information and knowledge upon which sound and objective evaluation of the results of the land reform recently undertaken in Taiwan can be made and valuable references given for use by those countries which are considering a land reform of their own.

I. Scope

This study is to be both intensive and encompassing. It will begin by explaining whether or not there had been a real need for undertaking such an extensive and drastic land reform in Taiwan. For it was to

cost the nation and the American AID huge amounts of money and materi-

als.[1] And it was to result in profound and revolutionary impacts upon

the country's social and economic structures. In various respects, the

impacts of this land reform had been the interruptions, or dissolutions,

of social and economic systems and life orders of many sections of the

population in Taiwan. In the enforcement of the various programs, there

was tremendous rish of arousing a rebellion of the powerful landlords

and their political, kinship, and economic alliances. The risk thus

taken was especially imminent at such a time when the power of making

and enforcing land reform laws was, by and large, in the hands of the

so-called "mainlanders," whereas, those upon whom the regulations were

applied were all natives of the province. There could have been a great

tragedy if there had indeed been no serious need for such a gigantic

undertaking.

Actually, drastic land reform had been an urgent need both on the

Chinese mainland and in Taiwan for a long time. Then why had not the

Government gone about such a badly needed reform earlier? Why had it

been done after the Kuomintang Administration was defeated by the Chinese

Communists and they had retreated to Taiwan? Were there reasons other

than, or in addition to, the need for such a reform? To find the

answers to these questions, this study will inquire into the real

reasons for which the land reform was designed and carried out. This by

no means implies that the inquirers are suspicious of the Administration's sincerity or motivation in improving the farm people's living conditions. We do, however, wish to know if there were any concerns not openly stated by the authority which could have been treated with the solution of the land problems. In other words, the study has an interest in finding out whether the Government used land reform to solve problems not related to land.

Any kind of social or economic reform has its objectives. There are the immediate, or meet-the-urgent-need objectives, and the long-term, or prepare-for-the-future objectives. Collaterally, anyone who makes a study on any social or economic reform or reconstruction program cannot but be engaged in searching for the endeavor's objectives. Our study will pay a considerable amount of attention to the revealing of the authority's objectives in the various programs of the land reform. It will try to analyze the nature and significance of these objectives and their relations to the current conditions of the land tenure, the farm-tenancy system, and the farm people's life as a whole, to the traditional land policies in China, and to the present Government's political and economic philosophies and principles.

The study's chief effort in this respect will, however, be the projecting, or assuming, of a number of far-reaching, or socio-economic-improvement objectives, and the searching for indications of the achievement of these objectives. Such objectives, though not explicitly proclaimed in the legal provisions of the program, could not fail to be affected by any land reform of significance. Because the realization of such objectives would have great effects on practically every important phase of the rural people's life and on some areas of the life of the nation's other people, any inquiry into this subject would make the periphery of the study very wide indeed. It would mean that the study would have to look into all such areas as the rural people's living conditions, in particular as well as in general, conditions of the farming business, technical as well as economic, the rural people's education and cultural activities, their community participation or socialization, and others, to see whether the land reform has had any effects on these phases and so given rise to important changes.

Whether or not there have been any effects, and whether or not such effects will have been of any significance, depend largely on the extent to which the overt results of the land reform have been favorably accepted and utilized with constructive purposes. If, for example, the limitation of the farm-rent rate and the transfer or redistribution of the landownership have to a great extent been enthusiastically accepted by the tenant-farmers and have been used as a stimulation to lift their work morale and, in turn, increase their effort in improving the farming business, then the land reform would very likely have profound effects on all aspects of the farm people's life and work. On the other hand, if the tenant-farmers have taken the two results half-heartedly, and have complained that such changes are too insignificant to bring much betterment to their miserable conditions, the progress of the land reform would have abruptly stopped at the lowering of the farm-rent rate and the transfer of the landownership from a certain number of landlords to a certain number of tenant-cultivators. As basis for this logic or deduction, inquiry into the farm people's feeling toward the result of the enforcement of the land-reform programs, and their ability and willingness to make some profitable use of those results, will constitute one of the important phases of this study.

It is easy to write about the content and meaning of the three importan programs which formed the main body of the land reform in Taiwan. It is als a simple matter to review the implementation of the programs and the achieve ment of those immediate goals of the undertaking. To accomplish these simpl tasks there are materials already in existence and data ready for use. But it is quite different to make inquiries into those far-reaching effects and to study the achievements, if any, of those socio-economically significant objectives, as were mentioned in the preceding paragraphs. No ready-made, published information and materials are available. Practically all the data had to be collected from the field by the research staff members them- selves. Furthermore, a great deal of the information required was from personal opinions, feelings, judgments, and experience. All of these are subject to individuals' prejudice, bias, self-centered interests, and lack of information. Should the data collected be heavily saturated with any of these elements, the outcome of the study would not only have no value but would cause misunderstanding of the results of the land reform.

In order to avoid so serious a mistake, or to diminish as much as possible the probability of making such a mistake, the collection of information or data was undertaken through three channels: interviews, sampling five types of farm people and five types of non-farm people; the use of literature which, without presumption, expresses opinions on results of the land reform; and the use of case studies.

The study not only had many kinds and large numbers of people involved;
it also covered a variety of territories or localities spreading all over
the province, and in each territory or locality, the different grades of
farm land and the various types of farming were taken into consideration.
That such a big coverage was made was based on the assumption that the
degree of the effects of the land reform might vary from place to place,
in accordance with conditions in various farm areas. In a rich farm area
the effects of the land reform, so the assumption went, could be different
from that in a poor area, and its effects on an agriculture predominated
by rice culture might not be repeated in one consisting largely of dry-
land crops. For instance, in most rich farm areas the farm rent had
always been extremely high. The tenants had been ruthlessly oppressed by
the heavy burdens laid upon them by the landlords. To these poor
peasants, the 37.5 per cent farm rent limitation must have been a tremendous relief and, therefore, they could not but have showed great appreciation toward it; whereas, in the poor, hilly areas where the crop production had been low and the farm-rental rates had originally also been
low, the rent-reduction program would have had very little, if any,
effect on tenants. The same assumption could be true concerning the
variation of the effects of the land-to-the-tiller program. In the
double-crop, paddy-field areas, assuming that the productivity of the farm
was high, the owning of one chia, or even one-half chia, of farm land
would mean a great deal to a forward-looking and hard-striving farm
family who had been poor tenants for many generations. On the other
hand, in the poor, hilly areas where very little could be produced on one

chia of land, a family could hardly subsist on such a small farm.
Consequently, their owning, or not owning, the land would make little
difference, as far as the betterment of a family's actual living condition was concerned. Supposing this to be true, then a family could
hardly be expected to become happy and optimistic toward life just
because the ownership of a little piece of poor farm land had been
transferred to their hands. With this much understanding, one should
not be surprised if one finds that the newly-become landowners have
little enthusiasm, or appreciation, toward land-reform programs, and
that the effects of the undertaking as a whole were slight.

II. Methods

In writing up the results of a study intended to be published or
made public in other ways, a scientist has the responsibility of
assuring his readers that the study was not made in a haphazard way,
but was conducted with carefully-devised, scientific methods. For
this reason, there will be a detailed description of the methods used
in this study.

One of the chief tasks in this study was the collection of information, opinions, comments, criticisms, feelings, experiences, and
statistical data concerning the results and effects of the land reform.
Together these formed the basis on which the findings of the study were
to be built. As mentioned previously, in making the collection, three
important channels were followed: 1) the interviewing of samples of
five types of farm people and five types of non-farm people; 2) the use

of literature which, without presumption, expressed comments on the under-

taking of the land reform and its results and effects; and 3) the use of

case studies. Of these three, the first was to be of the most importance.

1. Interviewing. The interviewing involved the preparation, or choice,

of samples, the construction of interview schedules or questionnaires, the

selection and training of interviewers, and the actual field interviewing.

The preparation of samples was itself quite a complicated matter. As was

pointed out in the preceding section, because the response to the effects

of land reform might have varied in degree in different areas, in accordance

with land classification and agricultural patterns, samples had to be taken

from different areas representing the various land grades and the numerous

farming types. This meant that the first step in the work of taking popu-

lation samples had to be the selection of study regions and areas.

a. The Selection of Study Regions and Areas

This selection was conducted according to three important criteria.

The first was that all the regions must be of important agricultural

land; the second was that they must have been heavily and directly

affected by the land-reform programs; and the third was that the methods

of farm operation in any one region or area must be much the same.

According to Professor Yi-tao Wang,[2] farm land mostly affected by

the land reform was the kind on which two crops of paddy rice were

grown annually; next was the land where one crop of paddy rice was grown;

third, land on which paddy rice could be grown only in a three-year, crop-

rotation system; fourth, the unirrigated land, or land on which no paddy

rice could be grown; land in the hilly areas was virtually unaffected.

The result of these considerations was that, in total, five regions were selected. Listing these from north to south of the Province: the Yilan-Taipei region, the Taoyuan-Hsinchu region, the Taichung-Changhwa region, the Yunlin-Chiayi-Tainan region, and the Kaohsiung-Pingtung region. No land on the east coast or in the mountains had been taken into consideration because the agriculture in these regions is far from being important, and the ownership of the land, or land tenure, had not been affected very much by the land reform.[3]

The selection of the study areas in each region was based on the economic classification of the farm land. It was also guided by the criterion that the type of farm management in the area should be the same on most, if not all, of the farms. In principle, each region had three areas, and the three areas corresponded to the different classes of farm land, i.e., high-class, middle-class, and low-class land. Our land classes did not correspond, however, with the land administration's land-productivity classification. The discrepancy was due largely to the fact that in most of the regions selected for study there was no land which belonged to the land administration's class one; the highest rates were only in class three or below. To study the effects of the land reform there should be no shortcoming in establishing our own land classification in accordance with the economic value given a piece of land by the local people

Another important factor related to the selection of the study areas was deciding the geographical size of an area. We used two criteria. One was similarity of economic land classification. That is, so long as the land classification remained uniform, the area should be as large as other factors permitted. The other criterion was that the numbers of different categories of farm households which had been directly affected by the land

reform should be large enough for sample-taking, and the samples thus selected

would not be concentrated in a small spot but evenly spread out. All these

rules were practiced for the purpose of making the findings of the study

representative of the facts as much as possible.

Since the selection of the areas in each of the regions was based on

a presently prepared, economic land classification, the study here needed

the assistance of the land administration divisions of the concerned

hsien governments, as well as of the district offices of the Provincial

Land Administration Bureau. The divisions and the district offices offered

information regarding the land administration's land productivity ratings

and the local land economic classification.

Basing choices on the above-mentioned criteria and the information

obtained from the various land administration offices, a total of fifteen

areas were selected for the study, three areas in each of the five regions.[5]

The 15 areas together had 36 townships. Six areas had three townships

each and nine areas had two townships each. Whether there should be three

townships or two townships in one area depended on the sizes of the town-

ships and the availability in them of adequate numbers of samples of the

various categories of population. The number of villages or li* required

in each township also varied according to the same principle.

B.   Population Sample Taking

As soon as the study regions and areas had been selected, the taking

of population samples was started. Before describing the manner in which

---

*Li is a village equivalent in a chen or urban township.

the samples were taken, it is necessary to state at this time that the numbers of samples of all categories of population listed in this study had been arbitrarily decided when plans were made. The numbers of the various samples to be taken must be the same as those already decided in the plan.[6] The procedure of the sample taking was, first, going to the Land Administration Division of each concerned Hsien Government and to each concerned District Office of the Provincial Land Administration Bureau to find out the numbers of the various categories of farm households in each of the selected areas. There are books in these offices wherein are recorded the farm households which had been directly involved in the land purchasing and land reselling programs of the land reform and those which had not been involved. The statuses and other information concerning these households are given in the lists. Here we found the total numbers of four of the five kinds of farm households in each of the townships in a selected area.[7] The five kinds are: (A) the former-landlord households, (B) the former-tenant households which had acquired land through the land-reform program, (C) the owner-farmer households which had not bought land through the land-reform program, (D) the tenant households which had not yet had the opportunity to acquire any land for their own, and (E) the hired farm-laborer households. Next, the work was to calculate how many samples of each of the five kinds of farm households should be taken in each of the townships of each area. The method was, first, to get the total numbers of each of the five kinds of farm households in each township of an area, then add together the numbers in each category in all the townships. Secondly, figure the percentage of the area's total numbers represented by each category in each township. For example,

we found that the respective total numbers of the (A), (B), (C), and (D) [8]
farm households of the Panchiao and Shulin townships in the high-
economic land-class area of the Taipei-Yilan region were 621 and 377; 483
and 571; 727 and 401; 359 and 412, respectively, and that the total numbers
of the whole area were 998, 1054, 1128, and 771, respectively. [9] The two
townships' percentages in the Panchiao-Shulin area's total numbers of the
various farm households were 62.2 and 37.8; 45.7 and 54.3; 64.4 and 35.6;
41.3 and 58.7, respectively. [10]

Then, to get the actual numbers of the samples of the four categories
of farm households, we multiplied the numbers shown in Appendix II, Table 3,
with the corresponding percentages in Appendix II, Table 6. For example,
the numbers of the (A), (B), (C), and (D) kinds of farm households of the
Panchiao-Shulin area in Appendix II, Table 3, were 33, 83, 16, and 16,
respectively. We first multiplied these numbers by the four percentages
of the Panchiao Township: 33 x 62.2; 83 x 37.8; 16 x 45.7; and 16 x 54.3.
Results of the multiplication were the actual numbers of samples of the four
kinds of farm households in Panchiao Township. They were 20, 38, 10, and
7, respectively. For Shulin Township, the calculation was 33 x 37.8;
83 x 54.3; 16 x 35.6; and 16 x 58.7. The actual numbers of samples of the
four kinds of farm households in this township were 13, 45, 6, and 9,
respectively. By adding the numbers of the two townships together, we got
the total numbers of samples of the four kinds of farm households in the
Panchiao-Shulin area as 33, 83, 16, and 16, respectively, which were the same
as those originally decided upon.

As has been mentioned in footnote No. 8, the numbers of samples of
the fifth type of farm household, that is, the hired farm-laborer house-

holds, of each study area, had to be obtained by asking that village officers with the assistance of the various concerned township Public Officers, tell us the numbers of hired farm laborers in the farm villages which they know well. The decision as to the number of such farm households to be taken in each village was made in accordance with the total number allotted to the township. When we had the townships' numbers, it was easy to figure the areas' numbers.[11]

After the sizes of samples of the five kinds of farm households had been decided and allocated, we went to the various township Public Offices to do the actual sample taking. In the township Public Office, there is a book titled "Book of Farm Households Acquired Land Through the Land Reform" wherein are recorded all the names and numbers[12] of the farmers who had acquired land through the land reform. The names of the landlords from whom the land was purchased are also recorded after the names of the land purchasers. This is the book we used to take samples of both the (A) type and the (B) type of farm household.

To take samples of the former-tenant farm households (B) we took down the total number of the land purchasers in the book. Next, we added a certain number of reserved samples to the number already decided for a township. Then the total sample number was divided into the total number of land purchasers to get the range number between two samples. After this range number was decided, the random system was used to take the samples.

Let us use the sample-taking in Panchiao township for an example. The total number of land-purchasing households in this township, according to its record book, was 851. The number of samples of this kind of farm household we decided was 38. To this number, twelve reserved samples were added. Now the total number of samples to be taken was 50. Eight hundred fifty-one is divided by 50 (851 ÷ 50) and the result was 17. Thus, 17 was the range number between two samples. We went back to the book. We took the first sample at No. 1, the second sample at No. 18, the third sample at No. 35, and so forth. When we came to a number which belonged to a name which had already been listed in the sample, this number was dropped and the next one was taken. In case the household of the next number had also been listed, we proceeded to take the next one, and so on. After all the needed numbers had been taken, they were then translated into names of the households. At the same time, the address of each sample household was also taken.[13]

The reason for taking in this kind of sample the numbers, instead of the names, of the household was that it would have taken too much time and trouble to get all the names from the book arranged in a list and then do the sample taking. As far as the objectiveness of the method and the avoidance of bias are concerned, the use of numbers should be just as good as the use of names. Therefore, it was believed that the use of numbers should be no less scientific than the use of names.

The sample taking of the (A) type of farm households was similar to that of the (B) type households. In most of the township Public Offices there was a book named "Records of Land Compulsorily Purchased From Landlords." In this book are recorded the names of the landlords whose land had been compulsorily purchased by the Government and then resold to their tenants. Each name has one or more numbers because each household had one or more lot of land to be purchased. In such townships the sample-taking formula was this: the total of the numbers of landlord-households in the book was divided by the sum of the already-fixed number of samples plus the number of reserved samples; the result was the range number between two samples. Then the random system was used to take the samples. For example, Tali township of Taichung Hsien had, according to the book, 457 landlord households whose land had been compulsorily purchased because of the land reform. But the total of these households' numbers was 902. In our study plan the number of samples of the (A) type of households was 12. By adding six reserved samples, the total number of samples of (A) type households in this township was 18. By dividing 902 by 18, we got the range number 50. We took the first household as our first sample, the fifty-first household our second sample, the one-hundred-and-first household our third sample, and so on till all the 18 samples were taken.

In those townships where the above mentioned book or record was lacking, the method of taking the samples was the same as that described in the foregoing, except that the total of the numbers of the type (B) households took the place of the total of the numbers of type (A) households. This was because in such townships the names and the numbers of type (A) households are recorded in the book of type (B) households and the numbers of the two are identical. For example, in Panchiao Township the total of the numbers of type (B) households is 851. The already fixed number of samples of type (A) households was 20. To this number we added 10 as reserved samples. The total number of samples to be taken was 30. We divided 851 by 30 to get the range number 28. We took the first of type (A) households as our first sample, the twenty-ninth household as our second sample, the fifty-seventh household as our third sample, and so on till all the 30 samples were taken.

A serious problem occurred in taking the type (A) household samples. It was discovered that almost no such households in the two kinds of books mentioned previously had an address under their names or number. This lack could make a selected sample useless, for the interviewer might never be able to find the sample. Fortunately, the people in the township public offices know the whereabouts of most of the resident-landlord households in their townships. Thus, we were able to add the addresses of the samples under their names. In a small number of cases the public office people knew only the village or the community where a certain sample lived but did not have a detailed address. We solved this problem by going into that village or community and consulting with the village officer about the sample's residence. There were cases, however, in which the landlord households taken for samples had moved out of the community, had cut all relations with the local people since the land reform, and no person in the township knew to what address they had gone. It happened that for our purpose they were the significant landlord households. If they were to be found and interviewed, assistance of the local census office had to be sought.[14]

For taking samples among the type (C) and the type (D) households, three kinds of census documents in the township public offices were used. Some township public offices have a kind of record called "Names of People From Among Whom Members of the Farm Tenancy Committee are to be Elected;" others have a book named "The Distribution of Ownership and Use of Farm Land." In the first book, dated 1952 or 1953, the names of the unaffected owner-

cultivators and names of the unaffected tenant-households are listed. In
the second book, dated 1953, we found that under the name of each farm
household there were two columns. In one column the household's own land
was recorded and in another its rented land was shown. An owner-cultivator
was identified by the fact that all his farm land was in the own-land
column, and a tenant household was identified by having all its farm
land listed in the rented-land column. The township public office people
firmly believed that if a household in either of the two books was an owner-
cultivator in 1953, it remained an owner-cultivator in 1963. In other words
it had not changed its status because of the effect of the land reform.
Many of the tenant-households, however, had changed to owner-cultivators or
part-owner cultivators since the implementation of the land-to-the-tiller
program. Therefore, it was all right to take samples of type (C) farm
households from among the owner-cultivators found in either one of the two
books, but it was impossible to do so for samples of type (D) households.
For samples of the current-tenant farm households, or tenant-farmers who
had not become owner-cultivators or part-owner cultivators through the
land-to-the-tiller program, we went to consult with the construction
department of the township public office. All the farm-lease contracts,
including the old ones and the current ones, within the territory of the
township, are kept in this department. We found all the current-tenant
households by working on these farm-lease contracts.

In a few of the 36 selected townships, however, we had to rely on the
townships' land officers for taking samples of both the type (C) households
and type (D) households. This was because we could not find any of the two
types of books nor the farm-lease contracts. Therefore, we had to ask the

local land officers to remember the current owner-cultivators and tenant

families in the various villages and to have their names and addresses

written down on paper. We emphasized with the land officers that they try

to remember all such households with no discrimination against one kind or

another.

Formulas used to take the samples of type (C) and type (D) farm house-

holds were the same as those used for taking type (A) and type (B) samples.[15]

The reasons for deciding to take a small number of samples of each of

these two categories were, first, that numbers of these two categories of

farm households in each township were relatively small, and, second, that

these farm households had not directly been affected by, or involved in, the

land-to-the-tiller program.[16]

As mentioned previously, there was practically no record in the

township public offices or in other public and private agencies about the

number, names and conditions of hired farm laborers. Therefore, in every

township we had to ask the township public office to introduce us to

village officers whom we asked to help us find them. We then selected our

samples from among those we found. In the selection we tried to have

representation from the different levels of laborers.[17]

Next, the taking of samples of non-farm households. There were five

categories of non-farm people: (1) people in significant businesses and

country store-keepers; (2) people in significant industries and those in

small trades; (3) people engaged in education and other cultural activities,

including college professors, writers, social-education workers, agri-

cultural-extension workers, and village school teachers; (4) people in

public services of all levels; and (5) leaders in rural communities who were not included in other categories. The total number of samples of these people was 500. The number of each category was 100, more or less. These 500 samples were to be distributed among the five regions. Each region should have 100 in total and 20 for each category. Each area should have 33, more or less; each township should have 16 or 11, depending on the number of townships which an area covers.

The taking of samples among non-farm people was also completed with the assistance of the township public office. They first suggested to our sample-taking personnel many names in each category of non-farm people in the local community. Then, according to their knowledge or information, they made a description of each person on the lists just prepared. Our personnel chose the ones whom they considered most appropriate for the samples. The number of samples so taken for each category was the number already fixed in our plan plus reserved samples, as many as fifty per cent of the regular samples. In some townships none of the significant industrialists, businessmen, educators, or persons of higher learning could be found. To solve this problem we selected people from other places but still within the territory of the area, or the region.[18]

The total number of population samples used in this study was 3075. Of this total 2575 were of the five kinds of farm households and 500 were non-farm people. Of the samples from farm households, 1250 had been tenant-cultivators before the land reform and had become small owner-farmers by acquiring land through the land-to-the-tiller program. They were called in this study 'the former-tenant households.' That they were not called 'owner-farmers' was to avoid possible confusion with the original owner-farmers. Five hundred and seventy-five were from the landlord households whose land had been compulsorily purchased by the Government because of the land-to-the-tiller program. These were called 'the former-landlord households.' Five hundred of them had been ordinary landlord households and 75 had had extra-large holdings. The number in each of the other three categories of farm households was 250. The reason for making such a range of sample sizes among the five categories of farm households was that the former-tenant households felt most strongly the results of the land reform and, therefore, they should have been our most important source of information. Following this presupposition, it would be logical to give much attention to the work and life of these people while trying to learn whether land reform had really given rise to significant socio-economic and cultural changes in the rural communities of Taiwan. Of next importance must have been the former-landlord households. These households had been deeply, and sometimes severely, affected by land reform: their farm rent had been drastically reduced by the 37.5 per cent limitation program, their farm land compulsorily purchased by the Government and many of them thus forced to take up entirely new occupations and adapt themselves to unaccustomed conditions. Even those who had been able with the land retained to continue to lead a farm life had also undergone a number of readjustments. Furthermore, during the whole time when the land-reform programs were being designed and implemented, the Government had both explicitly and implicitly made promises that landlord households whose land was required for the accomplishment of the land-to-the-tiller program would receive various kinds of assistance from the Government to make adjustments to new occupations and a new life. If anyone is competent to comment on the results and impacts of the land reform, it is these people; they should be given attentive hearings.

The importance of the other three categories of farm households is
less because they had not been directly involved in the action of land
reform. But their information, opinions, and feelings could well be more
impersonal, more objective, in comparison with those of the first two
categories. There would have been no harm done by interviewing many more
of them. But time and other factors made it impossible to have more than
250 in each of the categories.

The chief purpose of having the five kinds of non-farm people included
in the sample to be interviewed was to have information, opinions, and
feelings from persons who were more remote, rather than directly involved
in the land reform. It was hoped that their reactions would be still more
objective and impersonal. However, due to the shortage of time and other
difficulties, the number of samples in each of these groups could not
be limited to 100.

In each township the number of samples was augmented by a certain
percentage of reserved samples. Reserved samples were prepared for
addition in the event that there should be any loss of regular samples
because of unexpected factors. It was discovered when the interviews
actually took place that this preparation was greatly needed because some
of the regular samples could not be found due to wrong addresses. A few
others, it was found, had been dead for some time. Because township public
offices were slow in making changes on the death and life records in the
census book, dead people were still recorded as being alive and so had been
included among lists of persons for the study. There were also some who stubbornly refused to give cooperation to the interviewers. In such cases, the
interviewers were forced to give up and interview reserved samples instead.

c. The Construction of Interview Questionnaires

Ten different interview questionnaires had been designed for interviewing the five categories of farm households and the five categories
of non-farm people. There were questionnaires for: (A) landlord households, (B) former-tenant households, (C) owner-cultivator households,
(D) tenant households, and (E) hired farm-laborer households. The five
kinds of non-farm interviews were with people in businesses, people in
industries, people in education and cultural affairs, people in public
services, and people in rural community leadership.

In the designing of these questionnaires, all staff members and advisors of the project participated, as did several people who were informed
concerning the results of land reform and the recent developments in the
countryside of Taiwan. Discussion meetings were held and individuals'
ideas were exchanged. The drafting work was shared by three staff members,
and the project leader was responsible for the final shaping.

Questionnaire for interviewing the former-landlord households: In
designing this questionnaire, emphasis was laid on answering questions
concerning compensation for the land, the way in which the head of the
household had handled the land bonds and stocks. If these securities had
been sold, was the sale made at a profit at the par value, or below?
It was important to learn, too, how proceedings from the sale of land had
been used: invested in business, spent on increasing the comfort of life,
or used to send children to college? If the shares of stocks had been kept,
of what corporation is the owner now a stockholder? Other inquiries dealt
with whether or not the change from landlord to stockholder had been easy
and profitable, or with difficulties and losses. Then, sociologically, it

is of great importance to have information in regard to any change in the
psychology of these men, whether or not these people have, because of the
land reform, changed their values. Where once farm land was the most important tangible in the basic economic, social, and familial systems, had it
come to be merely one means of economic production; and had they further
come to believe that because times and economic structures had changed,
land as a means of production could be readily given up and other means
substituted without sentimental reluctance.

Another important question in interviewing the former landlords was
related to their change of occupation or livelihood. One of the hopes
held by the national economists, political policy-makers, and sociologists
in preplanning the land reform was that: after the landlords had given
up their land, they would have changed their traditional way of making a
living by collecting farm rents and entered into non-farm productive
enterprises. Such a change could be of great importance to the development of an entirely new social order. But to what extent had these transformations been accomplished; how much of each of the changes could be
specifically attributed to the effects of land reform; and what problems
or difficulties had been hindering such transformations or changes? These
were the questions asked in the interview.

One more question, important sociologically in studying the conditions
of the former landlords, was whether or not their traditional social
prestige, or community leadership, had gone with the loss of their land. If
the answer to this question were "yes," did this mean that factors which had
traditionally been responsible for putting a person in the community leadership remained unchanged? If, on the other hand, the answer were "no," did it

mean that a person's becoming a community leader, or continuing to stay in leadership, no longer depended on the ownership of a large amount of land, but on the possession of other merits?

Finally, it was also our interest to know whether many of the lesser landlords had, after land reform, become steady and progressive owner-cultivators of the land they had been allowed to keep. If they had done so, had such farm families formed a new group in the rural community and taken over some of the leadership roles vacated by those former, big landlords who had gone into businesses or other non-farm activities? And had they been getting along well with the new owner-cultivators, the former-tenant households?[19]

Questionnaire for interviewing former-tenant households: In this questionnaire, the important points were, how real and how large had been the effect of the 37.5% farm rent limitation program, the first phase of land reform, upon the tenant-farmers? Did it improve their living conditions and their farming business? Had their morale been lifted by the new, and more favorable rental rate? What had happened in the land-lord-tenant relationship after the implementation of this program? If there had been any significant changes in this relationship, had they, by extension, caused any disintegration or disorganization in the rural community as a whole?

Most people who had given thought to Taiwan's land reform would have said that the second phase of this great event, or the land-to-the-tiller program, had really and significantly changed the status of a great percentage of the tenant-peasants in this part of the world. There was rarely any argument opposing this assumption. What we needed, however, were

specific facts about the change, facts which could really support people
who attributed major changes to the effects of the transfer of landownership
from the landlord to the tenant. In order to give a fair treatment to the
effects of land reform, especially the land-to-the-tiller program, it
was important and necessary to find out which of the economic, social and
psychological changes that occurred in the past ten years could be rightfully credited to the change of land tenure and which must have been caused
by changes in other sectors of the people's life.

Specifically, it was important to know just how much land, on the
average, had a tenant household acquired through the sale of public land and
through the land-to-the-tiller program? Was the amount and quality of land
so acquired enough to arouse a family's spirits and hopes so that it began
to look forward to a prosperous future? If the land had not been as good
as the new owner had wished, had he and his family been willing and able
to make any significant improvement on it? If yes, how had the improvement
been made? Made with whose assistance, if any?

The acquisition of landownership was accompanied by a number of financial
obligations. The important ones were payments of the land price, the land
tax, and other levies or contributions based on landownership. It had been
said, time and again, that these obligations became a burden so heavy for
the new, small landowners that many of them became materially, as well as
morally, frustrated and returned to the old condition of apathy. Some even
had to sell the land they had just acquired in order to fulfill those
obligations. It was of great significance that we find out just how much
truth there was in these statements.

On the other side of the question, many people have claimed that the
land-reform programs gave to the tradition-bound and matter-of-fact minded
peasants the incentive and means whereby changes and improvements were made
in their way of farming. We designed questions to find out the amount of
truth in these claims, too. Changes in the way of farming are seen on
nearly all farms. Then it is important to ask which of the changes can
be attributed either directly or indirectly to the effects of the land
reform, and which should be considered results of other public and private
efforts. How much of the increase in agricultural production, for example,
is due to the higher spirits and harder work aroused, or motivated, by results
of the land reform? And how much should be accounted for as resulting
from agricultural research, vocational-agricultural teaching, and agricultural-extension work? Or is it not closer to the truth to say that the
increase is a result of all these programs combined?

In general, the living conditions of the farm people in Taiwan have
been significantly improved in the past ten years. People who have had one
thing or another to do with the land reform are apt to say that the improvement is all due to effects of the 37.5% farm rent limitation, the sale of
public land, and the land-to-the-tiller program. Others say that the land-
reform programs have made a contribution, maybe an important contribution
to the improvement, but certainly they are not the only factors. People
who have a grudge against the land reform like to belittle, or to completely
write off, any merits which the program might have had. It was our intention
to hear directly through this questionnaire from those who became owner
cultivators through the land reform, to learn first hand whether or

not their living conditions had really been improved, whether or not the land-reform programs had had anything to do with recent changes, and if they had, how much, and in what manner, did they contribute?

It was also important to learn whether or not land reform had in the past ten years brought about social change in the former-tenant households. Accordingly, we put into this questionnaire questions as to whether or not the change in their status had brought to the former-tenant family a new attitude toward education and an incentive to send children to educational institutions higher than the primary school. Had the new owner-cultivators become more interested in activities organized for agricultural-extension purposes? Another way of detecting social changes here was to inquire whether or not the new owner-cultivators and their families had, since the completion of land reform, become positive or active in community parti-cipation. By community participation we meant taking part in the various community organizations and social activities. We also meant making contri-butions in kind or in cash to the community's social-welfare and/or public-work projects. Another criterion of positive community participation is the taking of an active role in any group activities, not just being physically there. Finally, for the sake of the promotion of democracy in rural Taiwan, it is of importance to know whether or not landownership had made the former-tenant families active in local political affairs, whether they took part in local elections by actually going out to cast their ballots, by running for public offices, or by helping a friend to win an election.[20]

Questionnaire for interviewing owner-cultivator households: As was pointed out previously, the 'owner-cultivator households' are those whose lands were not acquired through the recent land reform and who had not been directly affected by the programs. These households were differentiated from those who, through assistance of the land reform, had recently changed from tenant households to owner-cultivator households. The chief purpose of these interviews was to learn whether or not in the past ten years they had made changes in land utilization, farm operation, community participation, desire for education, living conditions, etc., similar to those made by the former-tenant households. If the answer were affirmative, where had these households gotten the inspiration, the information or know-how, and the means to effect the changes? Would the finding of such changes here imply simply that any kind of owner-cultivator households might have made similar changes during the past ten years whether or not there had been land reform? Would such an inference be objective, justified, or fair to the land reform?

The principal elements in this interview were, by and large, like those contained in the questionnaire for former-tenant households. This was so because only when results have sprung from similar questions answered by different groups can they be subjected to comparison. The primary concern, however, was in finding out whether or not these households had been influenced by the land-reform programs, in one way or another. For example, an original, owner-cultivator household might also in the past ten years have made improvement on its living houses, its land utilization, its farm operation, etc., and it may have made these improvements with its own motivation and means. On the surface, the land-reform programs then had nothing to do with the changes made by, or occuring in, this household. But could the people of this household say with certain accuracy that they had not been influenced in any way by the activities and the spirit of those who had been directly involved in the land reform, nor been affected by a new atmosphere created by land reform in the rural communities? To be sure great care was taken in the interview to avoid inducing people to falsely say favorable words for the land reform.[21]

Questionnaire for interviewing tenant households. The chief reason for interviewing tenant households in this study was to see whether recent changes had occurred in the households which had no opportunity to buy land either through the sale of public land and the land-to-the-tiller programs, through their own efforts. If there were changes, from what source had thes households gotten the inspiration, the interest, the know-how, and the means to make the changes? If the tenant households also had been able to make progressive changes, would it mean that land reform might not be the only factor, or an indispensible factor, in any agricultural, social, and educational improvements? If, however, in the past ten years most of the curren tenant households had not experienced any significant changes such as those being experienced by the former-tenant households, we would then be able to say that the land reform did have important bearing on the improvement of th small farmers' agricultural, social, and living conditions.

Chief questions in this questionnaire concerned actual benefits which tenant households had received from the 37.5% farm rent limitation program and the ways in which the benefits had been used or spent. We were also concerned in this instance with what had been the small farmers' attitude or opinion in regard to using the saved farm rent for improving immediate living conditions, for increasing the farm input, or for home building or remodelling. Next were questions about changes in farm operation, in cultivation methods, in cropping systems, and in possession and use of farm tools. What had been the factors responsible for the changes? The third group of questions were related to the tenant households' living conditions. Had there been any changes in the family's food consumption, housing conditions, clothing, sanitation and health, etc? If the answer were affirmative, did the family attribute the changes to the 37.5% farm rent limitation program? What other factors might there be? The fourth group of questions dealt with the family's education. Had family members changed their attitudes toward the desirability of education? Had there been changes to the extent to which the family members were being educated? What had been the chief factors responsible for these changes? The last group of questions in this questionnaire concerned the present tenant-farmers' interest in their local community's social and public affairs. Had they become more involved during the last ten years in community organizations, public construction projects, and local elections? If yes, what had been the influences which made them so?[22]

Questionnaire for interviewing the hired farm laborers. The purpose of interviewing the hired farm laborers was to learn whether or not their employment had been affected by the land reform. Usually, only landlords' farms need to hire farm help. Inasmuch as the landlords' farms had been either liquidated or reduced through the land-to-the-tiller program, the hiring of farm help could be expected to have disappeared, or at the least to have decreased considerably. In either case, it could be assumed that many farm laborers had been deprived by land reform of the opportunity for jobs on the farms. If this should be true, it would be of importance to inquire whether farm laborers had been able to make any readjustment in the changed situation, and what kind of readjustment had been made? Another matter of interest was the quality of the hired farm laborers, and whether it had undergone any change due to the new conditions. Any change of this kind could, of course, be either positive or negative in nature. Positive change could mean that the hired farm laborers had become, under the new social and economic atmosphere, willing to learn new jobs and new methods and to improve their work efficiency. On the other hand, they could have been depressed by separation from their long-time employers, by the difficulty of finding new employment, and by the hardship of trying to readjust themselves to the new situations.

There were two groups of questions in this questionnaire. One group consisted of inquiries about employment opportunities, traditional and new, of farm laborers in the past ten years and how much they had been able to adapt to the new situations. The second group concerned possible change in laborers' quality, that is, their work efficiency.[23]

Questionnaires for interviewing the five kinds of non-farm people. The chief reason for interviewing non-farm people was to find out how persons with no direct involvement in the farm business, and persons who do not depend directly upon farming for their living, had come to look upon the land reform and what had been their opinions in regard to the consequences of this big event. An old Chinese proverb says: "For people inside of the case, its lines become blurred whereas those outside of it see things more clearly." It was our assumption that non-farm people could be more objective, and less sentimental, than their fellow citizens of the farms in making comments on the results and effects of the land-reform programs.

In interviewing people in industries and other significant businesses, our inquiry was concentrated on work opportunities and actual choices made in the entry of the former-landlords into industries and businesses after the completion of land reform. Attention was also directed to the existing world of industry and business and whether they had been kind and helpful in welcoming newcomers, or had left them alone to struggle with their fate. Had advantage been taken of the newcomers' lack of experience? Were there those who tried to steal or "devour" their investments? It had been reported frequently in the past ten years that former-landlords founded businesses with funds from the sale of their lands, but fell into bankruptcy after a short period. In interviewing the business people, we tried to find out how much truth there had been in these reports.

Considerable importance was attached to interviewing storekeepers in the local market towns. Our assumption was that by measuring the volume of buying and selling between the country stores and newly-established, owner-cultivator households, we should be able to determine fairly accurately the degree of improvement in economic and cultural conditions of the householders since land reform. In the same way, any changes in the former-landlord households could be discovered. The next step was to see whether the storekeepers would relate the changes to the effects of the land reform.

Teachers in the community schools and people engaged in other kinds of cultural activities might have been interested in the implementation of the land reform and in the consequences of its enforcement. It should be of interest and significance to find out what these people felt and believed about the effects of land reform upon life and work in the

118

farm households, as well as upon the life and work of other groups of
people. When interviewing school teachers, we inquired especially closely
concerning the farm people's attitudes toward school and toward sending
children to school since they had been affected by the land reform. At the
township level, we expected to find out from agricultural-extension people
whether or not the transfer of landownership made the former tenant-farmers
more interested in the extension programs and activities.

People in the local governments and other public services were
expected to be able to tell us whether there was any difference between
the way the small farmers today were discharging their public obligations,
especially the payment of taxes, and the way they did it before. It was
assumed that if the obligations were being met more willingly and readily
than before, it might mean that these farmers were economically better off
today than before, and that they had less grudge against the Government.
If this were true, would it not be right to say that the land reform had
benefited the public-service people too? People in the township public
offices were asked this question.

Finally, interviews had been prepared with community leaders, other
than the samples in the above-mentioned four categories. Community leaders
were asked to make their own comments, of whatever nature, on the manner
in which land-reform programs had been implemented and on the effects the
programs had so far produced.[24]

d. Selection and Training of Interviewers

The selection of 30 interviewers was completed in the space of two
weeks. Originally we had hoped that the selections could be made from

among the senior and junior students of the Agricultural Extension and
Agricultural Economics Departments of National Taiwan University. It was,
however, later discovered that these students were to go to military training immediately after their graduation from the university. Because of
this situation, we were forced to select interviewers from among sophomore
students. It was fortunate that the number of sophomore students was
large and that we were able to find the best ones for our selection.
The best ones were those who had a Taiwan rural background and had
recently taken a course in Interviewing Farm Households.

Two other means helped to remedy, to some degree, the shortcomings in
having to use sophomore students as interviewers. They were, first, to
have a well-qualified team leader accompanying the interviewers in each
study region. The team leader's duty was to help his interviewers with
problems concerning the questionnaires and interviewing, and to check for
any mistakes that might have been made by the interviewers. In addition,
the team leader was responsible for keeping up the interviewers' morale
during the hot summer days.

The other remedy was thorough and intensive training for the interviewers. It was a good thing that all the interviewers-to-be were students
who had, in one degree or another, been influenced by the project director
and other faculty members who were helping with the research. It was our
belief that all the young men were attentive and serious in the training.

All questionnaires had been tested before the formal interviewing
took place. In the pretest each of the interviewers had interviewed at
least one from each of the five categories of farm households and one from
each of the five categories of non-farm people. The pretest of question-

naires had been closely observed by the project leader, the chief assistants and the team leaders. Therefore, it was also a pretest for the interviewers

e. The Field Interview

In recounting now the way in which field interviews were conducted, there will be no attempt to report on the details of the work. This account will only mention and explain the difficulties, problems, and impasses met during the task. The purpose of doing this is to let the reader know that the results of this study were by no means all satisfactory and that the chief reasons for dissatisfaction were the encountering of many difficulties problems, and impasses while the task was being done.

Altogether there were thirty trained interviewers. They were divided into five groups corresponding to the study's five regions. This allotted six interviewers to each region. These six people were then subdivided into three couples. Each couple was charged with the interviewing of all the samples in one study area. In each study region there was a supervisor whose responsibility it was to supervise the interviewer's work by giving them help and advice when difficulties, problems, or questions arose in the interviewing or in understanding the meaning and implications of certain questions in the questionnaires. Another duty was the holding of meetings with all interviewers in the region to discuss various problems concerning the interviewing or concerning the daily life of the interviewers This task was undertaken in group meetings, or privately, with individuals. When the interviewers felt weariness, fatigue, and low morale, due to the sample people's uncooperativeness, the hardship of working in the hot summer, and other frustrations, it was the supervisor's duty to cheer them up and replenish their spirits, courage and persistence. All five supervisors employed in this interview were young staff members of the Department of Agricultural Extension of National Taiwan University. The director of this study and the two assistants to the director also made frequent trips to the study regions to convene with the regional supervisors and, occasionally, with the interviewers. They gave advice and pep talks to both supervisors and interviewers.

Despite all precautions and all kinds of assistance, the interviewers met with difficulties and frustrations. The first kind of difficulty was the non-cooperation of some of the farm-household samples. In most of the cases, the non-cooperation was caused by the farmer's being suspicious of the interviewer's purpose in doing the interviewing. Many farm people were inclined to believe that the interviewers were Government agents, or were doing the job for the Government, so that later the tax bureau could make use of the information for fixing of tax rates. Regardless of the large amounts of effort put up to dispel this fear, a number of the samples refused to be convinced. The great harm from this suspicion was that such samples tried to hold back information by not answering questions or by saying they didn't know or could not answer, or by giving superficial answers just to get the matter over with. Another reason for non-cooperation was that most members of farm families were very busy with farm work at the time when the interviews were undertaken. These samples felt that they were very much bothered, and their work was being interrupted, by the interviewing. When their dislike became intense, it was displayed in non-cooperation. To a great extent, this was understandable and the interviewers had sympathy for such households. A way to overcome this difficulty was to meet the samples at noontime, or in the early evening, when they were off from work.

Difficulties with former-landlord households arose when many a sample started the interviewing with bitter complaints against the land reform. They were so undone by their bitterness that no normal and intelligible conversation could be carried on. Some of the interviewers were very much embarrassed and could not bring the situation under control. Thus, the interview became futile. It was only after the interviewers learned how to divert an old man's "steam" and keep him pacified that normal and informative conversation was resumed. It is interesting to relate here that quite a few of the former landlords who were interviewed were angry and shouting at first, but after a while when the emotion was gone, they did confess that many of the mistakes made and the sufferings which afflicted them were largely their own fault. It was because of their own carelessness, listening to and accepting rumors concerning the value of the stocks, opening a business too large in size and too extravagant in personne taking up partners whose character and capability were questionable, etc. Others of the former-landlord samples were simply too timid to tell what they really felt and believed.

Many of the farmers interviewed complained that it was very difficult for them to remember things and figures from ten years ago and that, therefore, it was impossible for them to make a comparison between conditions ten years ago and those of today. Things they did remember had little relevance for us, and those things we wished to have remembered were forgotten. It was also a bad state of affairs when sample farmers could not really understand nor appreciate the meaning and the purpose of the questions asked and, consequently, the answers they gave were superficial or beside the point. In case the interviewer was unable to do a good interpretation, or was incapable of conveying the true purposes of the study, the information, or data, recorded in the interview schedules became of very little use. Still worse was that some of the interviewers themselves were unable to comprehend and grasp the basic points of the inquiries. The supervisors and the project director then had to explain to them what was wanted.

Record-keeping, the keeping of accounts of important matters, was still lacking in a majority of the ordinary farm households. It was true even in many of the landlord households. In conjunction with their being unable to remember things which happened some years ago, this constituted the chief obstacle for the interviewers and their obtaining adequate and accurate information from these farm samples. This difficulty inevitably reduced the richness of the results of the study. Fortunately, all these defects had been anticipated, and it was precisely because of this anticipation that the interviews with non-farm people and the use of literature and case studies were added to the interviews of the farm people.

Last, but not least, was the interference which resulted from the observation of certain customs and traditions, or the violation of certain others. In Taiwan the rural people, and small-town people as well, were still conscious of the power, or the binding force, of a number of mores and tabus. The use of certain terms, certain ways of expressing one's ideas and emotion, or inquiry into certain affairs could all be taken as an offense, or a bad omen, by the household being interviewed. When and if this happened, the interview could as well have been terminated; if completed, it had little usefulness. It was a pity that at some times such failures occurred without the interviewer's knowing the reason.

Notwithstanding the meeting of all these difficulties and frustrations, the interviewers did their best to bring the interview to a relatively successful conclusion. A successful conclusion meant that all samples had been interviewed (some reserved samples had to be substituted for the regular ones who either could not be found or refused to the end to give cooperation) most of the questions had been answered, and most of the answers contained a certain amount of reliable information. That this was possible at all was due partly to the constant assistance given to the interviewers by the supervisors, the project director and his two assistants, by many of the agricultural-extension agents of the local farmers' associations, and by staff members of the township public offices, and partly to the interviewers own ability in overcoming the difficulties.

f. The Processing of the Raw Data

The raw data thus gathered then had to go through processes of classification, tabulation, calculation, and summarization. Before the start of these steps, all questionnaires, which had been filled out and turned in by the interviewers, had to be checked yet another time. The purpose of this checking was to correct obvious mistakes, serious omissions, and ambiguities in answers. If such defects were found, the interviewers were called in to make any corrections that were possible with the best knowledge that they were still able to recall, or they were sent back into the field to make repeat interviews.

The processing of the raw data was done by persons other than the interviewers. Therefore, there had had to be a selection and training of

another group of workers. The criteria for choosing and training this
group of workers were chiefly: ability to do neat work, ability to put
materials into tabular forms, and ability to make accurate calculations.
Many answers were made in words, sentences, or statements. The summarization and classification of these words, sentences, and statements took
intelligence, understanding, and a facility in conceptualization. To
meet the requirements for these abilities, the training of this group of
workers needed not only time but, also, the trainers' thorough understanding and appreciation of the significance and objectives of this
study, and their capability to instill these things into the trainees.
Throughout the duration of the processing, a number of meetings were
held between the project director and his assistants (trainers) and the
workers (trainees). Great efforts were made to make the processed
products as lucid, neat, accurate, and objective as possible.

The application of statistical measures was of great importance in
the processing of the raw data. Practically every item relating to
quantity had to be converted into percentage before it could become
meaningful. For this reason, a person who was well trained in statistics
played an important part in the making of this study. His work was to be
of equal importance to the writing of this report concerning the findings
of the study.

2. The use of literature. Literature used in this study included
both special reports on the operation and results of the land reform and
writings in which the land reform and its results and effects are mentioned
indirectly or casually. More attention was given to the latter than to

the former. Dr. Hui-sun Tang's Land Reform in Free China had been, however, extensively used because there was considerable confidence in the authentication of the materials in the book and because of the fact that the author was one of the chief architect-administrators of this land reform and widely known for his integrity. Included, also, were a large number of other works which are not reports on land reform but contain materials useful to this study. In addition, books and articles dealing with land reform, and the results of land reform in other countries, were extensively read and used as references.

The reason for giving attention to such literature as folk stories, novels, and essays on traveling or visiting in the countryside, was that in such materials any mention of the land reform and its results was, in most cases, done in a casual manner. In other words, the work deals with subjects other than land reform, but things concerning land reform have been used to make up a story. In this context, the mentioning, or the telling, would not have been done for propaganda purposes. For this reason, such information was considered close to the fact. For example, a story was written chiefly to depict the scene of the wedding of a farm family. But in the narrative it is said that the wedding was made possible because the family had become better off because of the reduction of farm rent. The writer was not particularly interested in, or conscious of, the reduction of farm rent in the land reform. It was mentioned by him offhandedly and casually. But the information was used in the story. It was assumed in this study that this information in such a story had much greater truth, or a greater convincing power, than the same given in any official report on land reform.

Another example was in a rural-life story telling about the struggle and hard work and frugal living of an originally poor, but later well-to-do, farm family. It told in a matter-of-fact way how the old man of the family and his old wife worked on the farm and at home with much greater energy and enthusiasm after the ownership of the one _chia_ of tenanted land was added to their meager property through the land-to-the-tiller program. The theme of the story was the hard life and work of a poor, but advancing, farm family. In such a family the people's life experience was not necessarily always limited to hardship. There were occasions when things of excitement and promise sprang up. Holding onto the excitement and the promise, the family members could, at one time or another, enjoy high morale and the hope of a bright future. But what were the things which gave rise to such occasions? The author listed a number of them. The limitation of the farm rent and the acquirement of additional landownership were included in the list. No special emphasis was given to them. Such a casual mention serves the purpose of this study better than materials in which the results, or effects, of these two programs were far too much overplayed.

However, what is said in the foregoing need not be interpreted as meaning that all official and specialized works on land reform had been considered of no value, or little value, and, therefore, had been banished from the list of references. Neither was it assumed that all mention in other types of literature must be valuable and appropriate for use. A considerable amount of screening, evaluation, and judgment-making were given before any of the materials were finally accepted.

3. <u>The use of case studies</u>. Information and data collected by the
interview method have, in general, the shortcoming of being shallow and
fragmentary. They are better for quantity than they are for quality.
For example, they do not, and they cannot, present to the reader a whole
story, a story with integrated facts, life-filled facts, facts touching
the deepest layers and most hidden corners of a family's experience with
the results and effects of the land reform. It was believed that, to a
great extent, the findings from case studies could make up the deficiencies of interview materials. Therefore, several case studies have been
made in this project. One study tells the story of a former-landlord
household which made a success of the change of occupation after its
land was compulsorily purchased by the Government, while in the other
one it was a failure. In still another instance, a former-tenant
household was examined to see how it had been affected by the land reform.
Proper use of such stories in the study might result in a strengthened
report with more meaning and flavor.

Notes

[1]"JCRR has appropriated a total of NT$20,277,246 by way of financial assistance for the implementation of land reform in Taiwan in the course of the last five years. The expenditures incurred by the various levels of government for the same purpose must have been more than this." Hui-sun Tang, Land Reform in Free China, p. 21.

[2]Professor Y. T. Wang, Department of Agricultural Economics, National Taiwan University. Professor Wang played an important role in the planning and implementation of all the recent land-reform programs in Taiwan. He has made several studies on the results of the reform. He has kindly accepted our invitation to be one of the advisors of our study.

[3]The selected regions, together with their respective degrees, of agricultural significance are shown in Appendix I, Table 1.

[4]Professor Arthur W. Peterson of Washington State University, Pullman, has advised us that "In general, the productivity of the land by the government for official purposes shows a high correlation with economic land classes within the rice regions. The productivity ratings are not as useful in the non-irrigated regions. The following grouping of productivity classes would correspond to economic land classes within my experience: Land Class I equals productivity classes one through six. Economic Land Class II equals seven through ten, inclusive. Economic Land Class III equals 11 through 13." A letter from Professor Peterson, dated February, 1964.

[5]For details see Appendix I, Table 2.

[6]The reader is referred to Appendix II, Table 3, for the various numbers of the various population samples.

[7]Appendix II, Table 4, shows the total numbers of the four kinds of farm-household samples in all the study areas.

[8]The land administration offices in the areas do not have figures of this kind of farm households. Samples of such farm households had to be obtained in the villages through assistance of the village officers.

[9]Appendix II, Table 5, shows the total numbers of the various farm households in all the study areas and in the townships.

[10]For percentages of all the townships in the study areas, the reader is referred to Appendix II, Table 6.

[11]Appendix II, Table 7, shows sizes of samples of all the five kinds of farm households in all the concerned townships, the study areas in the five regions.

[12]One name may have more than one number, depending on how many ventures in land purchasing he had had. He got a number for each time. Therefore, the numbers are many more than the names in the book.

[13]Appendix II, Table 8, shows names and addresses of samples of type (B) households in all the townships, the areas, and the regions.

[14]Appendix II, Table 9, contains the names and addresses of type (A) household samples of all the townships, areas, in the five regions.

[15]Appendix II, Table 10 and Table 11, show names and addresses of samples of type (C) and type (D) farm households respectively.

[16] This is to answer Professor Arthur W. Peterson's inquiry: "It is not clear to me why you have different size samples in 'each category of the population.' Personally, I think that categories three, four and five on page 2 might be the most significant categories in your study. Your plan, however, calls for a smaller sample in these three categories. Is this because you expect it to be difficult to find families who fall in these three categories?" - Peterson's letter, February 24, 1964.

[17] Appendix II, Table 12.contains names and addresses of samples of hired farm-laborer households, or type (E) farm households.

[18] Appendix II, Tables 13, 14, 15, 16 and 17, contain the names and addresses of the samples of the five categories of non-farm people.

[19] For details see Appendix III, Questionnaire 1.

[20] For details please see Appendix III, Questionnaire 2.

[21] For details please see Appendix III, Questionnaire 3.

[22] For details please see Appendix III, Questionnaire 4.

[23] For details please see Appendix III, Questionnaire 5.

[24] For details please see Appendix III, Questionnaires 6, 7, 8, 9 and 10.

Chapter Four

LAND REFORM AND MORALE

I. Emotional Response: A Precondition toward Acceptance

II. Former Tenant-Farmers

III. Present Tenant-Farmers

IV. Original Owner-Farmers

V. Farm Laborers

VI. Landlords

VII. Non-farm People

VIII. Conclusion

The major thesis of this chapter is a theory: that deep emotional response, that is response charged with either intense love or resentment, is a precondition to acceptance of the profound and far-reaching effects accruing from a program of social and economic reform. To put it another way, one must first feel some deep affection toward a program of change before he can go beyond enjoyment of its immediate, tangible benefits to an understanding acceptance of effects which are so penetrating that his way of living, and even his personality, will probably undergo transformation. Following a brief expounding of this theory, this chapter will proceed to describe and analyze data collected in our survey concerning the emotional responses of the farm people toward the land reform in Taiwan.

I. Emotional Response: A Precondition to the Acceptance
of Far-reaching Effects

It is theorized that any person who has been really affected or changed
by a social movement must first have reacted from his heart toward the forces
of change brought to bear upon him by the movement. If the reactions are
especially charged with intense emotions, the effect will go deep, perhaps
transforming the man himself. By reaction from the heart we mean response
which rises out of strong feeling, be it of pleasure or loathing, with a
blessing or a curse, with hope or dread. A person may, for example, have
heard of a social-welfare program which is intended to extend educational
opportunities to everyone in the community. It may be that someone in his
own household had accepted this opportunity. But, somehow, the program had
not become appealing to this person, and his reaction toward it was one of
indifference. He has no grudge against it but shows no favor toward it
either. In such a case, it would be very unlikely that he would make the
effort to take the opportunity for himself. Consequently, the undertaking
of such a program could hardly have any far-reaching effects upon him. On
the other hand, if he had had a strong feeling, say a positive faith,
toward the objective of the program and had become convinced that it
could accomplish great benefits among people who formerly had been without any opportunity for getting an education, he would then certainly take
the opportunity himself if he needed it. He probaly would do all he could
to see that others also got it. In doing so, he might deeply involve himself in the matter and might even become one of its volunteer workers.
Eventually his philosophy of life and his whole personality might undergo
a considerable transformation.

The same reasoning can be applied in estimating the probable effects of land reform upon the farm people. We would expect that if land reform was to give rise to significant changes in the farm people's economic, social, cultural and technological concepts and activities; or, in other words, if the reform was to achieve the second set of objectives described in the first chapter of this book, it must first of all be able to arouse strong feelings in the farmer's heart, be able to stir up a response heavily charged with emotion. Had the tenant-cultivators taken the 37.5% farm rent limitation program as merely a matter of getting a higher share of the crops they had produced, and the land-to-the-tiller program as merely a way of acquiring ownership of the land they had been cultivating—that and nothing more—the whole land reform in Taiwan would have soon been forgotten by the people.

On the other hand, if the results of the two programs had been greatly appreciated by the small farmers, especially by the great masses of tenant-cultivators, their effects would be quite different. The gratitude of small farmers would have been followed by the hope that the good things received from these programs might constitute a springboard whereby more promising goals, or something like owner-farmer's status, economic prosperity, social advancement, etc., could be achieved in the near future. If this had been the case, land reform could not but have profound and lasting effects upon the farm people.

The truth in this reasoning becomes more apparent when the immediate and tangible results of a land reform are as small and insignificant in their economic benefits as were the results of land reform in Taiwan. The crops or money saved for the tenant-cultivators by the 37.5% farm rent

limitation program had really not amounted to much. If formerly a
tenant had had to pay one half of his 100 kg total crop for the year--that
is, 50 kg--the farm rent limitation program reduced his obligation to 37.5 kg.
It saved for the tenant only 12.5 kg of his crop. The land-to-the-tiller
program, it is true, helped the tenant-cultivator to acquire the ownership of the land he was cultivating, but the area of the land was small.
It was so small that the ownership of it did not signify very much,
especially in terms of realistic, practical economics. Therefore, unless
the tenant-farmers for some traditional, social and/or family reasons had
made sentimental attachments to the programs in landownership and rent
limitation, all their results would have soon been forgotten, and gone
from the people's attention. Only when a poor, tenant household, which
heretofore had never been privileged to own any amount of land, felt
extremely happy about the promise and possibility of the land-to-the-tiller
program would the ownership of even such a very little piece of land mean
a great deal to its members. It must be in this way that the result of
the program might become a motivating power, capable of pushing the household into continuous progress.

What has been said in the foregoing must not, however, be construed
as meaning that man's subjective feeling, or his personal like or dislike,
can outweigh in value the practical, tangible, economic factors in
determining whether a social-welfare program shall have profound and far-
reaching effects. This is not its meaning. It means rather that all such
results as the limitation of farm rent, the wiping out of evil practices
in the traditional farm-tenancy system, the transfer of landownership from
landlords who did not actually cultivate the land to its tenant-cultivators,

were good and important, and they were the things which ought to give,
or were intended to give, happiness and a lift of morale to the poor
peasants. But whether or not the peasants had really been made happy
or really had had their morale lifted was entirely a subjective matter.
Some were happier and did have higher morale, and others were unchanged.
Our basic premise here is that only upon those who were really happier
and who did experience a lift in morale, would the immediate results
of the land reform carry farther and farther until significant changes
occurred in the farm people's economic, social, and cultural activities.
Such changes, can, then, be called "profound and far-reaching effects."
For those who did not feel any deep affection toward the land reform,
the undertaking's results stop at the 37.5% limit on their farm rent
and the acquiring of a small piece of farm land.

It is, then, because of a deep appreciation for, and a sentimental
attitude toward, the immediate results of the land reform as prerequisites
for the achievement of profound and far-reaching effects, that the subject
of "Land Reform and the Farm People's Morale" is to be treated before any
others in this study.

II. The Former Tenant-Farmers' Emotional Response toward Results of the Land Reform

It has been a common belief, popularly expressed, that the 37.5%
farm rent limitation, the revision of the farm-lease contracts, the
abolition of unfair practices in the farm-tenancy system and the transfer of landownership to tenant-cultivators made the tenant-farmers very
happy and tremendously improved morale. As to the amount of truth in
this belief, we have the following indications:

1. <u>Toward the 37.5% farm rent limitation.</u> First, let us consider tenant-farmers who had first been benefited by the 37.5% farm rent limitation program and later on by the land-to-the-tiller program. Such farmers are called the "former tenant-farmers" in this study. When the 1250 samples were interviewed, the first question asked them was whether they had really felt happy when the 37.5% Farm Rent Limitation Act was put into practice. About 90 per cent gave a positive answer. An immediate common derivative of this subjective condition was an attitude of hopefulness or optimism toward life and the future of the family's farm business: about 80 per cent from this same group of samples said they had experienced such a derivative; 18 per cent said they had not; and 2 per cent did not know what to say.

When this happiness and hopefulness occurred, they had not stopped at the stage of mere feelings, or simple, emotional expressions of a state of mind. They, instead, had gone on to become the moving power behind concrete actions. In other words, they had been converted into the terms of practical living. In the farmers' various kinds of new activities one senses their happiness and hopefulness. This translating of feeling and perception into action is of much greater importance to this study than its expression only in words. For it is action which tells us whether feelings and perceptions are truly in existence and are charged with meaning and energy. In Taiwan tenant-cultivators expressed their happiness about the rent-limitation program by considerably increasing their efforts for improving farm operation and crop production. Those who became owners of little pieces of land suddenly increased their interest in making the best use of these lands. For instance, of the 1250 samples of former

tenant-farmers interviewed, 68 per cent said that after the farm rent
limitation act was put into practice, they became eager to put increased
amounts of capital and labor into the cultivation of the rented farm; about
13 per cent said that they were willing to increase the input; while 17
per cent said that they had not felt any change in this respect. To
summarize it, happiness about the reduced, farm-rent rate and hopefulness
toward the future had motivated more than 80 per cent of the tenant-cultivators to increase the amounts of capital and labor invested in the operation of their rented farms. Only a little more than 17 per cent reported
that this land-reform program had not made any change in the amount of
input in their farm operation.

If the happy and hopeful tenant-farmers had become willing to increase
the input on their rented farm, it was even more probable that they should
have increased their efforts to improve their operations on the land
owned by themselves. Of the 1250 tenant farm households, 34 per cent owned
little pieces of farm land before the land-to-the-tiller program. Of
these households 70 per cent reported that they increased their interest
and efforts in order to raise the production of their own land; 24 per
cent said that they had not made such a change; about 6 per cent could not
say if they had made it or not.

The information in the foregoing can be summarized as follows:

The Former Tenant-Farmers' Emotional Responses to the 37.5%
Farm Rent Limitation Program (taken from 1250 samples)

A. Being happy about it:		
Really happy	1120	89.60%
Indifferent	111	8.88
No answer	19	1.52
Total	1250	100.00

B. Hopeful toward life or
   future of the farm business

Hopeful	996	79.68
No such feeling	231	18.48
No answer	23	1.84
Total	1250	100.00

C. Willingness to increase
   input in farm operation,
   motivated by hapiness
   and hopefulness

Very willing	852	68.16
A little willing	156	12.48
As usual	216	17.28
No answer	26	2.08
Total	1250	100.00

D. Interest and effort
   in improving own land

More interest and effort	294	70.17
As usual	102	24.34
No answer	23	5.49
Total	419	100.00

2. <u>Toward the land-to-the-tiller program.</u> It was taken for granted that if the tenant-farmers had been happy about the 37.5% farm rent limitation, they must have been more so after the transfer of landownership from the landlords to themselves. Therefore, the 1250 samples were not asked in the interview whether they were happy when they first received a certificate of landownership. There were, however, questions which were designed to detect such a feeling. For instance, interviewees were asked if they would like to purchase still more land if it were permitted. More than 82 per cent answered "yes;" 17 per cent answered "no." Those households which wished to purchase yet more land must have experienced a great glee in the first purchase, whereas those giving negative answers were disinterested because they had felt no great pleasure in the purchase that was already done. It might have been that these latter persons reasoned that they would not be able to purchase

any more land anyway. Then why make oneself a fool by saying yes? It might also have been that they believed themselves to be unable to operate more land than they already had.

In general, a farmer's happiness lies in having full freedom in use of his land. That means that he can plant any kind of crop, use any kind of system, and make any kind of improvement according to his own wishes and knowledge, governed only by market conditions and natural forces. A tenant-cultivator usually does not have this kind of liberty. Only farmers who own their own land do have it. Therefore, the most realistic reason for former tenants to be happy about gaining ownership of their land was that they would thereafter have freedom of use. When the 1250 samples of former tenant-farmers were asked if they felt that they now had freedom of choice, 84 per cent gave affirmative answers. When they were making such answers they felt happy. They felt happy because they did have that important freedom. Furthermore, this freedom implies being independant, being free from the dominance of the landlords. There is no need to say that this feeling of freedom must have been accompanied by a feeling of happiness. There were other changes in the former tenant's way of farming and conditions of living, and in practically every one of these changes, one can sense the feeling of happiness.

Information given in the above may be summarized in a tabular form as follows.

A. A tenant household found great pleasure in the purchasing of land and, therefore, it wished to purchase as much land as permitted. One thousand two-hundred-fifty samples were asked to comment on this assumption.

Yes	1030	82.40%
No	216	17.28
No comment	4	0.32
Total	1250	100.00

B. A reason for your being happy about having your own land is that you can use it as you please.

Yes	1053	84.24
There was no such feeling	183	14.64
No answer	14	1.12
Total	1250	100.00

According to the words of the former tenant-farmers themselves, a great majority of them were very happy about the 37.5% farm rent limitation and the transfer of landownership from the landlords to them. In other words, these small farmers had genuine love for those immediate, tangible, economic results of the land reform. Also, a great many of them had transformed this feeling of affection into a power which then gave rise to hopefulness toward the future of life and willingness to invest more capital, labor, and interest in an effort to improve the farm operation. The happiness experienced in the purchasing of land was evidenced in the fact that a great majority of the tenant-farmers wished to buy as much land as possible. In a word, their morale was raised to a great extent.

Most people will praise a thing, sometimes praise it lavishly, as long as the benefits from it are free, or the flow of grace is smooth and is a one-way affair with the accruals being theirs. But whenever a price, or an obligation, is required or requested in return for the profits received, regardless of how light and reasonable the price or obligation may be, the recipient will rise at once in protest or complaint. Should anything happen to slow the receipt of benefits, interfere with, delay or change them from short-term to long-term, the original affection or happiness aroused by them will also diminish and the giver of the benefits, whether a person or an institution, will begin to receive complaints instead of compliments.

In this regard, many of the former tenant-cultivators certainly belonged to the masses. They were very happy about the transfer of landownership to them from the landlords. Their happiness had not been affected too much by the fact that a fair price had to be paid. That the payment had not significantly dampened their happiness was because the tenants had been informed of it earlier, and they had taken it as a matter of course. It was helpful, also, to have the payment divided into 20 installments paid over a period of ten years, each installment never amounting to more than the single, semiannual payment the tenants had formerly paid under the 37.5% farm rent limitation regulations. But, as soon as the old tenant-cultivators discovered that as a result of having the landownership, they also had to shoulder all other obligations such as land tax, irrigation water charges, and several other levies which were assessed on landowners, many of the new, small landowners were immediately grieved. They made no effort to disguise their dissatisfaction and, instead, they showed ungratefulness toward the Government.

The following information should, to a great extent, bear out what has been said in the preceding paragraphs. The 1250 samples of former tenant-farmers were first asked: When it was difficult to muster enough money to pay the price of and/or the taxes on the land, did you ever have the feeling that the obligations borne by an owner-farmer were too heavy and did you, therefore, wish you were still a tenant-cultivator? A little more than 14 per cent answered they frequently had had such feelings; about 35 per cent said they had felt so occasionally; 51 per cent claimed they had never had these feelings. The second question was: Since you have owned the land and had to pay the land taxes and the irrigation water charges, have you ever felt that the obligations are too heavy and that, therefore,

becoming an owner-farmer is not altogether a good thing? About 60 per cent

of the samples answered "yes," 39 per cent answered "no." Despite these

unpleasant feelings, very few of the newly-established, owner-farmers would

really wish to return to the old status of tenant-cultivator. For instance,

only 6 per cent of the 1250 new, owner-farmers said "yes," they would prefer

being a tenant-cultivator under the 37.5% farm rent limitation system rather

than being an owner-farmer charged with a number of obligations; but 92 per

cent said "no." A few households did not give any answer to this question.

III. The Present Tenant-Farmers' Emotional Response toward the Land Reform

By "present tenant-farmers" we mean those farm people who were still

tenant-cultivators after the completion of the public farm land sales

program and the land-to-the-tiller program. In other words, it means

those tenant-farmers who have not had the opportunity to purchase the land

they have been cultivating through the land-reform programs. Were these

people happy about the 37.5% farm rent limitation program? Of the

250 samples interviewed, 90 per cent said that they were really happy; only

8 per cent admitted that they didn't have much of a feeling. What happened

to these 8 per cent of households? Why should they have been so different?

According to information recorded in most interviewers' diaries, a few

samples of this category of farm households had rented either a very small

or a very poor plot of land. In the former case, the tenant-cultivator

could receive only very little benefit from the 37.5 per cent farm rent

limitation program, and in the case of the latter, the household might not

have been affected by the program at all, because the rental rate on a very
poor piece of farm might never have exceeded 37.5 per cent. Therefore, it
was natural that such tenant households felt no special thrill over the
limitation on farm rent.

Like the former tenant-farmers, the present tenant-cultivators had
also let their happiness give birth to hopefulness and optimism toward
life and the future of their farm business. As many as 80 per cent of the
250 samples said so; only 18 per cent said they did not have such an
experience. Furthermore, 81 per cent of these households confided that
they had, at one time or another, been led by their optimism to dream that
someday, not far off, they might become owner-farmers. Only 17 per cent
said that they did not have such a dream. In addition to the dream of
becoming owner-farmers, happiness and hopefulness had also generated in
these realistic land-tillers the motivation and energy for taking practical
action to improve cultivation of their rented land. About 92 per cent of
the 250 samples gave the answer "yes" to such a question as: Since you
have been receiving through the 37.5% farm rent limitation program a
greater share of the crops you produced, are you now very glad to do
better than before on the rented farm? Only 7 per cent said that they
had made no difference. This answer could be interpreted in two ways: It
may be that these households had already done their best, no more could be
added, regardless of whether there were a rent reduction. Or it might be
that some of the tenants had been so depressed that they could no longer
become stirred or interested by any change short of one involving life
or death.

Among those who did feel happy about the farm rent limitation, the majority were willing to spend more money and labor on their rented farms. Of the 250 samples about 79 per cent said they had done so; only 20 per cent reported that they had not done this.

A summary of the above findings would be as follows:

The Present Tenant-Farmers' Emotional Responses to the 37.5% Farm Rent Limitation Program (taken from 250 samples)

A. Being happy about it

Really happy	226 households	90.40%
Indifferent	19	7.60
No answer	5	2.00
Total	250	100.00

B. Hopeful toward life or future of the farm business

Hopeful	200	80.00
No such experience	44	17.60
No answer	6	2.40
Total	250	100.00

C. Interest in doing better in the operation of the rented farm (motivated by the happiness and hopefulness)

Very interested	229	91.60
Made no difference	17	6.80
No answer	4	1.60
Total	250	100.00

D. Wish to become an owner-farmer

Having such a wish	203	81.20
Having none	42	16.80
No answer	5	2.00
Total	250	100.00

E. Willingness to spend more money and labor on the rented farm

Willing	196	78.40
Did not have this idea	50	20.00
No answer	4	1.60
Total	250	100.00

A great number of the present tenant-farmers had once been very much disappointed by the fact that they had no opportunity to purchase the land under their cultivation. They could not purchase it because their rented lands happened either to be among those in the quota which the landlords were allowed to retain for their own livelihood, or to be, for one reason or another, exempted from the Government's compulsory purchase. In either case, because the Government did not purchase the lands from the landlords, there could be no resale of the same to the tenants. Although these unfortunate tenant-farm households were well informed of these circumstances, many of them still could not but be saddened by their bad luck. Their ineligibility to purchase land had not only broken their dreams of becoming owner-farmers, but it must have also considerably dampened their happiness and again lowered their spirits which had risen because of the rent limitation program. In turn, their enthusiasm toward the Government's efforts to improve the small farmers' living conditions must have also been adversely affected.

According to our survey, 52 per cent of the 250 samples reported that they had been disappointed by the fact that they could not purchase the land; 47 per cent said that they had not been so affected. If assumptions in the preceding paragraphs are true, then it should be considered fortunate that not too many, just a little over one-half, of the present tenant-farmers had been unhappy about the result of the land-to-the-tiller program.

IV. The Original Owner-Farmers' Emotional Response
toward the Results of the Land Reform

By "original owner-farmers" we mean those who had been owner-farmers before the undertaking of the land reform. They are separated here from those who had become owner-farmers entirely through the aid

of the land-to-the tiller program. The original owner-farmers, by
and large, had only slight feeling toward the outcome of the various,
land-reform programs. This is understandable, because they had not
been much affected by these efforts. Even though 68 per cent of the
250 samples of such farm households expressed favorable opinions
about the land reform as a whole, only 16 per cent said that they
themselves had really been affected. More than 82 per cent of them
complained that the programs had done nothing directly to them or
for them.

What kind of feeling did the original owner-farmers have while the
land-reform programs were being carried out? A majority of them, that
is more than 74 per cent of the 250 samples, felt that they should remain
unconcerned because none of the programs had anything to do with them.
Only less than 12 per cent said they were disappointed by not having the
opportunity of purchasing land; less than 6 per cent had the thought that
they might be hurt; and 7 per cent had unspecified feelings, or no feeling
at all.

For a few of the original owner-farmers, the land reform had an
indirect but desirable result. As it happened, some landlords had
stubbornly refused to give sympathetic support to the 37.5% farm rent
limitation program. They chose to sell their land at a low price rather
than be subjected to the limitation rules. Others were able to know in
advance the main points of the Government's design for purchasing the
landlord's land compulsorily and, being advised by selfish ideas, these
landlords also preferred the private sale of their land at low prices over
waiting for the Government to make the public purchase. Given these

opportunities, some of the original owner-farmers had been able to take
advantage of this situation and bought land at greatly reduced prices.
For these few households the land reform was an unexpected good-luck affair.
But a great majority, 85 per cent, felt that land reform brought no evident
benefit to them.

In spite of these facts, most of the original owner-farmers, that is,
83 per cent of the 250 samples, considered that the land reform as a whole
was successful. More than 55 per cent believed that the economic conditions
of a majority of the tenant-farmers had been improved because of the land-
reform programs; about 24 per cent felt that about one-half of the tenant-
farm households had enjoyed improvement in their economic status through
the land reform. Only 20 per cent thought that it had done very little in
helping the tenant-farmers.

In the interview, some of the original owner-farmers made criticisms
of the land reform. Their criticisms can be summed up in 14 points: (1)
The tenant-cultivators got all the benefits while the landlords suffered
all the losses. (2) The Government became a big landlord and made a huge
profit. (3) The land which a landlord was allowed to retain was too
little. (4) The ratio between the double-crop paddy field and the single-
crop paddy field was not fair. (5) The amount of land sold to one tenant
household differed too much from that sold to another. (6) Some tenant
households were not able to keep the land sold to them and thus the Government's efforts had been wasted. (7) Since the completion of the land reform
many small farmers could no longer rent any land at all. (8) The land
reform gave rise to many farm-tenancy disputes. (9) There was no security

or guaranty on the corporation stocks issued by the Government. (10) The Government gave consideration only to the benefits of the tenant-farmers; it did not take good care for the landlords' livelihood after their lands had been compulsorily purchased. (11) Many tenant-farmers had not done their best on the land sold to them by the Government. (12) The land classification made for the land reform was not in accordance with the real conditions. (13) Due to the land reform many small landlords had lost all the means on which their livelihood depended. (14) Since land reform tenant-cultivators could no longer receive sympathetic understanding from their landlords when in difficulty.

It is quite obvious that most of these criticisms stemmed from a lack of right information, or from the possession of wrong information. There is no doubt that some of the original owner-farmers were relatives, friends, or alliances of the landlords and, therefore, they prejudicially spoke on the side of the landlords. This is, however, by no means intended to say that the Government had done nothing wrong or that the land reform had put everything right. It was for the sake of being objective or impartial that our interviewers had requested the farmers to make any criticisms on the land reform, on the whole, as well as on particular items, with a completely free mind; and whatever kinds of criticisms were collected are authentically presented here.

In summary, all of the original owner-farmers' opinions about the land reform are put together as follows:

A. Was the land reform in whole a good thing?

Yes	170 households	68.00%
No comment	68	27.20
Not good	6	2.40
No answer	6	2.40
Total	250	100.00

B. Extent to which the land reform had been successful

Very successful	108	43.20
Moderately successful	99	39.60
No comment	40	16.00
No answer	3	1.20
Total	250	100.00

C. Feeling when the land reform was to be carried out

Fear to be hurt	14	5.60
Unconcerned	186	74.40
Disappointment	29	11.60
Others	18	7.20
No answer	3	1.20
Total	250	100.00

D. Concrete influence received from land reform

Had	40	16.00
Had not	206	82.40
No answer	4	1.60
Total	250	100.00

E. Bought land at low prices because of land reform

Yes	26	10.40
No	223	89.20
No answer	1	0.40
Total	250	100.00

F. Opinion as to the number of tenant-farmers whose living conditions improved because of land reform

Most have improvement	138	55.20
About one-half have improvement	59	23.60
Very few have improvement	50	20.00
No answer	3	1.20
Total	250	100.00

G. Opinion about being unable to purchase land through land reform

Not unfair	174	69.60
Unfair	24	9.60
Other feelings	37	14.80
No answer	15	6.00
Total	250	100.00

V. The Farm Laborers' Emotional Response
toward the Results of the Land Reform

In order to know whether or not farm laborers had had any emotional

responses toward the outcomes of the land reform, it was necessary to see

first how the land reform affected these people's opportunities of

employment and thus their livelihood. From reports made by those farm

laborers who were interviewed, the following pieces of information were

taken concerning their being employed on farms or in non-farm jobs since

the completion of the land reform:

1. Of the 250 samples of farm laborers, more than 82 per cent felt

that it had been harder after land reform to make a living as a laborer on

the farms. About 47 per cent attributed the new difficulty to such factors

as the increase of total population, the increase of general unemployment,

and the shortage of industrial as well as farm jobs. Only 16 per cent

thought it was because most farm households were nowadays making the utmost

use of their own labor. Then 12 per cent gave as reasons: too-low farm

wages, the farm-labor-exchange system, the use of farm machinery, and others.

About nineteen, 8 per cent,gave no answer. Although 36 per cent of the

samples blamed land reform for the difficulties, as many as 46 per cent

disagreed and said there was no relationship between land reform and

these changes.

2. About 49 per cent of the samples sadly said that in the decade

since the land reform, there have been increasing numbers of farm people

looking for employment opportunities. The chief reason for this increase,

according to those who made the statement,was that the number of family

members increased, the amount of farm land remained the same as before, and, as a result, many small farm households were forced to send some of their members out seeking gainful employment. But the other one-half of the 250 samples had different opinions in this regard. Some said that there had not been this kind of change in any significant degree; and others reported a decrease in the number of farm people seeking to be hired by other farm households. Reasons for the decrease, according to these people, were that many of the known or professional farm laborers had gone to the cities or towns for work in non-agricultural activities. They earn more there, in terms of cash, than from working on farms. Other people, especially the young ones, who do not have enough work to occupy themselves in the farm villages have practically all gone to the factories to become industrial workers or to learn a trade in the cities. Large numbers of young farm women went either to factories to be textile workers or to city homes to be domestic helpers. Then, also in recent years, most of the owner-farmers and the well-to-do tenant-farmers were willing to do all the work on their farms and homes by themselves. In this way they have not only saved a considerable amount of money but also have engaged everyone in the family in active and positive roles in the development of the family's economy.

Has there been any causative relationship between these changes and the land reform? About 40 per cent out of 190 people who gave answers to this question said "yes," the land reform gave rise to these changes; while 57 per cent answered "no," there was no relationship between the two.

3. There is no doubt that a majority of the former-landlord households, if they still continue farming, can no longer afford, or no longer have need for, hired labor. Both the original owner-farmers and those

who have just acquired this status have been infused by a kind of spirit or atmosphere with a motivation to work more diligently and to save more money so that someday in the near future they may become well-to-do and upper-social-class families. While being possessed by this kind of mood, they tried to use the least hired labor that conditions would permit. This observation was drawn from the fact that about 76 per cent of the 250 samples interviewed reported that the farm families had since land reform been hiring less farm labor. About 66 per cent attributed the decrease to the fact that nowadays most farm households were making the utmost use of their own labor.

With all these mixed, complicated, and sometimes contradictory opinions in regard to the impact of land reform upon their employment and livelihood, it is safe to conclude that the farm laborers as a whole have had no strong, sentimental feelings toward the land reform. Or, we can say that the farm laborers' feelings toward this have been diverse and perhaps ambivalent. On the one hand, their feelings might be bitter because after the carrying out of the land-to-the-tiller program, most landlords could no longer employ as many farm laborers as they did before. A great majority of the farm households have of late been depending chiefly on the labor supplied by their own members. As a result, most farm laborers have been having difficulty in finding farm employment. Their difficulty can be attributed ultimately to the impact of the land reform.

On the other hand, because of the development of new industries and businesses in the cities and towns, it has been much easier than before for unskilled labor to find menial and manual jobs. Those who are young

and pre-middle-aged could even get into the short-term training programs
in the factories and become skilled workers in a comparatively short time.
Furthermore, for those who continued to work on farms, earnings were now
much better. For these reasons, the farm laborers soon got over their
early discouragement and they became unconcerned about the outcomes of
the land reform. Bar the first one or two years after enforcement of
the land-to-the-tiller program, the farm laborers' attitude toward the
land reform was one of indifference.

Why not? These people received from the programs no specific or
important benefits. Although a sentence in the Land Law, and provisions
in the land-to-the-tiller program, stipulated that the landlord's excessive land should be compulsorily purchased by the Government and then
resold to the"tenant-cultivators and/or farm hands" who were cultivating
it, actually very few farm laborers, or farm hands, had been given this
opportunity. Therefore, farm laborers had no reason to praise the land
reform or to be really happy about it. On the other hand, none of
these people's interests, or rights, or opportunities, had been seriously
hurt by it, so they would not have become bitter against it either.

VI. The Landlords' Emotional Response
toward the Results of the Land Reform

It would be quite natural for one to assume that the landlords'
emotional responses to the land reform, especially toward the 37.5% farm
rent limitation program and the land-to-the-tiller program, must have
been sore and bitter. They were indeed, according to the results of our
survey. Of the 575 samples interviewed, men who were once owners of

ordinary or extra-large holdings, more than 78 per cent admitted that they
were angry and upset about both the limitation on their farm rent and the
compulsory purchase of their farm land. Only 20 per cent said that they
were able to remain calm and to show no sign of bitterness. The truth of
this latter statement is questionable, though there were indeed a small
number of cases in which the landlords had really been persuaded, and had
been quite relaxed on the matter of relinquishing a part of their property.
There were others, also in small number, who had been in non-farm businesses
for some time already and had wished to convert their land property into
business capital. For them the land-to-the-tiller program had been a
help rather than a loss. They certainly could afford to stay quiet.

Whereas most tenant-farmers had expressed their happiness and hopefulness over land reform by amplifying and vitalizing its immediate results,
that is, letting these results become the motivating power toward improvement of their economic and social conditions, the embittered landlords
had tried to avenge their grievance, or to make up their losses, by
undermining the success of the operation of the various programs. As
has been mentioned previously, when the 37.5% farm rent limitation program
was being carried out, quite a number of landlords tried by one means or
another to withdraw their land from rental on the pretext that it was to
be for their own cultivation. Withdrawing the land meant termination of
the lease contract. Though the termination of a lease contract might have
been made to appear to be a voluntary act on the part of the tenant-
farmer, it was basically always the result of threats or inducements
which came from the landlord. This landlords' scheme of sabotaging the
farm rent limitation program had at one time become quite a serious threat.

From the beginning of 1950 to the end of June, 1951, there had been 16,349 cases of lease terminations and tenancy disputes, which increased to a total of 35,313 one year later.[1]

One can imagine what kind of resentment the landlords must have had toward the reform program. But due to the Government's careful preparation and the precautions so minutely taken, very few landlords had had the chance to do anything damaging to its operation, except that quite a few of them had tried, successfully, to keep as much of their land as possible under the retention regulation by hastily and legally breaking up a large extended household into a number of small nuclear units. A few other landlords had received information about the land-to-the-tiller program in advance, and had time to make dispositions of all excessive lands according to their own wishes so that their land had escaped compulsory purchase. Whether or not the private disposal had been better than being purchased by the Government was another matter. At the time the social mood was such that the mere fact of being able to get away from the grasp of the Government was considered lucky or heroic.

The landlords' grudge against the Government was almost universal. There were, however, landlords whose additional complaint was due to the Government's mistaken purchase of land which was under joint ownership of two or more small cultivators and on which these people and their families were altogether dependent for their living. It was true that the regulations governing the enforcement of the land-to-the-tiller program made land under joint ownership subject to compulsory purchase. But the Government should have sympathetically made exceptions in certain special cases. Denying special consideration to unusual cases, or following the rules with unbending rigidity, would have left such families, as the one

mentioned in the above illustration without their only means of making a

living. This surely was not the intent of land reform. Such has been the

line argued by many of the former landlords in the interview.[2]

Another serious complaint made by landlords who were able to analyze

the situation was to hold the Government at fault for its use of the stocks

of the four corporations issued to compensate the landlords in the land

purchases. The landlords did not complain about the corporation stocks

per se. Rather, they scorned the Government for its failure to make any

guaranty of the value of the stocks. They were bitter because the Govern-

ment did not do anything to protect the worth of the securities but let

them be considerably damaged by purported scare rumors and by ignorance

of the holders themselves so that their market values suffered drastic

declines. The rumors and ignorance caused a large number of the landlords

to dispose of their stock shares quickly. As soon as the stocks were so

cheaply sold out, the landlords realized that 30 per cent of the prices

of their sold land had been lost. What else could these unlucky persons

be led to but bitterness?[3]

Some of the landlords' resentment toward the land reform originated

at quite a later time. There were landlords who became bitter when the

cash from the sale of the stocks was used up, when there was no prospect

of finding any easy way of making a new start, or when the whole family

was so depressed that it lost the will to work. At such moments these

former landlords would dwell only on memories of the "good old days,"

that is, the easy days of living on farm rents. The more they cherished

the past the angrier they became toward the land reform which, as they believed, caused all their latter-day miseries. Others became acutely

resentful after suffering repeated failures in trying to build up new

businesses or in trying to enter new occupations, through which most

of the family's savings or life securities had been lost.[4] In either

case, these situations arose five or more years after the completion

of the land reform.

From what has been said in the foregoing, one should be able to deduce

that there were landlords who at a later time had ceased to become ever

more indignant, perhaps had even become grateful toward the land reform. Mo

landlord families who became active farmers after the land-to-the-tiller

program had evolved into solid, well-managed, owner households. Their

living no longer came from collected farm rents but from fruits of their

own labor and wisdom. In the old days they had had the feeling of being

superior and yet, at the same time, dependent on others. Their life was eas

going, careless, lacking in spirit and meaning. After they became actual

farmers, especially after the reestablishment of their household on the

achievements of their own hard labor and alert planning, they acquired a

new feeling. They felt that they were independent and honest people. They

no longer had to feel guilty for occasionally taking other people's things

to maintain their own living. They felt in themselves the energy, the

determination, and the outlook for a positive, bright future. These feel-

ings made them realize that the old form of life had been decaying anyway,

and that the new way was leading toward economic prosperity and social

esteem. Therefore, they were glad that they had undergone all the changes.

If the changes had really been started with the undertaking of the land

reform, then why should they continue to be angry about it? The number

of thus-changed landlord households was quite large at the time of
the interview.

There were also landlord families which had been successful in
establishing themselves in new businesses or occupations after the land
reform. With such achievements they became not only materially comfortable
and secure but also socially respectful or admired. Their young folks
had, in most cases, become highly educated people or were studying in
institutions of higher education. In a word, theirs were families to be
respected by the modern world, by people of the modern civilization. They
no longer had any intimate relationship with the old, agrarian community.
Inasmuch as the origin, or the starting point, of this evolution was to be
found in the compulsory purchase of their land by the Government, the land
reform was not a bad thing after all.

There is no need to say that those landlords, though a small number,
who have become important or well-known members in the world of industry
and big business have been very happy and have taken no grudge against
the land reform. Except for a few, such landlords had indeed never been
unhappy about the affair because they had never suffered any significant
loss from it.

VII. Feelings and Observations of Non-farm People

The non-farm people interviewed in this study included local leaders,
merchants, small industry operators, local government employees, and
people engaged in cultural works. Samples from only two of these categories were asked about their feelings toward the land reform and their
observations of the farm people's emotional responses.

A. The land reform was fair and sound
  1. in regard to the 37.5% farm rent limitation

Yes	86 households	86.00%
No	14	14.00
Total	100	100.00

  2. in regard to the land-to-the-tiller program

Yes	83	83.00
No	17	17.00
Total	100	100.00

B. A need for land reform

Yes	90	90.00
No	8	8.00
No answer	2	2.00
Total	100	100.00

C. Land reform made tenant-farmers optimistic and hopeful

Began to be so	53	53.00
More so than before	34	34.00
Not so	6	6.00
No change	4	4.00
No answer	3	3.00
Total	100	100.00

D. Land reform made tenant-farmers work harder in improving farm operation

Began to be so	25	25.00
More so than before	67	67.00
Not so	3	3.00
No difference	4	4.00
No answer	1	1.00
Total	100	100.00

E. Land reform made tenant-farmers interested in community participation

Began to be so	41	41.00
More so than before	38	38.00
Not so	4	4.00
No change	16	16.00
No answer	1	1.00
Total	100	100.00

F. Land reform made tenant-farmers interested in social welfare activities

Began to be so	35	35.00
More so than before	20	20.00

Not concerned	7	7.00
No change	36	36.00
No answer	2	2.00
Total	100	100.00

1. The local leaders' feelings and observations. The first question put to local leaders concerned whether they felt that the 37.5% farm rent limitation program was fair and sound. Of the 100 samples 86 answered "yes " while 14 said "no." In regard to the land-to-the-tiller program, 83 said it was fair and sound while 17 felt that it was not. Did these people feel that there was really a need for land reform in Taiwan? Ninety said there was such a need.

Had these people witnessed the tenant-farmers' becoming hopeful or optimistic toward life and the future of their farm business? Fifty-three of the 100 reported that the tenant-farmers had begun to be hopeful or optimistic; 34 said they had become more hopeful and optimistic than before. Only a few said that they had not seen such changes and a few others reported seeing them become less hopeful or optimistic. A great majority of these samples had noticed that since the land reform the tenant-farmers had either started to have an interest, or had increased their interest, in the improvement of their farm operation, in the promotion of community participation, and in the expansion of local social-welfare activities. These findings are summarized as follows:

G. Land reform made tenant-farmers interested in local politics

Began to be so	46	46.00
More so than before	23	23.00
No change	25	25.00
No answer	6	6.00
Total	100	100.00

H. Land reform made landlords pessimistic toward life and work

Yes	74	74.00
No, optimistic	2	2.00
No change	20	20.00
No answer	4	4.00
Total	100	100.00

I. Land reform reduced landlords' interest in community participation

Yes	66	66.00
No, increased	3	3.00
No change	30	30.00
No answer	1	1.00
Total	100	100.00

J. Land reform reduced landlords' interest in social welfare

Yes	68	68.00
No	29	29.00
No change	3	3.00
Total	100	100.00

2. _Local government employees' opinions and observations_. Ninety-five per cent of the local government employees told the interviewers that they were interested in, or had paid attention to, the results or the benefits of the land reform. About fifty-five per cent of these people believed that the land reform was directly, and indirectly, responsible for the improvement of the farm people's living conditions, the rise of their educational level, and the growing prosperity in the farm villages. They said they noticed that after land reform, especially after acquirement of land-ownership, most new-owner farmers became interested in local politics and their spirits were good in dealing with the government employees. In their opinion, these facts indicated that the results of the land reform had made the formerly unhappy peasants into happy farmers. If this was true, the newly-established, owner-farmers must have thought favorably of the land reform.

VIII. Conclusion

We may then conclude that in the past decade, the former tenant farmers have been grateful to the Government for the acomplishments of the land reform. Practically all the accomplishments have been profitable for these people's life and work. No wonder a great majority, if not all, of them have been very happy about it. This happiness considerably raised their morale and, in turn, the higher morale generated hopefulness and optimism toward the future of the farm business and of life itself. Hopefulness and optimism gave birth to realistic actions: actions of working harder, thinking more deeply, and putting more labor, capital, and technology into land utilization and the improvement of crop cultivation. The immediate goal was to increase farm production. Thus, the former tenant-cultivators, who had received benefits first from the 37.5% farm rent limitation act and later acquired landownership through the land-to-the-tiller program, at first had statements of praise for the land reform and no words against it. Later, however, when they found that it was not easy to bear all obligations such as the payment of the land price, the land tax and other levies, and the discharging of water bills, then complaints arose. A few then expressed dissatisfaction with the outcome of the program and forgot most of their early praises for the Government.

The present tenant-farmers, that is, tenants who have not had the opportunity to become owner-farmers through the land-to-the-tiller program, were also happy and praised the land reform when they received benefits from the 37.5% farm rent limitation program. But a great number of them became disappointed and spoke bitter words against the Government when they learned that they would not have the opportunity to purchase the land under their cultivation.

There were also present tenant-cultivators who did not have much good feeling toward the land reform because the lands they cultivated were either too small, too fragmented, or too poor in quality. Under these conditions, the 37.5% farm rent limitation program could not bring them benefits of any significance if there were any benefits to them at all.

A majority of the original owner-farmers had, at one time or another, praised the land reform. They praised it not because they themselves had received much benefit from the programs, but because they observed that a great majority of the tenant-cultivators had profited substantially and that, thereby, obvious improvements had been made in their farm business and in their living conditions as well. However, some owner-farmers in this category must have been misinformed about the policies, principles, methods, and objectives which the Government held and employed in the land reform, or they had prejudicially taken sides with the landlords whose land had been compulsorily purchased by the Government. Probably it was for such reasons that they made some unfair, ill-founded criticism of some features of the land reform.

The farm laborers had mixed and ambiguous reactions toward the land reform. At one time, immediately after the enforcement of the land-to-the-tiller program, they were frightened by the possibility that none of the landlord households would be able to continue to hire farm laborers once their land had been purchased by the Government. Nor would the original-owner farm families and the newly-established owner families be able to hire. The most these families could do, or so the farm laborers figured, would be to hire day-laborers for a few days whenever they found the work too much to be handled by themselves. Later on, however, as industries, commerce, and other non-farm enterprises continued to develop in ever-increasing volume, the demand for labor, including both unskilled and skilled, increased with great speed, and the farm laborers, as well as other unoccupied but able-bodied people in the rural communities, found the situation gradually improved. Gradually they had less trouble in finding one way or another to make a living. When they were no longer threatened by the possibility of facing total unemployment, the farm laborers became unconcerned about the eventual results of the land reform.

We did, however, hear the opinion that since land reform there have been more people in the countryside looking for gainful employment on the farm. According to this opinion, the reason for this condition was that many farm families had a surplus of labor. At the same time the families had been badly in need of money. Under these circumstances, it was natural that they wanted their surplus labor to become employed. At the same time there was also information that in many of the prosperous farm regions that, in the past decade, there had constantly been a shortage of farm labor. The shortage could become acute in especially busy farm seasons. At any rate, the land reform had actually had very little to offer to, or take from, the farm laborers and, consequently, they had not had any kind of strong feeling toward it.

As for the landlords whose farm rent had been reduced and whose farm land was compulsorily purchased, their first reaction toward land reform had been almost unanimously resentful. In a later stage, however, there had been obvious changes occurring in differing degrees in individuals under differing conditions. In some landlord households resentment was terribly intensified when all cash from the sale of the stock shares

was used up, the remaining land bonds were diminishing rapidly, the outlook for finding a new livelihood was bleak, and the family members' will
to accept hardship in order to gain revitalization was nonexistent. But
a large number of the comparatively small landlords, with the land which
they were allowed to keep, had been able to adapt themselves to the conditions of a sober, middle-class, farm-owner family and had actually entered
upon land cultivation. Some landlords felt that the new way of life and
new socio-economic status were not so bad as had been imagined and that
the new ways were even better than life in the old days. For these people
the bitter period was over, and they began to look for a promising future.
There were also a small number of landlords for whom a change of occupation,
or entering into industry, had been successful. They happily established
themselves in a new world. Their young people entered colleges and univer-
sities and acquired the training and qualities for leading a modern, urban
life. Thus, these families would soon be dissociated from anything agrarian
and conservative, or traditional, in nature. When it was discovered during
interviews that there had been a relationship between a family's change of
occupation and the land-to-the-tiller program, these families either openly,
or secretly, praised the land reform.

Among non-farm people the opinions of only the local leaders and
local government employees were solicited. Many local leaders interviewed
expressed favorable and enthusiastic feelings toward all programs of the
land reform. Their observations were that a great majority of former tenant
farmers and present tenants were very happy about the land reform, that they
had transformed their happiness into hopefulness and optimism and, in turn,
the hopefulness and optimism had motivated them to take practical measures

to improve not only their farm operation but their productive capability in every aspect of life. The local government employees also reported that according to their observation, the tenant-cultivators received most of the benefits of the land reform and, therefore, they were the people who bore the greatest gratitude toward the program and the Government. This gratitude has already made the formerly poor peasants over into modern farmers who are far advanced in economic, social, and cultural activities.

Notes

[1] Hui-sun Tang, Land Reform in Free China, p. 50.

[2] Such arguments have been recorded in the interviewers' diaries.

[3] In the interviewers' diaries.

[4] See interviewed diaries.

Chapter Five

LAND REFORM AND AGRICULTURAL IMPROVEMENT

I. Recent Agricultural Improvements in
Taiwan
   1. Increase in Crop and Livestock
      Production
   2. Changes in Farm Technology
   3. Increase in Farm Input
   4. Beginning of Farm Planning

II. Agricultural Progress Made by the
Former-tenant Farm Households
   1. Average Size of Farm
   2. Land Improvement
   3. Improvement in Farm Operation
   4. Improvement in Cultivation Methods
   5. Improvement toward Mechanization
   6. Increase in Per-hectare Production
   7. Relationship between Land Reform
      and Agricultural Improvement

III. Agricultural Improvements by Other
Farm Households
   1. Made by Original-owner Farm
      Households
   2. Made by Present-tenant Farm
      Households
   3. Made by Former-landlord now
      Active-farmer Households

IV. Non-farm People's Observations
   1. Local Leaders in Rural Communities
   2. School Teachers, Agricultural-Extension
      Workers, and Staffs of Cultural Programs

V. Conclusion

It has been emphasized from the beginning of this study that whether or not land reform in Taiwan had really been successful would be judged by whether or not it had made contributions toward improvement of the farm people's living conditions. Such improvement should, in general, be a result of progress or improvement in their farming business. Under this proposition the first sign of any realistic success of the land reform should be seen in its relationship with the recent agricultural progress in Taiwan. The preceding chapter was devoted to analysis of qualitative findings of our survey. The chief task of the present chapter will be to present statistical findings of the survey.

I. Recent Agricultural Improvements in Taiwan

Before we can discover whether there is a relationship between agricultural improvement and land reform, we must first learn whether, in fact, such improvements do exist, and if they exist, then we must ascertain their degree of significance. Our search will cover four aspects of agricultural economy: production rates, technology, input rates, and planning.

1. Crop and livestock production. The years 1955 through 1964 are taken as the base period, and rice, sugarcane, sweet potato, banana, peanut, tobacco, soybean, and hog raising are the commodity base, on which analyses are to be made. This decade was chosen because land reform was completed in 1954. By 1955 it can be expected to have begun to show results. The commodities chosen are broadly representative; in Taiwan rice production is of first importance in the agricultural economy and accounted in 1965 for approximately 35.05 per cent of the

total value of agricultural products, while sugarcane, sweet potato,
banana, peanut, tobacco, and soybean accounted, respectively, for 10.14,
7.74, 3.03, 2.67, 1.40, and 1.15 per cent of the total agricultural
value. The total livestock production accounted for 26.18 per cent of
total agricultural value and of this portion, hog raising claimed 17.61
per cent.[1]

The per-hectare production of rise increased continually from 1955
to 1964. This was true for both first-crop and second-crop productions
of each year. For instance, the per-hectare production of first-crop
rice was 2,323 kg and the second-crop averaged 2,033 kg in 1955. For
the years from 1956 to 1964, the pairs of figures are: 2,672 + 1,988;
2,689 + 2,077; 2,715 + 2,211; 2,725 + 2,131; 2,719 + 2,324; 2,896 +
2,331; 3,081 + 2,340; 3,226 + 2,516; and 3,317 + 2,645, respectively.
The difference between the 1955 production and the 1964 production was
994 kg for the first crop and 612 kg for the second crop. There was a
42.8 per cent increase in the first and a 30 per cent increase in the
second. The compound increase for the whole year was 36.87 per cent.[2]
The aggregated compound increase for the ten-year period was 26.39 per
cent and the average annual increase was 2.64 per cent. This was due
to the 1.42 per cent decrease in 1959.

The per-hectare production of sugarcane alternately increased and
decreased in the same ten-year period. In the 1954-55 term, for instance,
the per-hectare production was 78,121 kg. In the 1955-56 term it dropped
to 69,782 kg, a 10.67 per cent decrease. From here on there were
continuous increases in three consecutive terms. The percentages of
increase were 3.30, 2.71, and 10.02. In the term of 1959-1960 production

decreased again by 13.56 per cent. In the following term, 1960-61,
there was a 12.16 per cent increase. But in the term 1961-62 a big
decrease cccurred--15.66 per cent. From the 1962-63 term the production
again turned upward. The increase that year was small, only 5.25 per
cent. The following term, 1963-64, it was even smaller, only 2.68 per
cent. Taking the per-hectare production of the 1954-55 term as 100 per
cent, the per-hectare production of the term of 1963-64 was 92.16 per
cent. There had been 7.84 per cent decrease at the end of the ten-year
period.[3]

This up-and-down swing in sugarcane production has been related
much more closely to the fluctuation of prices in the international
sugar market than to pure production factors. When the international
sugar price was high,the cane growers used all efforts to grow the crop
and production was then high. When the price dropped significantly, the
growers immediately lost interest.

The point is, however, that when the international sugar price
was high. the growers regained their incentive. In addition, the newly-
bred, high-yield varieties of the crop and the improved cultivation
methods had boosted per-hectare production to a very high point. This
writer had,in February 1966,an invitation from the Taiwan Sugar Corporation
to conduct a consultation tour in its six important sugarcane growing
areas. The purpose of the tour was to study with the corporation's
extension personnel what should be the effective measures of organizing
the sugarcane growers into groups and infusing the groups with incentive
for greater production through better production methods. The writer
made contacts with a number of the best individual growers and some

well-organized, effectively-functioning groups. He was informed that
in the main sugarcane growing areas such as Tainan hsien, growers who
developed high, group morale and learned the best cultivation methods
in their highly efficient associations, increased per-hectare production
of sugarcane from 90,000 kg in 1962 to 180,000 kg in 1965.[4] In these
particular cases the increase was 100 per cent. But even in the
second-class sugarcane areas good growers were able to achieve the
same rate of increase.[5]

The per-hectare production of sweet potato had also been increasing
in the ten-year period, except the year 1963. In Taiwan sweet potato
can be cropped several times a year. The average total annual yield
per hectare for 1955 was 9,928 kg. In 1956 this was increased to
11,154 kg. For the years 1957, 1958, 1959, 1960, 1961, and 1962, the
figures were, in kilograms, 11,774; 12,934; 12,766; 12,654; 13,713; and
13,180. In 1963 it suddenly dropped to 9,469 kg. Production of the
intercropped (hu-tsu) sweet potato and the year's first crop were
especially low. That drop was probably caused by bad weather and the
typhoon. In the year 1964 the yield per hectare increased considerably,
from 9,469 kg to 13,609 kg. The year's first crop ran as high as 15,592
kg. Comparing the per-hectare production in 1955 with that of 1964,
the increase for the ten-year period was 3,681 kg or more than 37 per
cent. The aggregated increase was 47 per cent, and the average annual
increase was 4.7 per cent for the ten-year period.[6]

Despite the frequent and serious damages inflicted practically
every year by the typhoons on the banana groves, the per-hectare
production of banana increased in every year of the ten-year period.

In the first nine years the annual increase was not conspicuous; but
the production of 1964 was almost twice that of 1955. The figure for
1955 was 7,934 kg and that for 1964 was 14,813 kg, an increase of
6,879 kg and 87 per cent. The production per plant was generally uniform
in the first nine years of the ten-year period, except for a considerable
drop in 1956 and a slight rise in 1960. But in the last year, that is,
1964, the increase was very significant. It rose from 7.88 kg in 1955
to 12.79 kg in 1964. The difference was 4.91 kg or a 62.30 per cent
increase.[7] This big increase was, no doubt, the result of the signing of
banana marketing contracts between the Republic of China and Japan, by
which the Chinese banana has secured a most dependable market in Japan.
With this market secured, the banana growers gained incentive to grow the
fruit and to make great efforts to better both per-hectare and per-plant
production.

The per-hectare production of peanuts in the years 1960 and 1961
were 1,017 kg and 1,061 kg, representing a significant increase. The
increase was significant over the 693 kg of 1955. But in 1963 production
dropped from the previous year's 992 kg to 967 kg. The next year,
however, the per-hectare production rose to 1,148 kg. In comparison
with the production of 1955, the increase was 455 kg, or 65.65 per cent.
The first crop of peanuts of 1964 did especially well. Its per-hectare
production was 1,256 kg, about 28 per cent larger than the first-crop
production of the previous year (1963).[8] The aggregated increase was
30.80 per cent. The difference between the production of 1955 and that
of 1960 was 324 kg. The increase was 46.75 per cent. This was for a
four-year period. The average annual increase for these four years was

11.70 per cent. This is added to the annual increases of 1961 to 1964 inclusive and subtracted from the 6.5 per cent decrease of 1952. The average annual increase for the ten-year period was 3.1 per cent.

For tobacco per-hectare production increased from 1,863 kg in 1955 to 2,138 kg in 1962, an increase of 275 kg and 14.76 per cent. The per-hectare production in 1963 dropped somewhat, but it gained handsomely in the next year. The 1964 figure was 2,277 kg, 414 kg more than had been produced in 1955. This was an increase of more than 22 per cent.[9] The average annual increase was around 2 per cent for the ten-year period.

For soybeans the increase was much better than for tobacco. Comparing the 1,132 kg per-hectare production of 1964 with 700 kg of 1955, the difference was 432 kg, a 61.71 per cent increase. Taking the ten-year period as a whole, however, the increase had been gradual and small in amount from year to year. The increase between 1956 and 1957, for instance, was 101 kg or 14.33 per cent, and that between 1961 and 1962 was 69 kg or only 7.62 per cent. The average of the percentages was 11.[10]

Another crop in which increase of production can be discerned is that of citrus fruits. In 1955 there were 5,245.96 hectares of citrus orchards, 2,635,266 harvested, citrus fruit plants, and the total production of citrus fruits was 30,235,059 kg. In 1964 the number of harvested plants increased to 7,021,123, the number of hectares of orchards to 13,361.10, and the total production of citrus fruits to 102,341,439 kg. The differences between these two years were 4,385,857 plants, 8,115.14 hectares, and 72,106,380 kg. Percentage-wise, they were 166,43, 154.69, and 205.41. The increase in each factor was great, but the increase in production was greatest. Per-plant production was 11.48 kg in 1955 and 14.58 kg in 1964, an increase of 3.10 kg and 27 per cent. Per-hectare production was 5,763.45 kg in 1955 and 7,659.71 kg in 1964, an increase of 1,896.26 kg, or 33 per cent. The average annual increase of production was 3.3 per cent.[11]

The increase of production in citrus fruits had been considerably retarded by lack of success in controlling diseases and insects in orchards and young plant nurseries. The disease which does the greatest damage in the fruit-bearing orchards is the so-called huang-lung disease. It is a virus disease, very hard to eradicate. Entomologists, agricultural-extension workers and the growers have expended a great deal of effort, but so far there has been no significant success. The most critical and deplorable problem is that there are not yet strict and effective legal or social measures to enforce quarantine in the nurseries. Nurserymen still have plenty of freedom to neglect sterilization of the soil and seedlings and to sell stocks infected by virus, germs, and the larvae of insects. Quite a few people, including college professors, made investments in the development of citrus-orchard industries in recent years. At the beginning stages, the young plants grow splendidly and everything seems to be fine. But no sooner are the growers' happy feelings expressed than a large number of the plants are found sick, withering, and dying. Within a few years, a whole orchard may be depleted of trees and its investors gone bankrupt. As a whole, however, in the past decade, great strides have been made in agriculture in Taiwan, in terms of total production, as well as per-hectare or per-plant production. Some crops have made greater increases than others. Some yields have been jumping up and down a bit over the years, whereas others show gradual and steady increases.

Among Taiwan livestock the hog is of first importance. If there has recently been any improvement in the hog-raising business, it is in the mortality rate in the hog population, susceptibility to serious diseases, and weight at maturity. In the year 1955 the total number of hogs farrowed was 2,081,959. Of this number, 48,156, or 2.31 per cent, died before reaching slaughtering age. The mortality rate was 2.31 per hundred or 23.1 per thousand. In 1964 the total farrowing was 2,644,488; the number dead before maturity was 32,581 or 1.23 per cent. The mortality rate was 1.23 per hundred or 12.3 per thousand. It had dropped about one-half in the ten-year period.[12]

The above mortality rates were the average for all breeds of hogs. The rate varied from breed to breed. For the native hogs, for instance, the mortality rate in 1955 was 3.08 per hundred or 30.8 per thousand. In 1964 it was 3.7 per hundred or 37 per thousand. There was an increase instead of a decrease. For the Western hogs, that is, hogs bred of imported, Western stock, the mortality rate in 1955 was 6.29 per hundred or 62.9 per thousand. This was three times as high as that of the native hogs. In 1964, however, the rate dropped considerably from 6.29 to 2.30, or from 62.90 to 23.00 per thousand.[13] This is readily explainable. When the Western hogs were first imported to or raised in Taiwan, the animals were not adjusted to the natural environment and methods of care in the new "home." Many of them had to die before reaching maturity. After ten years the acclimation was about completed, and, as a result, the number of deaths dropped. The hog farmers' gain in experience was also a factor. When the Western hogs were new, the Chinese farmer did not have much knowledge of feeding them and keeping them from becoming sick. During ten years the farmers must have learned new ways, accumulated new experiences in raising Western hogs. As a result, more hogs lived to maturity; only a small number of them had to die young.

But in this period it was the hybrid hogs which did the best in every way. The hybrid hogs were bred by crossing the native and the Western stocks. Quantitatively, hybrid hogs accounted for 91.28 per cent of the total number in 1955 and more than 97 per cent in 1964. The mortality in hybrid hogs was low from the beginning. It was, for instance, 2.03 per hundred, or 20.3 per thousand, in 1955; 1.17 per hundred, or 11.7 per thousand, in 1964. This was a great drop.[14]

Serious diseases which caused great losses to hogs were Swine Cholera, Swine Plague, and Swine Erysipelas. In 1955 the incidence of Cholera was 41,098 in 2,081,959 head. The rate was almost two (1.974) in every hundred or 20 in every thousand. In 1964 the rate dropped considerably. The total was 1,333, only .05 per hundred, or one per two-thousand head. In 1955, of the 41,098 new cholera cases, 14,537 head, or 35.37 per cent, died; 1,979 head, or 4.82 per cent, had to be killed; but 24,570 head, or 59.78 per cent, recovered from the disease. A few, .03 per cent, were still sick at the end of the year. In 1964 the number of cases dropped greatly, but the number of deaths was high. It was 639 out of 1,333, 47.93 per cent. Another sixty, or 4.51 per cent, had to be killed. Only 634, 47.56 per cent, recovered from the disease.[15]

The number of cases and the number of deaths from Swine Plague were much fewer than those from the Swine Cholera in the two years 1955 and 1964. In 1955 the number of new Swine Plague cases was 11,237. This was only a little over one case per two hundred hogs. In 1964 the rate increased to .98 or about one plague case in every hundred hogs.[16] In 1955 the number of hogs that died of Swine Plague was 2,329 or 20.72 per cent of the hogs which had contracted this disease. The number of sick hogs which had to be killed was 197 or 1.75 per cent of all the sick cases. Those which had recovered from the disease numbered 8,684 or 77.28 per cent. In 1964 the number of deaths was 3,674, out of a total of 26,005 sick cases. The death rate was 14.12 which was much lower than that of 1955. The number of sick hogs which eventually recovered from the disease was 22,173, or 85.26 per cent, which was much higher than that of 1955.[17]

In 1955, 17,603 out of 2,081,959 head became ill of Swine Erysipelas. The sickness rate was .83. In other words, fewer than one hog in each one hundred became sick with this disease. The 1964 rate was only one-half of one per cent. The death rate was 12.56 per cent in 1955 and 12 per cent in 1964. In 1955, 195, or a little more than 1 per cent, of the sick hogs had to be killed, while in 1964 the number was 56 or only .4 per cent. In 1955, 15,180, or 86.23 per cent, of the sick hogs recovered from the disease while in 1964 the number was 12,232 or 87.63 per cent.[18]

When the purpose in raising hogs is no longer limited to the making of manure and compost, as farmers of the old days used to believe, but includes earning some cash profit, the job of hog raising cannot be simply keeping the animals alive and free from disease. It must also include efforts to find better ways to feed the hogs, to make them grow healthy and become matured or fattened in the shortest time possible. In this sense, any improvement or progress made in the hog-raising business would mean that in addition to having lower sickness and death rates, the animals grow and fatten faster than before, so that with a similar cost and comparable length of time, the farmer can sell his hog, either as livestock or as meat, with more kilograms of weight and thus more dollars accruing.

According to the Agricultural Yearbook quoted formerly, the average weight per head of hogs at slaughtering time was 78 kg in 1955. This increased to 88 kg in 1964, a 12.82 per cent gain. What factors brought about the increase? The answer to this question is not given in the Yearbook. Most probably it resulted from better feed, better feeding, better sanitation, and better selection of breeds. In the last ten years great efforts have been made by the hog breeding-and-feeding research and experiment institute of Taiwan Sugar Corporation. A program called "Synthesized Hog Feeding" is now under vigorous promotion by joint forces of JCRR and the Province's Agricultural-Extension Service. It emphasizes the effectiveness of making various synthesized feeds and better methods of feeding. The purpose is to shorten the time required to mature a hog. In order to achieve this goal, the selection of breeds and the maintenance of sanitation must also be taken into serious consideration.

180

The preceding paragraphs concerning recent agricultural advancements in Taiwan are indicated in these figures:

A. Changes in per-hectare production of seven crops:

Crop	Per-hectare production in 1955	Per-hectare production in 1964	Change: + increase - decrease	Aggre. Increase	Av An In
Rice	1st crop + 2nd crop = 4,356 kg 100%	1st crop + 2nd crop = 5,962 kg 136.87%	+36.87%	26.39%	2
Sugar-cane	78,121 kg 100% 90,000 kg 100%	70,999 kg 92.16% 168,000 kg 186.67%	-7.84%* +86.67%**	6.30 86.67	0 43
Sweet Potatoes	9,928 kg 100%	13,609 kg 137.08%	+37.08%	47.00	4.
Banana	1. Per hectare 7,934 kg 100% 2. Per plant 7.88 kg 100%	1. Per hectare 14,813 kg 186.70% 2. Per plant 12.79 kg 162.30%	1. Per hectare +86.70% 2. Per plant +62.30%	87.00 62.30	43 31
Peanut	1. Whole year 293 kg 100% 2. 1st crop (1963) 982 kg 100%	1. Whole year 1,148 kg 165.65% 2. 1st crop (1964) 1,256 kg 127.90%	1. Whole yr. +65.65% 2. 1st crop +27.90%	30.80	3.
Tobacco	1,863 kg 100%	2,277 kg 122.22%	+22.22%	22.22	2.
Soybean	700 kg 100%	1,132 kg 161.71%	+61.71%	11.00	5.

*Based on <u>Taiwan Agricultural Yearbook</u>, 1965 Ed. figures.
**Based on the writer's report on "Observation Tour in Taiwan Sugar Corporation Sugarcane Growing Areas," 1966.

Crop	Per-hectare production in 1955	Per-hectare production in 1964	Change: +increase -decrease	Aggre. Increase	Average Annual Increase
	1. Number of hectares of citrus orchards 5,245.96 ha 100%	1. Number of hectares of citrus orchards 13,361.10 ha 254.69%	+154.69%		
Citrus fruits	2. Number of bearing plants 2,635,266 100%	2. Number of bearing plants 7,021,123 266.43%	+166.43%		
	3. Per-ha production 30,235,059 5,245.96 ha = 5,763.45 kg. 100%	3. Per-ha production 102,341,439 kg 13,361.10 ha = 7,659.71 kg 132.90%	+32.90%	33.00	3.30
	4. Per-plant production	4. Per-plant production 14.58 kg 127.00%	+27.00%	27.00	

B. Changes in hog mortality and in amounts of damage caused by hog diseases

(1) Mortality

a. For all breeds of hogs

Description	1955	1964	Changes
Number of hogs farrowed	2,081,959 head	2,644,488 head	+ 562,529 head
Number of hogs died	48,156 "	32,581 "	- 15,575 "
Mortality rate:			
per hundred	2.31	1.23	- 1.08
per thousand	23.10	12.30	- 10.80

b. For native hogs only

Number of hogs farrowed	158,383	71,814	- 8,569
Number of hogs died	4,892	2,654	- 2,238
Mortality rate:			
per hundred	3.08	3.70	+ 0.62
per thousand	30.80	37.00	+ 6.20

c. For Western hogs

Number of hogs farrowed	12,751	5,049 head	- 7,702 head
Number of hogs died	802	116 "	- 686 "
Mortality rate:			
per hundred	6.29	2.30	- 3.99
per thousand	62.90	23.00	- 39.90

d. For hybrid hogs

Number of hogs farrowed	1,910,516	2,567,332 head	+ 656,816 head
Number of hogs died	38,916	29,809 "	- 9,107 "
Mortality rate:			
per hundred	2.03	1.17	- 0.86
per thousand	20.30	11.70	- 8.60

(2) Disease damage

Changes in amounts of damage caused by hog diseases

a. Swine Cholera	1955	1964	Change
No. of new cases	41,098	1,333	− 39,765
Rate of new cases	1.97%	0.05%	− 1.92%
No. of deaths	14,537	639	− 13,898
Rate of deaths	35.37%	47.94%	+ 12.57
No. of hogs killed	1,979 head	60 head	− 1,919 head
Rate of hogs killed	4.82%	4.51%	− 0.31%
No. of cases recovered	24,570	634	− 23,936
Rate of cases recovered	59.78%	47.56%	− 12.22%

b. Swine Plague	1955	1964	Change
No. of new cases	11,237	26,005	+ 14,768
Rate of new cases	0.05%	0.98%	+ 0.93
No. of deaths	2,329 head	3,674 head	+ 1,345 head
Rate of deaths	20.72%	14.12%	− 6.60%
No. of hogs killed	197 head	235	+ 38
Rate of hogs killed	1.75%	0.90%	− 0.85%
No. of cases recovered	8,684	22,173	+ 13,489
Rate of cases recovered	77.28%	85.26%	+ 7.98%

c. Swine Erysipelas	1955	1964	Change
No. of new cases	17,603	13,958	− 3,645
Rate of new cases	0.83%	0.52%	− 0.31%
No. of deaths	2,212 head	1,670 head	− 542 head
Rate of deaths	12.56%	12.00%	− 0.56%
No. of hogs killed	195	56	− 139
Rate of hogs killed	1.10%	0.40%	− 0.70%
No. of cases recovered	15,180	12,232	− 2,948
Rate of cases recovered	86.23%	87.63%	+ 1.40%

2. <u>Progress in agricultural technology.</u>[19] The changes or improvements
in agricultural and livestock production described in the previous section
have not come about by themselves or by chance. Most have been the results
learning and adopting new and better agricultural technology. In other word
it is chiefly because the farmers have used new and better methods, techniqu
and tools in the farming business that the production of crops and livestock
has increased and that agriculture as a whole has improved. It is, therefore
advisable to make a brief examination into the recent changes in agricultura
technology in Taiwan.

Technology here has a broad sense. It includes not only techniques,
methods, and tools, but also ways and manners of doing things or making a
living. Changes for the better in agriculture, as in other sectors of
human life, can be caused by using changed (meaning new and better)
techniques, methods, and tools. They can also be caused by using changed
ways and manners. Many changes result from the use of both changed
techniques, methods, tools and changed ways and manners.

The changed techniques, methods, tools, ways, and manners accountable
for the agricultural improvements in Taiwan must be numerous, but they can
be grouped into the following categories: (1) methods and manners of crop
cultivation, which can be further broken down into intercropping, selecting
and planting of new crops, adopting new cropping systems, new methods and
techniques in crop culture, new knowledge and new practices in selecting
seeds and young plants, the organizing of collectives for cultivation of
paddy rice, and using new, power-driven farm machinery; (2) new methods and
techniques of prevention and control of plant and animal diseases and pests,
new technology and systems of farm irrigation, changed methods in land

improvement and utilization, changed methods in the making and using of

fertilizers, changed ways and manners of harvesting and handling field

and garden crops, new methods of caring and feeding for domestic animals

and poultry, and changed techniques and procedures of marketing farm

products. Because of limited space it is impossible to go into the details

of each item mentioned above. Instead, a brief description of only one or

two specific new methods, or techniques, of each category will be given.

In the category of crop-cultivation methods and techniques, the

promotion and improvements of intercropping systems are to be mentioned

first. Intercropping means that a second crop is planted between the rows

of the first crop, in the same field and before the first crop is harvested.

The purpose of the practice is simply to grow more crops in the same field

within a certain span of time. It makes more economical use of the land

and brings higher receipts from the same farm in the same period of time.

It is true that farmers in Taiwan have for a long time been practicing

this system. But in the old days intercropping was casual and haphazard.

Casual in that some farmers did it occasionally and half-heartedly, not giving

serious thought to it and,for this reason,expecting no regular or significant

harvest from it. Haphazard in that the farming business was not carefully

planned, if there was any planning at all. No thoughtful effort was made

to avoid difficulties or to make sure that the crop would grow and make a

harvest.

Today the intercropping method is quite differently applied. Farmers

now take it as an important way of increasing the family's farm receipts.

They consider the second crop thus planted just as important as the first

one and,therefore,expect a regular harvest of it. Today's improved

intercropping system is characterized by careful selection of the right
kinds of crops for intercropping, by calculation of the right or suitable
time for planting the second crop so that there will be no interference
between the two crops, and by consideration for the treatment of the land
so that its productivity would not be depleted. In other words, today's
intercropping is practiced with serious purpose and careful planning. For
this reason, the system has become an important means of increasing annual
production while farming the same amount of land. Because this system now
plays an important role in the agricultural development of Taiwan, it has
become one of the objectives toward which programs in research, education,
and extension services are jointly working.

New agricultural technology is also in evidence in the selecting
and planting of profitable new crops. Farmers in Taiwan have learned in
recent years of new demands for farm products in both domestic consumption
and overseas markets. In the interest of greater profits, they quickly accept
advices from the agricultural research and extension services and plant new
crops. Most of the new crops are produced primarily for marketing, domestic
and foreign, and they yield profits greater than the traditional crops can.
The new crops all require new techniques, methods, and tools for planting,
cultivating, harvesting, and processing. The farmers have to learn new
things if they are going to have any success. Thus, accepting and planting
new crops really means adopting or developing new and improved agricultural
technology. Furthermore, the planting and handling of new crops must have
effected some change in the farm people's ways of doing things as well as
their manners of making a living.

In the past fifteen years, a considerable amount of work has been done

find more efficient, fruitful, and practical ways of laying out a new
crop-rotation system and organizing crop production, livestock raising,
home-industry undertaking, and marketing of various products into one
unified, farm-economy system. It is believed that when and if such a system
is possible, a farm family's land, labor, capital, talent, and time should
be most efficiently used and thus produce the greatest economic results
and nonmaterial satisfaction. Before any large-scale industrialization
shall have developed, a large portion of Taiwan's population will continue
to depend on agriculture for a living. If they wish to have a decent
standard of living, they will have to produce more on each farm. The size
of the farm, the amount of land, will remain generally the same. So, the
only way to increase production will be by planting more productive and
more saleable crops, by practicing improved intercropping systems, and by
developing a comprehensive farm economy which can make the best use of all
family labor, farm lands, and best develop the potentials of both land and
people.

Such a comprehensive, farm-economy system would include several
elements. They are the multi-planting system (this is also understood as
the intercropping system), the crop-rotation system, the livestock-raising
system, and the farm-product processing system. The meaning and purpose of
multi-planting or intercropping have been stated in a previous section. In
building a new, crop-rotation system, the agronomists are emphasizing crops
which can most profitably use large amounts and types of labor and need
the shortest length of time to grow. Inasmuch as large amounts of labor
are already there, it would be better economy to make good use of them for
increasing production. This is the first principle.

The second principle is that when labor is abundant, required growing time is short, and market demand is high, the more crops that are grown in a given length of time, the greater the farm receipts will be. To the farmers in general this is new knowledge and improved practice. Their application brings a farm family greater income.

But the practicality of these systems depends very much on three conditions, one of which is improvement in agricultural technology. It means that the farmers have to have the skills, or the know-how, to cultivate the more profitable new crops. Mushrooms, asparagus, bananas, hybrid corn, etc., are all profit-making crops nowadays in Taiwan. And most of the farmers do have the up-to-date techniques and knowledge for raising them and preparing the produce for marketing. As a result, big profits are being made in the cultivation of any of these crops.

The second condition concerns land improvement. This means that in many cases when a new crop is to be planted, the physical condition of the farm land has to be improved. Irrigation facilities, for instance, might be lacking where needed or in poor repair. In Taiwan today land improvements are needed in most of the farm areas.

The third condition is the availability of a market for certain farm products. Today if any new crop is added to cultivation, it is added to meet a demand in the market. In other words, it is planted for sale, not for home consumption. There must be frequent changes in demand or there must be an available market for a given farm product before a farmer will spend time and effort to learn the necessary techniques and to actually raise the crop. In the last fifteen years products produced by Taiwan farmers won markets in many foreign countries.

There are improvements in techniques and methods of preparing the
soil, of applying fertilizers, and of cultivating. Formerly the farmers
did these tasks according to traditions or by following their grandfathers'
practices. Today they are using different methods. Improvements in methods
result from research projects conducted by the Taiwan Provincial Agricultural
Research Institute, by the three colleges of agriculture, by the district,
agricultural-improvement stations, and by the agricultural-vocational schools.
The farmers of today not only use the new methods of doing these tasks, they
also have learned the rationale and merits of the improved methods. For
instance, they know that the soil should be so prepared that its texture,
its ph quality, and its pliability are suitable to the growing of the young
plant. They not only use new methods of applying fertilizers, but also
know the nature, the functions, and the characteristics of the various
kinds of fertilizers, and why one is better than another. The farmers are
now using a new method to transplant rice seedlings which enables them to
grow many more plants than before in the same piece of land. The use of
this new transplanting method, together with the new way of preparing the
soil and the new way of applying fertilizer, has brought about a significant
increase in the per-hectare production of rice.

Taiwan's agriculture is gradually becoming mechanized. In comparatively rich farm areas small tractors have been increasingly in use for
plowing, planting and transportation. Other kinds of machinery are being
used in cultivating, threshing and processing farm products. Mechanized
implements are especially productive and rewarding in controlling plant
diseases and insects. The mechanized sprayers, for example, save many
crops from being ruined by infestations. Tractors and improved plows

enable the farmer to plow to much greater depth, and deep plowing helps
to increase crop production.

Until recently, Taiwan's agriculture had been considerably handicapped
by over-fragmentation of farm land and the minuteness of privately-operated,
individual farms. On such farms the farming business could hardly be
operated with any efficiency at all. If and when such a farmer had the
good luck to find a non-farm job and was able to make a living on that
job, he would either have just left the farm or would have cultivated it
half-heartedly. Either situation would naturally reduce his agricultural
production. This has been especially true in recent years when many farm
people found work in industries and in the cities. In the past five years,
however, there has been a "Farming Together" or "Joint Cultivation,"
program under promotion. "Farming Together" means that several farmers
whose lands are adjacent organize themselves into a farming group. They
pool their labor, materials, and implements and conduct their farming
tasks together. At the harvesting of a crop they share the costs and the
receipts according to the amount of land each farmer owns and the other
contributions each one has made.

The advantages of this system are that, first, farmers can use
better and more varied kinds of farm implements to do better and more
efficient jobs. They can even buy mechanized equipment. Second, the
work of controlling diseases and insects can be done coordinately and at
the same time, which is the only effective way to have the insects all
destroyed. Third, farming together is a favorable condition under which
new crops, new ideas, and new methods are likely to be adopted and used.
When a new idea is adopted, it is adopted for the whole area, by the

whole group of farmers, not just by one or two at a time. Fourth, many small pieces of farm land which had hitherto been left to waste can be well taken care of, and it is not necessary that the owners give up on non-farm jobs and return to farming. They can let others in the group do the cultivating and pay the costs accordingly. The costs are always low in such a system.

Taiwan is situated in tropical and subtropical zones. The climate is always warm. For this reason, plant insects and diseases are abundant at all times of the year. If unchecked or uncontrolled insects and diseases can considerably reduce the amount and the quality of farm products. To meet this threat, entomologists, microbiologists, and agricultural-chemists have been working hard to find more effective ways, methods, materials, and equipment. One such agency is the Taiwan Provincial Plant Protection Technology Examination Commission. Each year it holds meetings to examine the merits and faults of each of the new methods, new equipment, and new materials submitted by the various research organizations and individuals for the preventing or controlling of plant insects and diseases. Numerous aids have been discovered and made available to the farmers. For instance, most farmers now have learned the methods of treating seeds or seedlings with insecticides or fungicides before the field planting. As a result, losses from diseases and insects have been greatly reduced.

Taiwan's agriculture consists of paddy rice, sugarcane, sweet potato, and a number of other secondary crops, fruits, and vegetables. Paddy rice accounts for more than 35 per cent of the total value of agricultural products. Paddy rice needs irrigation most of the time, but many other crops need water, too. For this reason, irrigation water is always in great demand. In the old days irrigation methods were not ideal, and large amounts of water were wasted, or not fully utilized, in one area while in other areas there was a great shortage. About fifteen years ago the rotation-irrigation system was invented and refined, and the irrigation problem was solved to a great extent. This was abetted by the building of several big dams, of which the Shihmen Dam is the most renowned, and the digging of deep, artesian wells. Thus, the supply of irrigation water has been immensely expanded. Irrigation methods have been further improved by new knowledge in regard to the most suitable time of irrigation for specific crops and the right amount of water for each crop.

In summary, the agricultural-research institutions and the agricultura experiment stations in Taiwan have, in the last 15 of 20 years, done a great deal in finding or devising better techniques, methods, equipment, and ways in farm production to bring about improvements in agricultural technology. Also, the agricultural-extension service, sponsored by such agencies as the Farmers Association, the Taiwan Sugar Corporation, and the Provincial Food Bureau, has been working diligently to teach the farmers the uses of the new technology. After having witnessed the efficiency and effectiveness of the new ways, most farmers are happy to make the change and the resultant spread of technological changes has played an important role in achieving significant improvement in the agriculture of Taiwan.

3. _Increase in amounts of farm input._ Even new crops and improved technology may not always increase farm production. To make a crop successful the farmer has to put into the farm fertilizers (the crop's food), irrigation (the crop's water), cultivation, weeding, protection

from insects and diseases, and a number of other tasks. All the materials
and efforts thus spent by the farmer for the production of his crop are
called farm input. Within limits, the greater farm input the farmer makes,
the greater would be his crop production.

In the past fifteen years, agricultural economists of Taiwan have done
a great deal of research to find out the correlations between amounts of
input and amounts of production, and conditions of the market of agricultural
products. Farmers have learned the concepts of capital investment, entrepre-
neuring, and the cause-effect relations between input and output. They now
understand why profit is an outcome of business investment. One who wishes
to gain great profit must first make a large capital investment. Input is
investment; output is production. Profit is the difference between input
and output. A majority of farmers have even become acquainted with the
idea that in order to make larger profits, their input might be enlarged
by borrowing capital funds. And not a few of them are actually doing that.
As the farming business has become increasingly commercialized and the
farmers more enterprise-minded, greater emphasis is being placed on the
amount of input as the most important factor in determining the size of
production. Increased input usually means increased production. Increase
in production means, in most cases, improvement in an agricultural economy.

4. The beginning of farm planning. When agriculture was in its
primitive stage there was practically no farm planning. As soon as there
was anything which could be called advancement, planning began to appear.
Farm planning means the farmer, either by himself or together with his
family, first does some thinking and laying out, then plants according to
what has been considered and laid out. It is a general belief that planning

is necessarily concomitant with advancement in agriculture. But in the old days, the planning, if it could be called planning at all, was largely subjective figuring or wishful thinking. It had very little, if any, objective basis. In other words, pertinent conditions and factors, both natural and human, were overlooked and not taken into consideration. This was so chiefly because farming was considered the farmer's, or the farm family's, private affair. The importance of the natural factors, such as weather and natural calamities, was obvious and, of course, well known, and there was a popular belief that agriculture as a livelihood heavily depended on heaven (nature). But being aware of the existence and importance of natural factors is one thing, taking them into consideration in planning crop production and livestock-keeping is quite another. The old-time farmers had the awareness but did very little about making use of it.

In the last ten years this situation has changed. Farmers have been taught to do intelligent planning. This means considering possibilities on objective bases, taking all objective factors, natural as well as economic, into careful consideration. Plans are now laid in logical order so that they can be carried out in sequent steps. The Rural Economy Division of JCRR, in cooperation with the Department of Agriculture and Forestry, sponsored a program with the chief purpose and function of assisting farmers in planning. Such planning was done at the beginning of a year and was evaluated on its results at the end of each stage. Emphasis was laid on combining the business of farming with any other economically productive activities being carried on at home so that the two should be mutually complimentary and supplementary. The Agricultural Economics Departments of National Taiwan University and the Provincial Chung Hsing

University, in cooperation with the farmers' associations or with the agricultural-extension service, conducted a farm-and-home-planning program. Its main feature was that it sent well-trained, township-level agricultural-extension workers to selected farm homes to persuade and help the farmer and his adult family members do effective planning of their farm and home economic enterprises. The procedure in such planning was, first, that all adult family members sit down together in a meeting. Their first consideration is then the cooperative nature of the family's farm and home business. All the members must work cooperatively. Each member has his role, his obligations to fulfill, his right to express opinions and ideas, to give suggestions, to join in making decisions, and also the right to share with the others the resultant weal and woe. Then comes an exhaustive and informative inventory of the family's current capital funds, materials, sources of power, natural and human resources, and its deficits, if any. The third step is the establishment of goals for the farm and home enterprises. The last step is to draw up a comprehensive plan for the year, basing it on the inventory and the possibilities of getting outside help if it is needed. The chief function of the plan will be to make the most efficient and economical use of whatever capital funds, materials, and other resources are available for the achievement of family goals.

In the year's conduct of the farming and home-economic enterprises, consultation with the plan should be frequently made. Examination and evaluation of progress should be taken at appropriate times in order to point up problems and difficulties or any falling back, to see if the goals are being achieved, and to what degree. Any necessary revision of the plan must be made at the right time. A few years after the beginning of this program, practically every farm community had some farm families who had become acquainted with the main points of farm planning, and more than a few of them practiced it.

II. Agricultural Progress Made by the Former-tenant Farm Households

The following sections present the farm people's achievements in, and the non-farm people's observations on, agricultural progress and the relationship between agricultural progress and land reform. Agricultural improvements made by the former-tenant, or new-owner, farm households are to be described under the following headings.

1. A brief examination on the size of the farm. There is a close relationship between the size of a farm and the quality of its farming business. In general, the larger the farm, the higher the quality of farming, that is, the greater the possibility of developing farming to a better quality. Therefore, it is necessary to know first the average size of the farms owned by former tenants.

There were changes during land reform in the amounts of farm land operated by such farm households. Before land reform each of the 1250 survey samples operated an average one-and-one-half hectares (1.523 ha) of farmland. Of this amount 1.24 hectares were rented land, 0.229 hectare owned, and 0.059 hectare of unspecified other nature. Through the public, farmland-sales program and the land-to-the-tiller program, these households each acquired an average 1.038 hectares of farmland. Immediately after land reform these farm households operated an average 1.455 hectares. The amount had changed again by the time this study was undertaken, and the figure stood at 1.296 hectares of farmland, plus a bit of forest and fishpond land. In comparison with the pre-land-reform amount, there had been a decrease of 0.227 hectare. In comparison with the amount immediately following land reform, the decrease was 0.159 hectare. At any rate, small farms have been getting smaller and smaller every year since land reform, shrinking from 1.523 hectares, then to 1.296 hectares.[20]

The shrinkage in size had, of course, no direct or obvious relationship to the land reform. It was a natural result of urbanization, industrialization, and the growth of pupulation. In other words, one cannot blame the land reform for the decrease. But when this point was brought up in interview, the small farmers could not but associate the shrinkage with the land reform. For instance, they were apt to say that after land reform they were not only unable to get additional land they needed, but, on the contrary, they had less land than before. Such a statement or comparison had the effect of dimishing favorable feelings toward the accomplishments of land reform. This dissatisfaction of the small farmers brought up again and again the fact that the land reform in Taiwan had tackled only the problem of undesirable distribution of rights to land ownership. It had so far done nothing about the minuteness of the size of the farm. Notwithstanding all the good things achieved, the lack of effort toward solution of this problem had a considerable, limiting effect on the impact of the land reform. Insufficiency of land, as compared to the amount required for profitable farm operations, has always been one of the most serious obstacles to improving the farmland situation.[21]

2. Land improvement. Despite the scantiness of its farmland, a household puts great value on it and takes the best possible care of it, as do good farmers all over the world. One way of taking good care of a

farm is to make continuous improvement on it. Of the 1250 sample households, 80 per cent reported that they had made special efforts to improve
the land after ownership of it was transferred to them. Less than 18 per
cent admitted that they made no change in this respect. But in making no
change they could have considered that they had made all the necessary
improvements prior to land reform.

What kinds of land improvement had been made in the last ten years
since land reform? The question received a total of 2545 answers. Of
these, 18 per cent said improvements were made in the shape and topography
of the farm; 15 per cent made general soil improvement; 13 per cent built
irrigation and drainage facilities and systems; 16 per cent practiced deep
plowing; 7 per cent made changes to better cropping systems so that the
productivity of the land could be increased, or saved from being depleted;
2 per cent consolidated lands to lessen the disadvantages of fragmentation;
3 per cent made new layouts of their farms; 24 per cent made improvements in
their way of applying fertilizers; 2 per cent made improvements which could
not be specified. That these households had truly made special efforts to
improve the land which they had purchased through the land-to-the-tiller
program, as well as the small pieces originally owned by them, was verified
by their neighbors, the original owner-farmers. Of the 250 samples of the
original-owner farm households, 90 per cent gave affirmative answers to
such a question as, "Have you really noticed (or do you really agree) that
a great majority of the tenants who became owner-farmers through the land
reform are far more interested than before in improving the productivity
of the farmland they now own?" What is, however, of greater significance
and interest than that 84 per cent of these owner-farmers also made

improvements of various sorts on their farmland, is that their doing so was in a great many cases because of the influence of the former tenant-farmers.

3. Improvement in farm operation. Within this category are selection of better ways of using the farmland, and freedom in selecting the kind and number of crops to be planted or enterprises to be undertaken.

Of the 1250 former-tenant households, 86 per cent emphasized that since land reform they had been enjoying the freedom of selecting uses of farmland and that this freedom had had considerable bearing on the success and efficiency of the farming business. The possibility of success is usually much greater on the farm where the operator has freedom to select his way of farming than on the farm where all decisions are made by the landlord. A majority of these households, 64 per cent, now enjoyed that freedom. But the number of those who had not experienced such a change was also large: 34 per cent. Perhaps the size of their farms had not increased and, consequently, they were still not able to have much room for change and experimentation. When the farm was owned and controlled by the landlord, the tenant had very little choice and often he worked with little enthusiasm and with meager success. But under the new conditions, where he was free to try whatever enterprises which he felt would be most profitable, it was natural that the farmer and his family should do their best to win success. For instance, 64 per cent of the former-tenant farm households said that multicropping on their farms increased greatly since land reform. Only 35 per cent reported no such increase. Some of these might already have had a high use of this technique, leaving no room for any further increase.

Ownership of the farmland also made the farmer willing to use more fertilizers, to increase the frequency of irrigation, and to do more toward effective insect and plant-disease control. Such was reported by 94 per cent of the 1250 sample households. However, ownership of the farmland had not been the only factor in these changes. The need to produce more food to feed increased numbers in the family circle was another force impelling the farmer to increase input. A majority of the samples said that if they were still tenant-farmers, they would still have had to put in more effort so that the land could produce more, but they might not have done it as willingly.

The increase of farm input after land reform is shown in the following illustration: Before land reform the amounts of fertilizers applied on paddy rice, sweet potato, sugarcane, and vegetables per hectare were 446.23 kg, 302.77 kg, 614.69 kg, and 428.95 kg. Ten years after land reform the amounts were 638.56 kg, 745.34 kg, and 592.64 kg. The increases were 192.33 kg, 193.83 kg, 130.65 kg, and 100.69 kg in absolute amounts and 43.10, 64.02, 21.25, and 23.47 in percentage. The amounts of money spent on agricultural chemicals for these crops per hectare were, respectively, 198.10, 57.50, 148.75, and 104.35 N.T. dollars before land reform. Ten years after its completion the amounts changed to 367.43, 184.41, 185.44, and 337.60 N.T. dollars. The increases in absolute amounts were 169.33, 126.91, 36.69, and 233.25 N.T. dollars, and 85.48, 220.71, 24.67, and 223.54 per cents.

4. _Improvement in cultivation methods._ Most former tenant-farmers became interested in learning new and better cultivation methods after completion of the land reform. For instance, about 31 per cent of the 1250 samples interviewed said that after the land reform they began to

have this interest; 25 per cent became very much interested; 27 per cent became interested, though not much, in learning new and better cultivation methods. Together, these three categories accounted for more than 80 per cent (82.40%).

The new cultivation methods, which had actually been adopted by new owner-farmers, included improved methods in the use of fertilizers, new and better methods of controlling insects and diseases, techniques of deep plowing, straight-row-and-close-planting method, improved intercropping, seed treatment, new broadcasting methods, improved irrigation or watering, thinning and pruning methods, etc. There were many others not mentioned here.[22] In addition, these new owner-farmers also adopted new crops and new varieties, or strains, of old crops. They were able to break themselves away from many of the traditional practices which kept farmers planting the same varieties of crops generation after generation. The possibility of this breaching of tradition would be chiefly attributed to the new owner-farmer's willingness to learn from agricultural-extension programs about new methods, ideas, and equipment; and their willingness is attributed to the high morale aroused by the change from tenant-cultivators to owner-farmers through the land-to-the-tiller program.

For various reasons, however, the number of new owner-farmers who participated directly in the different agricultural-extension programs has not been large. For instance, at the time of this study only about 19 per cent of the 1250 former-tenant households had members taking part in the village-level, farm-study classes; the remaining 80 per cent had not participated. Their participation in other extension programs was also scant. Only 15 per cent were readly involved; 20 per cent reported occasional participation, while 35 per cent reported none at all; 30 per cent gave no answer to this question.

If the farmers had not attended those agricultural teaching activities, how and where did they learn about better cultivation methods and new crops? According to findings in other rural studies,[23] most Taiwan farmers received new farming information from their neighbors and friends, from personal contacts between farmers and agricultural-extension agents, and by reading farm magazines and bulletins. Also, according to other sources, the number of farmers participating in farm-study classes had been much larger than that told by the farmers themselves.[24]

5. Changes in the utilization of farm implements, or movement toward mechanization. There was a notable increase in the number of important farm implements possessed by the former tenant-farmers after land reform. Before land reform 212 of the 1250 households had threshing baskets, 412 had threshing machines, 2 had modern water pumps, 14 had sweet potato slicing machines, 46 had mechanized sprayers, and none had a tractor. At the time of the study the number of households which had threshing machines increased to 509, while the number of households which had threshing baskets decreased to 167. There were modern water pumps in 87 households, sweet potato slicing machines in 96, mechanized sprayers in 353, and tractors in 22.

The use of modern farm implements has some bearing on the farm household's socio-economic status. A farmer who is plowing his field with a tractor and modern plow feels superior to his neighbor who is working with an old-fashioned plow drawn by a waterbuffalo, and the latter admits his inferiority. A young farmer likes the modern and mechanized sprayer more than he does the primitive one, not just for its higher work efficiency but also because the modern, smart implement makes the young farmer see himself as modern and smart in comparison with one who does not have this machine.   In harvesting rice, the use of the threshing machine, instead of the traditional threshing basket, is a good indication of the farm household's higher socio-economic status. At home the women-folks are proud of the sweet potato slicing machine and any other modern or improved gadgets in performing domestic tasks. Thus, it is safe to say that many new owner-farmers had acquired modern farm implements partly for their work efficiency and partly because of the implication of improved social and economic status.[25]

6. Increase in per-hectare production. Farmers reported that per-hectare production of many crops had increased since completion of the land reform. With paddy rice, for instance, the per-hectare production in 1963 averaged 3,177 kg. The average total amount of rice harvested that year was 7,106 kg per household. There is a great discrepancy between the two figures. Most of the households interviewed must, at this point, have contradicted themselves. When asked about the per-hectare production, they intentionally reported less, but when asked about the year's total harvest, the real figures were given. At the beginning of Section II of this chapter, it is recorded that at the time of the interview the average amount of farmland operated by those small farm households was 1.296 hectare, provided that the household had planted paddy rice on its whole farm both the first crop and the second crop in that year. The result would have been that the 1.296 hectare had produced, in total, 7,106.4 kg of rice. The per-hectare production ought to be between 5000 kg and

6000 kg. This estimation conforms remarkably to the per-hectare production figure quoted from the 1965 edition of the Taiwan Agricultural Yearbook at the beginning of this chapter.

The per-hectare production of sweet potato in 1963 averaged 13,329.72 kg. The actual harvest of sweet potatoes in this year averaged 9,896 kg. In answering the question regarding per-hectare production, the farmers gave the figures estimated, according to production in the previous one or two years. When asked about the total harvest of this crop in that year, the actual amounts were reported, hence the 9,896 kg figure. In 1963 the production of sweet potato was especially low.[26] The estimated, per-hectare production was 2,418 kg, or 22 per cent larger than the production before land reform.

The per-hectare production of sugarcane increased most greatly. Before land reform it was 33,855.88 kg. It was 61,893.34 kg in 1963, an 83 per cent increase. The per-hectare production of corn increased 25 per cent, from 1,500 kg before land reform, to 1,875 kg. For peanuts the increase was not big, only less than 5 per cent, from 2,364.6 kg to 2,475 kg. The per-hectare production of soybean increased conspicuously, from 549.66 kg pre-land reform, to 1,221.58 kg after it, an increase of 122 per cent.

In summary, the data presented in this section are condensed as follows:

A. Average Size of Farm Operated by Former-Tenant Households Before and After Land Reform

Before L.R.	Immediately After L.R.	Ten Years Later
1.523 ha	1.455 ha	1.296 ha

B. Land Improvement

(1) Number of Households who Made Improvements

With special efforts	1000 households	80.00%
Effort same as before	223	17.84
No answer	27	2.16
Total	1250	100.00

(2) Kinds of Improvement

Land shape & topography	640 answers	18.05%
General soil improvement	541	15.26
Irrigation & drainage imp.	475	13.40
Deep plowing	569	16.05
Better cropping system	241	6.80
Reconsolidation	72	2.03
New layout	112	3.16
Techniques of fertilizing	837	23.61
Unspecified improvements	58	1.64
Total	3545	100.00

(3) As Observed by Original Owner-Farmers

Confirms claims of new owners	225 households	90.00%
No comment	25	10.00
Total	250	100.00

(4) Land Improvement Done by Original-Owner Farm Households

Improvements made	209 households	83.60%
No improvements made	18	7.20
No answer	23	9.20
Total	250	100.00

C. Improvement in Farm Operation

(1) Freedom of Selecting the Best Use of Land

Appreciate the freedom	1079 households	86.32%
No such appreciation	163	13.04
No answer	8	0.64
Total	1250	100.00

(2) Latitude in Choice of Crops

Rate it as a prime advantage	799 households	63.92%
Do not feel so	423	33.84
No answer	28	2.24
Total	1250	100.00

(3) Increase in Multicropping Index

Yes	804	64.32
No	432	34.56
No answer	14	1.12
Total	1250	100.00

(4) Increase in Amount of Farm Input

Increase reported	1174	93.92
No increase reported	46	3.68
No answer	30	2.40
Total	1250	100.00

(5) Increase in Amounts of Fertilizers and Agricultural Chemicals Per Ha of Crops

	Before L.R.	Ten Years After L.R.	Increase Amount	%
Paddy rice				
Feritilizers (kg)	446.23	638.56	192.33	43.10
Chemicals (in $)	198.10	367.43	169.33	85.48
Sweet Potato				
Fertilizers (kg)	302.77	496.60	193.83	64.02
Chemicals (in $)	57.50	184.41	126.91	220.71
Sugarcane				
Fertilizers (kg)	614.69	745.34	130.65	21.25
Chemicals (in $)	148.75	185.44	36.69	24.67
Vegetables				
Fertilizers (kg)	428.95	529.64	100.69	23.47
Chemicals (in $)	104.35	337.60	233.25	223.53

D. Improvement in Cultivation Methods

(1) Interest in Learning Better Cultivation Methods

Began to have interest	380	30.40%
Very much interested	311	24.88
Some interest	339	27.12
Still no interest	190	15.20
No answer	30	2.40
Total	1250	100.00

(2) As Observed by the Original-Owner Farm Households

Yes	223 households	89.20%
No	19	7.60
No answer	8	3.20
Total	250	100.00

(3) Participation in Farm-Study Classes

Participation	232	18.56%
No participation	998	79.84
No answer	20	1.60
Total	1250	100.00

(4) Extent of Participation in Various Farm-Study Activities

Active	189	15.12%
Occasional	250	20.00
None	442	35.36
No answer	369	29.52
Total	1250	100.00

E. Changes in Number of Households Possessing and Using Major Farm Implements

	Before L.R.	Ten Years After L.R.
Threshing Machines	412	509
Modern water pumps	2	87
Sweet potato slicing machines	14	96
Mechanical sprayers	46	353
Tractors	0	22

F. Increase in **Per-hectare** Production

	Before L.R.	1963	Increase in
Paddy rice	2,602.19 kg (?)	5,000-6,000 kg	115.21%
Sweet potato	10,911.74	13,329.72*	22.16
		9,896.00+	-9.30
Sugarcane	33,855.88	61,893.34	82.82
Corn	1,500.00	1,500.00	25.00
Peanuts	2,364.60	2,364.60	4.66
Soybeans	549.66 (?)	549.66 (?)	122.00 (?)

7. Relationship between land reform and farm improvement. According to the foregoing, there should be no doubt that the former-tenant households have made significant progress in their farming business. But is there any relationship between their agricultural progress and the land reform? If there is any, how much? The answer to this question is to be found first in the facts which follow.

Eighty per cent of the 1250, former-tenant households admitted at the interview that they had been making more improvements on the farm because the land had become their own. Some of these households, 393, had owned small pieces of land prior to land reform. After land reform, 307, or 78 per cent, of them began to make serious improvements on these small pieces. Their interest in doing so also came from their status as owner-farmers. This was admitted by 72 per cent of the 307 households. Those who did not recognize a relationship between the improvement and land refor gave reasons such as: desire to increase the farm's productivity; a respons

---

*The normal or possible per-hectare production.
+The actual per-hectare harvest of this year.
(?)Since the pre-land reform amount is uncertain, this percentage is also uncertain.

to the increase of population, coupled with its concomitant, the scarcity

of land; a desire to improve the family's living conditions; because most

other farmers were making improvements; the high land tax.

Five-hundred-and-eighty-five households reported increasing the number

of their farm implements after land reform. Was the increase due to their

having become owner-farmers? Less than one-half, (249), or about 43 per

cent of them said "yes;" 56 per cent said "no;" and a few did not answer.

Three-hundred-eighty-six, or 31 per cent, reported that they had bought

mechanized farm tools after land reform; and about one-half of them admitted

having been influenced in their purchases by land reform. Specifically, the

influences were given as (1) stabilization of ownership and operation of the

farm made the household both financially and psychologically able to buy

better and more durable implements; (2) after land reform the household had

more income and decided to use the increase to purchase more valuable, more

efficient, and more fashionable farm tools; (3) ever since the household

acquired its own land through land reform, it had been trying to make the

best and utmost use of it, and mechanization best serves this purpose; and

(4) once the household owned the land, it could be used as collateral in

buying costly farm equipment.

A majority of the households, or more than 68 per cent, denied such a

relationship. These households said that their reasons for buying mechanized

farm tools were (1) to effectively control insects and diseases; (2) to work

more efficiently; (3) to increase production; (4) to improve irrigation water

sources; (5) because mechanized farm tools were more fashionable; (6) because

there is a practical need of mechanized farm tools; (7) because they needed to

earn extra income by helping neighbors, and mechanized farm tools served the purpose well. None of these reasons necessarily excluded a relationship between the buying of mechanized farm implements and the effect of land reform. For instance, one may say that a household's chief purpose in buying a sweet potato slicing machine was to save labor and time in preparing the hog feed; but one should not overlook the possibility that it might have been largely due to the effect of the land reform that this household was able to do the buying. The effect consisted mainly in the extra money saved, or produced, by the land-reform programs. After land reform 38 per cent of the 1250 households had sold their inferior water buffalo and bought better ones. About 36 per cent of these households attributed this change to land reform. The change in status from tenant to owner, for instance, ought to be, or needs to be, accompanied by the possession of a superior water buffalo; increased income enabled the household to buy a better animal; the land could be used as collateral to make the change.

Had land reform anything to do with the increase of per-hectare production of various crops? Nine-hundred-and-sixty-four households gave answers to this question. Of these, 54 per cent said "yes," there was a relationship between the two. They stated it in such terms as ownership of the farm, possession of all commodities produced, need for increased production to cover land purchase and taxes, and having freedom to make the most productive use of the land. Those households which denied such a relationship attributed the increased production to increased amounts, and improved methods, in the application of fertilizers; more effective control of insects and diseases; improvement of irrigation and other farm technology and cultivation methods; farmers' hard work; better choice of crops and crop varieties; increase in capital investment or input; favorable natural conditions; and

incentive to produce more because of the great increase in population.
Again, none of these reasons would necessarily exclude a relationship
between land reform and increase of production. The results of land
reform should have either made these purposes possible or produced the
preconditions, or the needed motivation, or driving power.

III. Agricultural Improvements by Other Farm Households and Their Relations to Land Reform

In the preceding section, agricultural improvement efforts made by
farm households, other than former tenants, have been mentioned occasionally.
In the present section a thorough and systematic report is to be made.

1. _The original-owner farm households._ A great majority, more than
88 per cent, of the 250 sample households observed that farm people, as a
whole, had become more devoted to the improving of the farming business in
the ten or twelve years since completion of land reform. Only a small number
of them did not make such observations. In farm villages the influence of
household upon household was great and effective. People were apt to take
inspiration from each other, especially if the inspiration had bearing on
lifting up a family's economic and social status. Thus, a great majority,
or 87 per cent, of the original-owner samples admitted that they became more
industrious because they noticed that most other farm households were working
harder than before.

In the years after land reform a majority of the original-owner households also tried to make more use of their farmland by increasing the numbers
of plantings, which we have called the index of multicropping. They had a
need to do so, according to their reports in interviews. The number of

family members had increased, and the cost of living had increased, too.
The farm then had to produce more in order to support the family. They
also got the idea of multicropping from neighbors and friends, for everyone
talked about finding ways to produce more, and making additional plantings
was one of the measures recommended and adopted. The agricultural-extension
service was another source for such ideas, as well as other farm information
By talking with the farm advisors, or by participating in extension programs
a farmer learned of various suggestions for improving his farming.

Since land reform many original owners had also made changes in the
kinds of crops planted. To be exact, 41 per cent of the 250 samples made
some such changes. While a small number made the changes because of the
influence of the neighbors, a majority did so in the belief that such
changes might make them greater profits.

More than 85 per cent of the original-owner households increased farm
input after land reform. For instance, prior to land reform these households had applied an average 500.16 kg of fertilizer and NT$180.62 worth
of agricultural chemicals, per hectare of paddy rice; 311.11 kg of fertilizer and NT$45.00 worth of agricultural chemicals, on sweet potato; 570.87
kg of fertilizer and NT$97.14 worth of agricultural chemicals, on sugar-
cane. Ten years after land reform these figures changed to 694.95 kg and
NT$483.34; 426.8 kg and NT$152.56; and 643.58 kg and NT$485.00, respectively.
In percentage, the increases were 39 and 168; 37 and 239; 13 and 399. In
the agricultural-chemical item, the depreciation of the value of the NT
dollar, and the resultant inflation in commodity prices, has to be taken
into consideration.

The original-owner households also made changes in cultivation methods after land reform. In paddy rice culture, for instance, more than 41 per cent of the sample households began the practice of treating seed before planting; 16 per cent started thin broadcasting in the seedling nurseries; and 36 per cent adopted the straight-row-close-planting method of transplanting the young shoots. In the cultivation of other important crops, such as sweet potato, sugarcane, soybeans, peanuts, winter wheat, jute, vegetables, bananas, citrus fruits, etc., numerous new and better methods were in wide use.

Where had they learned the new methods? Agricultural-extension agents were, by far, the most frequent source. Next were neighbors, friends, and relatives. Farm magazines like The Harvest and Farmers' Friend were important sources. Next in order were the agricultural-improvement stations, the "Farmers' Hour" radio programs, and the farm-observation tours. Quite a few farmers had been able to devise new and better methods out of their own experience and thinking.

There was improvement, also, in the farm implements used by these households. Before land reform, for instance, 118 households had a rice threshing machine; 16 had a modern water pump; 17 had a sweet potato slicer; 35 had a mechanized sprayer; but none of them had a tractor. Ten years after land reform the figures changed to 144; 62; 39; 91; and 17, respectively.

In this respect, it is interesting to see the process of change reflected in the sources of farm power. The changes occurred in three different progressions: (1) human labor only---> human labor + animal power---->human labor + animal power + tractor and other mechanized farm tools;

(2) human labor only---> human labor + animal power + power-driven farm tools

and (3) human labor only---> human labor + animal power. At the time of this

study, ten years after completion of the land reform, 28 per cent of the 250

original-owner households were in the first category; about 16 per cent were

in the second; and 50 per cent were in the third. This means that there wer

still 50 per cent of the original-owner farm households who had not at this

time achieved any mechanization.

The following chart summarizes findings concerning original-owner farm

households:

A. Effort expended in farm work:

Working harder	221 households	88.40%
As usual	28	11.20
Less diligent	1	0.40
Total	250	100.00

B. Working harder because of other farmers' influence:

Yes	217	86.80%
No	18	7.20
No answer	15	6.00
Total	250	100.00

C. Improved the land because of other farmers' influence:

Yes	209	83.60%
No	18	7.20
No answer	23	9.20
Total	250	100.00

D. Became more interested in farm study:

Yes	223	89.20%
No	19	7.60
No answer	8	3.20
Total	250	100.00

E. Made utmost use of farmland in the recent years:

Yes	159	63.60%
No	90	36.00
No answer	1	0.40
Total	250	100.00

F. Increased amount of input:

Yes	213	85.20%
About the same	29	11.60
Decreased	1	0.40
No answer	7	2.80
Total	250	100.00

G. Adopted new cultivation methods:

(1) Paddy rice

Seed treatment	186	41.43%
Thin broadcasting	70	15.59
Straight-row	162	36.08
Others	31	6.90
Total	449*	100.00

(2) Sweet potato

Improved intercropping	72	75.79%
Young plant sterilization	20	21.05
Others	3	3.16
Total	95**	100.00

(3) Sugarcane

Intercropping	24	24.48%
Ratoon	46	46.94
Stock sterilization	28	28.58
Total	98	100.00

H. Made changes in crops planted:

Some changes	78	31.20%
Many changes	24	9.60
No changes	147	58.80
No answer	1	0.40
Total	250	100.00

I. Reasons for making the changes:

Others made them	27	26.47%
For profit	71	69.61
No answer	4	3.92
	102	100.00

---

* one household might have adopted several new methods; therefore, the
total is greater than 250.

** only 95 households adopted any new methods.

J. Changes in number of households possessing and using major farm implements:

Farm Implements	Before L.R.	After L.R.	Increase
Rice thresher	118 households	144 households	22.03%
Modern water pump	16	62	287.50
Sweet potato slicer	17	39	129.41
Mechanical sprayer	35	91	160.00
Tractor	0	17	170.00

K. Increase in per-ha production:

Crops	Before L.R.	Ten Years After L.R.	Increase Amount	%
Paddy rice	3,718.08 kg.	4,809.95 kg.	1,091.87 kg.	29
Sweet potato	12,115.17	14,873.26	2,758.09	22
Sugarcane	110,102.60	122,510.60	12,408.00	11
Corn	2, 175.00	3,000.00	825.00	37

Was there any relationship between progress on original-owner farms and the land reform? There was a relationship, but it was indirect. As reported previously, 87 per cent of the 250 samples admitted that their increased diligence on their farms was chiefly due to the influence of other farmers. By 'other farmers' they meant the former-tenant but now-owner farmers. The former tenants worked more diligently after they became owner-farmers, and their diligence, with its attendant successes, cast an influence upon the original owner-farmers so that they, also, started to work harder and, as a matter of course, also enjoyed success. Success gave rise to more interest and greater determination. Land reform had, then, created an atmosphere of happiness, hopefulness, and diligence in which no morally-conforming farmer could do otherwise than work hard.

2. The present-tenant farm households. The farming business of those were still tenants at the time of this study had also undergone some changes or progressed. First, as has been pointed out in the preceding chapter,

tenants became happier than before in operating their rented farms because

after land reform they were able to get a much larger share of what they had

produced. Thus, they were encouraged to make special efforts in improving

operation and, therefore, increase production. Special efforts included

increased amounts of farm input, learning and adopting new and better culti-

vation methods, changes in crops and cropping systems, and the purchase and

use of improved farm tools.

When asked whether after the enforcement of the 37.5% Farm Rent Limitation

Act they had, or had not, become willing to spend more capital and labor on

the rented farm, more than 78 per cent of the 250 tenant households gave

affirmative answers. Only 20 per cent said they had made no change. As

previously mentioned, 59 per cent of the households reported using the money

saved by the farm-rent limitation to improve their farms. More specifically,

the tenant households, like the other farm households, had, since land

reform, increased both the amounts of fertilizers applied on the three chief

crops of paddy rice, sweet potato, and sugarcane and the amounts of money

spent on agricultural chemicals. Before land reform the amounts of ferti-

lizers applied on paddy rice, sweet potato, and sugarcane, per hectare, were

463.76 kg, 381.76 kg, and 558.42 kg, respectively. The amounts of money

spent per hectare for controlling insects and diseases on these crops were

NT$123.45, NT$30.00, and NT$275.00, respectively. Ten years after land

reform the amounts of fertilizers per hectare were 637.58 kg, 509.39 kg,

and 898.33 kg; expenditures on agricultural chemicals were NT$423.60,

NT$154.52, and NT$230.00. The increase of fertilizers were 173.82 kg,

127.58 kg, and 339.91 kg, in absolute amounts, and 37.48, 33.41, and 60.87,

in percentages. The increase in agricultural-chemicals expenditures was

NT$300.15 and NT$124.52 for paddy rice and sweet potato; for sugarcane there was, however, a NT$45.00 decrease. In percentage, the increases were 243.13 and 415.07, and the decrease was 16.37, but effects of inflation should be kept in mind.

Increase of farm input had not been limited to capital or farm supplies but also applied in the amount of labor. As many as 80 per cent of the tenant households reported that they put in much more work than before. Only about 19 per cent said they made no change. It is not known whether the lack of change indicated that these households had already been working to their utmost or that land reform had not given them the incentive to work especially hard.

Most farms in Taiwan are in great need of water at the growing seasons. Whether or not a household was working especially hard on its farm can, in one way, be gauged by how much labor its members spent on finding and getting the necessary water to the fields. At the time of this study, a majority, about 64 per cent of the tenant-farm households, complained that the irrigation water on their farms was far from being enough, certainly not abundant; and more than 70 per cent of them spent a great deal of extra labor to find and transport water to the fields.

As with other farmers, the tenant households also learned and adopted new and better cultivation methods following completion of land reform. In paddy rice culture, for instance, they had started to practice one, two, or more of such new methods, such as seed treatment, thin broadcasting, straight row-close-planting, and others. In the cultivation of sweet potato they had begun to use the improved intercropping system, the sterilization of young shoots, and others. In growing sugarcane they had adopted the intercropping method, the ratoon method, the sterilization of seedlings, and others. Since land reform the number of tenant-farmers who had come into contact with agricultural-extension agents had increased. Many of them had warm feelings toward the extension staffs.

In the possession and use of modern, or improved, farm tools, the tenant-farm households made progress, too. Before land reform, for instance, 80 of the 250 households had a rice threshing machine; none had a modern water pump; 1 had a sweet potato slicing machine; 22 had a mechanized sprayer; none had a tractor. At the time of the interview the thresher was owned and used by 105 of these households, 13 had a modern water pump, 26 had the new, sweet potato slicer, 42 owned a mechanical sprayer, and 3 owned silage-making machines. Almost every household had more farm tools ten years after land reform than before it.

A result of the increase in farm input, the improvement of cultivation methods, and the modernization of farm implements, was the increase of per hectare production of the various crops. Before land reform, for instance, the average per-hectare production of paddy rice of these households was 3,020.66 kg. At the time of this study the production was 3,842.82 kg, up by 822.16 kg, or 27.22 per cent. The increase of sweet potato was 7,051.23 kg, or 48.71 per cent, from 14,473.77 kg before land reform to 21,525. kg ten years after. As for sugarcane, the pre-land-reform, per-hectare production was 48,000 kg, and it changed to 65,555.4 kg ten years after land reform. The increase was 17,555.4 kg, or 36.57 per cent.

The statistics given on the preceding page can be tabulated as follows:

A. Farm input:

(1) Number of households reporting

Increase	196 households	78.40%
No increase	50	20.00
No answer	4	1.60
Total	250	100.00

(2) Increase in fertilizers and agricultural chemicals

Crops & Materials	Before L.R.	Ten Years After L.R.	Increase Amount	%
Paddy rice				
Fertilizers (kg)	463.76	637.58	173.82	37.48
Chemicals (in $)	123.45	423.60	300.15	243.13
Sweet potato				
Fertilizers (kg)	381.76	509.39	127.63	33.41
Chemicals (in $)	30.00	154.52	124.52	415.07
Sugarcane				
Fertilizers (kg)	558.42	898.33	339.91	60.87
Chemicals (in $)	275.00	230.00	-45.00	-16.37

(3) Labor input

Reported increase	200 households	80.00%
No increase	47	18.80
No answer	3	1.20
Total	250	100.00

(4) Additional efforts to obtain irrigation water
(159 households were in need of water)

Yes	112	70.44
No	43	27.04
No answer	4	2.52
Total	159	100.00

B. Adoption of new cultivation methods:

(1) Paddy rice

Seed treatment	170	38.99
Thin broadcasting	77	17.66
Straight-row	164	37.61
Others	25	5.74
Total	436	100.00

(2) Sweet potato

Improved intercropping	59	88.06
Sterilization of young shoots	7	10.45
Others	1	1.49
Total	67	100.00

(3) Sugarcane

Intercropping	20	37.74
Ratoon	25	47.17
Sterilization	8	15.09
Total	53	100.00

C. Changes in number of households having improved farm tools:

Tools	Before L.R.	Ten Years After L.R.	Increase Amount	%
Rice thresher	80	105	25	31.25
Modern water pump	0	13	13	-
Sweet potato slicer	1	26	25	250.00
Mechanical sprayer	22	42	20	90.91
Tractor	0	0	0	0
Silage maker	0	3	3	-

D. Increase in per-ha production:

Crops	Before L.R.	Ten Years After L.R.	Increase Amount	%
Paddy rice (kg)	3,020.66	3,842.82	822.16	27.22
Sweet potato	14,473.77	21,525.00	7,051.23	48.71
Sugarcane	48,000.00	65,555.40	17,555.40	36.57

A relationship between the agricultural improvement of a tenant-farm household and the effects of land reform is obvious. First, the 37.5% farm rent limitation freed tenants from the oppressive pressures of traditionally heavy rent. This relief had not only given the tenant a great lift in morale, but also additional money, or produce, saved from the payment of rents, and it enabled him and his family to make significant advances. Secondly, while it is true that there were other factors, or forces, which made contributions to the achievement of agricultural progress, if there had not been the lift in morale, the saved money, the optimistic atmosphere, and a host of other favorable conditions created by the effects of the land reform, most, if not all, of the other factors might have had no effect. Notwithstanding the fact that a large number of the tenant-farmers did not realize, or refused to admit, this relationship, it is, nevertheless, a fact that only farmers who are free from any kind of oppressive servitude, in the form of extremely heavy rent, have the desire, or the capability, of making spontaneous, agricultural improvement.

3. _Agricultural improvements among former-landlord but now active-farmer households._ It has been pointed out previously that a great number of the former ordinary, or small-landlord, households became authentic farming households after completion of the land-to-the-tiller program. They began cultivating the three hectares lawfully retained by them from the Government's compulsory purchase of land. Many of these reorganized, and revitalized, households made conspicuous progress in the farming business. This was not surprising, because they had much larger farms, and other conditions were better than for other categories of farmers. Of the 500 ordinary-landlord samples, 40 per cent had either continued to be, or

became, farming households. Of these households more than 55 per cent admitted that they were far more diligent than pre-land reform in operating the farming business; 32 per cent said that they had been diligent long before, and that after land reform most farm people worked harder, so naturally they, too, continued to farm diligently. This means that more than 87 per cent of the former-landlord households which had continued to be, or newly became, farming households were, at the time of this study, working especially hard on their farms.

Of the 202 former-landlord, but now actually-farming households, more than 67 per cent had a rice thresher; 15 per cent had modern water pumps; 10 per cent had a sweet potato slicer; 40 per cent had mechanized sprayers; and 6 per cent had tractors. On the whole, the farm implements of these households were better than those of other categories of farmers. With much larger farms, better farm implements, and other more favorable conditions, and diligence, these households had high per-hectare production for most of the crops.

IV. Observations from Non-farm People

A number of the non-farm people commented on the agricultural progress made by the different categories of farmers and the relationship between agricultural progress and land reform.

1. Observations from local leaders in rural communities. Fifty per cent of the local leaders interviewed in rural communities observed that, after the tenant-cultivators had acquired the ownership of the land through land reform, they made drastic changes in the kinds of crops planted and in the cropping system practiced. Objectives of their changes were higher

rates of production, more plantings in a year, more by-products, and increased total farm receipt.

Eighty-six per cent of these local leaders verified the claims of most of the farmers that they had considerably intensified the utilization of their farmland after land reform. Again, their purpose was to get more production from the land. An important way of improving production was to have more adequate irrigation for crops, which needed irrigation badly. Therefore, the new owner-farmers, as well as the original farmers, spent a great deal of labor and capital seeking water. As a result, after land reform the acreage of farmland having access to irrigation facilities had been considerably expanded.

Practically all the local leaders observed that after land reform farmers of every category had increased the amount of fertilizers applied on important or money-making crops. The quality of fertilizers, and the ways of applying them, had also been improved a great deal. Farmers had become more concerned, and more energetic, in the prevention and control of farm insects and diseases. They were spending much more labor and money on such tasks than before land reform. The local leaders also bore witness to the fact that in approximately ten years after land reform farmers had become interested in learning, and adopting, new and better ideas and cultivation methods. The methods most commonly adopted were the straight-row-close-planting, deep plowing, seed treatment and seedling sterilization, improved crop varieties, the growing of green manure crops, and various techniques of insect and disease control. The local leaders reported that as a result of these efforts and improvements, the per-hectare production of paddy rice rose from 3,164.84 kg before land reform to 3,554.83 kg in 1963. The increase was 389.99 kg or 12.32 per cent.

2. Others queried. Eighty-nine per cent of the 100 teachers, agricultural-extension agents, and people of cultural activities who were queried, commented that after the tenant-cultivators had become owner-farmers, they also became much more interested and enthusiastic about township-level, agricultural-extension education. Women in the new-owner households were also more interested in new ideas and better methods of homemaking.

V. Conclusion

In the ten years following the completion of land reform agriculture in Taiwan had shown a considerable amount of progress. This progress was chiefly a result of the farm people's willingness to work especially hard, to increase farm input to their utmost limits, and to learn, and practice, many new and better methods and techniques. Their willingness was aroused by their happiness, high morale, and hopefulness toward the future of the farming business and farm life in general. Where did these feelings come from? This writer has concluded that, in significant degree, they came from accomplishments of the land reform.

Notes

[1]Taiwan Province Agriculture Yearbook, Department of Agriculture and Forestry, Taiwan Provincial Government, July, 1965, pp. 42-43.

[2]Ibid.

[3]Ibid., p. 97.

[4]Report on Touring the Taiwan Sugar Corporation Sugarcane Growing Districts, 1966, by Martin M. C. Yang.

[5]According to information recently issued by the Taiwan Sugar Corporation, it is reported that high production of sugarcane depends very much on the crop's variety and the amounts and kinds of fertilizers applied. At its sugarcane experiment station, five new varieties have been tested. They are F146, per-hectare production 265,000 kg; F151, per-hectare production 252,000 kg; F153, per-hectare production 278,000 kg; F155, per-hectare production 260,000 kg; and F156, per-hectare production 314,000 kg. In the years 1965 and 1966, farmers in one of the best sugarcane growing areas, P'ingtung County, already planted the variety F152. One of the growers got the highest per-hectare production of 260,000 kg. (Report on "Observation Tour on the Sugarcane Experiment Farm Testing the High Production Varieties;" report on "Observation Tour on Farmer Heng Hsien-wu's F152 Sugarcane Farm." These two reports were written by Mr. Kwang Ti, published in the Taiwan Sugar Corporation's bulletin, Tai-tang Tung-hsun, or Taiwan Sugar Corporation's Information, Vol. 36, No. 18, 1966.)

[6]Taiwan Province Agriculture Yearbook, p. 71.

[7]Ibid., p. 216

[8]Ibid., p. 101.

[9]Ibid., p. 99.

[10]Ibid., p. 83.

[11]Ibid., p. 128.

[12]Ibid., pp. 230-31.

[13]Ibid., pp. 230-31.

[14]Ibid., pp. 230-33.

[15]Ibid., p. 253.

[16]Ibid., pp. 230 and 254.

[17]Ibid., p. 254.

[18]Ibid., p. 255.

[19]Most of the materials in this section are from "Changes in Agricultural Technology Affecting the Rural Community" (Unpublished manuscript in Chinese) by Martin M. C. Yang, 1965, Chapters IV and V.

[20]Before land reform, the average amount of farm land operated by a tenant household was one-and-one half (1.5) hectares. The reason that it could have been so much was that then most of the landlords had all their farm land rented to the tenants. During land reform, the public, farm-land sales program sold a total amount of farm land less than that originally cultivated, or occupied, by the tenants. The diminution was due to striking out of the list of land for sale a number of bad or unproductive lands. The land-to-the-tiller program also sold less total amount of farm land to the original tenant-cultivators because each landlord household was allowed to keep an

average of three hectares of farm land for its own cultivation. About the
same number of cultivators bought, in total, much less land than they used
to operate. The result was that the average amount of land each of the
former tenant-cultivators had been able to buy, through either of the two
programs, was almost one-half hectare less than that which they operated
as tenants. Later on, a large number of the new owner-farmers had the
opportunity of renting some farm land again, from either the original landlords or other land owners. As a result, the average size of individual
farms operated by these households after land reform was larger than that
which they purchased. It was much closer to the pre-land reform amount.
At the time of the study, Taiwan's industrialization and urbanization had
already taken a considerable amount of farm land for the building of factories and living houses. A great number of the farm households could not
resist the good prices offered for their land and each might have sold some.
Consequently, there was shrinkage in the total amount of farm land and
shrinkage in the size of each farm.

[21]Under all standards, the average size of the private, individual farm
in Taiwan today is too small. The farmers themselves complain bitterly that
their land is too little. The agricultural economists tell people every day
that the present size of farms would forever keep Chinese agriculture from
developing into a modern, progressive agriculture. The Government regrets
that, at present, there is little, if anything, that can be done to significantly change the farm land scarcity situation. The farming situation, as a
whole, has, however, not been as bad as some people think it would be. In
considering this land-shortage problem, one should keep in mind a number of
conditions which have bearing on the success or failure of the operation of

a small farm. Productivity of the farm, the cropping system, farm technology, the amount of input, the use of the land, marketing of farm products, the character of the farmer and his family, climate and other natural elements, are all powerful factors which can, under favorable conditions, make the operation of a small farm quite successful. By successful, it means that the farmer and his family can have a decent standard of living from their work on the farm.

[22]See "Changes in Agricultural Technology Affecting the Rural Community."

[23](1) A Study on the Results of the Application of the Various Agricultural Extension Methods (in Chinese) by Martin M. C. Yang and Tseng-Shien Wu; (2) A Study on the Farmers' Response to Agricultural Extension Education (in Chinese) by the same authors; (3) A Study on the Diffusion of Agricultural Information (in Chinese) by Tseng-Shien Wu.

[24]Taiwan Sugar Corporation reports on Annual Business Report of Taiwan's Farmers' Associations; and the Organization of Sugarcane Production Study Classes.

[25]Martin M. C. Yang, "Changes in Agricultural Technology Affecting the Rural Community," Chapter VI, Section 4.

[26]See Section I of this chapter, paragraph on per-hectare production of sweet potato.

Chapter Six

CHANGE OF OCCUPATION OF THE LANDLORDS

I. The Government's Way of Inducing
   the Landlords to Change Occupation

II. The Landlords' Own Efforts toward
    Change of Occupation

III. Difficulties in Change of Occupation

IV. Other Observations
    1. Observations of the Rural Town
       Business People
    2. Observations of the Rural Town
       Industrialists

V. Conclusion

It has been pointed out several times in the preceding chapters that one of the important objectives of the land reform was that the landlords, especially the big ones, should give up their farm land and go into occupations not dependent on the collection of farm rents. Generally, there were two ways which a landlord could take in changing his occupation. One way was devised by the Government; the other was devised by himself.

I. The Government's Way of Inducing
   the Landlords to Change Occupation

In order to help the landlords achieve this objective, the Government purposely paid three-tenths of the land prices in shares of stocks of four, Government-owned corporations. The Government's

intention had been widely and clearly publicized, and measures to carry
out the payment, and realize the objective, were put into practice. But
the degree of success in the change of the landlords' occupation is still
a question. Some answers have been given, but their truthfulness is in
controversy. The task in this chapter is to make an objective, and close-
to-fact, answer to this question. It is to be done with data collected
in the survey.

Supposedly, once the landlords accepted the shares of stocks of the
four corporations and became owners, or shareholders, of those enterprises, they would consider such ownership and investment as a new occupation. At least a portion of their living expenses would be derived
from the earnings of the stocks. Actually, however, this presumption had
not proven true, except with an extremely small number of very big landlords. Holding of several hundreds, or several thousands of shares of
corporation stocks, had not given those landlords, who remained in farming and become active farmers, the slightest idea of changing occupations. Except for a small number, landlords who did not remain in farming were also uncertain and confused regarding what they ought to do with
their shares. They had heard the "change of occupation" talk, but they
did not understand exactly what this talk meant or how a change was to
be accomplished. Very few of the landlords realized that owning a corporation's stock meant ownership in the enterprise, nor did they believe
that their livelihood could come from the earnings of the corporation.

Because of their ignorance that their stocks represented the
property and business of the corporation, and the consequent significance
of their holding stocks, the great majority of landlords did not place

much value, or importance, on their shares of stock. Therefore, when rumors, perhaps purposely-planted, broke out implying that the stocks of the four corporations would soon become worthless, and that the wisest thing to do was to get rid of them at the earliest opportunity, a great many of the holders sold their shares at great losses. A few of them spent the money in a short time for an easy life or for other non-productive purposes. Our survey discovered that each of the 500 ordinary landlords received an average of 4406 shares of stocks, of which 732 shares were in the Manufacturing and Mining Corporation, 1460 shares in the Taiwan Paper Corporation, 575 shares in the Agricultural and Forestry Corporation, and 1639 shares in the Taiwan Cement Corporation. The 75 big landlords received an average 39,762 shares, of which 5347 shares were in the Manufacturing and Mining Corporation, 17,834 shares in the Taiwan Paper Corporation, 4423 shares in the Agricultural and Forestry Corporation, and 12,358 shares in the Taiwan Cement Corporation. Instead of retaining their shares of stocks, more than 98 per cent of the ordinary landlords, and about 91 per cent of the big landlords, sold them either in one lot or in several lots. All, except the stock of Taiwan Cement, were sold at prices far below par value which was NT$10.00. The average loss was NT$4.03 per share. Taiwan Cement averaged NT$10.74 per share, less than NT$1.00 above par. More than 48 per cent, (48.47), of the ordinary landlords, and more than 45 per cent, (45.58), of the big landlords gave as the prime reason for their quick sale of the stocks their urgent need of money. A second reason was that, at the time, these people saw no advantage in keeping them. And then, of course, they had heard that the value of the stocks might soon depreciate, so much that the holders would suffer very great losses.

The way in which proceeds from the sale of the stocks was spent
is the next subject of significance. Of those landlords who sold their
stocks, only 62 per cent of the ordinary ones, and 85 per cent of the
big ones, remembered how the money was spent. About 35 per cent were
unable to tell, or did not want to tell, what they did with the money.
Of those who remembered, 60 per cent of the ordinary landlords, and
60 per cent of the big ones, spent it on everyday living. A number of
them also spent for such other things as education, house-building or
repairing, medical care, marriage, buying land, agricultural improvement,
buying furniture, and paying debts. Among the big landlords, there were
a few who used the money to run for political office. Less than 10 per
cent of the ordinary landlords, and a little over 17 per cent of the
big ones, used it to establish a factory or a business. A great
majority of both the ordinary and the big landlords, 73 per cent and 65
per cent, admitted that they had known that the way they were spending
the money was not wise, but they spent it anyway.

The above findings show that the Government's effort to persuade the
landlords to change occupations and to enter industries or businesses, by
paying the land price with corporation stocks, had almost completely
failed. It is true that there had been a few, exceptional cases in which
landlords were very successful in one or two of the four corporations.
Several of the present, major stockholders and management personnel of
the Taiwan Cement Corporation are former, large landlords. They are now
considered very successful and capable industrial leaders. They truly
changed their land investment into industrial investment. Among former

landlords as a whole, however, the plan was a great failure.

What were the reasons for this failure? One direct reason was that more than 90 per cent of the landlords had blindly sold their shares of the stocks. Why did they have to sell them? Cheng Ch'eng-chang, a reporter of the China Daily, in reporting a survey of opinions and attitudes toward the various measures and results of land reform said, "In regard to the compensation made to the landlords for the purchase of their land, the land bonds in kind are considered by the landlords most dependable and, therefore, generally welcome. In regard to the stocks of the four corporations, I have so far met no landlord who shows any interest in those Government-operated enterprises. They are, first, doubtful about the appraisement made on the fiscal value of the properties of the four corporations. They feel the evaluation is too high. Secondly, the number of shares of stocks they have in any one of the corporations is too small--so small a number it can hardly give a holder power to control, or even to influence, the policy and management of the corporation. In case the policy is wrong and the management bad, the value of the stock would certainly depreciate. If it does, to whom can the stockholders go for redress? One of the big landlords whose 80 hectares of land had been compulsorily purchased by the Government openly stated that the Manufacturing and Mining Corporation is the most criticized business among the Government-operated enterprises."[1]

The validity of this opinion is difficult to check because Cheng failed to tell in his report how many landlords he had interviewed. But the appearance of such a report in one of the influential, daily papers could not fail to have a vast effect on the minds of the landlords who were then holders of the stocks. There was suspicion that some shrewd spectators took advantage of this report and spread word that the four corporations really were in a shaky position, that the value of their stocks might soon drop drastically, and that the longer the holders kept the stocks, the greater their loss would be. Thus, it is very possible that the landlords' own ignorance, plus Cheng's report and the subsequent speculators' rumors, were the causes of the landlords' quick sale of their shares of stock.

At this point, an appropriate question would be: who were the buyers of those stocks? There is no record in which answers to this question can be found. It is, however, public knowledge that today each of the four corporations is managed, or largely owned, by a few native-born, wealthy persons who were big landlords before land reform. These few, former landlords were tremendously successful in their change of occupation; but their success was at the expense of the livelihood of a large number of their own kind. Today, the Taiwan Cement Corporation is very prosperous and makes great profits. The Taiwan Paper Corporation is also doing well. The other two, the Manufacturing and Mining Corporation and the Agricultural and Forestry Corporation, are not as profitable, but they have not gone bankrupt either.

In regard to this matter, one more point should be raised and discussed. This concerns the debate over whether or not at the very beginning, the Government ought to have taken measures to guarantee the value of the stocks. Some people argue that if the Government had taken such a step, the landlords might not have been so susceptible to the influence of reports, such as that made by Cheng Ch'eng-chang, or to the effects of rumors spread by speculators. Then, they might not have

foolishly sold their stocks so hurriedly and so cheaply. The People's

Assembly of the Hsinchu County did recommend to the authority concerned,

the Executive Yuan, that the Government provide guarantees on the par value

of the stocks.[2] But the Government did not agree. The authority in the

Executive Yuan responded to this recommendation by saying that because the

four corporations had already been sold to the people, they had become

private enterprises, and the private owners, or stockholders, should be

entirely responsible for their growth,or decline, for the increase, or

decrease, of the value of their stocks. The Government, it continued,

was no longer in a position to interfere with the operation of the

corporations and, therefore, could not provide the guaranty in any way.[3]

Legally, and from a free-enterprise-capitalism point of view, this

response did not include anything which could be subject to criticism. But

at a time when a great majority of the people were inexperienced and naive

in modern business investment and business management, and when the big,

wealthy speculators were so selfishly determined to grab whatever money, or

property, they could lay their hands on, the adoption of such a laissez-fair

policy must have equalled the abandoning of a poor, meek lamb to the mercy

of a pack of vicious wolves. What chance could the lamb have! If the

Government had the wisdom and the determination to put the land-to-the-

tiller program into practice, i.e., to force all landlords to sell their

land, it ought also to have the wisdom and determination to take the neces-

sary steps to protect the chief interests of all landlords, not just the

interests of a few. If an outright guaranty on the stocks' par value was

not advisable, then other measures should have been taken to help the landlords help themselves, to avoid their selling so quickly and at such great losses. In one way or another, the Government should have helped the new stockholders to strengthen the corporations' organization, personnel, policy-making, and management. It should have seen that the corporations were on a sound business basis and that their operations enabled them to make some profit, or, at least, not lost money. These words may sound idealistic. But unless, and until, this is the case, land reform will be considered successful only for one side, the tenants. As to what actually happened, it was rather unfair to the majority of landlords, who had generally been loyal to the Government and had obediently accepted its compulsory purchase of their land.

In summary, the results obtained by the Government's methods to bring about the landlords' change of occupations is shown as follows:

A. Numbers of shares of corporation stocks received by each landlord:

1. The 500 ordinary landlords

Corporation	Number of shares of stocks per landlord
Manufacturing and Mining	732 shares
Taiwan Paper	1460
Agriculture and Forestry	575
Taiwan Cement	1639
Total	4406

2. The 75 big landlords

Manufacturing and Mining	5347
Taiwan Paper	17834
Agriculture and Forestry	4223
Taiwan Cement	12358
Total	39762

B. Numbers of landlords who sold stocks early:

Ordinary landlords	492 landlords	98.40%
Big landlords	68	90.66

Prices received	Par value	Market price	Loss, gain

1. Ordinary landlords

	Par value	Market price	Loss, gain
Manufacturing and Mining	NT$10.00	NT$ 3.58	NT$ 6.42-
Taiwan Paper	10.00	6.76	3.24-
Agriculture and Forestry	10.00	6.76	3.24-
Taiwan Cement	10.00	10.59	+0.
Average	10.00	6.92	3.08-

2. The big landlords

	Par value	Market price	Loss, gain
Manufacturing and Mining	NT$10.00	NT$ 5.07	NT$ 4.93-
Taiwan Paper	10.00	6.99	3.01-
Agriculture and Forestry	10.00	6.62	3.38-
Taiwan Cement	10.00	10.89	+0.
Average	10.00	7.39	2.61-

C. Uses of proceeds:

1. The ordinary landlords

Remembered how spent	304	61.79%
Did not remember	196	38.21
Total	500	100.00%

On living expenses	202	66.45%
Business investments	28	9.21
Building or repairing houses	19	6.25
Education	25	8.22
Paying debts	9	
Buying land	5	
Buying furniture	4	9.87
Marriage	2	
Farm improvement	3	
Other	7	
Total	304	100.00%

2. Big landlords

Remembered how spent	57	76.00%
Did not remember	18	24.00
Total	75	100.00%

On living expenses	34	59.65%
Business investment	4	7.02
Capital for changing occupation	6	10.54
Education	4	7.02
Running for office	2 ⎤	
Savings in bank	2 ⎬	15.77
Other	5 ⎦	
Total	57	100.00%

D. Information from sources, other than the survey, reveals that a small number of the big landlords had become large stockholders of the corporations and are regarded as successful businessmen or industrialists. For these few, the change of occupation, through Government methods, had been successful.

II. The Landlords' Own Efforts
toward Change of Occupation

Ideally, all landlords who had not chosen to remain in farming ought to have made some effort to change their occupation and enter a new way of life. Actually, however, this was not the case. According to the survey, only 28 per cent of the 500 ordinary landlords and 36 per cent of the large landlords had considered, or planned, a change of occupation upon completion of the land-to-the-tiller program. A majority, 71 per cent, of the ordinary landlords and 61 per cent of the large landlords had had no such plan even one or two years following land reform. A significant finding was that of the 354 ordinary landlords and 46 big landlords who had no idea of changing occupation, only 60 per cent of the former, and 50 per cent of the latter, reported that the reason for their not having such an idea was that they wished to remain in, or begin, actual farming. The rest did not give this reason. Why not? It could be that they were already in business or other non-farm occupations at the time of the land reform, so there was no need for them to think of a change. It could also be interpreted, however, that these people had been in an easy life too long. They had not experienced the need, or acquired the necessary knowledge, to think about change and make plans in regard to the family's livelihood. At the moment when their land was gone and their accustomed life was crumbling, many of these landlords must have been in great confusion and suffered great bewilderment. They badly needed a plan for the future. Yet with the land bonds in kind, and the money from the sale of corporation stocks, they and their carefree fami continued a life of spending and wasting. They did not have plans, provi- sions, or understanding, about what would happen in the future.

But had the 139 ordinary landlords who did plan their change of occupation actually made the change? No, only 72 per cent actually changed; 28 per cent did not. This means that only 20 per cent of the 500 ordinary landlords actually changed occupations in the year or two following completion of the land-to-the-tiller program. Among the 75 large landlords, the proportion was less than 30 per cent.

Occupations into which these landlords entered included businesses related to commerce, store operation, handicraft manufacturing and selling; public services such as local government and community organizations; operation of small factories; processing of farm products; transportation; commercial services, such as the hotel business, photography, watch repairing, and others.

Some landlords had to make more than one change of occupation, usually because they had suffered a loss in the previous one. The survey discovered that the number of landlords who succeeded in new occupations were smaller than the number who suffered losses or bankruptcy. Cited as factors for success were good management, good location, fair prices, good credit, acting at the right time, knowing the trend of a certain business, having sufficient capital, and others. Factors causing failure were the absence of the advantages just listed.

According to data recorded in the interview schedules, and as presented in the preceding paragraphs, the landlords' change of occupation through their own efforts had also been less successful. Only a small percentage had made it, successfully escaping any serious loss in their new ventures. If, however, a closer examination is made, and if information gathered in other ways were consulted, one would get a somewhat different picture, a picture which looks much better than the one just presented. In the diaries kept by the interviewers, in which they listed discoveries which could not be written in the questionnaire forms, three significant facts have been revealed which have important bearing on this subject.

One is that many a landlord who had not chosen to continue farming was, at the time of the interview, in another kind of non-farm business or occupation. Some had been in business, public service, or school teaching before land reform. After land reform they continued to do what they had been doing previously. Quite a few of them had even become grateful to the land reform because it was this program which had made them sell land, add money to the business, and thus see the old enterprise improve and expand. It was land reform that prompted their decision to convert a stagnant and problematic land investment into a growing and a promising

business investment. When the land was gone and the investment transformed, an energetic and enterprise-minded landlord felt a new freedom
from the numerous agrarian and traditional bondages and was able to
concentrate all his means and mind on the development of his business,
or on another modern enterprise.[4]

Of those who went into businesses, or other non-farm occupations
after land reform, a small number entered immediately, but most of them
suffered several years' confusion, or uncertainty, before they realized
that they had to make a livelihood, in one way or another, outside of
farming. Few had found it possible to succeed on the first try. More
often, they made several attempts before succeeding in an occupation outside of farming. There must have been a great deal of floundering, suffering, wasting, and losses. At any rate, a majority of the former
landlords must have reached the same conclusion as the one reported in
Bernard Gallin's study. In his case study in the village of Hsin Hsing
of Taiwan, Bernard Gallin reports a former landlord's statement, "Despite
his bitterness, however, he admitted that now the landlord no longer can
spend all his time playing around, drinking, gambling, and seeing shows.
Now, in order to live, he must go out to work and do business. In the
old days, if the landlord played a lot and needed more money to finance
his entertainment, he could just raise his rents."[5]

The second fact discovered in the diaries is that those landlords
whose residences were close to towns, cities, or important transportation
lines, enjoyed the advantages of comparatively more opportunities, and
greater possibilities of success, in starting businesses of various kinds.
These landlords had, in general, much more knowledge, wider acquaintance-

ships, and,therefore, greater courage in taking up new ventures than those who lived in relatively insular, rural communities. Landlords, for instance, whose homes were in villages near Taipei, Taichung, and other booming business towns had entered large or small business operations in great number.

A third fact is that a large number of the landlords interviewed had confused the interviewer's question regarding change of occupation with the one which concerns undertaking new, or expanded, supplementary jobs or enterprises. When a landlord mentioned taking up a new supplementary job, it might have meant that he had, in fact, entered a new occupation. There had been difficulties for both the landlord and the interviewer in differentiating a "supplementary job" from a "new way of making a living." There were a number of so-called "supplementary undertakings" which overlapped the areas of farming and non-farming activities. It was also true that a certain landlord might have been in the farming business at home and, at the same time, been a nominal, full-time staff member in the township public office. Which was his regular occupation, and which was supplementary work? It was difficult to make the differentiation.

The chief reason for the discrepancy between the statistical data recorded in the questionnaires and the information in the interviewers' diaries and in other documents may have been that in the questionnaires, the landlords were asked if they had changed occupations immediately after the completion of the land-to-the-tiller program, whereas, facts recorded in the diaries were observations, or discoveries, made at the time of the interview, which took place more than ten years later.

In those ten years, many landlords, who had failed to make a change in occupation immediately after land reform, must have made it later on.

This section is summarized as follows:

A. Numbers of landlords having early plans for change in occupation:

    1. Ordinary landlords

Had ideas or plans	139	27.80%
Had no ideas or plans	354	70.80
No answer	7	1.40
Total	500	100.00

    2. Big landlords

Had ideas or plans	27	36.00
Had no ideas or plans	46	61.33
No answer	2	2.67
Total	75	100.00

B. Reasons for not having ideas or plans:

    1. Ordinary landlords

Intent to remain in farming	213	60.17
No reason given	141	39.83
Total	354	100.00

    2. Big landlords

Intent to remain in farming	23	50.00
No reason given	23	50.00
Total	46	100.00

C. Numbers of landlords actually making a change:

    1. Ordinary landlords

Actually made change	100	71.94
Had ideas but no actual change	39	28.06
Total	139	100.00

Only 100, or 20 per cent, of the 500 ordinary landlords made a change of occupation.

    2. Big landlords

Actually made change	22	81.48
Had ideas but no actual change	5	18.52
Total	27	100.00

Only 22, or 29.33 per cent, of 75 big landlords made a change of occupation.

D. According to data from other sources, the ratio of landlords' changes of occupation, of becoming engaged in a way of life not dependent on the collection of farm rents, was much better than the above data would indicate. There are three additional facts to be noted:

1. Quite a few of the landlords, especially the big ones, were already in business before land reform; and a number of them succeeded in entering business, or other non-farming jobs, in the first few years following completion of the land reform.

2. Still more landlords got into non-farming livelihoods not long before the time when our interviews took place.

3. Landlords who had been located close to cities, towns, main communication lines or business centers, had found it easier to enter business than those who were far away from such places.

E. Big landlords had, in general, been able to enter comparatively large and modern businesses or industries, whereas, the small and ordinary landlords had to pick up many kinds of non-farming jobs.

III. Cause of Difficulties in the Landlords' Change of Occupation

Many landlords complained to interviewers that the primary reason for their failure in changing occupations was that they felt lost and were in great confusion about life in the future. At the time when their land had been compulsorily purchased, and they saw tenants get the land without undergoing any struggle or hardship, they were bitter and bewildered. They were possessed by hatred, fear, and faintness of heart. These emotional conditions lay at the root of their confusion. Added to these were their ignorance in the operation of any business and their lack of will power to face a strange, uncharted future. What they needed most of all at that time was understanding sympathy, sincere reassurance about their future, and practical guidance from responsible authorities. Instead, the Government evidently felt that after the land had been taken away, the land reform had been accomplished, and its job was done. Thus, the former landlords were left alone, miserable and distressed in darkness. No one came to offer help, or advice, about what to do next. The Government gave attention and consideration only to the tenants. The landlords were deserted. It is understandable that under such circumstances, few landlords were able to plan, or even to think of a change of occupation, and still fewer could actually make any careful change.

The second reason was that landlords, who had not been in business or known anything other than living on farm rents, were usually ignorant concerning the operation of any business. If the Government was really sincere in its proposition that these people should enter business, or other kinds of non-farming undertakings, it should have conducted some sort of business or trade training programs for landlords who intended going into business or a trade. Indeed, some of the landlords had made a petition to the Government for such help. That the Government had not met its responsibility in this respect not only disappointed many of the landlords, the default was followed by a great many mistakes, and losses, in landlords' trying to enter the world of business and industry. There is no doubt that the Government had really wanted to see the landlords become established in business or industry, but its negligence in establishing training programs for the landlords was naive and inexcusable.

The third reason given by the landlords was shortage of funds. Concerning this problem, many landlords had wished that the Government had paid the full purchase price of their land at once, or paid it in two or three years at the most, instead of in ten years. They **argued** that if the Government really cared about the landlords' well-being, it would have provided that the land be paid for in full at one time. If this had been the case, a landlord could immediately have had a large sum of money for capital to make an adequate start in a business investment. Adequate investment is always one of the important conditions for business success. Instead, the land prices were paid in twenty, equal installments spread over a period of ten years. The amount of each installment was too small to start any sound business. This argument, of course, ignored the most fundamental purpose of the land reform, which was to get rid of the evils of the traditional, tenancy system and to help the tenant-cultivators establish themselves as owner-farmers. No tenant would be able to make full payment for the land at one time, or in less than ten years.

The landlords also argued that in paying the landlords with stock shares, the Government should have provided that the percentage be higher than 30, and that the shares be concentrated in fewer holdings, rather than so thinly scattered among all of them. It is common sense that anyone who wishes to participate in the operation of an enterprise must have a large enough bloc of its stock. Instead, the Government's provision gave a small number of shares to every landlord. The number was so small that it neither gave the holder any sense of ownership in the business, nor power in controlling it, ncr security in depending on it for even part of his living. This was why most of the landlords attached very little importance to the holding of their shares and why they often sold the shares in a very careless manner. Some landlords suggested that the Government should let them choose any one, or two, of the corporations according to their judgment, and then pay their land price with the stocks selected.

Ideally, and from a businessman's point-of-view, these were all intelligent suggestions. But the Government would have had great difficulties in putting such measures into effect. Who, for instance, would choose the landlords in whose hands the shares of stocks should be concentrated? Would not the concentration, if really made, give rise to a small number of new, big-business people and leave a large number of small, ordinary landlords out of favor? Would this be fair? In regard to the percentage of the corporation stocks, opinions have also been diverse. There must have been a great number of landlords who would certainly have opposed a percentage greater than 30. At the time, just after completion of the land-to-the-tiller program, many people preferred the land bonds in kind rather than shares of corporation stocks.

Finally, in many cases, the landlords themselves were responsible for the failure, and the losses suffered in the change of occupation, or in the establishment of a new business. In business operation, the most common mistakes made by the landlords were: (1) too heavy investment in the physical plant; (2) over-hiring of personnel, in order to include relatives and friends, for whom the proprietor then had great difficulty in arranging duties and commanding their services; (3) too much emphasis on hierarchy, so that persons in high positions, or in leadership positions, seldom took part in work which required physical labor and soiled clothing; and (4) carelessness in selecting partners. These mistakes had mercilessly pushed numerous naive and careless businessmen into bankruptcy, or ruined the possibility, and opportunity, for development of a business.

IV.   Other Observations on the
Landlords' Change in Occupation

The former landlord's own information and evaluation of their experience, in regard to change of occupation, might have been too subjective, too fragmentary, and too saturated with their unpleasant feelings. In trying to free the survey from all such shortcomings, people of businesses and small and medium-sized industries were interviewed. The purpose was to look for facts and problems relating to failures, as observed by uninvolved people. The following is information given by business men and industrialists in small towns.

1. Observations of the rural town business people. Of the 100 business people interviewed in the towns, 31 per cent believed that after land reform the former landlords became more interested in, and more energetic about, going into business or industry. About the same number of people, 32, took an opposite stand. They felt that a majority of the former landlords had become pessimistic, or discouraged, about establishing businesses or industries for themselves. Twenty-three people said a minority of the former landlords took a positive attitude, and 25 of them said a minority of the landlords took a negative attitude. In expressing their varied observations on the former landlords' attitudes toward going into business, our samples were, again, almost equally divided. This can, however, be a reflection of the landlords' confused, or uncertain, mental situation in the early period after land reform. Their confusion made other people's observations confused, too. Probably that is why the data presented above looks so very paradoxical.

Concerning what former landlords had done about their stock shares,
most town business people stated that a great majority had sold the shares;
only a small number had kept them.

Seventy of the 100 samples believed that there had been few landlords
who entered business after their land was purchased by the Government.
Asked whether they had any specific idea about the number of landlords who
had gone into businesses, more than half of the samples said, not many;
the number was small. Only 27 of them said, many. Three of them did not
answer the question. But in answering another question, 49 of these people
listed a total of 750 persons whom they knew had entered business after
land reform. On the average, they named more than 15 people each. This
seems to be inconsistent with the first statement which said, not many, or,
the number was small. As to the success, or failure, of the landlords who
had entered new businesses, about half of the samples thought that the new
business people had been doing all right. Only a few of them said they had
been doing very well.

Altogether, the samples mentioned 13 kinds of businesses which the
former landlords had entered. They included buying and selling on the
markets; operating financial organizations; operating general stores and
wholesale businesses; operating appliance stores or department stores;
managing theaters; dealing in grains; selling agricultural chemicals and
Western drugs; operating soda fountains or cold drink parlors, textile shops,
stationary shops, trade agencies, and van or moving services.

Fifty-four per cent of the business people believed that the Government
had had no significant success in its objective of transferring the landlords from the land into business and industry; only 20 per cent of them

thought it had been achieved; 26 per cent could not answer the question.

How should the Government have aided the landlords in changing occupation? Only 30 of the 100 samples could answer this question, and their answers were: by making business loans available at low interest rates; by offering knowledge, technical training and employment guidance; by guaranteeing the value of the corporation stocks; by paying the landlords in cash instead of stocks and land bonds; by reducing the rates, or amounts, of the various kinds of taxes; by encouraging people to establish new enterprises; and by letting the landlords sell the retained land.

2. Observations of the rural town industrialists. The industrialists had no consensus on how many of the former landlords had considered industry as a new occupation. In regard to the kinds of landlords who might have thought of changing their occupation to business or industry, about half, or 43 per cent, of the rural town industrialists thought it was the large landlords; less than half, or 45 per cent, thought it was those landlords who had had some middle-level education. Only a few people thought that other kinds of landlords also had the idea of going into business or industry.

What kinds of occupational opportunities were available in the years immediately after land reform? Twenty-eight people mentioned industries; 42 said businesses; 19 thought of government services and teaching. A few mentioned professional work, employment in civic organizations, and others.

A great majority, 83 per cent, had observed a general trend in the years following land reform: people who had money and had been informed of new economic affairs were likely to leave the farm for business or industry. Varied reasons were thought to have produced the trend. People had begun to complain that farming was hard work and its cash income smaller, and less predictable, than the income from business. They saw that business and industry earned more profits, ran less risks, required funds were easier to get, and the work was lighter. They noted that businesses and industries were then in a period of fast growth. Also, many people had lost interest in land or farming as an investment because they were afraid there might be another land reform after a few years. Gallin's case study supports this generalization.[6]

Had the Government clearly advised the landlords to sell their land, to make investments, or actively enter business or industry? Thirty-six per cent of the industrial people interviewed answered,"yes,"while 57 per cent said,"no." If the Government had really given such advice, would the landlords have understood its meaning and significance; would they have paid attention to it? A few people said most landlords did understand and had paid attention to the Government's advice. But more people believed that only a small number of the landlords understood and paid attention to it.

What was the attitude and reaction of the industrial people toward this kind of advice coming from the Government? The answers to this question suggest that the number of business and industrial people who took a favorable attitude, and expressed welcome to the landlords, were greater than the number of people who took an opposing stand and were afraid of the competition from the landlords or other newcomers.

About half of the 100, rural town industrialists reported that some of their landlord relatives, or friends, had entered businesses, or industries, after land reform. According to these people's information, although the number of landlords who succeeded in businesses or industries was comparatively small, those who met bankruptcy or suffered serious losses were also few. The majority were experiencing normal conditions. Of those

who were within such conditions, some liked to say the business was not good,

while others preferred to say they were "just getting along."

A great percentage of these people felt that the landlords' most fre-

quent difficulties were: lack of knowledge and experience needed in business

or industrial operations, too little capital for making necessary shifts and

business maneuvers, insufficiency of technical assistance, lack of management

capability, and inability to counter the keen competition in the business

world. What could, or should, the Government, or society at large, have

done to help the landlords? A comparatively large number of the industrial

people suggested Government loans at low or reasonable interest rates, to-

gether with some sort of supervision to see that the loans were really used

to strengthen business. Also, more technical assistance should have been

given by the Government or other appropriate agencies.

In summary, the observations and opinions were quite divided and in-

conclusive. Some people felt sure that to a great degree, the changes of

occupation had been successfully carried out, while others assumed a more

pessimistic point of view and ascertained that the efforts had largely

failed. Here, we must take into consideration the possibility that the

business people and industrialists in those rural towns could have been

narrow-minded and jealous when the landlords invaded their sphere of

interests. They might have considered the coming of the landlords a threat

to their economic stake. If this were true, they would certainly have made

discouraging statements about the matter. I am not suggesting that this

had actually caused these differences of opinion; but simply that something

of this nature could have been operating here.

Observations of the Rural Town Business People and
Industrialists on the Landlords' Change of Occupation

A. The rural town business people's observation:

1. Took a positive attitude toward going into business
   and industry

Number of landlords	Number of business people thought so	
All	5	8.48%
Majority	31	52.54
Minority	23	38.98
Total	59	100.00

2. Took a negative attitude toward going into business
   and industry

All	10	14.92
Majority	32	47.76
Minority	25	37.32
Total	67	100.00

3. Beliefs concerning disposition of corporation stocks

	Sold	Kept	Bought	Unknown
All landlords	17	1		21
	23.95%	1.85%		75.00%
Majority	45	10		3
	63.38%	18.52%		10.71%
Minority	9	43	3	4
	12.67%	79.63%		14.29%
Total	71	54		28
	100%	100%		100%

4. Personally acquainted with landlords who entered business
   after land reform

Yes	70	70.00%
No	28	28.00
No answer	2	2.00
Total	100	100.00

Number of landlords known to enter businesses: 49 business
people listed 750 landlords, an average of 15 per person.

B. The rural town industrialists' observation:

1. Estimates concerning the number of landlords who had considered changing their occupation to business

Great majority	24	24.00%
More than half	29	29.00
Less than half	21	21.00
Very few	22	22.00
No answer	4	4.00
Total	100	100.00

2. Opinions as to what kind of landlords thought of changing their occupation

Big landlords	43	43.00%
Above middle class, educated	45	45.00
Other kinds	3	3.00
No answer	9	9.00
Total	100	100.00

3. Opinions concerning opportunities for a change of occupation

Industries	28	28.00%
Commerce	42	42.00
Public services	19	19.00
Professional	8	8.00
Civic organization	1	1.00
Others	2	2.00
Total	100	100.00

4. Estimates of change as a general trend: people of funds and enlightenment likely to go into business and industry

Yes	83	83.00%
No	15	15.00
No answer	2	2.00
Total	100	100.00

5. Opinions regarding Government's advising of landlords who went into business

Yes	36	36.00%
No	57	57.00
No answer	7	7.00
Total	100	100.00

6. Evaluations of the landlords' reaction to Government's advice

A majority paid attention and understood	13
Few paid attention	22

7. Evaluations of business people's attitudes toward this advice

Approving	22	22.00%
Welcoming	7	7.00
Opposing	7	7.00
Fearing competition	15	15.00
No answer	49	49.00
Total	100	100.00%

V. Conclusion

From what has been presented, it is clear that those landlords who were already in business, or some other type of livelihood having nothing to do with farms, before the enforcement of the land-to-the-tiller program generally mildly objected, or did not object at all, to the Government's compulsory purchase of their land. They either passively agreed to sell the land or happily took the opportunity to shift their land investment to a business investment. A second group of landlords, who had been able to go into businesses or other non-farm occupations and make a comparatively satisfactory living immediately after completion of land reform, made few, or none, of the bitter complaints heard against land-reform programs. They were completely occupied with their new work. They had little time to think of earlier injustices. A third group of landlords were those who entered business and failed the first time, perhaps a second time, but finally succeeded. While they were suffering hardship because of failure, they spoke many bitter words about land reform. When the suffering was over and the business became stable, they not only forgot the pains inflicted by the land reform, but they also realized that their early failures were chiefly their own fault. Once they had come to this realization, land reform was no longer the target of attack. Only those landlords who were not in any one of these three groups, who made neither a plan for change, nor a decision to remain in farming or to start actual farming, said harsh words and bore hard feelings toward land reform from the very beginning up to the present.

In view of these facts, it should be obvious that (1) any kind of land reform, which involves the compulsory purchase of land, ought to be undertaken after as many landlords as possible are already in business, or in other enterprises, which have little to do with farm land directly, and/or (2) it is made easy for landlords to enter new occupations after their land has been purchased. If such conditions are not present, the Government ought to do everything possible to promote or create them. In other words, if a democratic, land-reform program is to escape formidable and bitter opposition from the landlords, it is most important that the authorities have various means ready and available to assist the landlords change their sources of livelihood.

Actually, only a small number of Taiwan's medium and big landlords continued to prefer the life of collecting farm rents. A great many of them really wanted to go into businesses or industries. But because many did not have the necessary knowledge or experience, or the courage or determination, they either failed in their tries or never tried at all. If the Government had really done its best to help them, their early feelings and opinions about land reform might have been different. There is no doubt that the change of the landlords' occupation was one of the Government's primary objectives in the land-reform movement. But, unfortunately, the Government neglected its responsibility to extend assistance which the landlords needed so badly.

The long-range goal of land reform in Taiwan, and in mainland China as well, should not be limited to, or even emphasized too strongly, a mere redistribution of the ownership of the farm land. It must also emphasize enlarging the size of individual farms. Under present conditions, the smallness of the farms is such a serious deterrent to modernization and mechanization that significant advances can hardly be hoped for. A most rational way of enlarging the size of farms is to reduce the size of the agricultural population, i.e., shift as many farmers as possible to occupations other than farming. If this is difficult at the present time to absorb a large number of small farmers into business and industry, the Government should at least take the opportunity offered by land reform to make all necessary kinds of help available, and to encourage at least the exlandlords to change their occupations into non-farm activities.

The chief point to be stressed here, however, is that today, any land reform should not merely emphasize the redistribution of landownership or the correction of agrarian injustices. Its chief objective ought to be farms of efficient and economical sizes, upon which the most modernized and productive agriculture can be developed. Only with this kind of agriculture will a progressive, prosperous, and culturally-advanced, agrarian community be possible. Such a community is the ultimate objective of any kind of land-reform program. In this sense, the land problem in Taiwan is still far from being resolved. The reform undertaken ten years ago did not achieve the goal emphasized in this chapter; and one of its proudest accomplishments, the redistribution of landownership, might later become a hindrance in the development of a modernized agriculture.

This does not mean, however, that the undertaking of the past land reform should be regretted. Under the circumstances which existed at that time, where many landlords owned large tracts of land, each tract being cultivated by a large number of tenants, the farm-tenancy situation was extremely miserable. Therefore, the solution of this tenancy problem became the first objective of the land reform in Taiwan.

Notes

[1]Facts about the Implementation of the Land-to-the-Tiller Program in Taiwan, edited by Yi Teng, p. 635.

[2]Ibid., Chapter II, pp. 418-19.

[3]Ibid.

[4]Ibid., p. 368. Interviewer Heng Shun-liang's diary, August 14, 1964.

[5]Bernard Gallin, Hsin Hsing, Taiwan: A Chinese Village in Change, p. 113.

[6]"To these landlords, especially to many urban people, the Land Reform Program made it evident that it was no longer profitable or even safe to invest their capital in the land. Instead, these people, in addition to their forced participation in industry through being paid in shares of stock for expropriated land, have now in many cases begun to shift their excess capital willingly into industrial, commercial, and small business activities in urban centers and in smaller market towns. When money was invested in small market towns, it usually went into financing light industry or small businesses and often meant that the investor needed new technical knowledge. In some cases, the landlords or their sons became greatly involved in business activities, gradually sold off portions of the three chia of land which they had been allowed to retain under the land reform act, and used the money for additional investments." --Gallin, pp. 113-14.

Chapter Seven

LAND REFORM AND FARM LIVING CONDITIONS

I. Changes Over-all
    1. Former-tenant Households
    2. Current-tenant Households
    3. Former-landlord Households
    4. Original-owner Households
    5. Hired farm-laborer Households
    6. Observations from Non-farm People
    7. Summary
    8. Factors Inhibiting Change

II. Changes in Specific Areas
    1. Food Consumption
    2. Sources of Drinking and Cooking Water
    3. Housing Conditions

(Continued in Chapter Eight)

Both in planning and in launching land reform, the authorities had time and again proclaimed that the highest objective of this great undertaking was to enable farm people to enjoy an improved livelihood. At the end of the decade following completion of land reform, people from practically every walk and level of the nation believed that farm people in Taiwan had indeed progressed to conditions much better than those of ten years earlier, and that the betterment could be attributed largely to the effects of the land reform. In general, their belief was not far from the truth. But just what was the truth remained in question. Some

objective research was needed, and, for this reason, it was that our survey
included information from non-farm informants, as well as from the farm
people themselves. It was our purpose to learn from the farm people themselves, and from non-farm people as disinterested observers, whether living
conditions of farm households really had improved. If, indeed, there had
been improvement, how great was it and to what extent was it attributable
to land reform? Notwithstanding the argument that the reports given by
our particular samples might not be entirely unbiased, it remains nevertheless true that people who had actually experienced the reform, or who had
observed it first-hand, should have information of greater authenticity and
authority than those who lived outside the rural communities. This does
not mean that information contained in governmental and journalistic reports
is to be wholly excluded from consideration, however.

I.   Changes Over-all

First, let us consider the farm people's daily life as a whole.
Later we will go deeper into conditions in those specific areas such as
food consumption, housing, clothing, and others. The reason for making
such a separation is that while in some cases their daily life may be
better than before land reform, one or two specific areas may still be
relatively unchanged, or vice versa. If there were cases in which the
household's daily life was on solid foundation, but the consumption, or
expenditure, in one or two specific areas was still poor, or if the
household's daily life was on a shaky basis, yet the family members were
indulging a fondness for eating good foods and enjoying extravagant
entertaining whenever they could get hold of some money, this lack of

consistency, whether of the first kind or the second, could cause considerable error in appraisals of the household's living conditions. For convenience then, living conditions in the five categories of farm households
were evaluated separately.

1. <u>Former-tenant farm households</u>. Sixty per cent,(59.84),of these
1,250 households reported that their daily life as a whole had become better
since land reform. The number of households which reported no betterment was,
however, also large. It was more than 38 per cent. Chinese people are usually
modest in talking about their own living conditions. They seldom admit to
being well-to-do, or that life is getting better and better. As long as they
don't complain, it means that things are going well. The common expression
they use is "<u>ma-ma hu-hu</u>," equivalent of "so so." But they have no inhibitions
about discussing the conditions of their neighbors. For these reasons, we must
qualify the statements made by sample households concerning their own
daily living conditions, and at the same time take into account the
evaluations made by them of their neighbors. This study took special pains
to ask each sample about the living conditions of his neighbors, that is,
neighbors of his own kind. The result was that about 75 per cent of the
samples said they had seen improvements in their neighbor's daily livelihood. There is a difference of nearly 15 per cent between the number of
households admitting improvements in their own living conditions and the
number of households attributing the same to their neighbors.

2. <u>Current-tenant households</u>. A smaller percentage of current tenants
reported improvements in their daily living conditions. Of the 250 samples,
for instance, 42 per cent admitted that their living conditions had been more
or less improved in the ten years since land reform. About 37 per cent said

there had been no change in their living conditions, and about 21 per cent complained that theirs had actually deteriorated in the ten years. These households also had the characteristics mentioned in the preceding paragraph. About 57 per cent of them said they had noticed improvements in the living conditions of their neighbors of their own kind. Less than 25 per cent denied such an observation. There were, however, more than 11 per cent who thought that their neighbor's living conditions had deteriorated since land reform.

3. _Former-landlord households_. It has been commonly supposed that for great majority of the landlords the land reform's immediate effects were hard and that, therefore, living conditions in these households must have been adversely affected. To a considerable extent this assumption was proved by the survey to be true. Of the 500, ordinary, former-landlord households, less than 8 per cent reported improvements in living conditions. Thirty-five per cent said there had not been much change, but almost 57 per cent complained that their living standards had declined. The former landlords did not make a habit of praising the other fellow's living conditions. Only a very small number of the 500 said they had observed progress in the daily life of other households of their own kind. More than 16 per cent said there had not been much difference, while 80 per cent said that conditions for all of them had become hard due to the effects of the land reform. Similar information came from among the 75, former, big-landlord households. Less than 7 per cent of them reported improvement in their living conditions; 32 per cent said there had not been change of any significance; but more than 61 per cent declared that they had been suffering hardship since land reform. Among these households there was also a great majority, 88

per cent, who said that living conditions of the other landlord households were just as bad as theirs.

4. <u>Original-owner farm households</u>. Opinions of the 250, original, farm households were, by and large, similar to those described above. For instance, only 30 per cent of these households reported improvement in their living conditions; 45 per cent observed not much difference; and 23 per cent complained that they had been living in hardship.

5. <u>Hired farm laborers</u>. Like the landlords, farm laborers were also pessimistic about their low living conditions. According to these people, their poor living conditions were due to difficulty in finding employment. Eighty-two per cent of the 250 samples reported that since land reform it had become harder for farm laborers to find ways of making a living. A small percentage of them said there had not been much difference, but only a few said that it had become easier. About living conditions, again a great majority, 72 per cent, said that they had experienced deterioration in the past ten years. A small portion felt that there had not been much change. Only a few households reported bettered conditions.

6. <u>Observations from non-farm people</u>. Observations made by non-farm people were somewhat different from opinions expressed by the farm people. Of the 100 samples from among local community leaders, 87 per cent said that living conditions of the former-tenant farm households had improved in the last ten years. As for living conditions of the former-landlord households, 82 per cent of these local leaders had not observed much change. Among the 100 teachers and other cultural workers, 92 per cent believed that living conditions of most farm households had improved in the last ten years. Practically all of these samples answered "yes" to the question as to

whether, after completion of land reform, more farm families had been willing and able to send children to educational institutions above the elementary school. This observation indirectly indicated improvement in the farm people's living conditions, since, otherwise, they would not have been willing and able to give their children more education.

Business people in the rural towns held more conservative opinions. Of the 100 samples interviewed, only 66 believed that living conditions of farm households were better than before land reform; 22 per cent thought there had not been much change. But a majority of them reported that their business dealings with farm people had increased in volume; that the farm families had been receiving bigger incomes; and that the farm people's spending had increased in the ten years since land reform. All these changes were signs of improvements in living conditions of the farm households. Among the 100, rural town industrialists, 81 agreed that economic conditions of the farm people had become better ten years after land reform. Seventy-seven per cent to 89 per cent believed there had been increased spending for manufactured farm tools and other farm articles, house building materials and furniture, and other factory-made consumer goods.

For lucidity, all information in the above may be condensed as follows:

A. Former-tenant farm households:

	Households Reporting	
	Number	Percentage

Own conditions

	Number	Percentage
Improvement	748 households	59.84%
No improvement	477	38.16
No answer	25	2.00
Total	1,250	100.00

Neighbors' conditions

	Number	Percentage
Improvement	930	74.40
No improvement	281	22.48
No answer	39	3.12
Total	1,250	100.00

B. Current-tenant farm households:

Own conditions

	Number	Percentage
Improvement	105	42.00
Not much change	92	36.80
Deterioration	52	20.80
No answer	1	0.40
Total	250	100.00

Neighbors' conditions

	Number	Percentage
Improvement	142	56.80
Not much change	62	24.80
Deterioration	28	11.20
No answer	18	7.20
Total	250	100.00

C. Former-landlord households:

1. Ordinary-landlord households

Own conditions

	Number	Percentage
Improvement	39	7.80
Not much change	175	35.00
Deterioration	284	56.80
No answer	2	0.40
Total	500	100.00

	Households Reporting	
	Number	Percentage

Neighbors' conditions

Improvement	7	1.40
Not much change	82	16.40
Deterioration	400	80.00
No answer	11	2.20
Total	500	100.00

2. Large landlord households

Own conditions

Improvement	5	6.67
Not much change	24	32.00
Deterioration	46	61.33
Total	75	100.00

Neighbors' conditions

Improvement	2	2.67
Not much change	7	9.33
Deterioration	66	88.00
Total	75	100.00

D. Original-owner farm households:

Own conditions

Improvement	77	30.80
Not much change	113	45.20
Deterioration	57	22.80
No answer	3	1.20
Total	250	100.00

E. Hired farm laborers:

Finding a job

Easier than before	12	4.80
Harder than before	206	82.40
Not much change	32	12.80
Total	250	100.00

Living conditions

Improvement	20	8.00
Not much change	49	19.60
Deterioration	181	72.40
Total	250	100.00

F. Observations from   Households Reporting
    non-farm people: Number   Percentage

1. Local community leaders (about former- tenant households only)

	Number	Percentage
Improvement	87	87.00
No change	2	2.00
Deterioration	8	8.00
No answer	3	3.00
Total	100	100.00

2. Teachers and cultural workers (about farm households as a whole)

	Number	Percentage
Improvement	98	98.00
Not much change	2	2.00
Total	100	100.00

Education as an indicator of improved living conditions

	Number	Percentage
Increase in education	99	99.00
No increase	1	1.00
Total	100	100.00

3. Rural town business people (about farm people as a whole)

	Number	Percentage
Improvement	66	66.00
Not much change	22	22.00
No answer	12	12.00
Total	100	100.00

Increase in farm income

	Number	Percentage
Increase	77	77.00
Decrease	14	14.00
No change	9	9.00
Total	100	100.00

Increase in farm purchasing

	Number	Percentage
Increase	43	43.00
Not much change	29	29.00
Decrease	27	27.00
No answer	1	1.00
Total	100	100.00

Increase in farm purchasing interest

	Number	Percentage
Increase	49	49.00
Not much change	29	29.00
Decrease	22	22.00
Total	100	100.00

	Households Reporting	
	Number	Percentage

4. Rural town industrialists (about farm people as a whole)

	Number	Percentage
Improvement	81	81.00%
No improvement	18	18.00
No answer	1	1.00
Total	100	100.00%

Purchasing power and willingness to spend for manufactured good

	Number	Percentage
Increase	77	77.00
No change	14	14.00
Decrease	7	7.00
No answer	2	2.00
Total	100	100.00

7. _Summary_. An average two-thirds, 67 per cent, of the former-tenant farm households reported living conditions generally improved in the ten yea after completion of land reform. Less than one-half, 49 per cent, among current tenants admitted improvement in their living conditions. That fewer current tenants than new owners had experienced improved living conditions, is understandable. The new owners had benefited from both the farm rent limitation program and the land-to-the-tiller program, whereas, the current tenants benefited only from the first, i.e., the farm rent limitation progra

Most samples in each of the two landlord categories complained of deter orated living conditions. Usually their complaint was justified. It was justified if only because it was human to complain of suffering and loss after property had been taken away, disregarding the fact that it was not a property confiscation but a proper, though compulsory, purchase with fair compensation. It was also justified by evidence that many of the former-landlord households did have to make a considerable reduction in living expenses. Many of them had suffered tremendous hardships, or austerity, in the period when the money from the sale of their corporation stocks was gone and they had not yet been able to find any new way of making a living. Hard experiences such as these are likely to stay in people's memory for a long time. In the interviews, which took place only five or six years after these sufferings, some of the questions must have touched spots still tender from their pain. Hence the complaining. Most, 77 per cent, of the farm laborers-for-hire also expressed dissatisfaction and cited difficulties in finding jobs and deterioration in their living conditions. These people based their complaints on an alleged probability of unemployment which was largely unfounded in fact. Farm laborers had, in the old days, been hired either on annual or daily bases, by landlords or large-farm tenants, and it was assumed that after land reform, there would be no landlord households left, that the number of large farms would also be considerably reduced, and that, therefore, there would be much less employment for farm laborers. In actuality, the assumption had not proven entirely true. New developments in farming throughout the province in the recent decade had created demand for a great deal more farm labor than before. It is true that only a few farm households now hired on long-term bases. But daily hiring had increased considerably because of new cash crops and new cropping systems, which required constant help of hired laborers. The decrease in long-term hires had really been caused by the farm laborers themselves. It was they who did not want the annual hire. Their chief reason for this was their distaste for being tied to a particular farm. If they were not tied, they could move about according to their own choice or wishes. When the demand was heavy and farm wages were handsomely high, they went to work on the farms. When the demand began to drop and wages were slipping, they changed directions and moved toward the cities or non-farm businesses where opportunities for daily, or seasonal, employment were available.

Among the actual farmers, the original-owner households were those least touched by land reform. Very probably this was the reason why the living conditions in a large percentage, 45 per cent, of these farm households had not undergone much change. If there had been changes, these people were not particularly conscious of them. But because farming in general had made good progress and the national economy was growing, about one-third of these households enjoyed improvements in their total living conditions too. It should be remembered, however, that at the same time, 23 per cent of them suffered deterioration.

The non-farm people's observations on this matter were very optimistic. Practically all local community leaders, as well as the school teachers and other cultural workers, believed that the living conditions of farm people had been greatly improved. There is, however, a question about the validity of their observations. It is possible that community leaders, perhaps in one way or another connected with government agencies and authorities or with the ruling party, might have had personal motives in praising the results of land reform. School teachers and other cultural workers must have assumed that inasmuch as all the land-reform programs had been greatly beneficial to the tenant households, the living conditions in these homes could not but have improved. On the other hand, opinions of business people and industrialists had been somewhat conservative because these people had had direct business dealings with the farm people. Thus, they had reason to carefully watch the economic conditions of the farr

people, those who were their customers and also those who were their farm-
produce suppliers. Under their scrutiny, too, were the living patterns of
farm households. Furthermore, whether in small town or big city, business
people are always careful and shrewd. They speak comparatively carefully-
measured words. Therefore, the information from them should be more
dependable than that given by the other non-farm people.

8. <u>Factors inhibiting change</u>. Although a great majority of the former-
tenant farm households, about one-half of the current-tenant households, and
many original-owner households reported general improvement in their living
conditions, the fact remains that a considerable portion of each of these
groups complained either of lack of progress or of deterioration in living
standards; this should not be passed without explanation. According to
information recorded in the interview schedules, the interviewers' diaries,
and other documents, the following factors pertain.

In the ten or so years following reform, there had been a rapid growth
of population. The number of marriages, and the number of children per
marriage in the several categories of farm households, had risen considerably. In a twelve-year period, 1952-1964, the population of the 1,250
former-tenant households increased by 2,838 persons, from 9,609 to 12,447.
This was a rise of 29.53 per cent. Each one thousand people increased by
295.3 persons in the twelve years, by 24.6 persons each year. In 1952
the average number of persons in each of these households was 7.69, and
it had increased to 9.96 by 1964. This meant an increase of more than
two persons per household. People who have been concerned about the
relation between the growth of population and the increase of farm production fear that the hard-won increase in production of agricultural

commodities can very possibly be immediately consumed as food by the increased population, with no rise at all in the general living standard. In concrete terms, for illustration, each household's annual receipt has increased an average 800 kg. An average person's annual requirement of food is around 370 kg. For two persons the requirement would be 740 kg. Each household increased in size by two-plus persons. Thus, very little could have been realized from the additional resources (the approximate amount saved by the farm rent limitation) beyond these added living requirements. If there is ever to be anything with which living conditions can be improved, it must come from increased farm production. According to information given in Chapter V, most of the farmers had shown some increase in their farm production, but it will continue only when there are no serious natural calamities to damage agriculture.

Unfortunately, there has been no way to keep the natural calamities from coming, and the second factor delaying agricultural growth was bad weather over the two or three years before the survey was taken, such as typhoon, drought, unexpected frost or cold spells, etc. There had been heavy damage to farm lands and crops and considerable reduction of income for many farm households. These adversities had undoubtedly brought very hard times to ordinary, small farmers. When the interview questions touched on living conditions, the still-fresh memories were awakened. It was only natural for the people to complain that their living conditions had become worse instead of better.[1] Since, however, the calamities had not occurred everywhere in the province, farm households in districts where farming had not suffered any serious setbacks in those years reported improved living conditions.

Many of the former- and current-tenant farm households had built
new houses or repaired old ones in the years after land reform. Undoubtedly,
the new buildings, or extensive repairs, had cost a great deal. Not only
would the increase in household income have been spent, but considerable
debts might have been incurred for these purposes. In order to finance
a son's or brother's marriage, or to show the family's new status after
land reform, a new house had to be built or, at the least, the old house
had to be manifestly repaired or remodelled. It had been a common
observation a few years after land reform that new houses started to
appear in farm villages throughout the province and that toward the end
of the ten-year period, they were to be seen in practically every part of
the countryside. Most of these new or remodelled houses belonged to
former- and current-tenant households. As was pointed out above, either
building or remodeling must have cost a great amount of money and the
cost must have drained off a great deal from the increased farm production,
or funds which ordinarily would have gone into other aspects of living.
In the minds of most farm people, 'living' meant food consumption. 'Good'
living meant adequate and superior foods and 'poor' living meant the
opposite. When a household had adequate housing but its food was inadequate,
or inferior in quality, the family head complained that their living
conditions were poor. This, then, was the third factor accounting for the
finding that there were still so many farm households whose living conditions had not improved.

The fourth factor concerned education. After land reform many a farm
household became ambitious to send its boys, perhaps even its girls, to
middle schools and colleges. Nearly all the middle schools and colleges

276

were located in towns and cities far away from the farm villages. Study in such schools or colleges was expensive. An ordinary, farm household usually had to be very frugal in its daily-living budget in order to support a boy, or boys, in school. Thus, it would be unlikely to have any funds left for improving its living conditions.

In spite of all these explanations, there must be farm households whose lack of improvement in general living conditions must be attributed to such factors as the shortage of necessary means, the bondage of old traditions, lack of motivation for advancement, and having been beyond the reach of the effects of land reform.

II. Changes in Specific Areas

In studying changes or improvements in farm living conditions, one should not be satisfied with information concerning only general daily life. One should go farther to know the details in each area of the livelihood. This section concerns the recent changes in such specific areas as food, housing, furniture and facilities, clothing, transportation and communication, and the maintenance of health and sanitation.

1. <u>Food consumption</u>. Before land reform, about 27 per cent of the 1,250 former-tenant farm households ate pure, polished rice; about 67 per cent ate rice plus sweet potato; 10 per cent had sweet potato only; and a very small number ate unspecified other foods as the main staple. As to what were the supplementary foods, of the 2,032 answers received, about 3 per cent constantly had meat and fish in meals; 15 per cent constantly had fish and occasionally had meat; 41 per cent had vegetables only; and a few households had unspecified other foods. But ten years after land

reform, the figures had changed as follows: main staple, 55 per cent polished rice; 43 per cent rice and sweet potato; a few households, sweet potato only. Supplementary foods were, for 9 per cent, constantly meat and fish; 21 per cent had fish always and meat occasionally; 28 per cent had meat or fish infrequently; 37 per cent had vegetables only; and 4 per cent had unspecified other foods.

There were increases in consumption of both main and supplementary foods. Improvement in the main food consumption was indicated in the increased number of households using pure, polished rice and the decreased number of households using other staples. Polished rice had, up to the time of the study, always been considered a superior food. An increase in the number of households using it as the main food meant improvement in the food-consumption aspect of the households' living conditions. Using both rice and sweet potato, rather than using sweet potato only, was an indication of better resources for living. Any increase in the eating of meat and fish was a further sign of improvement. The reason is obvious. Improvement in food consumption is reflected in increased quantity, that is, rise from inadequate amounts to adequate amounts, but another indicator is in change from foods popularly considered to be 'inferior' food stuffs to 'superior' food stuffs. When the living standard is already above subsistence level, any true improvement in food consumption will include considerations of the food's nutritional values and its cultural signi-ficance as well. Living standards in most tenant households in Taiwan at the time of the study were above subsistence level. Therefore, in making judgments about changes in their food consumption, reference to nutritional and cultural factors ought to be included.

Sample households were, therefore, asked whether or not, ten years after land reform, more attention was being paid to the nutritional value of foods consumed. More than 43 per cent answered "yes;" 54 per cent said they had been paying attention to this matter before and had no need to change after land reform. A few households said they were not paying attention to this matter. The samples were also asked whether their women had after land reform become interested in learning new cooking methods from the home demonstration agents or other sources. Only 17 per cent of them said "yes" while 80 per cent said "no." Those who said "yes" meant that their women had joined home-improvement study classes organized by home demonstration agents and those spare time meetings in the farm villages. Cooking, sewing, homemaking, child care, etc., were taught and practiced. The number of farm women attending such meetings had not yet become large.

Although interest in learning new cooking methods had been widely aroused, especially among the younger women, many young, married women were constantly under the surveilance of their conservative mothers-in-law and did not dare ask permission to attend the study meetings. What they could do was to learn individually from neighbor women or cousins who had attended the meetings. Another way was to listen to the radio. The extension agencies sponsored radio programs on home economics. Still another channel through which at least the educated, rural women could learn new methods and new things was the reading of farm magazines. In each issue of the Farmers' Friend, The Harvest, and Life in Farm Villages, many new methods of cooking and food preservation were discussed and illustrated. The "Food for Health" program, which as its name implies, is a basic program, taught farm women and 4-H Club girls how to save food values when cooking vegetables and rice, and how to plan and serve healthful, yet economical, meals. The program urged the raising of more fruits, vegetables, and livestock for family use to increase health and reduce expenses. Accomplishments of the "Food for Health" program were reported[2] as follows:

Improved Practices	Number of Families Adopted Practice
Rice cookery	2,879
Vegetable cookery	2,866
Dietary: Green and yellow vegetables	28,036
" : Fruits	1,324
" : Year-round vegetables	1,531
" : Dried beans and peanuts	1,219
Egg storage	888
Dietary: Balance for three meals	1,849
Slaughter of pigs	679
Others	256

In 1958 there were in the province 296 Home Improvement Clubs with 5,142 farm women members.[3] They were concerned with foods, nutrition, and better cooking methods. These members might well have influenced other farm women five times their own number, as the report estimated.

The current-tenant farm households had undergone similar changes in food consumption. Of the 250 samples, for instance, 33 per cent before land reform ate pure, polished rice; 65 per cent ate rice and sweet potato; about 3 per cent ate sweet potato only for the main food. These figures had changed to 49 per cent, 50 per cent, and less than 1 per cent by the time of the survey. An added sixteen per cent of the households were using pure, polished rice as their main food.

There had been only slight changes in uses of the supplementary foods. Before land reform, about 9 per cent of these households could afford to have meat and fish all the time. Ten years after the figure was somewhat more than 14 per cent. Before land reform, 30 per cent of the households had only fish as supplementary food. Ten years later the figure was between 30 and 31 per cent, and the proportion of households which could have only vegetables was 59 per cent.

A little over 41 per cent of the households said they had been giving more attention to nutrition since land reform, but more than 58 per cent said they had continued the same as before. Only about 30 per cent of them had made changes in their methods of cooking, as a measure toward better nutrition.

The original-owner households did a little better than the current tenants, but less well than the former-tenant households. About 22 per cent of the original-owner households moved up to join the 48 per cent who had been eating pure, polished rice. The households eating rice plus sweet potato had been 51 per cent before land reform, and dropped to 29 per cent ten years after.

Their consumption of supplementary foods had changed very little. Before land reform, about 14 per cent had meat and fish, 19 per cent constantly had only fish, 29 per cent had fish and meat occasionally, and about 39 per cent had only vegetables. At the time of the survey these figures had changed to 19 per cent, 2 per cent, 22 per cent, and 38 per cent.

As to consciousness of nutritional and cultural values, the original-owner households had again gained more than had other farm households.

The number of households paying more attention to food nutrition at the
time of the survey had increased by about 5 per cent, about the same
number had acquired a desire to learn new cooking methods. Somewhat
more than half the total expressed some interest in these matters. The
samples were asked if their womenfolk had, after land reform, become
more interested in the demonstration programs of the township, farmer
associations. Half of the 250, original-owner households answered "yes;"
the other half said "no." It showed once again that women in this category were, at the time of the interview, more enlightened than those in
the tenant households.

Despite the fact that food production in Taiwan had been much more
than enough to meet the needs of the population, the farm people still
suffered from nutritional deficiencies until very recent years. This
was due chiefly to the people's lack of information about nutrition.
The situation has now improved to such an extent that the JCRR report[4]
says, "Through years of efforts from JCRR and various agencies, the
people on Taiwan have gradually become aware of the importance of nutrition in food preparation. This is primarily due to the efforts made by
various health agencies concerned and JCRR. More housewives now select
food on the basis of its nutritional value instead of its taste only.
The nutrient intake of the people, thanks to the increased agricultural
production and other factors, has made further improvement, as shown on
the following pages. Generally speaking, however, the people on the
island are still suffering from low intake of good quality protein, ribo-
flavin, calcium, and thiamine and, to a lesser degree, niacin, vitamin A,
and iron. Ascorbic acid deficiency is mostly seasonal."

Standard Daily Requirement of Nutrients

	Men	Women	Child-tending Women	Children (age 1-12)	Children (age 13-20)
Food energy, cal	2,300-4,000	2,000-3,000		1,200-2,300	2,400-3,800
Protein, gm	70	60	85-100	40-70	80-100
Calcium, mg	1,000	1,000	1,500-2,000	1,000-1,200	1,300-1,400
Iron, mg	12	12	15	6-12	15
Vitamin A, I.U.	5,000	5,000	6,000;3,000	1,500-4,500	5,000-6,000
Vitamin B1, mg	1.4-2.5	1.2-2.0	2.5-3.0	0.6-1.4	1.5-2.5
Vitamin B2, mg	1.8	1.5	2.1-2.5	0.6-1.8	2.0-2.5
Niacin, mg	15-25	12-20	25-30	6-14	15-25
Vitamin C, mg	60	60	80-120	25-70	75-100
Vitamin D, I.U.	-	-	300-600	300-600	400

Average Individual Daily Intake of Nutrients by Farm People

	From Animal Foods	From Plant Foods	Total
Food energy, cal	139.40	2,484.02	2,623.42
Protein, gm	7.20	51.82	59.02
Minerals, mg	108.29	1,512.70	1,720.99
Calcium, mg	38.35	480.08	518.43
Phosphate, mg	69.57	1,121.01	1,190.58
Iron, mg	0.37	11.61	11.98
Vitamin A, I.U.	92.82	5,385.81	5,478.63
Vitamin B1, mg	0.07	1.41	1.48
Vitamin B2, mg	0.04	0.68	0.72
Niacin, mg	1.56	11.43	12.99
Vitamin C, mg	0.73	198.38	199.11

Average Daily Intake of Nutrients by Farm People (Adult male)

	Animal Foods	Plant Foods	Total
Food energy, cal	193.10	3,441.01	3,634.11
Protein, gm	9.97	71.78	81.75
Minerals, mg	150.00	2,095.45	2,245.45
Calcium, mg	53.12	526.49	579.61
Phosphate, mg	96.37	1,552.88	1,649.25
Iron, mg	0.51	16.08	16.59
Vitamin A, I.U.	128.57	7,460.79	7,589.36
Vitamin B1, mg	0.10	1.95	2.05
Vitamin B2, mg	0.05	0.94	0.99
Niacin, mg	2.16	15.82	17.98
Vitamin C, mg	1.01	274.80	275.81

Daily Per Capita Apparent Nutrients Availability on Taiwan

	1948	1953	1957	1958
Food energy, cal	1,911	2,282	2,340	2,314
Protein, gm	41.7	53.42	56.8	56.6
Animal protein, gm	8.1	12.49	14.1	14.6
Calcium, mg	209.6	241.2	270	285
Iron, mg	7.4	8.8	9.4	9.4
Vitamin A, value I.U.	4,842	4,425	4,421	4,679
Thiamine, mg	0.97	1.18	1.25	1.25
Riboflavin, mg	0.41	0.51	0.52	0.56
Niacin, mg	10.5	12.31	13.17	13.09
Ascorbic acid, mg	98	92.84	93.2	96.72

The Research Institute of Taiwan Land Bank made a study on the economy of former-tenant households before the payment of land price in full in 1964.[5] According to this study, the nutritive quality of foods consumed by these farm households is much better than is indicated by the JCRR's 1959 general report just quoted. The charts on pages 282 and 283 describe the standard, daily requirement of food nutrients for Chinese people in general; the average, individual, daily intake of food nutrients by farm people of Taiwan; and the average, daily intake by an adult Chinese man. All the charts are adaptations of those contained in the Taiwan Land Bank Study.

There were still a large number of the farm families whose food consumption had not improved over conditions existing before land reform. Several reasons were given for this: (1) Increase of population. Each family's limited increase in income had largely been used to feed added family members. (2) Increased education. Many farm families now were sending children to middle schools, then colleges, or technical-vocational schools. Many farm parents hoped that at least some of their

children could enter occupations other than their own,and realization of
this ambition required education. Therefore, these families were frugal
in daily living so that money could be saved for schooling. (3) After
the landownership was transferred to the former tenants, their financial
obligations increased tremendously. (4) Some households invested any
added income in farm improvement or in developing supplementary enterprises,
rather than using it for better food or other comforts. (5) There were
still farm families so committed to the virtue of being thrifty that
their consciences just could not let them have any material enjoyment.

Food consumption in former-landlord households had not undergone much
change. It had not deteriorated because of the change in their socio-
economic positions. Before land reform all landlord households had
undoubtedly used the superior main foods, either pure,polished rice or
other good grains. Ten years after land reform their conditions remained
practically the same. Only in supplementary foods had there been some
slight changes. Some of the ordinary, landlord households could no longer
have meats, fresh fish, and high-quality fresh vegetables all the time.
This change was due either to decrease of income or to influence of
those factors mentioned above as affecting consumption trends.

A. Changes in food consumption in former-tenant households:

Food	Before L.R. No.	%	10 yrs. after L.R. No.	%	Change No.	%
(a) Main foods						
Pure,polished rice	332	26.56	688	55.04	+356	107.00
Rice, sweet potato	771	61.68	535	42.80	-236	30.61
Sweet potato only	126	10.08	6	0.48	-120	95.24
Others	21	1.68	21	1.68	0	0
Total	1250	100.00	1250	100.00		

(b) Supplementary foods	Before L. R.		10 yrs. after L. R.		Change	
	No.	%	No.	%	No.	%
Meat and fish constantly	64	3.15	185	8.94	+121	189.00
Fish, constantly	301	14.81	440	21.27	+139	46.18
Meat or fish, occasionally	830	40.85	584	28.23	-246	29.76
Vegetables only	801	39.42	774	37.41	- 27	3.37
Others	36	1.77	86	4.15	+ 50	139.00
Total	2032	100.00	2069	100.00		

The heading "Number of Households" spans the Before L. R. and 10 yrs. after L. R. columns.

(c) Households aware of nutritional values

Aware, changing habits	541	43.28
No change	669	53.52
Paying no attention	36	2.88
No answer	4	0.32
Total	1250	100.00

(d) Women interested in new cooking methods

Interested	215	17.20
Not interested	995	79.60
No answer	40	3.20
Total	1250	100.00

B. Changes in food consumption in current-tenant households:

(a) Main foods

Polished rice	82	32.80	122	48.80	+ 40	48.78
Rice, sweet potato	162	64.80	126	50.40	- 36	22.22
Sweet potato	6	2.40	2	0.80	- 4	66.67
Total	250	100.00	250	100.00		

(b) Supplementary foods

Meat and fish	36	8.55	65	14.25	+ 29	80.56
Fish	127	30.17	139	30.48	+ 12	9.45
Vegetables	241	57.24	235	51.54	- 6	2.49
Others	17	4.04	17	3.73	0	0
Total	421	100.00	456	100.00		

(c) Households aware of nutritional values

Aware, changing habits	103	41.20
No change	146	58.40
No answer	1	0.40
Total	250	100.00

(d) Women interested in new cooking methods	Number of Households				
	Before L. R.		10 yrs. after L. R.		Change
	No.	%	No.	%	No.	%
Interested			74	29.60		
Not interested			175	70.00		
No answer			1	0.40		
Total			250	100.00		

C. Changes in food consumption in original-owner households:

(a) Main foods

	No.	%	No.	%	No.	%
Pure polished rice	120	48.00	174	69.60	+ 54	+45.00
Rice, sweet potato	128	51.20	73	29.20	- 55	-43.00
Sweet potato only	1	0.40	2	0.80	--	--
No answer	1	0.40	1	0.40	--	--
Total	250	100.00	250	100.00		

(b) Supplementary foods

	No.	%	No.	%	No.	%
Meat and fish, constantly	56	13.79	75	19.08	+ 19	+33.93
Fish, constantly	77	18.97	82	20.87	+ 5	+ 6.49
Fish and meat, occasionally	116	28.57	86	21.88	- 30	-25.86
Vegetables only	157	38.67	150	38.17	- 7	- 4.45
Total	406	100.00	393	100.00		

(c) Households aware of nutritional values

	No.	%
Aware, changing habits	127	50.80
No change	106	42.40
Not paying attention	8	3.20
No answer	9	3.60
Total	250	100.00

(d) Women interested in new cooking methods

	No.	%
More interested	130	52.00
Not interested	114	45.60
No answer	6	2.40
Total	250	100.00

(e) Women interested in home demonstration agents' teaching

	No.	%
Very interested	36	14.40
Interested	76	30.40
Still not interested	117	46.80
No answer	21	8.40
Total	250	100.00

D. Changes in food consumption in former-landlord households:

1. Ordinary landlords

(a) Main foods

	Number of Households				Change	
	Before L. R.		10 yrs. after L. R.			
	No.	%	No.	%	No.	%
Pure polished rice	457	91.40	446	89.20	- 11	- 2.4
Others	43	8.60	54	10.80	+ 11	+25.5
Total	500	100.00	500	100.00		

(b) Supplementary foods

	No.	%	No.	%	No.	%
Meat and fish	265	37.27	218	51.05	- 47	-17.36
Fish	99	13.93	104	24.36	+ 5	+ 5.00
Meat	69	9.70	56	13.11	- 13	-18.84
Vegetables	260	36.57	30	7.03	-230	-88.46
Others	18	2.53	19	4.45	+ 1	+ 5.56
Total	711	100.00	427	100.00		

2. Big landlords

(a) Main foods

	No.	%	No.	%	No.	%
Pure polished rice	72	96.00	71	94.67	- 1	
Others	3	4.00	4	5.33	+ 1	
Total	75	100.00	75	100.00		

(b) Supplementary foods

	No.	%	No.	%	No.	%
Meat and fish	49	41.88	29	27.36	- 20	-40.82
Fish	15	12.82	20	18.87	+ 5	+33.33
Meat	10	8.55	4	3.77	- 6	-60.00
Vegetables	33	28.21	47	44.34	+ 14	+42.42
Others	10	8.54	6	5.66	- 4	-40.00
Total	117	100.00	106	100.00		

E. Reasons given for lack of improvement in food consumption:

	No.	%
Increase of family size	386	41.69
Saving money to pay land price	86	9.29
Saving money to pay taxes	94	10.15
Natural calamities	81	8.75
Education costs	73	7.88
Sickness	68	7.34
Marriage costs	25	2.70
Crop failure	34	3.67
Purchasing farm tools	29	3.13
Purchasing additional land	5	0.54
Other farm investment	5	0.54
Others	40	4.32
Total	926	100.00

2. <u>Changes in the sources of drinking and cooking water</u>. Changes in sources and ways of getting drinking and cooking water reflect some measure of improvement in living conditions. For instance, a community whose people carry drinking and cooking water from a shallow pond or a little stream in two pails is usually considered as having a living standard lower than that of the village whose residents draw water from artesian wells and transfer it to houses through either a carefully built pipe or an improvised bamboo tube.

Of the 1250 former-tenant households, about 38 per cent reported improvement in such forms as a change from getting water from open ponds or streams to drawing water from artesian wells; from drawing water from deep wells to using modern water pumps; from getting water from wells to using the community water systems; and other unspecified forms. Some of the 61 per cent who reported no change might already have been getting water from deep wells or using water pumps before land reform. Undoubtedly, some were still relying on primitive ways at the time of the survey.

This writer observed that a great number of the rural townships in Taiwan had built their own reservoirs in the past ten or fifteen years. A township reservoir supplies clean water to all households in the township center through systems of pipes. Many of the large and medium farm villages also had clean water, but households had to carry it from a number of public faucets on the village streets. This was why a number of households reported that the water improvement was accomplished through the help of the township government, the farmers' associations, the district water bureau, the township health stations, or the Provincial Food Bureau. If the improvement were simply the boring of an artesian well and the installing of a water pump, it could very likely have been a household affair, or a project among several close neighbors.

The current-tenant households were in a similar status on this matter at the time of the interview. Before land reform more than 23 per cent of the 250 samples carried drinking and cooking water from ponds and streams; 64 per cent of them got water from wells; a little over 3 per cent had water pumps, and a few households got water from a running system, or in other unspecified ways. After land reform these figures changed to 10 per cent, 52 per cent, 22 per cent, 9 per cent, and 7 per cent.

Among original owners there were also some changes. Before land reform about 19 per cent used drinking and cooking water from ponds and streams; 66 per cent had wells; 4 per cent had water pumps; 5 per cent had running water; and 6 per cent got water from other unspecified sources. After land reform the figures changed to 11 per cent, 39 per cent, 35 per cent, 9 per cent, and about 2 per cent.

The above data are summarized as follows:

A. Former-tenant households:

1. Change

Improvement	473 households	37.84%
No change	766	61.28
No answer	11	0.88
Total	1250	100.00

Among the 766 households which reported no change, there might have been a number of them whose drinking and cooking water was already from wells or sources other than open ponds or streams.

2. Kind of improvement

From drawing water from wells to using water pumps	252	53.28
From well water to running water	102	21.56
From open pond and stream to wells	63	13.32
Unspecified	52	10.99
No answer	4	0.85
Total	473	100.00

3. Sources of assistance for improvement

Township government	91	65.47
Water Bureau	12	8.63
Farmers association	11	7.91
Public Health Station	4	2.87
Food Bureau	5	3.60
Sugar Cane Growers Service Society	1	0.72
Neighbors and friends	12	8.64
Others	3	2.16
Total	139	100.00

B. Current-tenant households:

Water Source	Before L.R.		After L.R.		Change	
Ponds & streams	58 house-holds	23.20%	25 house-holds	10.00%	-33	- 57.00
Wells	160	64.00	131	52.40	-29	- 18.13
Water pumps	8	3.20	54	21.60	+46	+575.00
Running water	3	1.20	22	8.80	+19	+633.33
Other	21	8.40	18	7.20	- 3	- 14.29
Total	250	100.00	250	100.00		

C. Original-owner households:

Water Source	Before L.R.		After L.R.		Change	
Ponds & streams	47 house-holds	18.80%	27 house-holds	10.80%	-20	- 45.22
Wells	165	66.00	97	38.80	-68	- 41.21
Water pumps	10	4.00	88	35.20	+78	+780.00
Running water	13	5.20	22	8.80	+ 9	+ 69.23
Other	15	6.00	4	1.60	-11	- 73.33
Total	250	100.00	238	95.20		
No answer			12	4.80		
			250	100.00		

Food is prepared in the kitchen. Conditions in the household's
kitchen have a close relationship with conditions of food consumption
and water supply. Therefore, we should make brief mention of kitchen
improvements in the farm households. In the past decade the home-
improvement education conducted by extension agents had persuaded many
farm households to make improvements in their kitchens. Traditionally,
the kitchen was the most gloomy and disorganized place in the household.
The women working in it suffered fatigue and irritation all the time.
The food prepared in such a kitchen could hardly meet decent standards
of cleanliness and safety to health. Therefore, the home economics and
extension agents paid first attention to improvements in the farm
kitchens. To be truthful, our survey, undertaken among the 1250 former-
tenant households, did not show that the agents had had any significant
success. Only a little over 30 per cent of the samples reported kitchen
improvements after land reform. A majority, more than 56 per cent,
admitted to no manifest change. But information from other sources[6]

indicated that by 1964 a majority of the farm villages in Taiwan had been reached by the work of the extension agents and in most of these villages there were home improvement, study classes. In these classes the most often discussed and demonstrated subjects had been related to the improvement of kitchens. Furthermore, practically all rural people under 25 years of age had attended schools and had learned there the importance of having a clean and comfortable kitchen. Many had seen for themselves the convenient and clean kitchens in modernized homes. They must have been influenced to want a clean and well-arranged kitchen in their own homes.

3. Housing conditions. Conditions of a household's living quarters account for a great portion of the comfort or misery in its everyday life. Therefore, many a family would take the first opportunity to make changes or improvements in housing once the means were available.

Of the 1250 former-tenant households, 38 per cent built new living quarters in the ten years following land reform. About the same number, 39 per cent, had done repairwork on old houses. But the numbers of households which built, repaired, or remodelled could have been much larger than the survey revealed. Most households which were tenant-cultivators before land reform had been living in very bad conditions. After land reform they had the additional resources of saved farm rents or of increased agricultural production, and the first thing they did was to repair the old houses or to build new ones. The repairing and building were motivated not just by realistic necessity but also by the demands of new, higher socio-economic status and their high morale. Owner households ought to live in houses better than tenants' straw huts.

In one way or another, most former tenants vouched for what has just been reported. For instance, about 48 per cent of them said that their old houses had been in very bad shape. Their repair or replacement was really an urgent necessity. Even if they did not have the money, they still had to do it, with borrowed money if need be, and they were able to borrow because they now owned land. About 19 per cent of these households did the repairing or building because their children were growing up, and they were in great need of more rooms. More than 12 per cent said they improved their homes because they had money, and with higher social status, they wanted to have better houses. Others gave the realistic reason that the old houses had been destroyed, or severely damaged, by typhoons. This reason was cited by more than 17 per cent of the households.

Most of the new houses built by the former tenants were brick-cement-tile, one-story, single-unit houses. Some were two-story buildings, and a very few of them were traditional, mud-straw huts. It is safe to say that the great majority of the new houses in the farm villages were of good materials and in modern styles. Adoption of new materials and styles reflected the farm people's breaking away from old traditions and their growing taste for things in the modern mode.

A home's interior condition and decoration are generally a good index of the household's socio-economic-cultural level. A bright, clean home, neatly arranged, with decoration are signs of the upper levels, whereas, dark, unclean, disorderly, or bare rooms reflect low standards. There has been, however, a kind of irrational agrarian axiom which was in direct contradiction with this general rule. It holds that the truly prosperous farm home will have a yard full of chicken droppings, pig manure, and all kinds of refuse, and inside the house there will be articles, utensils, etc., scattered or piled up everywhere, without any order or arrangement. This disarray was supposed to imply that the people of the household were so busy with farm work and cooking that they hardly had time to do any cleaning and arranging. It is only a poor family, which does not have a good farm to work on, does not have pigs and chickens to keep and feed, nor many children to raise and discipline, that can afford the time, energy, and thought to do cleaning and decorating. Thus, in an inverse way, cleanliness implies a scarcity of the things which a normal, or prosperous, farm household ought to have. Should this tradition still prevail in any rural district, then a dirty, disorderly, undecorated home there may not necessarily mean a low-living standard. In general, especially nowadays, however, the expected rule holds true.

At the time of the interview 33 per cent of 796 former tenants reported that the inside walls of their living quarters were whitewashed or papered. They gave as the reasons for the whitewashing or papering: It is nice or good looking (35 per cent of the households); it helps keep the house clean for the family's good health (about 31 per cent); it makes for better lighting in the house (12 per cent); it indicates the raised living standard, etc. About 63 per cent reported having papered, or whitewashed, in the ten years after land reform. Only 20 per cent had done it before land reform.

The floors of the living quarters characteristically indicate the level of the household's standards. Mud floors reflect, in most cases, poverty or low standards while cement- or brick- paved floors signify improved standards. In this regard, one should be informed of the fact that cement only recently became a cheap, widely used building material in the ordinary farm villages. Formerly, only rich families lived on brick-paved floors. All others lived with floors of mud, or hard-beaten earth. There was no intermediate material between brick and mud or earth. It was only in the last twenty or thirty years that cement floors began to appear in farm homes. A change from a mud floor to a cement floor represented a marked improvement in housing.

Of the 1250 former tenants, 46 per cent now had cement floors; 51 per cent had floors which were not paved with cement or with bricks, therefore must have been mud floors. Of those households whose floors were paved with cement, 51 per cent added the paving in the ten years after land reform; about 26 per cent already had it before land reform; and a similar number could not remember when the floor was first paved. All told, then, only a little over 23 per cent had made the improvement of changing mud floors to cement or brick paving.

The amount and kinds of furnishings in a family house mean a great deal to the household's living standard, not only in material worth and physical comfort, but also culturally and socially. About one-half of these 1250 farm households had been able to add new pieces of furniture or appliances to those they already had in the house. The total number of the new pieces was 935, of which 37 per cent were radio sets; more than 25 per cent were electric fans; 22 per cent, ordinary tables and chairs; 6 per cent, upholstered chairs; 4 per cent, sewing machines; the remaining 6 per cent were cabinets and chests of drawers, electric phonographs, beds, electric cookers, electric irons, kitchen cabinets, clocks, refrigerators and television sets.

As to their reasons for these purchases, about 54 per cent of the 598 households said it was out of necessity; 46 per cent reported it was intended to show that their living conditions had been improved. There were even 13 per cent who felt that the house furnishings in an owner's household ought to be different from, and better than, those in a tenant household, both in amount and in quality. As to cultural considerations, 19 per cent of the households believed that there should be paintings, calligraphic scrolls, pictures, or other artistic works decorating the walls in the living room, dining room, and bedrooms. Although this is a small percentage, it, nevertheless, indicated that among the small-farmer households, appreciation of living was no longer limited to material sufficiency, but had begun to seek aesthetic or spiritual satisfactions. This is far above a peasant-living standard. When had this kind of consciousness arisen? More than 63 per cent of the 238 former-tenant households which answered this question said it began to grow after they had become owner-farmers through the land reform; 32 per cent claimed that they had had such tastes even before land reform.

Another indicator, which is closely associated with housing conditions, is the source of artificial light for daily use. In the primitive and peasant stage of living, artificial light came mostly from crude-oil burners and candles. When resources for living were improved, light usually came from various types of kerosene lamps; still later, gas light would appear. But thus far the highest degree of attainment in man-made sources of light is the electric lamp. Today the city people no longer experience, or remember, the delight which came from the first use of electric light. But in the rural districts of Taiwan the coming of electric power to a farm village and the installation of electric lights in a home still represents a significant step in the progress of the farm people's livelihood. The Government's long-established, rural-electrification program had made it much easier and faster to get electricity into farm homes. Even so, the farm households had to pay their shares of the costs before the light could actually arrive. For instance, the installing of electric lamps in 951 households cost NT$875,134. Each household paid an average charge of more than NT$920.

Our study found that more than 91 per cent of the 1250 households had electric lights and that 55 per cent of these homes acquired it after land reform. In the farm villages, at the time of the interview, the use of electric light in a home denoted higher social status, at least in the opinions of more than 38 per cent of the former-tenant, now-owner households.

Ten years after land reform, changes in the housing conditions of the current-tenant farm households were observed at the time of the survey as these: About 62 per cent of the 250 samples had repaired or remodelled their old houses; of these, 39 per cent did a complete rebuilding and about 62 per cent did partial repairing. In most cases of complete rebuilding, the homes were re-done in new styles and with better materials. The most frequent change was the replacement of the old mud and straw hut with a brick-and-tile, one-story house. Another important difference between the old and the new was that the old houses had had very little window space. The so-called windows were simply a couple of holes in the walls with a few wooden bars as a frame. In the new houses there were real windows with standard wooden framing and panes. Some homes which had been rebuilt were now quite modern structures, but most farm

homes were still in the traditional pattern with minor modifications.
Reasons given by current-tenant families for repairing or rebuilding
their houses were much the same as those given by the former-tenants,
now-owners, as mentioned above.

At the time of the survey, 65 per cent of these households were living
in brick-and-tile, one-story houses; less than 18 per cent were still in
straw huts; a few lived in bungalow-shaped, but solid, modern buildings;
and some homes were of unspecified types. Before land reform more than
85 per cent of the houses occupied by these tenant households had mud
floors; only a little more than 12 per cent had cement floors. After
land reform there had been some change, though not much. The number
of houses with mud floors decreased, to less than 65 per cent. This was
a 20 per cent decrease in the ten years. The number of houses with
cement floors increased from just over 12 per cent to about 33 per cent.
This, too, was an improvement of 20 per cent. At the time of the survey
less than one-half of these tenant households had whitewashed, or papered,
the interior walls of their houses. More than 55 per cent of them still
left the walls bare and dark. In most cases (70 per cent) in which
whitewashing or papering were done, it had occurred after land reform.

The degree of electrification in the current-tenant households was
just as high as in the homes of the former-tenant, now-owner households.
At the time of the survey about 95 per cent of the tenant homes had
electric lights; more than 60 per cent of these had been installed in the
ten years following land reform. The average installation cost was NT$916.

About one-half of the 250 current tenants added furniture in their
houses after land reform. Among the new pieces, about 40 per cent were

electric fans; 31 per cent, sofa chairs, tables, and plain chairs; about 15 per cent, radio sets; about 13 per cent, sewing machines; the remainder were miscellaneous pieces. Just one-half of these households declared that the new furniture was a necessity, whereas, the other one-half admitted that it was meant to show improvement in their living conditions. Only a small number, a little over 11 per cent, had cultural or decorative articles such as paintings, calligraphic scrolls, or pictures in the house. Practically all these families acquired their aesthetic tastes and the art objects in the years after land reform.

More than 40 per cent of the 250 original owners had built new houses after land reform. The new homes were of brick-and tile, or brick-and timber, and some were two-story structures. Others were still in the farm-village house style. The average cost of the new buildings was NT$70,529. More than one-half of the households had done repairing on their old houses. In most cases, repairs were major ones, such as a new roof, or changing a mud-straw hut into a brick-and-tile structure. The average cost of such repair was NT$6,765. Where had the households gotten the money they needed? More than one-half, 57 per cent, said it came from their own farm's production. About 25 per cent had borrowed from relatives, friends, or financial institutions. Some households used earnings from their supplementary enterprises. A few used the proceeds from sale of other possessions. Another small number earned it through a variety of miscellaneous activities.

More than 70 per cent of the households which had repaired or rebuilt houses did the job mainly because the old houses were about to collapse or because the children were growing up and there was an urgent need for more rooms. Others had had to repair or rebuild because typhoons or other calamities had destroyed them. There were also households which did the rebuilding because when their socio-economic conditions had improved, they felt that they ought to have better living quarters.

Over one-half, 58 per cent, of these households had whitewashed or papered their interior walls. Many had done so in the years after land reform. Before land reform 60 per cent of the households had lived in houses with mud floors; about 33 per cent had houses with cement floors; a few had brick floors. Ten years later these figures had changed to more than 34 per cent; and about 59 per cent, respectively. There was no change in the number of brick floors, but the increase in cement floors was more than 20 per cent.

There were households among the original-owner farmers whose homes did not have electric lights at the time of the survey. The number was very small, less than 4 per cent. About one-half of the households had had electricity even before land reform. The average cost of installation in these households was much larger than in the tenant households, NT$2,092 as compared with NT$916.

More than one-half, 56 per cent, of these original-owner households had added new pieces of furniture. The total number of the new pieces was 270 which included more than 30 per cent radio sets; 28 per cent electric fans; about 18 per cent tables and chairs. The others were sofa chairs, electric phonographs, sewing machines, electric irons, bicycles, etc. Most, 67 per cent, of the households which added new pieces of furniture said it was out of necessity that they did the buying. Others, about 32 per cent, admitted that the presence of new and modern furniture showed the rise in their living standard. A small percentage had paintings calligraphic scrolls, pictures, or other objects of art to decorate their homes. And those which had these things acquired the taste in the ten years after land reform.

The former-landlord households made few changes in their housing conditions. In most cases, change was not needed because they had had comparatively good houses for a long time. Only those who had had to move from their original homes to enter new business undertakings had to have some change in the housing conditions. About 40 per cent of these households had moved to a better house; 28 per cent moved to a similar house; and less than 9 per cent went to an inferior house. In many a case, the housing of a former-landlord household at the time of the survey no longer represented the true level of its living. In other words, a former-landlord household might have difficulty otherwise in maintaining a decent living standard, but its house was still the old and magnificent residence.

Ten years after land reform the great majority of former-landlord households were still living in good houses. Of 208 households which gave answers to questions regarding their housing conditions, more than 66 per cent had brick-and-tile houses; about 19 per cent had Western-style, two-story houses. A small number lived in Japanese-style, wooden houses. The interior of most landlord houses was whitewashed, or papered, or panelled. There were draperies on windows, art pieces on walls, and ornamental objects in the main rooms. Most of these homes had radio sets, electric phonographs, electric fans, electric irons, sofa or easy chairs, sewing machines, organs, refrigerators, etc., among other furniture of

good quality. These houses were floored with bricks, with patterned and
transparent cement, or with wood and tatami. All had electric lights.

To summarize the data on housing conditions:

A. Former-tenant, now-owner households:

(a) Housing built after land reform

New houses built	476 households	38.08%
Did not build	761	60.88
No answer	13	1.04
Total	1250	100.00

Kinds of houses built

Brick-and-tile, one-story	234 units	79.60%
Cement, one-story	17	5.78
Two-story	6	2.04
Partial brick	4	1.36
Straw-and-mud blocks	26	8.84
Other	7	2.38
Total	294	100.00

(b) Housing repaired

Did repair house	487 households	38.96%
Did not repair	730	58.40
No answer	33	2.64
Total	1250	100.00

Kinds of repair

Replace straw roof with tile	45 units	10.53%
Roof repair	259	60.65
Wall repair	49	11.48
Whitewashing	16	3.74
Remodelling, complete	17	3.97
Remodelling, partial	35	8.23
Other	6	1.40
Total	427	100.00

(c) Reasons for building and repairing houses

Old house collapsing	427 households	47.87%
Children growing up	165	18.50
Old house destroyed by calamities	154	17.27
To show improved socio-economic status	111	12.44
Moved to a new place	13	1.46
Other	22	2.46
Total	892	100.00

(d) Interior walls

Whitewashed or papered	263 houses	33.04%
Bare wall	522	65.58
No answer	11	1.38
Total	796	100.00

Purpose of whitewash or paper

Sanitation	113	30.70%
Appearance	130	35.32
Better lighting	44	11.96
Had rebuilt the house	51	13.86
Show higher living standard	17	4.62
Influenced by neighbors	9	2.45
Other	4	1.09
Total	368	100.00

When done?

Before land reform	101	20.12%
After land reform	316	62.95
Could not remember	85	16.93
Total	502	100.00

(e) Flooring

Paved, cement or bricks	574	45.92%
Unpaved*	635	50.80
No answer	41	3.28
Total	1250	100.00

When paved

Before land reform	147	25.61%
After land reform	292	50.87
Could not remember	135	23.52
Total	574	100.00

(f) Lighting

Electric	1140	91.20%
Not electric	108	8.64
No answer	2	0.16
Total	1250	100.00

Electricity installed

Before land reform	492	43.16%
After land reform	625	54.82
Could not remember	23	2.02
Total	1140	100.00

---

*Unpaved floors were not necessarily mud floors. Some might have been wood, tatami, or other types.

(g) Furnishings

Added new pieces	560	44.80%
None added	678	54.24
No answer	12	0.96
Total	1250	100.00

Item added

Radios	347 units	37.11%
Electric fans	238	25.45
Tables, chairs (plain)	202	21.60
Sofa chairs	53	5.67
Sewing machines	38	4.06
Electric phonographs	10	1.07
Beds	9	0.96
Electric irons	7	0.75
Electric cookers	7	0.75
Kitchen cabinets	4	0.43
Clocks	3	0.32
Refrigerator, television	2	0.21
Other	2	0.21
Total	935	100.00

Reasons for adding

Necessity	320 households	53.51%
To show better living	274	45.82
No answer	4	0.67
Total	598	100.00

Owner households should have better furnishings than
tenant households

Should	160	12.80%
Should not	955	76.40
No answer	135	10.80
Total	1250	100.00

(h) Rooms should be decorated with art pieces

Yes	238	19.04%
No	999	79.92
No answer	13	1.04
Total	1250	100.00

First believed in need for art objects

After becoming owner-farmers	151	63.45%
Before land reform	76	31.93
Could not remember	11	4.62
Total	238	100.00

B. Current-tenant households:

    (a) Houses rebuilt or repaired

Yes	154 households	61.60%
No	96	38.40
Total	250	100.00

        Kinds of repair

Complete	59	38.31%
Partial	92	59.74
No answer	3	1.95
Total	154	100.00

        Type of rebuildings: converting mud-straw huts to brick-tile houses.

        Reasons for rebuilding

Old house collapsing	122	70.93%
Children growing up	21	12.21
Improved comfort	11	6.40
Other	18	10.46
Total	172	100.00

    (b) Interior whitewashed or papered

Yes	110	44.00%
No	139	55.60
No answer	1	0.40
Total	250	100.00

        When done?

Before land reform	31	28.18%
Recently	77	70.00
Could not remember	2	1.82
Total	110	100.00

    (c) Floors

Kind of floor	Before L.R.		After L.R.		Change	
Mud	214	85.60%	162	64.80%	-52	- 24.30%
Cement	31	12.40	82	32.80	+51	+164.50
Other	5	2.00	6	2.40		
Total	250	100.00	250	100.00		

No. of households

    (d) Electric lights

Yes	236	94.40%
No	14	5.60
Total	250	100.00

When installed?

Before land reform	78	33.05%
After land reform	143	60.59
Could not remember	15	6.36
Total	236	100.00

(e) Furnishings

Added	121 households	48.40%
None added	129	51.60
Total	250	100.00

Items added

Electric fans	56 units	39.16%
Sofa chairs, tables	44	30.77
Radio sets	21	14.68
Sewing machines	18	12.59
Other	4	2.80
Total	143	100.00

Reasons for adding new pieces of furniture

Necessity	65 households	50.00%
Show better living	63	48.46
No answer	2	1.54
Total	130	100.00

(f) Art pieces

Owned art pieces	28	11.20%
Owned none	219	87.60
No answer	3	1.20
Total	250	100.00

C. Original-owner households:

(a) Housing built after L.R.

Built	101 households	40.40%
Did not build	147	58.80
No answer	2	0.80
Total	250	100.00

Kinds of construction: Brick-and-tile, one story; Western, two-story; brick-and-wood; traditional farm house (brick, stone, and tile).

(b) House

Did repair	129	51.60%
No repair	114	45.60
No answer	7	2.80
Total	250	100.00

Kinds of repair included complete remodelling and partial repairing.

(c) Reasons for building and repairing

Old houses collapsing	74	39.57%
Children growing up	62	33.16
Old houses destroyed	28	14.97
Better living conditions	23	12.30
Total	187	100.00

(d) Sources of money

Farm production	137	57.08%
Borrowing	59	24.58
Supplemental work	25	10.42
Miscel. earnings	12	5.00
Sale of possessions	7	2.92
Total	240	100.00

(e) Interior whitewashed or papered

Yes	145	58.00%
No	105	42.00
Total	250	100.00

When started

Before land reform	44	30.35%
After land reform	64	44.13
Could not remember	37	25.52
Total	145	100.00

(f) Floors

Kind of floor	Number of Households Before L.R.		After L.R.		Change	
Mud	150	60.00%	86	34.40%	64	- 42.67%
Cement	82	32.80	147	58.80	65	+ 79.27
Brick	16	6.40	16	6.40	0	0
Other	1	0.40	0	0	1	0.40
No answer	1	0.40	1	0.40		
Total	250	100.00	250	100.00		

(g) Electric lights

Yes	241	96.40%
No	9	3.60
Total	250	100.00

When installed

Before land reform	114	47.30%
After land reform	106	43.99
Could not remember	21	8.71
Total	241	100.00

(h) Furnishings

Added	140	56.00%
None added	109	43.60
No answer	1	0.40
Total	250	100.00

Items added

Radio sets	82 units	30.37%
Electric fans	76	28.15
Tables, chairs	48	17.78
Sofa chairs	27	10.00
Chests-of-drawers	12	4.44
Electric phonographs	8	2.96
Sewing machines	8	2.97
Electric irons	4	1.48
Bicycles	5	1.85
Total	270	100.00

Reasons for adding

Necessity	100	71.43%
To show better living	40	28.57
Total	140	100.00

(i) Art pieces

Owned pieces	66	26.40%
Owned none	176	70.40
No answer	8	3.20
Total	250	100.00

When bought?

Before land reform	26	39.39%
Recent years	40	60.61
Total	66	100.00

D. Former-landlord households:

(a) Moved from former home

Yes	78	13.57%
No	497	86.43
Total	575	100.00

(b) New house as compared to original house

Better	30	38.46%
Similar	24	30.77
Not as good	7	8.97
No answer	17	21.80
Total	78	100.00

(c) Types of housing

	Before L.R.		After L.R.		Change	
Brick-and-tile	121 answers	62.05%	141	64.38%	+20	+16.53%
2-story	30	15.38	43	19.64	+13	+43.33
Timber	10	5.13	10	4.57	0	0
Straw	7	3.59	3	1.37	- 4	-57.00
Stone	8	4.10	2	0.91	- 6	-75.00
Other	19	9.75	20	9.13	+ 1	+ 5.27
Total	197	100.00	219	100.00		

(d) Interior decorations

Decoration	Before L.R.		After L.R.		Change
Whitewash or paper	391 answers	42.55%	414	44.66%	+23 + 5.88
Window drapery	229	24.92	237	25.57	- 8 - 3.45
Art pieces	189	20.57	182	19.63	- 7 - 3.70
Antiques, heir-looms and others	110	11.96	94	10.14	-16 -14.56
	919	100.00	927	100.00	

According to these figures, the percentages of households which built new houses and/or repaired old houses were quite large among the former-tenant, current-tenant, and original-owner farmers. When the instances of building new houses are separated from repair of old houses, it is seen that the percentage of households which built is smaller than the percentage of households which repaired.

Reasons given for building new houses, remodelling old houses, and decorating or adding to furnishings, were largely practical ones. Only a small percentage of the households admitted that they simply thought they ought to have better houses to show off their recent economic progress.

Electricity had been installed in more than 95 per cent of the farm households at the time of the survey. This great progress was largely

attributed to the Government's rural-electrification program which had
been greatly assisted by JCRR funds. It should also be attributed to
the farmers' ability and willingness to pay the costs which were not
insignificant.

It must have been true that before land reform the energies of
tenant households were entirely devoted to the tasks of making a subsistence. They could hardly spare thought or means for beautifying
their homes, or for artistic enjoyment. After land reform the conditions
were changed. At the time of the survey, among each of the first three
categories of farm households, there was a modest percentage whose rooms
were decorated with paintings, calligraphic scrolls, pictures, and other
objects. This change could only have resulted from improvement of
economic conditions and increase of education.

Finally, the housing levels of the former-landlord households had
not undergone much change after land reform. Most of them had had good
houses when they were landlords. There was no need to make changes after
land reform. Those landlords who had entered businesses or industries
and moved to new places had usually gone into modern or Western-style
apartment buildings. There were, however, a few former-landlord households which had been faring very badly and had to move from good houses
into inferior ones.

Notes

[1]See the interviewers' diaries; reports on agricultural damages inflicted by the various natural calamities.

[2]Report on The Accomplishment of Agricultural Extension Education Work in Taiwan during 1958 by the Taiwan Provincial Farmers' Association, pp. 20-21.

[3]Ibid., Table 7. Distribution of Home Improvement Clubs in Different Townships (1958).

[4]JCRR General Report X, pp. 87-88

[5]An Analysis of Farm Family Economy of Owner Operations under the Land-to-the-Tiller Program in Taiwan, by Nien-tsing Lu, Chapter 10, pp. 233 - 46.

[6]JCRR General Report X, pp. 87-88.

Chapter Eight

LAND REFORM AND FARM LIVING CONDITIONS

(Continued from Chapter Seven)

4. Clothing
5. Transportation and Communication
6. Health Care

III. Relationship between Land Reform
and Changed Farm Conditions
1. Farm Rent Limitation Program
2. Land Reform in Total
3. Land Reform's Influence on
Specific Areas of Farm Life

IV. Conclusion

---

4. <u>Clothing</u>. Even the casual observer would notice that the clothes worn by people in Taiwan in the last ten years were much better than those worn before. Not only have city people been dressing themselves well; farm people have been doing so too.

(1) Former-tenant households. Of these 1,250 households, almost 59 per cent reported that their family members were either "much better" or "better" clothed than before land reform. The other 41 per cent did not say "better," only that the "difference was not big." Here the word "difference" meant change or improvement. Big, or not big, was a matter of

personal opinion. The change or improvement was stated in terms of quantity and quality. In quantity it was reported that the farmers after land reform had more work clothes, more dress suits for social functions, and they also had apparel for everyday wear at home. Formerly, a farmer usually would have only one or two suits or outerwear and these had to serve all occasions. Now he had the means and opportunity to own one or two sets of clothing for each of such purposes as working in the field, being at home, and going out visiting. The quality of clothing worn by villagers was quite similar to that found in the city. Everyday clothes were made of khaki materials, while clothes for dress occasions were usually of synthetic fabrics, woolen cloth, or silk. More than 90 per cent of the clothing of both men and women was in modern or Western styles, and special attention was given to cut and good looks.

When these households were asked whether they thought that farm people as a whole had become better dressed since land reform, 80 per cent gave affirmative answers. The betterment was expressed in the same terms as those given above. Another important point was that most farm people interviewed stressed the fact that farm people no longer had to wear clothes with holes or patches or garments made of gunnysack. These were often seen in the old days, before land reform.

Reasons for the improvement were given as: First, improvement of the farm people's economic condition and; second, the abundance, good quality, and low prices of textiles. These were the two most important reasons, each given by more than 33 per cent of the samples. Reasons next in importance were that the use or adoption of modern and luxurious things had begun to appear in the daily life of the farm households; being well-dressed and fashionable was one of the important factors accounting

for a person's social status; and people who had decent social positions

liked to wear better dress. Undoubtedly, all these are effective motives

for changes in habits of dress at any time in any society.

An American professor, while recently studying rural life in Taiwan,

observed that, "In the same spirit women now dress well not only for

festivals but simply to go to town. Because they are not afraid of being

criticized, or rather pay little heed to criticism when given, they dress

not only for their husbands and if unmarried, for young men, but for

style, which I suppose means for the sake of other women. Although an expert

might be able to distinguish a village girl from her urban sister because

of dress style when the former visits the city, I certainly could not.

A woman who had but an hour or so before been spreading the "night soil"

in the vegetable patch could be seen on the streets of Taichung in as

fetching an outfit as anyone in the city and wearing a hair style that was

as modern as those of London."[1]

In the farm households of Taiwan making the family's clothes was at

the time of the study still considered a regular task of the women.

Therefore, the possession of one or two sewing machines per household was

a matter of necessity, or at least it was no longer considered a luxury.

This did not mean, however, that every farm household had one or two

sewing machines. Women who did not have one had to do their sewing at

the neighbor's or give the business to a tailor's shop. The survey

found that almost 63 per cent of the 1,250 households had sewing machines.

Of this number less than one-half had bought the machine for themselves,

and more than one-half had gotten it through daughters-in-law who brought it as part of the dowry. With the possession of a sewing machine, a desire for new and modish clothing, and access to good but low-priced materials, many young women were willing to learn the art of making their own and their men's clothes. For instance, about one-half of the 1,250 households reported that their women had specially studied the cutting and sewing skills at sewing classes. Many other women learned the trade in informal ways, as from their own mothers, sisters, and neighbors.

(2) Members of the current-tenant farm households made similar observations. For instance, about 85 per cent of the 250 tenant-farm households reported that in the ten years after land reform the farm people, as a whole, had become self-conscious about the kind and quality of clothes they wore. Motivated by this, farmers and their families became interested in buying or making better clothes whenever they could afford to do so. More than 57 per cent of the 250 sample households reported that the clothes worn by their people at the time of the interview were either "much better" or "better" than those before land reform. About 43 per cent of them said there had not been much change in their clothing conditions.

According to these households, their clothing had improved in both quantity and quality. Their people were now able to have clothing suitable to various purposes and occasions, which had not been true in the old days. In quality their garments were comparable to those modern styles of the owner-farmers and varied suitably in accordance with seasons and occasions. No longer did tenant-farmers and their family members wear torn or patched clothes. Clothes made of gunnysack had also disappeared from the farm villages.

Concerning reasons for these improvements, opinions of the current-tenant farm households coincided with those given by the former-tenant-now-owner households.

More than one-half of the current tenants had sewing machines at the time of the survey, and in the same number of households there were women who had learned tailoring either in sewing classes or from mothers, sisters, or neighbors.

(3) When the 250,original-owner households were asked about the clothing conditions of farm people in general ten years after land reform, 90 per cent of them thought that considerable improvement had occurred. When the question was asked in reference to their own household members, about 65 per cent admitted great or moderate improvement in clothes. More than 35 per cent thought they had not made any significant change.

The clothing in these households also had improved in both quantity and quality. In quantity each person had more garments and more variety among them. In quality the new fabrics were much better and the garments were more up-to-date and stylish. People of these households, as had people of the other farm households, emphasized the fact that ten years after land reform no farm people wore torn or patched garments, except when working in muddy fields or messy barnyards. Clothes made of burlap had long disappeared from farm homes. Even the cloth flour bags were now seldom used for making men's or boy's summertime work shorts or shirts, as had been done in the old days. At the time of the survey practically all work clothes were made of khaki cloth or synthetic fibers.

Again, agreeing with farm people of the other categories, the original-owner households believed that the big improvement in their clothing conditions should be attributed chiefly to the improvement of the farmer's economic status and the availability of abundant, good, and low-priced textiles. They cited, also, the beginning among young people of a new boldness for spending money on luxurious things, the rise of the family's social standing along with its rising economy, and the new way of judging people's status according to their dress.

In this connection there was at least one factor on which the original-owner households surpassed those in the other two categories. More than 81 per cent of the original-owner households had sewing machines. Most had been bought in the years after land reform. In nearly all of these households, there were also women who had learned sewing, from other family members or from farm women's study classes.

(4) As for the clothing conditions of the former-landlord households, we discovered a small number of them who were clothed even better than before and another small number whose clothes were inferior to those they wore in the old days, but a majority of them had made no significant change. Those whose clothing had become inferior were in households which had not been able to succeed in any new occupation since their farm land had been purchased by the Government through the land-to-the-tiller program.

Changes in the various farm households' clothing conditions can be summarized as follows:

A. Former-tenant-now-owner households:

(a) Opinions on clothing conditions of farm people, in general, ten years after L.R.

Better	1,000 households	80.00%
Not better	198	15.84
No answer	52	4.16
Total	1,250	100.00%

(b) Clothing conditions of their own household members

Much better	172	13.76%
Better	563	45.04
Not much difference	510	40.80
No answer	5	0.40
Total	1,250	100.00%

(c) Improvement in quantity: Different clothes for different occasions or conditions, and more than one unit or suit in each kind of clothing: work clothes, dress suits, and everyday wear.

(d) Improvement in quality: Work clothes and daily wear were made of khaki cloth or synthetic materials. Dress suits were made of woolen or synthetic materials or silk. No farm people had to wear torn or patched garments, or clothes made of gunnysack, or cloth out of flour bags.

(e) Reasons for improvement

Economic improvement	579 answers	33.57%
Abundant dress materials	572	33.16
Modern living	271	15.71
Social importance of clothing quality	184	10.66
Improvement in social status	119	6.90
Total	1,725	100.00%

(f) Owned sewing machine(s)

Yes	786 households	62.88%
No	454	36.32
No answer	10	0.80
Total	1,250	100.00%

(g) Woman member learned to sew

Yes	548	43.84%
No	475	38.00
No answer	227	18.16
Total	1,250	100.00%

B. Current-tenant households:

(a) Opinions on clothing conditions of farm people, in general, ten years after L.R.

Better	211	84.40%
Not better	37	14.80
No answer	2	0.80
Total	250	100.00%

(b) Clothing conditions of their own household members

Much better	29	11.60%
Better	114	45.60
No change	107	42.80
Total	250	100.00%

(c) Improvement in quantity: same as A (c).

(d) Improvement in quality: same as A (d).

(e) Reasons for improvement

Economic improvement	124 answers	38.75%
Abundant dress materials	97	30.32
Modern living	57	17.81
Social importance of clothing quality	41	12.81
Other	1	0.31
Total	320	100.00%

(f) Owned sewing machine(s)

Yes	144 households	57.60%
No	103	41.20
No answer	3	1.20
Total	250	100.00%

(g) Woman member had learned to sew

Yes	141 households	56.40%
No	109	43.60
Total	250	100.00%

C. Original-owner farm households:

(a) Opinions on clothing conditions of farm people, in
     general, ten years after L.R.

Better	225 households	90.00%
Not better	21	8.40
No answer	4	1.60
Total	250	100.00%

(b) Clothing conditions of their own household members

Much better	65 households	26.00%
Better	96	38.40
No change	89	35.60
Total	250	100.00%

(c) Improvement in quantity: same as A (c).

(d) Improvement in quality: same as A (d).

(e) Reasons for improvement

Economic improvement	121 answers	32.70%
Abundant dress materials	123	33.24
Modern living	61	16.49
Social importance of clothing quality	44	11.89
Improvement of social status	21	5.68
Total	370	100.00%

(f) Owned sewing machine (s)

Yes	203 households	81.20%
No	47	18.80
Total	250	100.00%

(g) Woman member had learned to sew

Yes	202	80.80%
No	48	19.20
Total	250	100.00%

D. Former-landlord households:

Most former-landlord households made no significant change
in their clothing conditions. Only a small number of them
had more, and better, clothes after land reform, and only
a small number had become worse in this respect.

5. <u>Transportation and communication</u>. The survey discovered that 1,115 of the former-tenant households had a total of 2,143 bicycles, an average of two per household. More than 59 per cent of the 1,250 households in this category had purchased new bicycles since land reform. The same was true of current-tenant households. About 90 per cent owned bicycles at the time of the interview and most had bought them in the years after land reform. The original-owner and former-landlord households had an even higher ratio; the average number of bicycles per household was much more than two. Most machines had been bought after land reform.

People owned bicycles more from daily necessity than because of a desire to show prosperity, or so the interviewers were told by a majority of both former-tenant and original-owner households. The use of bicycles had increased considerably in the ten years after land reform.

The number and frequency of visits or trips away from home should indicate a household's, or a community's, conditions in respect to transportation. If there is frequent travel outside the local community, it must be that transportation facilities are relatively adequate. Therefore, our samples were asked if they had been making more frequent out-of-community journeys since land reform. Twenty-eight per cent of the 1,250 former-tenant households gave affirmative answers; 71 per cent said "no." A majority of those who did make more trips admitted that they had been able to do so because their economic conditions had become much improved after land reform. The findings were generally the same for current-tenant and original-owner households. Among the latter, however, the percentage of households which reported increased out-of-community traveling was much larger than in either the former-tenant or the current-tenant households.

The transportation used by the farm people was, first, bicycles for short distances; and second, buses and trains for long distances. More than 63 per cent of the former-tenant households agreed that in the ten years after land reform many more farm people were traveling by buses. They attributed this change to two facts: The bus service had become accessible to all but a few of the farm villages, and bus fares had been so reasonable that practically everyone was able to afford them. Besides, farm people had become quite liberal in spending money for this kind of purpose. Similar findings were made among current-tenant and original-owner households. In the past ten years farmers had been encouraged by the agricultural-extension agents to make organized, farm-observation tours to different areas. Most farmers were fond of participating in the tours. They learned new things and also enjoyed the pleasures of the trips.

More than 50 per cent of the former-tenant households stated that their writing and receiving of letters had increased in frequency after land reform. As reported previously in this chapter, among the new furnishings bought since land reform, the most frequent in all households had been the radio set. The radio has for some years been one of the most popular media of mass communication.

Other communications media which had become available to Taiwan's farm households in the decade after land reform were farm magazines, such as The Harvest and the Farmers' Friend, teaching circulars published by agricultural-extension agencies, mobile, information-education units, and various exhibits. The two-way communication channels, by which the farm people exchanged information, included agricultural-extension agents, neighbors and friends, farm-and-home study classes, 4-H clubs for rural youth, itinerant sales people, etc. All these had expanded tremendously in numbers and effectiveness in the years after land reform.[2]

Information presented in the foregoing can be summarized as follows:

A. Use of bicycles:

    (a) Former tenants

Owned bicycles	1115 households	89.20%
Number of bicycles per household	1.92	

    (b) Current tenants

Owned bicycles	222	88.80%
Number of bicycles per household	1.57	

    (c) Original owners

Owned bicycles	234	93.60%
Number of bicycles per household	2.32	

B. Bicycles bought after land reform:

(a) Former tenants	738	59.04%
(b) Current tenants	---	---
(c) Original owners	250	100.00%

C. Reasons for purchases (the first 3 categories of farm households together):

A daily necessity	850 answers	86.47%
Economic conditions better	109	11.09
No answer	24	2.44
Total	983	100.00%

D. Increased travel after land reform:

   (a) Former tenants

Yes	349 households	27.92%
No	886	70.88
No answer	15	1.20
Total	1,250	100.00%

   (b) Current tenants

Yes	49	19.60%
No	201	80.40
Total	250	100.00%

   (c) Original owners

Yes	93	37.20%
No	149	59.60
No answer	8	3.20
Total	250	100.00%

Few farm people would admit that they were interested in traveling because they were supposed to work hard all the time while at home. But, actually, many farmers today like to make tours out of their communities.

E. Increased use of bus service:

   (a) Former tenants

Yes	790	63.20%
No	447	35.76
No answer	13	1.04
Total	1,250	100.00%

   (b) Current tenants

Yes	165	66.00%
No	84	33.60
No answer	1	0.40
Total	250	100.00%

   (c) Original owners

Yes	180	72.00%
No	58	23.20
No answer	12	4.80
Total	250	100.00%

F. Reasons for increased use of bus service (the first 3 categories of farm households together):

(a) Bus service had become available in the rural districts and the bus fare was reasonable   664 answers   58.50%

(b) Farmers now have more money   31   2.73

(c) Combination of the two   421   37.09

(d) No answer   19   1.68
          Total   1,135   100.00%

G. Increased writing and receiving of letters (former-tenant households only):

Yes   659 households   52.72%
No   582   46.56
No answer   9   0.72
          Total   1,250   100.00%

H. Mass Media:

Since land reform, a great majority of the farm households in Taiwan keep in communication with the outside world through numerous kinds of mass-communication media. The important ones are radio, farm magazines, and agricultural-extension teaching materials.

6. Health care. As it has been pointed out previously in this chapter, one criterion of the living standard of a household is the quantity and quality of its health care. For this reason, our survey investigated environmental and personal sanitation and the upkeep of health in farm households during the years following land reform.

The first requirement for keeping a household in good health is a clean and neat environment inside and outside the home. It was rather a surprise to hear that more than 86 per cent of the 1,250 former-tenant households were paying attention to keeping the house and the yard clean and neat, and that more than 56 per cent of these households claimed they had been doing so before land reform. Information from the current-tenant households was similarly encouraging. More than 85 per cent of the 250 samples said they were trying to keep their living quarters clean and neat, and more than one-half of them had been doing so before land reform. The original-owner farm households were doing even better. Almost 94 per cent of the 250 samples declared that they were doing their best to keep their houses and yards clean and neat. Almost 63 per cent of these households said that the effort was not anything new. They had been doing so before land reform.

But, the observations of this writer, the interviewers, and many other non-farm people suggested there was some discrepancy between information given by these farm households and the real conditions in their homes and yards. There were, indeed, numerous farm homes and yards which could be considered clean and neat, but certainly their numbers could not constitute those high percentages. Therefore, we could not but feel that the farm households were boasting in this matter. Their boasting was understandable, however. Few people in any civilized society could easily admit carelessness in keeping one's own body and home clean and neat. A great majority of the farm people were sufficiently civilized to know that decent people live in decent homes with decent things. If they considered themselves decent people, which they proudly did, they had to say they gave attention to keeping their homes and yards neat and clean. Besides, the farm people could have had different standards of cleanliness and neatness; things not considered clean and neat by non-farm people might be clean and neat enough according to the farmer's yardstick.

The treatment which people seek for their own illness, or illness of
their beloved ones, is a criterion whereby their degree of enlightenment
and the decency of their daily life is measured. People who have a
high standard of living generally go to modern, scientifically-trained
physicians and use modern, scientifically-prepared medicines and
facilities in illness or in maternity cases. Those who go to see the
primitive "medicine man," who resort to ignorant and superstitious methods
or accept unclean religious articles, usually have a living standard
which is low in every way. What had been the standards in the various farm
households before and after land reform?

"Before land reform, when sickness occurred in your household where
did you go for consultation and treatment?" To this question 1,910
answers were collected from the former-tenant households. Of this number
33 per cent had gone to Western physicians;[3] more than 41 per cent relied
on Chinese, or traditional, medicine; over 11 per cent went to temples
and burned incense; about 9 per cent consulted their gods at home; less
than 1 per cent went to the local health station; about 3 per cent visited
unregistered or secret medicine men; and about 2 per cent resorted to
places or things unspecified. After land reform these percentages changed
to 69.47, 19.59, 2.46, 1.92, 2.58, 1.60, 2.33, respectively. The number
of people going to Western physicians for sickness treatment had increased
tremendously. Needless to say, this increase reflects an equal degree
of decrease in the number of people who went to backward or primitive
places or institutions.

Similar improvements occurred among the 250, current-tenant farm

households. Before land reform, only a little over 30 per cent of them
went to see Western physicians when they were sick. About 50 per cent
depended on traditional Chinese medicine. After land reform more than
72 per cent took advice and prescriptions from the Western physicians;
only 19 per cent still went to see the "Chinese doctors" or used Chinese
medicines. A few households still had faith in primitive or superstitious
religious rituals. The original-owner households had a much better standing in this matter. Even before land reform more than 40 per cent of
them had confidence in the Western physicians, and this percentage increased
to nearly 70 per cent after land reform.

"Before land reform, what did you do when one of your women was about
to deliver a child?" To this question there were 1,800 answers from the
first three categories of farm households. Of this number only a little
more than 1 per cent had been taking the women to a maternity hospital.
More than 47 per cent were getting help from a trained maternity nurse,
and about 51 per cent got help from an "experienced" person, either among
members of the same family or among the neighbors' elder women. A few
households had assistance from other unspecified sources. Ten years after
land reform the number of farm women who went to a hospital for delivery
was still very small, only a little over 4 per cent, but the number of
households which received help from trained,maternity nurses increased
tremendously. From 47 per cent before land reform the number had grown
to 81.2 per cent. The number of households which still depended on
"experienced" women for help decreased to less than 13 per cent. Up to
this date only the middle and upper classes of the city people, and the

rich and better-educated farm people,would believe that their women ought
to go to a hospital to deliver. That more than 80 per cent of the farm
mothers now had assistance from a trained and registered,maternity nurse
represented a considerable advance in this aspect of farm life.

The extent to which the people of a community have learned to take
medical measures to prevent outbreaks of disease is another index of
advancement. Generally speaking, people with advanced living standards
are accustomed to inoculations, physical examinations, and other preventive efforts toward controlling disease. Those who live only on a
subsistence level seldom realize the necessity for such measures and,
therefore, often refuse to accept them. As the standard of living
gradually rises, the number of people who believe in preventive efforts
also increases. By the same token, when the number of people who believe
in taking measures to prevent disease increases, it means that their
living standard is rising.

Before land reform about 33 per cent of the tenant-farm households
regularly took the two or three injections needed every year for the
prevention of epidemic diseases. Another 40 per cent of them took the
injections irregularly; and the others never took them. Original-owner
households did better. More than 38 per cent took the injections regularly
every year and the same percentage took them irregularly, while only 23
per cent never took them. After land reform the percentages changed
considerably. Almost 73 per cent of the former-tenant-now-owner households were taking the injections regularly; 25 per cent were taking them
irregularly; and only a very few households did not take them at all. Of
the current-tenant households, about 83 per cent took the injections

regularly, and less than 16 per cent took them irregularly. The original-owner households again ranked higher than the others. Almost 88 per cent of them took the injections regularly, and fewer than 12 per cent took them irregularly.

The farm households seemed to have very little affection for, or confidence in, the health stations located at the centers of the townships. Only 10 per cent of the former tenants, 12 per cent of the current tenants, and 17 per cent of the original owners said that before land reform they went to the health station whenever they needed treatment. The majority of persons in all three categories either had never gone there or had visited only a few times. After land reform the situation changed, but the change was not significant. Only 27 per cent of the first category, 33 per cent of the second, and 39 per cent of the third had made a call at the health station. Those who called only occasionally, or did not call at all, were still in heavy preponderance.

Explanation of this reluctance to call on the health station probably lies in the fact that the station's chief functions were prevention of epidemic diseases, disseminating information among the local population, and giving examinations and advice to expectant mothers. Most farm people in Taiwan are still unwilling to see a physician or anyone else who had anything to do with taking care of people's health, unless they are actually ill. The health station does not treat sick people, nor does it sell drugs. Therefore, it does not have much practical appeal for the ordinary people.

The information collected concerning improvements in health care can be summarized as follows:

A. Cleanliness of home and yard:

    (a) Former tenants

Paying attention	1,076 households	86.08%
Not paying attention	146	11.68
No answer	28	2.24
Total	1,250	100.00%

When begun?

Before land reform	606	56.32%
After land reform	466	43.31
Could not remember	4	0.37
Total	1,076	100.00%

    (b) Current tenants

Paying attention	213	85.20%
Not paying attention	32	12.80
No answer	5	2.00
Total	250	100.00%

When begun?

Before land reform	125	58.68%
After land reform	84	39.44
Could not remember	4	1.88
Total	213	100.00%

    (c) Original owners

Paying attention	234	93.60%
Not paying attention	8	3.20
No answer	8	3.20
Total	250	100.00%

When begun?

Before land reform	147	62.82%
After land reform	79	33.76
Could not remember	8	3.42
Total	234	100.00%

B. Source of care during illness:

    (a) Former tenants

	Before L.R.		After L.R.		Change	
Western physician	643 house	33.19%	1,131 house	69.47%	+488	+ 75.89%
Chinese medicine	786	41.35	319	19.59	-467	- 59.41
Temples and incense	214	11.26	40	2.46	-174	- 81.31
Family gods	170	8.94	32	1.92	-138	- 81.18
Health station	12	0.63	42	2.58	+ 30	+250.00
Unregistered physician	49	2.58	26	1.60	- 26	- 47.00
Others	36	1.89	38	2.33	+ 2	+ 5.56
Total	1,910	100.00	1,628	100.00		

    (b) Current tenants

	Before L.R.		After L.R.		Change	
Western physician	109	30.36	232	72.27	+123	+113.00
Chinese medicine	178	49.58	62	19.31	-116	- 65.17
Temple and incense	25	6.96	5	1.56	- 20	- 80.00
Family gods	39	10.86	10	3.12	- 29	- 74.36
Others	8	2.24	12	3.74	+ 4	+ 50.00
Total	359	100.00	321	100.00		

    (c) Original owners

	Before L.R.		After L.R.		Change	
Western physicians	164	40.29	246	69.68	+ 82	+ 50.00
Chinese medicine	156	38.33	79	22.37	- 77	- 49.36
Temple and incense	48	11.79	7	1.98	- 41	- 85.41
Family gods	33	8.12	11	3.14	- 22	- 66.67
Others	6	1.47	10	2.83	+ 4	+ 66.67
Total	407	100.00	353	100.00		

C. Source of care in childbirth:

    (a) Former tenants

	Before L.R.		After L.R.		Change	
Hospital	4	0.31	52	4.21	+ 48	+120.00
Trained maternity nurse	600	46.08	1,014	81.97	+414	+ 69.00
Experienced woman	696	53.46	171	13.82	-525	- 75.43
Others	2	0.15	0	0		
Total	1,302	100.00	1,237	100.00		

(b) Current tenants

Hospital	16	6.40	6	2.40	− 10 − 62.5
Trained maternity nurse	111	44.40	204	81.60	+ 93 + 83.7
Experienced woman	115	46.00	35	14.00	− 80 − 69.5
Others	7	2.80	5	2.00	− 2 − 28.5
No answer	1	0.40	0	0	
Total	250	100.00	250	100.00	

(c) Original owners

Hospital	2	0.80	17	6.80	+ 15 +750.0
Trained maternity nurse	136	54.40	203	81.20	+ 67 + 49.2
Experienced woman	103	41.20	20	8.00	− 83 − 80.5
Others	8	3.20	10	4.00	+ 2 + 25.0
No answer	1	0.40	0	0	
Total	250	100.00	250	100.00	

D. Preventive injections:

(a) Former tenants

Take regularly	409	32.72	910	72.80	+501 +122.4
Take irregularly	544	43.52	314	25.12	−230 − 42.7
Never take	288	23.04	17	1.36	−271 − 97.5
No answer	9	0.72	9	0.72	
Total	1,250	100.00	1,250	100.00	

(b) Current tenants

Take regularly	81	32.40	207	82.80	+126 +156.0
Take irregularly	92	36.80	39	15.60	− 53 − 57.6
Never take	75	30.00	2	0.80	− 73 − 97.3
No answer	2	0.80	2	0.80	
Total	250	100.00	250	100.00	

(c) Original owners

Take regularly	96	38.40	219	87.60	+123 +128.1
Take irregularly	96	38.40	29	11.60	− 67 − 69.7
Never take	58	23.20	0	0	0
No answer	0	0	2	0.80	
Total	250	100.00	250	100.00	

E. Use of the health station:

(a) Former tenants

Use it when needed	125	10.00	337	26.96	+212	+169.60
Seldom use it	464	37.12	594	47.52	+130	+ 28.02
Never use it	613	49.04	305	24.40	-308	- 50.24
No answer	48	3.84	14	1.12	- 34	- 70.83
Total	1,250	100.00	1,250	100.00		

(b) Current tenants

Use it when needed	30	12.00	83	33.20	+ 53	+177.00
Seldom use it	88	35.20	114	45.60	+ 26	+ 29.55
Never use it	122	48.80	53	21.20	- 69	- 56.57
No answer	10	4.00	0	0		
Total	250	100.00	250	100.00		

(c) Original owners

Use it when needed	42	16.80	98	39.20	+ 56	+133.33
Seldom use it	95	38.00	101	40.40	+ 6	+ 6.32
Never use it	100	40.00	47	18.80	- 53	- 53.00
No answer	13	5.20	4	1.60	- 9	- 64.62
Total	250	100.00	250	100.00		

These figures reveal an average increase of more than 75 per cent in numbers of households calling on Western-trained physicians when family members were sick. The number of households using trained, maternity nurses in childbirth increased by about 68 per cent, and the average number of households regularly taking preventive injections increased by 127 per cent. It has been assumed previously in this section that increasing reliance on modern, scientific, trained physicians and nurses, and scientifically-made drugs and instruments for the maintenance of good health and the treatment of disease, is indicative of a rising standard of living. If this assumption is sound, then living conditions in the farm households in Taiwan did improve during the ten years after land reform.

III. Relationship between Land Reform
and Changed Farm Conditions

That there had been improvements in the living conditions, both general and specific, of most farm households since land reform has been established. Our further task was to find out the relationship, if any, between these improvements and the land reform.

1. <u>Farm rent limitation program.</u> The 37.5% Farm Rent Limitation Act made savings, either of grains or cash, for the tenants. This meant increases in their annual incomes, and it was very possible that the added resources had been used to improve the conditions of the daily living. Before land reform farm-rent rates averaged 50 per cent of the main crop. The reformed rate was 37.5 per cent. The tenant household thus gained 12.5 per cent in farm receipts. The amount of paddy land rented by a tenant household before the land-to-the-tiller program averaged 1.5 hectares. The average amount of rice produced on such a farm was around 7,200 kg a year. Before the limitation on farm rent the tenant had to give at least 3,600 kg of this to the landlord. He could keep only the other 3,600 kg for himself and his family. After enforcement of the program, he gave only 2,700 kg, and his family kept 900 kg more than before. The cash value of 900 kg of rice in the early 1950's was about NT$2200. This was the average, and, in many cases, the value was much larger. For instance, where land was more productive, and the rice production higher, the old rental rate had been higher than 50 per cent, even as high as 60 per cent or more. It it were reduced from 60 per cent, the amount of grain so saved by rent limitation would have been 1,620 kg, or NT$3,904. To people of means, the addition of NT$2,220,

or NT$3,904, to its income would not have been important. To an ordinary-
tenant household, however, adding either of these amounts to its scanty

income would mean a great deal toward the improvement of its living

conditions.

The information collected among the former tenants agrees generally

with the preceeding data. About 65 per cent of these households reported

that before land reform, they paid an average 51 per cent (51.62%) of the

main crop as rent. In kind, it was 2,393.12 kg of grain per ha, per year.

If the tenant cultivated 1.5 ha of land in rice, the total rent in kind

would have been 3,489.70 kg of rice. If this was 51.62 per cent of the

total production, the total production would have amounted to 6,954 kg.

When the rent was limited to 37.5 per cent, the total rent would have

been reduced to 2,607.15 kg. The amount of grain thus saved would have

been 882 kg. In cash this would have been NT$2,145.62. If the old

rental rate had been 60 per cent, the amount saved would have been

1,564.65 kg, and NT$3,711, almost twice as much.

The income saved through farm rent limitation had immediate effects on

the recipient household's living conditions. The survey revealed that of

the 1,250 former-tenant households, more than 55 per cent used at least a

portion of the savings to improve their living conditions. More than 35 per

cent increased their spending on the religious and social activities which

were important parts of a farm household's daily life. Of the 250 current

tenants, more than 56 per cent reported having improved their diet; 40 per

cent built new houses, or repaired old ones. (When people spoke of "375

houses," they meant that these houses were built with funds saved through

the 37.5% farm rent limitation program.) Thirty-eight per cent purchased more and better furniture, and about 29 per cent reported using a portion of their gains to make the pai-pai[4] and other festivals more gay and joyous.

If gains in capability of making marriage arrangements for the family's male members is any sign of improvement in the household's living conditions, the saved farm rent made some good contributions to this effort. More than 46 per cent of the former tenants and 56 per cent of the current tenants arranged marriages for their family members within the four or five years following the establishment of rent limitation. Whether or not these marriages were made possible with the saved funds, people still called all the women in these matrimonial couples "375 wives" or "375 brides." And, in any case, the saved farm rent had another effect on these marriages, in that about one-half of them admitted that the marriage festivities had been more costly than would have been possible before rent limitation.

There is no doubt that rent limitation had resulted in improvement, in varying degrees, in the tenants' living conditions. What had been the effect of this program on the landlords? According to reports from more than 81 per cent of the 500 ordinary landlords, each had suffered an annual loss of 3,211 kg of rice, or NT$7,738.5. For the large landlords, the average annual loss was 18,697.2 kg of rice, or NT$45,060. The ordinary landlords must have felt the loss at once in their daily life. As for the large ones, although the amount of loss looked big, the effect on their daily life might have not been severe. These assumptions are supported by the fact that large numbers of the small and medium landlords complained bitterly that their livelihood had been threatened by the reduction of farm rent. They said that their loss was severe because they had been using practically every measure of grain and every dollar of cash. The household of a big landlord, however, could get along, as usual, despite its loss. At worst, it might have been deprived of some luxuries, but it would not have lost essentials for living.

2. <u>Land reform in total</u>. It is more important to seek a relationship between land reform over-all and the improvements in living conditions of farm households. To the question, "Would you attribute the recent improvement in your living conditions to the land reform?" about 88 per cent of the 748 former tenants said "yes" and about 11 per cent said "no." When asked to specify the relationship, more than 42 per cent reasoned that due to land reform, the farm, whether owned or rented, had become their property, the business of farming had become safer, and, consequently, farm production had considerably increased. With increased production, the improvement of living conditions became possible. Other relationships listed were: Farm income increased because of the reduction of farm rent; farmers became more willing to increase their investments in farming once they had acquired ownership of the farm through land reform; using the land as collateral, farmers were able to obtain loans for farm improvement and, in turn, increase income; thus, the general improvement of farm economy was due, in one way or another, to land reform.

Of the current-tenant farm households, 57 per cent reported improved living conditions, and 81 per cent believed that there was a relationship between their improvement and the land reform. They specified the relationship as follows. Through the farm rent limitation program, tenants were able to keep more of what they produced and, thus, they had the means to improve their living conditions. The rent limitation program provided that a lease contract could not be terminated before it was due to end. Thus, the tenant's right to continue using the farm was guaranteed, and he was willing to do the utmost to increase production. With the security provided in the new lease contracts, tenants felt safe in investing as much as possible in improvements which, in turn, increased production.

About 83 per cent of the original-owner households believed that land reform had been successful and expressed a general belief that most tenants had become economically better off because of the effects of land reform. These households also indicated that there was a small percentage of tenant households whose economic conditions had not become better since land reform because their resources had been drained by increase of family size, impact of natural and/or human calamities, unwise spending of money, etc. Land reform had some influence on the living conditions of these original-owner households too, although indirectly. Inspired by the progress of the transformed, tenant households, they also became more energetic, and more enlightened, in the farming business and other related enterprises and so increased their income. With increased income, their living conditions also improved.

In regard to the former-landlord households, the general opinion had been that their living conditions must have deteriorated on account of the reduction of farm rent and the compulsory purchase of their land. Actually, not all the landlords felt disadvantageous effects. As has been noted several times in preceding chapters, many of those formerly-declining or decaying landlord households had actually become better off because the change had required the whole family to unite, either in actual farming or in a diligent business undertaking, and to work hard and energetically. The result was a considerable improvement of

their living conditions. Those who had succeeded in new business undertakings had attained a still better livelihood than before.

The hired-farm laborers complained a great deal about hardship because many employers no longer gave employment after land reform. Actually, a considerable portion of these complaints had been results of
erroneous deduction or imagination. Laborers apparently reasoned that
since the landlords and big farm households had sold their land, they
would no longer need to hire any labor, and, thus, the farm laborers
would have little opportunity for employment. Without employment their
living conditions would have to deteriorate. Actually, as has been pointed
out previously, most former laborers had been able to find work in the
cities or in non-farm jobs. Furthermore, the demand in the farming
business for laborers had not decreased at all because of the change of
farming patterns. The new cropping systems, the considerable increase of
truck farming, the the new ways of harvesting and preparing farm products
being demanded by consumers on the international markets, all gave stimulus
which resulted in expansion of the labor market and a rise in farm wages.
The former alternation between busy and slack seasons was largely eliminated
because, after land reform many farmers entered into a highly diversified
type of truck farming. This kind of farming keeps farm workers busy all
year round. The result has been that the so-called farm laborers found
themselves in demand both on the farm and in the cities. Those who were
ambitious and diligent found steady employment, and their earnings were
uninterrupted and gradually increasing as well. With continuous employment and ever-increasing earnings, the living conditions of these households could not but become better. Needless to say, their betterment ultimately, and largely, can be attributed to land reform.

Most non-farm people also believed there had been a relationship
between land reform and improvements in living conditions of the farm
households. For instance, 98 per cent of those in education and other
cultural activities believed that living conditions of the farm people had
improved in the ten years after land reform, and 93 per cent of them held
that the improvement was related to land reform. They specified the
relationship in terms similar to those expressed by the farm people themselves, as mentioned in the preceding paragraphs. Eighty-seven per cent
of the local community leaders gave support to the belief that it was
land reform that made possible the improvement in the farm people's
livelihood. Most rural town business people, 77 per cent, agreed that the
income of farm households had increased and that, consequently, their
purchasing power had also increased. They agreed that all these changes
were related to the effects of land reform. The same opinions were discovered among the rural town industrialists.

In summary, a majority of the farm households of all categories had
experienced improvements in their general living conditions and the
improvements could either directly or indirectly, in greater or lesser
degree, be attributed to the effects of land reform. This statement had
been confirmed in the survey by a majority of the farm households themselves and by a majority of the non-farm people.

3. Land reform's influence on specific areas of life. In the area
of food consumption, for instance, many more households in all five categories now had better foods, higher nutritive qualities in their foods,
and, since the completion of the land reform, enjoyed new refinements in
cooking.[5] When former tenants were asked in the survey whether the im-

provements in their food consumption had any relationship to land reform, about 60 per cent of the 1,250 households answered this question, and more than 90 per cent of the answers were affirmative. In improvement of general living conditions in the current-tenant households and households of the hired laborers, there must be improvements in food consumption too. Since many of these households and a great majority of the non-farm people agreed that there was a relationship between land reform and the general improvements, the improvements in food consumption by these farm households must also have been a result of the land reform. The food consumption improvements in original-owner and former-landlord households had indirect relationships to land reform.

Relationship between land reform and improvements in the farm families' housing conditions was indicated, first, in the expressions "375 houses" and "375 brides" which were in popular use in the ten or so years after land reform. This meant that through the 37.5% farm rent limitation program the house was built and the marriage made possible.

Second, a large percentage of both former- and current-tenant farm households reported that they had built new houses or remodelled old ones with money which came from farm production. The farm production must have considerably increased before they could have enough money for such projects. According to information presented in Chapter Five, the farm production of these farm households did increase tremendously, and a great majority of both farmers and non-farmers interviewed admitted that the increases were results of the effects of land reform.

Third, it is a well-known fact that when any kind of family acquired a higher, more socially-desirable status, it would sooner or later start to do something, or establish some symbolic object, by which the new status could be observed and admired. Despite the fact that a majority of the former-tenant and current-tenant households said the building of new houses and the remodelling of old ones were out of necessity, the desire to show the "owner-farmer" status, or to indicate the rise in the family's economic position, played an important role in their motivation. It was by this avenue that land reform exerted its effects upon farm-housing conditions.

Having electricity in the house represented great progress in the daily life of farm households. In the minds of many people, this progress is totally credited to the implementation of the rural electrification program, jointly sponsored by JCRR and the Taiwan Power Company. With some deeper probing, however, it has been discovered that the land reform also had some effect on it. Land reform gave the farm households the impetus, determination, and means by which to increase their comfort and convenience through use of electricity. Determination grew from happiness and high morale, and the means were the result of improvements in farming and other economic undertakings. The happiness, the high morale, and the agricultural improvements in the former- and current-tenant households were, primarily, all the results of land reform.

Similar reasoning and analysis hold true in regard to relationships between land reform and improvements in clothing, drinking water, transportation and communication, and health care. The land reform had effects in these areas, and the processes by which the effects applied were similar to those seen in the other areas.

To summarize:

A. Relationship between land reform and changed living conditions:

    (1) Former-tenant households

Had a relationship	657 households	87.83%
Had no relationship	82	10.96
No answer	9	1.21
Total	748	100.00

        Relationship in specific terms

The farm is safe, cultivation good, increase in production	221	42.05%
Income increased by farm-rent limitation	74	14.06
Farm ownership increased farm input, farm production	61	11.58
Farm ownership helps get needed loans	3	0.57
General economy better after land reform	161	30.60
Other	6	1.14
Total	526	100.00

    (2) Current-tenant households

Had a relationship	85	80.95
Had no relationship	18	17.14
No answer	2	1.91
Total	105*	100.00

        Relationship in specific terms

Farm rent reduced, lease contract secured, better cultivation, more production	45	73.77
Other	16	26.23
Total	61**	100.00

---

* 105 of the 250 sample households admitted improvements in living conditions.
**61 households answered this question.

(3) Hired-farm-laborer households

Of the 250 laborer households, only 8 per cent said
their living conditions had become better; more than
72 per cent complained that their living conditions
had deteriorated; about 20 per cent said there had
not been much difference. More than 80 per cent
claimed changes in their living conditions, betterment or deterioration, after land reform; about 42
per cent believed the changes were results of land
reform; and 53 per cent thought there had been no
relationship between land reform and the changes.
Those who thought there was a relationship said that
their living conditions had deteriorated, and they
blamed this worsening on land reform because, they
said, many landlord households had sold their land,
were out of the farming business, and, therefore, no
longer needed farm laborers. More than 83 per cent
of these households advanced this argument.

(4) Local community leaders

Had a relationship	87 households	87.00%
Had no relationship	7	7.00
No answer	6	6.00
Total	100	100.00%

(5) Educators, artists, etc.

Had a relationship	93	94.90%
Had no relationship	5	5.10
Total	98*	100.00%

(6) Rural town business people
Change in farm household's economic conditions after L.R.

Improvement	66	66.00%
Not much difference	22	22.00
No answer	12	12.00
Total	100	100.00%

---

*98 out of the 100 sample households believed improvements in the farm
people's livelihood after L.R.

Relationship between L.R. and improvement

Yes	59	89.39%
No	6	9.09
No answer	1	1.52
Total	66	100.00%

Business dealings with farm households after L.R.

Increase	43	43.00%
Not much difference	29	29.00
Decrease	27	27.00
No answer	1	1.00
Total	100	100.00%

Relationship between changes and L.R.

Yes	48	68.57%
No	18	25.72
No answer	4	5.71
Total	70	100.00%

Changes in farm household's income after L.R.

Increase	77	77.00%
Decrease	14	14.00
No change	9	9.00
Total	100	100.00%

Relationship between income increase and L.R.

Yes	60	77.93%
No	13	16.88
No answer	4	5.19
Total	77	100.00%

Changes in farm household's purchasing power after L.R.

Increase	49	49.00%
Decrease	22	22.00
Not much difference	29	29.00
Total	100	100.00%

Relationship between changes in purchasing power and L.R.

Yes	45	63.38%
No	22	30.98
No answer	4	5.64
Total	71	100.00%

The former-tenant farm households doing more purchasing than before L.R.

Yes	66	66.00%
No	31	31.00
No answer	3	3.00
Total	100	100.00%

Relationship between more purchasing and L.R.

Yes	55	83.33%
No	10	15.15
No answer	1	1.52
Total	66	100.00%

(7) Rural town industrialists
Change in farm people's economic condition after L.R.

Improvement	81	81.00%
No improvement	18	18.00
No answer	1	1.00
Total	100	100.00%

Reasons for improvement

Land reform	53 answers	49.07%
Increase of farm product	30	27.77
Other	25	23.16
Total	108	100.00%

Changes in farm people's interest and ability to buy manufactured goods after L.R.

Increased	77	77.00%
Decreased	7	7.00
No change	14	14.00
No answer	2	2.00
Total	100	100.00%

Relationship to land reform

Had a relationship	57	74.03%
Had no relationship	20	25.97
Total	77	100.00%

Land reform may have positive effects on the development of industries

Yes	64	64.00%
No	27	27.00
No answer	9	9.00
Total	100	100.00%

B. Relationship between land reform and improvements in specific
    life areas:

    (1) Food consumption

        Improvement in food consumption a result of land reform

Yes	610	82.77%
No	52	7.06
No answer	75	10.17
Total	737	100.00%

    (2) Housing conditions

        Building and repairing of houses direct and indirect results
        of L.R.

Yes	703	73.00%
No	260	27.00
Total	963*	100.00%

        Relationship between installation of electric lights
        and land reform

Had a relationship	217	37.74%
Had no relationship	339	58.96
No answer	19	3.30
Total	575	100.00%

        Electric lights indicate higher social status

Yes	477	38.16%
No	679	54.32
No answer	94	7.52
Total	1,250	100.00%

    (3) Clothing

        There are no statistical data, or opinions, regarding
        relationships between improvements of clothing and land
        reform. But there must have been an indirect relation-
        ship. A chief reason for the farm people's being able
        to make, or buy, better clothes was the improvement of
        their economic conditions, and this was directly, and
        indirectly, related to effects of the land reform.

---

*Number of former-tenant-now-owner farm households who built or repaired
houses after land reform.

IV. Conclusion

A majority of farm households experienced improvements in general living conditions. Specific areas of daily life were also improved. Further, a majority of farm households agreed that improvements in living conditions, as a whole and in specific areas, had been generated by effects of land reform.

Notes

[1]Frank B. Bessac, "The Field Research Concerning the Social Consequences of the Land Reform in Taiwan," pp. 42-44.

[2]Martin M. C. Yang and T. S. Wu, A Study of the Results of the Application of Various Agricultural Extension Means and Methods in Taiwan (In Chinese), 1964.

[3]Western physicians means physicians using scientific methods, implements, and medicines; in general, physicians who are formally trained in medical schools or colleges.

[4]A seasonal, socio-religious festival; pai-pai means "worship."

[5]See section dealing with food consumption in this chapter.

Chapter Nine

COMMUNITY PARTICIPATION
AFTER LAND REFORM

I. Community Participation as Viewed by Farm People
   1. General Interests
   2. Specific Interests
   3. Depth of Participation
   4. Summary

II. Education as a Precondition for Positive Community
    Participation
   1. Education and Social Status
   2. Education after Land Reform
   3. Preference in Secondary and Higher Education
   4. Summary of educational preferences

III. Educational and Social Activities
   1. Farm Organizations Sponsored by Farmers'
      Associations
   2. Farm Organizations Sponsored by the Taiwan
      Sugar Corporation
   3. Community Participation by Tobacco Growers
   4. Community Participation by Banana
      and Citrus Growers
   5. Community Participation through Farmers'
      Organizations

IV. Participation in Farmers' Associations
   1. The Membership
   2. Farmers' Involvement in the
      Associations' Activities

V. Land Reform and Community Participation
   1. Land Reform and the New Community Spirit
   2. Land Reform and Schooling of Children
   3. Land Reform and Agricultural-extension Services

Modern and sophisticated community participation has considerable bearing on the progress of a community's economy, social organization, and cultural achievement, and, in turn, on the uplifting and enrichment of the people's daily living. The time has passed when a farm household can live and work largely by itself without having much contact with others. Farmers of today have to have up-to-date information and employ modern innovations if their farming is to be progressive and profitable; and the most effective, or economical, way of acquiring information is by associating with neighbors, friends, fellow villagers, and others who know the results of the newest agricultural research. Today farmers have to join forces and act collectively in order to receive significant assistance from outside agencies and to sell their products under the most advantageous conditions. Information received from well-organized institutions is, in general, more accurate, systematic, and abundant than that which is acquired in accidental or casual meetings. Furthermore, positive, willing, and informed participation in carefully programmed organizations will not only reap further knowledge and techniques but, also, it is this spirit which gives birth to new motivations, new resolutions, and new encouragements whereby one goes out to work more enthusiastically and efficiently for his own benefit and for the benefit of his community as well. Therefore, participation in well-considered community programs in carefully planned organizations is a process of intellectual enlightenment and moral socialization. It is from this point of view that a study of the farm people's community participation after land reform is to be undertaken in this chapter.

I.   Community Participation as Viewed by Farm People

1.   General interests. In the survey the 1250 former-tenant-now-
owner households were asked whether they had become more interested in
taking part in community social or group activities after they became
owner-farmers through the land reform. Only 21 per cent of these households answered "yes." About 67 per cent said they had made no change.
"No change" could have meant that they had already been interested in
social activities before land reform and so there was no need for them
to change. It could also have meant that they had not been interested
in such activities before land reform and had made no change after it.
Less than 9 per cent reported that they had become more disinterested in
community affairs.

These 1250 farm households were also asked whether they had felt
Quite similar information was discovered among the current tenants.
About 21 per cent of them had become more interested in community activities after land reform. More than 70 per cent reported no change in this
respect. Only a little over 2 per cent said they had become rather disinterested in the local activities.

These 1250 farm households were also asked whether they had felt
that after land reform the social positions of the former landlords had
collapsed and that, therefore, the opportunity of becoming social leaders
would pass to the owner-farmers. To this question, 48 per cent of these
households answered "yes;" 51 per cent expressed doubt. Did they believe
instead, that those who had changed through the land-to-the-tiller program
from tenant-cultivators to owner-farmers would take over the positions in

community affairs which used to be occupied by landlords and original-
owner farmers? Only 32 per cent said "yes" and 67 per cent said "no."

Less than 30 per cent of the original owner-farmers said they
became more interested in local affairs after land reform. About 60 per
cent of them said they had made no change while more than 10 per cent
admitted that they had lost interest in such activities. About 45 per
cent of these households believed that after the landlords had lost
their land-based social prestige, the owner-farmers would rise to take
their place in leading the community's public functions. About 54 per
cent expressed doubt in this matter. In regard to the speculation on
what role the former tenants might play in a village's collective life,
37 per cent of the original owner-farmers believed that the new owner-
farmers would take over the positions formerly occupied by the landlords
and themselves; 62 per cent were doubtful. Another interesting point
is that about 40 per cent of those original owners, who had reported
becoming more interested in community participation since land reform,
said that they became so because most of the other people in the
community had begun taking part in social activities; and about 50 per
cent had the notion that one earns respect from his fellowmen by being
active in his community's affairs. All these observations indicate that
after land reform many farm people did become active in community participation. A small number of them admitted that their reason for joining
any community organization was the idea of getting some kind of material
benefit out of it.

After land reform, or after the completion of the land-to-the-
tiller program, people were apt to expect that the former landlords

would have become discouraged and, therefore, disinterested in community functions. This had been true to an extent, but had not become as bad as had been assumed. Of the 500 ordinary landlord households interviewed, only a little over 34 per cent admitted discouragement. A majority of them, 55 per cent, said they remained unaffected; that is, if they had been active in such activities before land reform, they remained so afterward. A small number of them, 9 per cent, reported that they had become even more interested in giving assistance to such activities. One reason for this was that the local populace had continued to elect them, and support them as leaders, in the local organizations. Conditions among the former large landlords were somewhat different. The percentage of those who had become disheartened was as big as the percentage of those who had not. However, there were also a small number who had become more interested than before.

By and large, the hired farm laborers remained as shy as before in regard to participation in social groupings. They took part in unorganized and informal mass meetings or street-corner gatherings. But their inferiority feeling still prevented them from joining formal organizations, or associations in which people of higher social status predominated. Hired laborers might join certain community organizations in which their membership was prescribed by law or Government order. Such a membership carries little implication of genuine community participation, however.

Among non-farm people, the local community leaders had made some observations concerning the changes which occurred in the farm people's community participation. In summary, the local leaders observed that

if before land reform the membership of a community organization included landlords, owner-farmers and tenant-cultivators, leadership was
always in the hands of the landlords; especially capable owner-farmers
might also have the opportunity of holding responsible positions; but
tenant-cultivators had to be just plain, ordinary, insignificant members.
After land reform there had been a great change, according to the local
leaders. In many cases of social activities, the lead was taken by the
former-tenant-now-owners and the current tenants. The original owners
had been largely unaffected. Most former landlords either had left the
rural communities to pursue occupations in the cities or had become too
discouraged to have any interest in civic affairs. A majority of the
school teachers and other cultural workers had similar opinions. They
also observed that after the tenants had become owners, they seemed to be
no longer as timid and shy as before in meeting the school teachers and
in participating in social programs sponsored by the schools. They
had also become more concerned with conditions and problems of the local
schools, more responsive toward raising funds or collecting materials
for educational and social-welfare projects.

    2. **Specific interests.** Information concerning the actual member-
ships of certain community organizations and the degree or depth of
members' participation has been collected and analyzed. Eight community
organizations were considered: the farmers' association, the farm-
tenancy committee, the parents' association[1], the neighborhood-heads'
association, the volunteer fire-fighting squad, the public construction
control board, the boxing (exercise) team, and political party groups.

More than 64 per cent of the former tenants, more than 74 per cent of the current tenants, and about 54 per cent of the original owners reported that they had had membership in the farmers' association before land reform. In other words, before land reform about 70 per cent of the tenant-farmers and 54 per cent of the owner-farmers belonged to farmers' associations. That the number of owner-farmers was 16 per cent less than the number of tenant-farmers seems unbelievable. The explanation might be that some farmers in either of the two categories had not made accurate reports on this matter, or it might be that some owner-farmers felt so self-sufficient that they did not want to be bothered by membership in the association.

Before land reform very few farm people belonged to any of the other organizations mentioned above. About 3 per cent of the tenants and about 5 per cent of the owner-farmers had been members of their local farm-tenancy committees; about 3 per cent of tenants and 9 per cent of owners had belonged to a parents' association; about 13 per cent of tenants and 20 per cent of owners were in an organization of neighborhood heads; around 5 per cent of tenants and 4 per cent of owners had, at one time or another, been members of volunteer fire-fighting squads; less than 1 per cent of tenants and a little over 3 per cent of owners had even been on the community's public-construction control boards; 1 per cent of each group had joined boxing teams; and about 2 per cent of tenants and 5 per cent of owners had belonged to a political party.

At the time of the study, these memberships had not undergone any significant changes. Memberships of the farmers' associations included,

for instance, 52 per cent of the original owner-farmers. This represented
a 2 per cent decrease from the pre-land-reform figure. The number of
current tenants belonging to farmers' associations also had reduced by 4
per cent. Only the former tenants had increased their memberships, by
more than 4 per cent. In the other organizations, whether they increased
or decreased, the changes had all been trivial, except that both the original and the new owner-farmers had doubled and, in some cases, tripled their
memberships in political parties or local cliques.

Another point worth noting is that before land reform there must have
been some landlords, perhaps a great number, who belonged to farmers'
associations. After land reform some landlords became non-farm people and
others, who actually began cultivating the farm land retained by them, were
called owner-farmers. The farmers' association membership for these people
was not taken into consideration in this study. Because of this shortcoming
there might be some difference between the number of farmers' association
members recorded in this study and that recorded in other documents. What
this study emphasizes at this time is the change in farmers' association
membership in the above mentioned three categories of farm people.

3. Depth of participation. In regard to the degree of participation
in community organizations, the study discovered that 42 per cent of the
former tenants, 45 per cent of the original owners, and more than 51 per
cent of the current tenants participated out of their own wishes and attended
meetings or group activities frequently or regularly. Over 13 per cent of
the original owners, and 22 per cent of the former tenants, and 24 per cent
of the current tenants participated involuntarily and only occasionally.
About 20 per cent of the new owners and 28 per cent of the original

owners participated in community organizations because of election or
recommendation by fellow villagers. This kind of participation was
involuntary at the beginning but had their approval later. Still later,
the participation became a matter of honor or pride. It was discovered
that only a very small percentage of farmers in each category considered
their memberships largely nominal and seldom attended meetings or activities.
Did the farmers feel it a profitable or beneficial thing to have participated in community organizations? In each category a majority answered
"yes;" a small percentage felt it was very profitable; and around 30 per
cent declared the participation gained them nothing.

Another indication of the depth of a person's community participation
is the amount of material and non-material contributions he may make to
the organization or activity in which he takes part. About 60 per cent
of the former tenants said they had become more willing after land reform
to make contributions to community organizations or causes. About 14
per cent of current tenants and 11 per cent of the original owners said
they were not willing to make such contributions before land reform but
became willing after it. About 29 per cent of the former tenants and 42
per cent of the original owners said they were willing to contribute
before land reform and had become more willing after it. About 37 per
cent of the former tenants admitted that after land reform they still
had no interest in making contributions to social-welfare programs.
Quite a few original owners and current tenants said they had no interest
either before land reform or after it. A small number of these households
said they used to be willing to give toward social-welfare activities
but not so nowadays. Then, in each of the last two categories, there

were 30 per cent who expressed various opinions on this matter which cannot be classified simply as willing or not willing. Their opinions were qualified by many kinds of conditions.

There have been changes in the farm people's selection of community organizations and social-welfare activities to which they would give contributions. Before land reform, for instance, 33 per cent of 1,082 former-tenant households made contributions of labor, or money, to the building of local schools. At the time of the study, 50 per cent of 1,133 such households were doing this. Before land reform more than 26 per cent of them gave help toward construction or repairing of local roads or bridges. This percentage decreased to 18.53 ten years after. About 23 per cent of these households gave help toward construction and repairing of temples and shrines and made contributions to religious activities before land reform. The proportion was less than 7 per cent at the time of the study. Their interest in the improvement of water works or irrigation grew considerably. Only 11 per cent of them remembered making contributions to such work before land reform but the percentage was doubled at the time of interview.

Among the current tenants the changes found were as follows: Before land reform, 38 per cent considered contributions to the building and repairing of local schools their first choice; at the time of the survey, 45 per cent did so. The number whose first concern was with water works or irrigation changed from 16 per cent before land reform to 18 per cent after it. Those choosing to help temples, shrines, and religious work

decreased from 14 to 9 per cent. Those assisting with local roads
and bridges decreased from 24 to 20 per cent.

Among original-owner households, the changes had been somewhat
different. The number giving first consideration to local schools
jumped from 39 per cent before land reform to 51 per cent after. Interest in road construction and repair rose by 2 per cent, but interest
in water works and irrigation decreased by 4 per cent. Temples, shrines,
and religious ceremonies lost 12 per cent of their prime contributors:
17.86 per cent before land reform; 5.61 per cent after.

Despite their losses suffered through rent limitation and the land-
to-the-tiller program, some landlords continued contributions to
community construction and social-welfare projects after land reform.
It was true that at the time of the study, the number of landlord households which used to be willing to make contributions toward community
causes, heavier than those made by the general citizenry, had reduced from
pre-land reform 32 per cent to 13 per cent; and the percentage of those
not willing to make any such contributions had increased from 2.20 to
9.40; but it was also true that the number who were willing to contribute, in accordance with what the general community was able to do, had
increased from 64 per cent to 76 per cent. Among the extra-large landlord households, the changes had been much the same. Both before land
reform and afterward, the number willing to give first contributions to
educational causes was larger than for any other organization or cause.
In summary, changes among the landlord households, in preference for

organizations or civic causes, followed largely the same pattern as that found among the other three categories of farm people.*

It is now clear that both farmers and landlords had been increasingly independent and selective in choosing organizations and activities, except in the case of farmers' associations. The general trend had been that farm people in general have been quite ready to take part in educational, economic-productive, and constructional programs. They have begun, whether by intention or unknowingly, to shake off the influence and break the bonds with religious institutions and kinship networks. It is true that participation in pai-pai among rural people has continued to be strong and even become more extravagant as the farmers' income increased. But this is more a kind of momentary, spend-thrift showing-off than a part of their normal social life. It looks like a defiance by the younger generation against the frugality virtue of the

---

*In this regard, there has been a change which is not only interesting but also significant in the growth of grass-root democracy. Before land reform, the landlord and other wealthy-gentry households, which had the means and the desire to acquire a reputation, used to make large contributions to community-welfare projects. For instance, a dozen or so such households could by themselves meet fully the financial responsibilities allotted to the locality for building a township, public-health station. Thus, all ordinary villagers were exempted from giving anything, and the big and wealthy households were praised by both the Government and the local populace. After land reform, most of these wealthy households had given up their land and transferred their financial resources to industries and businesses in the cities. Their interest in community affairs also shifted, or was lost. In their stead, the ordinary households, including the original owner, new owner, and those better-off, current tenant-farmers, began to be interested in community welfare. As the interest increased in depth and intensity correspondingly with improvement in living conditions, these households gradually took up those responsibilities which used to be on the shoulders of a small number of wealthy households. From now on, it seems that responsibilities will be spread more and more generally over the community members. Only when the people in general are voluntarily accepting these responsibilities will grass root democracy grow.

older generation, or a deliberate breach of tradition in order to enjoy a wild expressionism. It cannot be considered to be 'community partici- pation' in its legitimate or usual sense. When local, political contests are underway, candidates belonging to big clans may try to gain support among their clan by arousing kinship-consciousness and unity to strengthen traditional kinship ties. But, in most cases, such efforts have not met any significant success. It is becoming more and more clear that an appeal for cooperative effort toward youth's educational advancement and toward community (or group) prosperity is much stronger than a calling up of past- family or clan glories.

4. Summary.

A. Changes in community interest:

   (1) Former tenant, now owner

Increase	260 households	20.80%
No change	835	66.80
Decrease	108	8.64
No answer	47	3.76
Total	1,250	100.00%

   (2) Current tenant

Increase	52	20.80%
No change	129	51.60
Decrease	6	2.40
Never been interested	50	20.00*
No answer	13	5.20
Total	250	100.00%

   (3) Original owner

Increase	73	29.20%
No change	115	46.00
Decrease	26	10.40
Never been interested	35	14.00*
No answer	1	0.40
Total	250	100.00%

*In the text this percentage is included in the category under "No change."

(4) Former landlord

    (a) Ordinary

Increase	45	9.20%
No change	267	54.60
Decrease	168	34.36
No answer	9	1.84
Total	489	100.00%

    (b) Large

Increase	6	8.00%
No change	37	49.33
Decrease	32	42.67
Total	75	100.00%

(5) Non-farm people: Many school teachers thought that after becoming owner-farmers through land reform, the former tenant-cultivators have become more interested in the schools.

Agree	86	86.00%
Disagree	13	13.00
No answer	1	1.00
Total	100	100.00%

B. Changes in roles in community participation:

(1) Former tenant

More leadership	378	35.90%
No change	638	60.59
No answer	37	3.51
Total	1,053	100.00%

(2) Current tenant

    (a) After the disappearance of landlords, the owner-farmers have more opportunities to become leaders in community organizations.

Agree	119	47.60%
Not necessarily so	127	50.80
Other opinions	4	1.60
Total	250	100.00%

(b) The new owner-farmers may take the leadership from the original owner-farmers.

Agree	80	32.00%
Not necessarily so	167	66.80
No answer	3	1.20
Total	250	100.00%

(3) Original owner

(a) Same as B (2)(a)

Agree	112	44.80%
Not necessarily so	134	53.60
Other opinions	3	1.20
No answer	1	0.40
Total	250	100.00%

(b) Same as B (2)(b)

Agree	93	37.20%
Not necessarily so	154	61.60
No answer	3	1.20
Total	250	100.00%

(4) Non-farm people

(a) Community leaders

More than 90 per cent of the local, community leaders interviewed observed that before land reform, all, or a great majority, of the leadership in community organizations came from landlords, while small owner-farmers played a few, minor leadership roles; tenant-cultivators were only followers. Ten per cent of the local leaders believed tenant-farmers also displayed some leadership. Had this situation changed after land reform?

Yes	67	67.00%
No	25	25.00
No answer	8	8.00
Total	100	100.00%

Since land reform, the farm people's interest in community affairs:

First appeared	41	41.00%
Increased	38	38.00
Remained as before	16	16.00
Decreased	4	4.00
No answer	1	1.00
Total	100	100.00%

(b) School teachers

After land reform, both former and current tenant-farmers have become confident enough to visit schools and to meet teachers on equal footings.

Agree	86	86.00%
Disagree	13	13.00
No answer	1	1.00
Total	100	100.00%

C. Community organization memberships:

(1) Organizations: farmers' associations, farm-tenancy committees, parents' associations, neighborhood-heads' associations, volunteer fire-fighting squads, public construction control boards, boxing teams, political party groups.

(2) Membership: Before land reform, about 70 per cent of the tenants and 54 per cent of the owners belonged to farmers' associations. Membership in any of the other organizations was sparse, from 1 to 20 per cent. At the time of this study, there had been no significant changes.

D. Depth of participation:

(1) Conditions of participation

	Former tenant		Current tenant		Original owner	
(a) Voluntary and regular	444	41.89%	110	51.64%	110	45.08%
(b) Involuntary and irregular	236	22.26	52	24.41	32	13.12
(c) Through village election	206	19.43	---	---	67	27.46
(d) Nominal participation	137	12.93	28	13.15	18	7.37
(e) Other	37	3.49	23	10.80	17	6.97
Total	1,060	100.00%	213	100.00%	244	100.00%

(2) Benefits of participation

	Former tenant		Current tenant		Original owner	
(a) Many benefits	123	9.84%	15	6.58%	17	6.80%
(b) Some benefits	643	50.72	140	61.40	145	58.00
(c) No benefits	346	27.68	73	32.02	66	26.40
(d) No answer	147	11.76	---	---	22	8.80
Total	1,259	100.00%	228	100.00%	250	100.00%

(3) Willingness to contribute to community organizations or causes

	Former tenant		Current tenant		Original owner	
(a) Willing	744	59.52%	---	---	---	---
(b) Not willing	457	36.56	---	---	---	---
(c) More willing than before	---	---	72	28.80	105	42.00
(d) Not willing before but willing now	---	---	34	13.60	28	11.20
(e) Willing before but not willing now	---	---	10	4.00	14	5.60
(f) Not willing before or now	---	---	39	15.60	21	8.40
(g) Other responses	---	---	76	30.40	78	31.20
(h) No answer	37	3.92	19	7.60	4	1.60
Total	1,238	100.00%	250	100.00%	250	100.00%

Former landlords

	Before L.R.				10 years after L.			
	Ordinary		Large		Ordinary		Larg	
(a) Contributing more than general standard	161	32.20%	40	53.33%	65	13.00%	15	20.0
(b) Contributing according to general standard	321	64.20	31	41.33	378	75.60	49	65.3
(c) Not contributing	11	2.20	4	5.33	47	9.40	8	10.6
(d) No answer	7	1.40	-	---	10	2.00	3	4.0
Total	500	100.00%	75	100.00%	500	100.00%	75	100.0

(4) Organizations or causes chosen

(a) Former tenant

	Before L.R.		10 years after L.R	
Schools, education	356	32.90%	564	49.78%
Road construction	285	26.34	210	18.53
National defense	26	2.40	13	1.15
Water works	121	11.18	232	20.48
Public health	10	0.92	8	0.71
Social welfare (relief)	38	3.51	28	2.47
Temple construction	197	18.22	66	5.83
Religious work	48	4.44	10	0.88
Others	1	0.09	2	0.17
Total	1,082	100.00%	1,133	100.00%

(b)   Current tenant

	Before L.R.		10 years after L.R.	
Schools, education	87	38.16%	102	44.74%
Road construction	54	23.68	46	20.17
National defense	3	1.33	4	1.75
Water works	37	16.23	41	17.97
Public health	5	2.19	4	1.75
Social welfare (relief)	11	4.82	11	4.82
Temple construction	27	11.84	17	7.45
Religious work	4	1.75	3	1.35
Total	228	100.00%	228	100.00%

(c)   Original owner

	Before L.R.		10 years after L.R.	
Schools, education	87	38.84%	118	51.08%
Road construction	38	16.96	42	18.18
National defense	3	1.33	4	1.73
Water works	41	18.31	34	14.72
Public health	0	---	2	0.87
Social welfare (relief)	15	6.69	18	7.79
Temple construction	38	16.96	12	5.20
Religious work	2	0.91	1	0.43
Total	224	100.00%	231	100.00%

(d)   Former landlord (both categories)

	Before L.R.		10 years after L.R.	
Schools, education	271	35.29%	332	46.50%
Road construction	130	16.92	119	16.67
Bridge building	102	13.28	73	10.22
Temple construction	128	16.67	82	11.49
Social welfare (relief)	67	8.72	45	6.30
Water works	41	5.34	37	5.18
Others	29	3.73	26	3.64
Total	768	100.00%	714	100.00%

According to their own words, farm people had not changed significantly in their community participation after land reform, except that
at the time of this study, whatever community participation they made
was usually voluntary and regular. Also, a majority admitted that there
were either many or, at least, some benefits gained from community participation. After land reform most farm people became more willing to
make civic contributions. As already pointed out, at the time of the
study, there was a general trend in farm communities to forsake religious and kinship organizations and move rapidly into educational and
particular-interest groups.

II. Education as a Precondition for Positive Community Participation

1. Education and social status. The kind and amount of education
a person has received, or the number of educated members in his household, has a great deal to do with his choices concerning community participation or social life. In general, education brings with it a higher
social status, and this education-based status is often the entree to a
community organization. A primary-school education still has such a
function in rural Taiwan today. It is, of course, also the base upon
which education at higher levels may be added. Because higher social
status usually provides incentive, qualification, and courage for the
individual or the household to take part in social activities, schooling
is, in a sense, a prime mover toward community participation. A fine
education, at high levels, inclines, however, to separate and so to
isolate the individual or household. A university graduate, or a college

professor, can seldom really mingle with the rank and file of the usual farm village. At best, he can serve as a leader of the group. But even so, he feels, in most cases, that he is floating above the sea of the great masses; he is not within it. The masses would not admit him as one of their pals. That is why the younger villagers, who have received middle-school or college educations, can never really return, much less stay in the farm villages; when they do try to stay, they feel they are no longer really in it and they, therefore, cannot be active in community life.

Formal education can confer a certain desirable social status upon an individual. Furthermore, should status be achieved in another way, some formal education may be needed to accompany or to maintain it. In this case, an effort usually follows to get the needed education. Education can help maintain status. Possession of social status, without its companion education, would be like wearing only formal dress with an essential part missing. One cannot go thus to any formal party. For instance, most owner-farmer households have traditionally had some amount of schooling. Otherwise, they would almost certainly be looked down upon by their neighbors. For this reason, it is assumed that after the tenant-cultivators in Taiwan had become owner-farmers through land reform, attendance in the primary schools of farm villages and rural towns would have increased considerably.

The kind of education which is comparatively more helpful in motivating people into group activity seems to be the informal, out-of-school, adult education. The latter-day, agricultural-extension services should be a most appropriate example. Farm people, including men, women, and youth, who have regularly, over a period of time, attended extension-service programs usually become very much interested and, therefore, active in village-level group activities. They can also overcome shyness sufficiently to join township-wide programs. Education which comes to them through exhibits, community fairs, observation tours and field days, annual conferences etc., is also effective in changing their traditional isolation and self-reliance into gregariousness and cooperation.

The reason for the socializing effects of informal education, in our case agricultural-extension services, probably lies in the fact that if it is of rich and appropriate content and effectively conducted, its subject-matter and methods will be inherently related to the farmers' daily life and work and it will always have congenial associations with the participants' practical experiences. The close relationship between teaching and practical experiences makes this kind of education immediately pertinent and useful. The 'students,' have the pleasure of feeling that what they have talked about in classes or meetings are exactly the things of which they can become masters. Practical gains and pleasant feelings encourage the farmers and induce them to return. This is true not only of Taiwan but of other countries as well. Where some kind of farmers' out-of-school education is effectively and universally undertaken, farmers take part, in one way or another, in community affairs. Each farmer in Denmark, for example, is, at any one time, a member of several, cooperative societies, and his community participation fills a considerable portion of his everyday life.

2. <u>Education after land reform.</u> Our assumption concerning school attendance proved to be well founded. Before land reform less than 63 per cent of the 1,250 former-tenant households sent all their children to primary school; about 28 per cent sent some of their children; and about 6 per cent sent none. After land reform the percentages were 92, 5.28, and 0.8.

The 250 current tenants did not have 'owner-farmer' status at the time of the study, but their socio-economic positions had, in general, significantly improved, and their desire for education had increased. Before land reform only 62 per cent of these households sent all their children to primary schools. Thirty-two per cent sent some of their children, and more than 5 per cent sent none. After land reform the percentages were 90.40, 7.60, and 1.20.

The original-owner households were greatly different. More than 77 per cent of the 250 said they had been sending all their children to primary schools long before land reform. Less than 19 per cent sent some, but not all, of their children, and a very small number sent none, for reasons unspecified. After land reform practically all the owner households sent every child to primary school. This is another indication that these households had not felt much direct effect from land reform. But the indirect impact was great. If those who were either current tenant-cultivators at the time of the survey, or tenant-cultivators only a few years before, were able and willing to send all their children to primary school, the original owners thought they ought to be more able and willing to do so.

The former landlords underwent no change in this regard. Most of their children went to primary schools both before and after land reform. However, there were a few who sent none of their children either before or after land reform. It must have been for some unfortunate reasons.

About 80 per cent of the 250 hired-laborer households reported that after land reform many more such households had been sending their children to school, presumably primary school. This change was largely due to the farm laborers' desire that their children have opportunity in occupations other than farm work or unskilled labor to avoid the bitter experience of being unable to read and write, and of being looked down upon for their lack of education. There were also other factors such as the new social trends, the new, farm-cultivation methods, the influence of neighbors who were educating their own children, etc.

According to observations of non-farm people, the above information is, in general, correct. Ninety-five per cent of the school teachers and others in cultural activities and practically all local community leaders agreed that in the ten years after land reform the number of farm children in primary schools increased greatly. What these people meant was that those many farm children entering primary schools after land reform might not have gone if there had not been some new motives or influences which changed traditional attitudes and persuaded farmers to voluntarily send their children to school. What were the new motives or influences? According to these non-farm people, after land reform most farm households became much better off economically and physically. Under the new conditions, they had the means and persistence to realize their desires for education. Developments in mass communication and

social education helped further their interest in giving their children
new opportunities through education.

Today most farm households hope that one or two of their children
will stay on the farm to continue the family's farming business but that
all the others will seek occupations away from the farm. They realize
that good, non-farm jobs with high earnings require formal education and
special training. Therefore, they must see to it that their children
have the required education and training. Finally, farm people have
noticed that high social and economic positions and special prestige
are won by those who have education, and that the higher the level of
education, the better the chance of getting into a desirable position.

Some people may say that it was because the primary school had
been made compulsory so that, under law, every normal, school-aged child
must attend for at least six years, that the farm families now send
their children to primary school. This is true, but the law could
hardly have been so effective as to make all the farm households send
their school-aged children to school. In other words, policemen alone
cannot send all school-aged children to school. Primary school was
compulsory before land reform. But many children of poor families were
kept home working instead of going to school. After land reform, if
these families had wished to do so, they could have continued just as
before. However, a great number of these same families changed their
attitudes and actions. They began to allow their children to go to
school. Their doing so was due less to the force of law than to the
reasons given above.

There had also been changes in regard to the amount of education that young farm people ought to have, or that their parents wished them to have. Even today, only the primary school is compulsory. If farm households had wished merely to comply with the law, they would have refused permission and support to their children in secondary schools and colleges. But, instead, the number of farm children in secondary schools increased considerably after land reform. Among the 1,250 former-tenant households, only 96 persons had ever attended, or graduated from, middle schools before land reform. This number had increased to 674 by the time of this study, an increase of 600 per cent. Before land reform from all these households, there was only one person in college. There were 32 college students ten years after land reform.

The 250 current tenants experienced a similar change in this respect. Before land reform 24 of their young people had attended, or graduated from, middle schools. At the time of the survey, their number had increased to 129, or 438 per cent. Before land reform all these households together had only 2 college students. Ten years later the number was 5.

Among the 250 original owners, the number of young people who had studied in, or graduated from, middle schools before land reform was 99. Ten years after land reform it was 304. On the average, each household had more than one student in middle school. They had 4 college students before land reform and there were 19 ten years after it.

The former landlords also registered increases in the numbers of their young people going to secondary schools and colleges. Before land reform the 575 landlord households together had 693 middle-school students. This number increased to 1,076 in ten years, up 55.27 per

cent. These households together had 149 boys and girls in college

before land reform. Ten years later the number was 272, an increase

of 82.55 per cent.

There are no data on numbers of children from laborers households

in secondary schools and colleges before or after land reform. There

is, however, information to the effect that more than 79 per cent of

these 250 households wished their children to have the opportunity for

secondary and college educations.

After the tenants became owners through the land-to-the-tiller

program, their attitudes and ideas in regard to children's education

can be summarized as follows: Their becoming owners made them realize

the importance of education, and they became willing to spend more

money on it. Education is a very important prerequisite to high earn-

ings. Education and discipline of children is the responsibility of

parents, and the current trend is toward educating all persons, each

according to his need and his means.

3. <u>Preferences in education above elementary school.</u> More than 57

per cent of parents in former-tenant households said that before land

reform they would have been satisfied if their boys had only a primary-

school education. Nine-and-one-half per cent said they would have liked

their boys to go through middle school. More than 6 per cent specified

senior, middle school; about 4 per cent said senior, vocational school;

more than 2 per cent said normal school; and about 14 per cent would

have wanted college or a university. For girls, about 66 per cent cited

primary school; 7 per cent, junior, middle school; about 3 per cent,

senior, middle school; less than 2 per cent, senior, vocational school;
about 3 per cent, normal school; and about 10 per cent, college or a
university. At the time of the study, less than 17 per cent (40 per
cent fewer) still felt that for boys, primary school was enough. About
11 per cent thought it should be junior, middle school; more than 10
per cent, senior, middle school; more than 7 per cent, senior, vocational
school; more than 5 per cent, normal school; about 41 per cent, college
or a university.

The drastic change has been that a much smaller percentage of
parents now were satisfied with a primary-school education for their
boys, and the number of parents who felt their boys ought to go to
college increased from less than 14 per cent to about 41 per cent.
For girls, although at the time of the survey about a third of the
parents still felt primary school education was enough, the number who
wished their daughters to have college educations increased by one-
seventh. We can conclude then that after the tenant-cultivators
acquired owner-farmer status through land reform, they became quite
ambitious for their children's education.

In this regard, the pattern of change among current tenants
appeared somewhat different. After land reform the number of parents
who still held primary school to be enough for their boys and girls was
only one-half as large as before land reform. The number who thought
that their children should go to college had increased three times over
by the time of the survey. Another finding was that after land reform
there was a great increase in the number of parents who thought their
girls ought to train in normal schools so that they could be teachers.

The original owners also reported great changes in their thinking about education. Before land reform only a little over 23 per cent of them had wished their children to go to college. At the time of the study, more than 52 per cent wanted it. The number who were satisfied with primary school had decreased from 36 per cent to 12 per cent.

Across all categories of farm people, the number of households wishing their children to study in junior, or senior, agricultural schools has decreased considerably in recent years. Each year the agricultural schools have difficulty filling up their enrollments. Only a small number of young people are interested in such schools.

In the recent years, since land reform, not only have many more farm households sent their children to colleges, they have even concerned themselves with the question as to whether parents ought to dictate to their children their subjects or fields of study. Of the parents in former-tenant households, more than 46 per cent were quite democratic on this matter. They felt that young people themselves should make the choice according to their interests and ambitions. Other parents thought that their children ought to be advised or guided in considering what to study in college. About 11 per cent said they would like their children to study medicine, and 8 per cent wished their children to study engineering. Then came agriculture, business, natural sciences, humanities, social sciences, and fine arts, each mentioned by a small number of parents.

Medicine has long enjoyed high earnings and, therefore, is popular among pragmatic-minded people. As far as earning is concerned, occupations ranking next to medicine are commerce and business, engineering,

and agriculture. During the Japanese administration, the small number of
Chinese young people who had the opportunity to enter institutions of
higher learning were allowed to study only medicine or agriculture, for
the Japanese authorities paid attention first to the elimination of epidemic diseases and the production of food and fiber.

Opinions of former landlords were different, although also pragmatic.
There was, too, a comparatively large percentage who wished their children,
especially sons, to study medicine. But very few of them took agriculture
into consideration. Next to medicine engineering was favored by parents.
For girls, most preferred normal school; the area in favor was liberal arts.

In the summer of 1959, a rural survey on a gigantic scale was conducted under the sponsorship of JCRR.[2] It covered 18 townships throughout the province. The people interviewed were mostly farmers, but there
were also some community leaders and other non-farm people living in the
township centers. In the matter of education,[3] the survey discovered
that the annual percentage of school-aged children attending primary
schools averaged 93 to 95. In the more prosperous townships, the average
rose to 98 or 99. Even in comparatively poor townships, the lowest figure
was just under 90. In each township there were a certain number of
school-aged children, both boys and girls, who, for some reason, did not
go to school at all. Usually there were many more girls than boys in
this group; if, for some reason, education could not be given to every
child, a boy usually got the priority, and a girl had to wait or, perhaps,
forsake the hope entirely.

The survey also discovered that since land reform practically every
township had to build new primary schools to take care of the greatly

increased number of children who had come up to school age. In a period

of six years, 14 townships built 24 primary schools. The capacity of

the schools varied from 150 students to 800 or 1,000. Many of the old

primary schools in the rural districts were repaired and new classrooms

were added to existing ones. Hundreds of millions of N.T. dollars were

spent for these purposes. But to this day, the cry for more schools

and classrooms is still loud in almost every rural community. In 1958,

for example, the people of Feng-yuan township called desperately for

help because they required at least 49 more standard classrooms if they

were to take care of all the boys and girls who were ready for school.

On the average, each of the 18 townships needed 21 new classrooms in

the year 1959.

One reason for the space shortage was the fast growth of population.

But another reason, just as important, was the farm people's new under-

standing of the importance of educating their children.

The survey also revealed large increases in the number of second-

ary schools and secondary-school students in the rural communities of

Taiwan. In the 18 townships surveyed, there were 19 general, middle

schools and 12 secondary, vocational schools, an average per township

of 1.7 secondary schools. The number of students in these secondary

schools was 24,003, of which about 74 per cent were boys. Obviously,

educational opportunities for girls above the primary school were fewer

than for boys. Many a girl agreed that priority should go to her bro-

ther, in case a choice had to be made, because it was said, she still

did not realize her own need for anything more than a primary-school

education.

The desire of rural families to have their children attend school developed considerably in the years after land reform, according to findings of the survey. Everyone strongly desired that all children should have at least an elementary education. The motives specified were interesting. They were, in order of frequency: (1) People's own experience of "sufferings through illiteracy and ignorance;" (2) improved living conditions since the land reform; (3) the wish to improve the social position of one's family; (4) that education makes possible a better job and, therefore, a better social position; (5) that some education was compulsory; (6) the importance of learning new technology, especially the new techniques of production; (7) the increased financial feasibility, owning to the free-education system; (8) the increased realization of the importance of education; (9) the desire to meet the needs of modern life.

In summary, it must be noted that the most manifest and universal advance made in rural Taiwan in recent years has been in the field of education. In every township investigated, primary-school attendance had risen. Where formerly many parents had to be called upon, reminded, even threatened before their children came to school, they now took the initiative and pressed for admission as soon as possible. A great, though still inadequate, effort is being made to provide the required classrooms and facilities -- a task of increasing difficulty as the school-age population rises. A higher proportion of parents than before feel ashamed if they cannot put their children through secondary school and college. This aspiration is largely social, but realistic calculations are stressed at the same time; both parents and children think that elementary education is insufficient to enable a person to secure

employment at a higher level than working on the family farm or in a

village shop.

4. Summary of educational preferences.

A. Emphasis on education:

(1) About 92 per cent of the former-tenant-now-owner farm households valued education because (a) it is important for the children of owner-farmers to have education; and (b) education is a means toward more desirable occupations.

(2) More than 85 per cent of the current-tenant households valued education because (a) most people are emphasizing education; (b) the Government builds schools and persuades people to send their children to school; (c) economic conditions have improved so that they have the means to educate their children.

(3) More than 90 per cent of the original-owner households valued education for the same reasons as mentioned above.

(4) About 70 per cent of the hired laborers valued education for similar reasons.

(5) About 80 per cent of the former-landlord households placed higher value on education because their children could no longer depend for their living on rents from farm land.

(6) About 97 per cent of the teachers and others in cultural activities agreed that after land reform, the farm people began to give more attention to education.

B. Children's primary school attendance:

(1) Former tenants

	Before L.R.		10 years after L.R.		Change	
All children attended	787	62.96%	1,150	92.00%	+363	+46.12
Some children attended	349	27.92	66	5.28	-283	-81.09
No children attended	73	5.84	10	0.80	- 63	-86.30
No answer	41	3.28	24	1.92		
Total	1,250	100.00%	1,250	100.00%		

(2) Current tenants

	Before L.R.		10 years after L.R.		Change	
All children attended	155	62.00%	226	93.40%	+ 71	+45.81
Some children attended	80	32.00	19	7.60	- 61	-76.25
No children attended	13	5.20	3	1.20	- 10	-76.92
No answer	2	0.80	2	0.80		
Total	250	100.00%	250	100.00%		

(3) Original owners

	Before L.R.		10 years after L.R.		Change	
All children attended	193	77.20%	242	96.80%	+ 49	+25.39
Some children attended	47	18.80	3	1.20	- 44	-93.62
No children attended	3	1.20	3	1.20	---	---
No answer	7	2.80	2	0.80		
Total	250	100.00%	250	100.00%		

(4) Former landlords (both categories)

	Before L.R.		10 years after L.R.		Change	
All children attended	538	93.57%	556	96.69%	+ 18	+ 3.34
Some children attended	30	5.22	10	1.74	- 20	-66.67
No children attended	2	0.35	2	0.35	---	---
No answer	5	0.86	7	1.22		
Total	575	100.00%	575	100.00%		

(5) Hired laborers

About 80 per cent of the hired laborers believed that after land reform many more among them were sending their children to primary schools.

C. Education above primary school:

(1) The 1,250 former-tenant households had

	Before L.R.		10 years after L.R.		Change	
	Number of students	Per Cent per household	Number of students	Per Cent per household		
Middle school students	96	0.08%	674	0.54%	+578	+600.00
Students in colleges	1		32	0.03	+ 31	+310.00

(2) The 250 current-tenant households had

Middle school students	24	0.10%	129	0.48%	+105	+437.50
Students in colleges	2		5	0.02	+ 3	+150.00

(3) The 250 original-owner households had

Middle school students	99	0.39%	304	1.22%	+205	+271.00
Students in colleges	4	0.02	19	0.08	+ 15	+375.00

(4) The 575 former-landlord households had

Middle school students	693	1.25%	1,076	1.87%	+383	+ 55.27
Students in colleges	149	0.26	272	0.47	+123	+ 82.55

(5) Of the 250 hired-laborer households,

A majority believed that people of their kind had a changed attitude toward education and that the new belief was that children of farm laborers ought to be educated beyond primary school.

D. Maximum level of education held desirable for farm children:

(1) Former tenants

	Before L.R.				10 years after L.R.				Change	
	Boys		Girls		Boys		Girls		Boys	Girls
Primary school	715	57.11	819	65.52	209	16.72	387	30.90	−506 − 70.77	−432 − 52.75
Junior middle	119	9.50	88	7.04	133	10.64	184	14.70	+ 14 + 11.77	+ 96 +110.00
Senior middle	78	6.23	35	2.80	131	10.48	96	7.67	+ 53 + 67.95	+ 61 +174.30
Senior voca-tional	40	3.19	20	1.60	91	7.28	45	3.60	÷ 51 +127.50	+ 25 +125.00
Normal school	28	2.24	34	2.72	67	5.36	122	9.74	+ 39 +139.30	+ 88 +258.82
College	169	13.50	124	9.92	512	40.96	302	24.12	+343 +203.00	+178 +143.55
Others	103	8.23	130	10.40	107	8.56	116	9.27		
Total	1,252	100.00	1,250	100.00	1,250	100.00	1,252	100.00		

(2) Current tenants

	Before L.R.				10 years after L.R.				Change	
	Boys		Girls		Boys		Girls		Boys	Girls
Primary school	141	56.40	166	66.40	69	27.60	80	32.00	− 72 − 51.06	− 86 − 51.81
Junior middle	31	12.40	19	7.60	38	15.20	40	16.00	+ 7 + 22.58	+ 21 +110.00
Senior middle	12	4.80	7	2.80	22	8.80	19	7.60	+ 10 + 83.33	+ 12 +171.43
Senior voca-tional ⎤ Normal school ⎦	17	6.80	8	3.20	30	12.00	28	11.20	+ 13 + 76.47	+ 20 +250.00
College	23	9.20	18	7.20	71	28.40	51	20.40	+ 48 +208.70	+ 33 +183.33
Others	26	10.40	32	12.80	20	8.00	32	12.80		
Total	250	100.00	250	100.00	250	100.00	250	100.00		

(3) Original owners (boys and girls together)

Level of Education	Before L.R.		10 years after L.R.		Change	
Primary school	90	36.00%	30	12.00%	- 60	- 66.67
Junior middle	33	13.20	29	11.60	- 4	- 12.12
Senior middle	21	8.40	24	9.60	+ 3	+ 14.29
Senior vocational Normal school	29	11.60	27	10.80	- 2	- 6.90
College	58	23.20	131	52.40	+ 73	+125.86
Others	19	7.60	9	3.60		
Total	250	100.00%	250	100.00%		

E. Preferences in higher education after land reform:

	Former tenants		Former landlords			
			Sons		Daughters	
	Answers	Per Cent	Answers	Per Cent	Answers	Per Cent
According to the young people's own interest	587	46.23%				
Medicine	212	16.69	151	29.09%	48	9.53%
Engineering	105	8.27	142	27.34	24	4.77
Agriculture	83	6.54	29	5.59	8	1.59
Business (including Law*)	29	2.28	27	5.20	26	5.17
Natural Sciences	16	1.26	23	4.46	11	2.19
Humanities/Arts College	13	1.02	8	1.54	63	12.53
Social Sciences	12	0.94				
Normal College	14	1.10	24	4.63	178	35.39
Fine Arts	1	0.08				
Others	13	1.02	115	22.15	145	28.83
Don't know	68	5.35				
No answer	117	9.22				
Total	1,270	100.00%	519	100.00%	503	100.00%

---

*In Taiwan, Law School includes business studies and social sciences.

It is interesting to note the percentage (46.23) of former tenants who were so enlightened and open-minded as to leave to their young people the matter of choosing the field for advanced study in accordance with their interest or ambition. Information about such opinions among current tenants and original owners is lacking, but it can be safely said that theirs must be, by and large, similar to those presented here.

III. Educational and Social Activities

Formal education gave to farm people, who had been largely illiterate and, therefore, looked down upon, some social status and a feeling that 'I am as good as others.' Such status and feeling can be of significant help in getting a farmer to join in some sort of social life or group activity. But it is not invariably so for every person. Farmer Wang may be a graduate of the township's First Primary School, but may yet feel that he is nobody and so refuse to participate in the parents' association on behalf of his children.

In rural Taiwan today there are numerous organizations and activities which give farm people both practical education and some social experience. They are learning to produce, whether in farming or related businesses, more efficiently and more profitably. But since this teaching is always conducted through doing, and the doing always involved group cooperation and, therefore, new personal interrelationships, the whole process of this kind of education is actually a new social life. This aspect of rural life can be much better evaluated today through the functions of the educational organizations than

through the traditional social or civic collections described in the
first section of this chapter. Since the most active organizations
among farm people are created by, or related to, the agricultural-extension service, it is necessary to understand this function of education in
Taiwan.

Since the restoration of Taiwan to China, the agricultural-extension
service has been conducted by different agencies such as the township
farmers' associations, the Taiwan Sugar Corporation and a number of
special, farm-production, processing, and marketing organizations.
In the following, we shall examine the agencies one by one to see how,
and to what extent, the farm people's community participation is promoted
and the agency's services utilized.

1. Farm organizations sponsored by farmers' associations.[4] Agricultural-extension services conducted by the farmers' associations exist
in three main branches: The Farm Advising Program, the Home Economics
Teaching Program, and the rural youth or 4-H Club Program. The chief
task of the Advising Program is to acquaint the farmers with new and
better crops, farm planning and management, techniques and implements,
agricultural economics, and marketing. The Home Economics Program teaches
farm women new and better ideas, methods, and materials in home making
and how to build a satisfactory home life. The 4-H Club's work is to
inspire young boys and girls to become good citizens through learning
skills and discipline, and by providing them with information which will
lead to good citizenship. Principal methods and mechanisms used in these
programs are personal contact, group projects, and community organization.

It is the down-to-earthness which makes this type of education more effective than others in turning a timid, group-shy farmer into a community-participation man.

The extension services undertaken by the other agencies have been primarily limited to farm advising. But the Taiwan Sugar Corporation has recently broadened the scope of its service, and its programs now cover virtually all the subject matter and interests described in the foregoing and employ the same methods and mechanisms.

Extension education fairly well blanketed rural Taiwan ten years after land reform: In 1964 85 per cent of the township-level farmers' associations were conducting extension programs. Each township had one farmers' association, so this meant that 85 per cent of Taiwan had agricultural-extension services. In 95 per cent of the townships, farm-advising service directly, or indirectly, reached all farm people. There were 544, township-level farm advisors and 35, county-level farm supervisors in 1966. About 50 per cent of all farm villages had agricultural demonstration projects. To emphasize the principle of working through group organizations, a number of extension supervisory committees were established. In 1960 these committees involved 316 persons on the county level, 2,772 persons at the township level, and 14,129 persons at the village level. Members of the township and village committees were, with but a few exceptions, farm people. There were also 2,668 village supervisory committees, and each committee averaged 5 or 6 members.

The most important extension unit at the village level is the farm-study class. A total of 4,416 such classes with 78,784 members

were recorded in 1966. Members of these classes were adult farmers.
At a farm-study class the farmers, the extension agent, and, on some
occasions, a farm specialist gathered together to discuss some particular problem existing in the locality and to exchange knowledge and
experience. On some occasions, civic affairs, current problems, and
social events were discussed along with farm innovations.

The demonstration-farm-household was another technique through
which better methods were shown and the farm people socialized. A
demonstration-household was a more advanced or enlightened farm household which was selected to plant a certain proved, but not yet extensively adopted, crop, using certain certified, cultivation methods.
If the result was good, the farm then became a model to demonstrate the
new crop and its good points to other farmers, with the anticipation
that other farmers might adopt the new crop and method of cultivation.
The chief objectives of such a project were (1) to install the demonstrating farmers as local farm leaders with a considerable amount of
socialization and (2) to establish the teaching (demonstrating and
showing) and learning (observing) relationship among the farmers themselves. Behind such projects there was the belief that farmers will
accept and adopt what they have personally seen to succeed, and that
one farm family gains confidence in its own capability after witnessing
the success of another farm family. In 1966 there were 4,035 demon-
stration-farm-households.[5] In 1960 there were 5,051 demonstration
fields. To these demonstration fields, 1,744 observation tours were
conducted for 120,036 farmers.

The township and village, agricultural-extension, supervisory committees and the village, farm-study classes could also call special meetings to discuss any emergency in farm affairs. Up to the end of 1960, the township supervisory committees had met 355 times for this purpose and 4,147 farmers had participated. The village committees had had 1,685 such meetings involving 17,121 persons. The village, farm-study classes called 14,838 emergency sessions and the farmers attending numbered 244,544.

There was also short-term job training for local farm leaders. In 1960, 7,958 persons participated in 135 such training meetings at the county level. At the township level 1,604 training meetings were held and 68,106 local leaders attended.

The recently created, and rapidly developing, joint-cultivation system is another effective way of instituting intimate and in-depth community participation. By joint cultivation it is meant that farmers of the same village who have adjacent fields enter into agreement to plant, cultivate, and harvest their crops cooperatively. They work together and pool farm implements. The great advantage of this system is that each participating household has the advantage of united labor, has more capital resources with which to buy better farm implements, has the benefit of concerted effort for insect and disease control, can adopt new crops and methods faster and with greater rewards than it could do individually. This system can also incorporate those small farms which it would otherwise not be worth-while to cultivate. And, finally, it makes the farms more productive. This system was started first in the cultivation of paddy rice and later on extended to a number of other crops. Up to the end of 1966, there were 296 joint, rice-cultivation projects on 4,732 hectares involving 7,291 farm households. There were also joint projects in such crops as sweet potato, peanuts, and soybeans in which 614 farm households participated. There is no need to emphasize that by joining in these joint-cultivation projects, the farmers and their families enjoyed a much fuller social life. The chief group activities in such projects are discussion study and talks centered on the dissemination of agricultural information, the exchange of experience, and the exploration of new crops, improved cultivation methods, better farm tools, etc. Recreation and civic discussion were secondary, but they served to make the meetings interesting and offered a change in the farm people's tiring routine. Participation was largely voluntary, but sometimes persuasion was necessary. Meetings were held in seasons when they would least interfere with the operation of the farm. And, importantly, there was almost no political talk or partisan indoctrination. A certain farmers' study organization was known by many people to be under the direction or influence of a strong partisan leader. At one time this writer happened to stop in a place where a meeting of this particular farmers' organization was being held. A party man was present. All the officers or leaders present at the meeting were introduced, except this party man. When all formalities and rituals had been taken care of, the party man was called up to perform his part. He quietly and modestly hung up the party founder's picture, read the party 'doxology,' and then retired to a back corner of the room without making any remarks. Thereupon, the farmers at the meeting immediately went into a discussion of some critical problems in regard to the harvesting of the sugarcane. The party man was heard from no more.

This incident showed clearly that political or partisan indoctrination was not welcome at the farmer's meetings and the party man knew it.

The home economics branch of agricultural-extension education had programs designed to get farm women and girls into group activities. In 1966 they were staffed by 235, township-level, home economics, demonstration agents employed by the farmers' associations and 4,488 volunteer local leaders. There were 2,244 home improvement study classes with a membership of 40,452 women. In addition, 1,201 irregular or emergency meetings, held to discuss special homemaking problems or topics, were attended by 38,301 women. Children's centers were operated in busy farm seasons. These centers had 1,522 classes in 1966 and enrolled 70,840 children. Large numbers of farm women were directly, or indirectly, involved in these projects, and they were effective in putting farm wives in touch with each other. Out of such interrelationships, community cooperation is born and strengthened. In addition to regular business meetings, the home-improvement classes sponsored home-industry training: weaving, knitting and sewing. There were, in 1966, a total of 558 such classes attended by 26,781 rural women.

Farm women's community participation can also be seen in the implementation of the various, home-life, improvement programs where women of different households, and different communities, work together. Thus, each woman's mind and world were widened. In 1966 there were 68,067 home-life, improvement projects carried out in rural homes.

To bring knowledge and socializing to the farm boys and girls under the age of 25, there were 4-H clubs with their work, civic, and recreational projects. The chief function of 4-H clubs is to plan and carry

through various group activities among rural youth related to farm
production, home improvement, health buildings, recreation, civic exercise,
and trade-skill training. At the end of 1964 there were 351, 4-H club
advisors or organizers, 4,756 local volunteer leaders, of whom about three-
fifths were men and two-fifths were women. These clubs had a membership of
64,825, of whom 42,767 were male and 22,058 were female. These members
undertook 4,867 work projects with an average participation of 13, boys
or girls or both.

In addition to the regular work projects and work discussion
meetings, 4-H club members organized recreational activities such as
movies and stage plays. In 1964 they put on 1,610 shows and involved
449,589 farm people. In 1966 the 4-H club members banded themselves
into groups or teams and went into such community work projects as
planting and caring for trees along public highways, construction or
repair of village roads, helping farmers in rice transplanting and in
the sterilization of rice nurseries, eradicating rats and insect eggs
in the rice fields, building or repairing irrigation canals, weeding
rice fields, cleaning ditches and drains, repairing dams, and others.
Altogether, 102,179 young people participated in these activities which
had both economic and social values.

4-H clubs also conducted method demonstrations for their own
members and for other farm young people. In 1959, 3,743 method demonstrations were attended by 13,956 young people who learned new ways
of doing things and also enjoyed with each other the experience of
group life. The clubs set up project-result exhibits which attracted
20,637 farm people. The numbers of members who participated in such

programs as <u>kuo-yu̇</u> (Mandarine Chinese) speech contests, demonstration talks, achievement-judging contests, educational tours, and physical check-ups were 2,264, 4,408, 13,668, 27,618, and 12,417, respectively.

These statistics show that in the seven years between 1959 and 1966, the farmers' association-sponsored, agricultural-extension service alone had been able to get about two million farm people, including men, women, and youth, into active community participation.

2. <u>Farm organizations sponsored by the Taiwan Sugar Corporation.</u>[6] Each year there are, on the average, about 150,000 private sugarcane growers. These are the objects of the services of Taiwan Sugar's agricultural-extension branch. The corporation regularly employs an extension staff of 1,700.

Formerly, the Taiwan Sugar Corporation did its extension work mostly through individual contacts. Its extension men went to grower households one by one, to encourage the farmers to plant more hectares in sugarcane and to teach them the best know-how for growing the crop. In recent years, however, extension personnel of the corporation have been deeply impressed by the conspicuous success of the extension work done through the various farmers' organizations. Because of this, the extension branch of the corporation also began to encourage and assist the surgarcane growers to organize themselves into study groups. This writer was asked in 1966 to make a special tour of these classes and to give advice concerning their organization and performance. At the end of 1966, more than 600 such classes were functioning. Each class averaged 20 to 30 active members, that is, growers who attended the study meetings regularly for as long as they continued to be sugarcane growers. Today the membership of these classes must be around fifteen thousand. According to the corporation's personnel who were in charge, they plan to establish 5,100 classes within a period of ten years. When this goal has been reached, there will be more than 150,000 sugar-cane-growing households participating in these classes. Assuming that each household averages three adult persons, there will be 450,000 farm people in direct, or indirect, community participation through this program.

The sugarcane growers' class is, in principle, a village-level organization. The growers of each village organized into one, two, or more study groups. Each group was to have from 25 to 30 members. Under ordinary conditions, one village will have from 25 to 60 households grow-ing sugarcane. If they number more than 40 but less than 60, there should be two classes. All sugarcane growers whose ages were between 20 and 45 could join the classes, or were persuaded to join. But they must be literate, or have had at least primary-school education. Each class elected its president, vice president, and secretary. All affairs of the class were democratically managed by the officers and members themselves, but the class was supervised and assisted by the local township govern-ment, the township farmers' association, and the corporation's branch office or plant located in the vicinity.

The primary function of a sugarcane study class was to see to it that members learned from sugarcane specialists and from each other the newest technology, the latest information about the biological and economic relationships between sugarcane and other crops, and the way in which the production of this crop fitted into the total agri-

cultural economy in a particular farm area. The relationships between
sugar production in Taiwan and the supply and demand for sugar on the
international market were frequently discussed at meetings. With such
discussions, the growers were constantly informed of the rise and fall
of sugar prices and the outlook for income from this crop. In order
to keep the farmers growing sugarcane, the corporation's extension
people, in cooperation with agricultural economists, needed to use
all available knowledge and arguments. This had always been the most
important topic for discussion whenever the international price of
sugar dropped and growing of sugarcane became unprofitable. Technical
information, exchange of field experiences, analysis of the farm economy,
and explanation of international conditions were all very helpful to the
participants and made them no longer feel isolated but, instead, a part
of a complex framework of human and business relations.

As did the classes sponsored by the farmers' associations, the
sugarcane growers' classes also had frequent production contests, mutual
aid or cooperative activities, joint-cultivation projects, programs to
increase knowledge of non-farm affairs, and community-welfare projects.
In summary, the total objective of the sugarcane study program was to
improve the farmer's knowledge and technique in the growing of sugarcane, and to fix the economy of this crop within the framework of the
household's, and the locality's, total farm economy. At the same time,
it also furnished opportunity, means, and atmosphere for socialization
among members.

At first, growers' classes included only men. Later women were
invited and some included both men and women. There were also classes

which were only for women. The inclusion of women greatly extended the influence of the classes.

For the past ten years, the Taiwan Sugar Corporation has been sponsoring an organization called "The Sugarcane Growers' Service Society," or Cheh-Nung Fu-wu She. Ninety-thousand sugarcane growers are now members. The Society's purpose is to help the sugarcane growers by rendering them various kinds of services through their own organization or group activities. According to latest reports,[7] the Society is now operating ten services. Some are as follows:

The Sugarcane Growers Insurance Program. This program covers maternity, accident, disability, life and old age. More than 84,000 growers have joined this program. It has paid benefits in 34,000 cases for a total of 20,000,000 and NT$400,000.

The Sugarcane Growers Mutual Aid Program. Under this program, the sugarcane growers help each other when any one of them is facing a crisis or has a particularly critical need. It is intended to supplement the Insurance Program, to take care of needs which insurance cannot meet. In 1965 the Mutual Aid Program had a membership of 39,000 people, and it had given help to 2,350 persons with payments totaling about NT$7,000,000.

The Guaranteed Loan Program. The purpose of this program is to help growers obtain loans they badly need so that they do not have to subject themselves to the exploitation of unscrupulous loan-sharks. The program offers loans in four categories: sugar storage; production loans, emergency, land-improvement loans; and loans against sugar storage certificates to help sugarcane growers avoid having to sell the

certificate for their sugar stored in the warehouse at a low price.
Production loans are intended to furnish money at reasonable interest
rates so that growers can finance their operations. Loans for special
occasions, or emergencies, cover such occasions as marriage, funerals,
sending a boy to college, and so forth. In a ten-year period, more
than 10,000 sugarcane growers have used this loan program to borrow
more than NT$100,000,000.

The Life Service Program. This program is intended to help the
growers include recreational and educational activities in their daily
lives. A farmer's life is strenuous and stern, and in the countryside
there is still a shortage of facilities, organizations, and atmosphere
for group recreation. This program is designed to promote such activities among sugarcane growers by furnishing them the needed facilities
and program plans. It also offers education scholarships and other
encouragements to rural youth.

The Purchasing Agent Program. This helps growers purchase certain
manufactured commodities, either at wholesale or at discounted prices,
to avoid exploitation by crooked merchants. The program resembles a
consumers' cooperative, and in the past ten years, it has purchased
for its members such articles as radios, motorcycles, sprayers, bicycles,
sewing machines, electric fans, and so on. The total savings must have
been hundreds of millions of N.T. dollars.

The Sugarcane Production Instruction Program. This program,
undertaken in conjunction with the Corporation's agricultural-extension
service, brings to growers the latest knowledge and techniques of sugarcane growing so that production can be increased to full capacity. It

frequently sponsors production contests and more than 27,000 growers have competed. It also conducts observation tours to let the growers see more advanced cultivation methods. Some 14,000 growers have taken part in such tours.

The Information Diffusion Program. Many media are used by the Society to spread information: One is its publication, "Sugarcane Message" (Cheh Pao); other means include color slides, pictures and illustrations, broadcasting, and movies. Just about all of the 200,000 sugarcane growers, their families, their neighbors, and friends have been reached by these programs.

Another type of service provided to growers allows them to obtain reasonably and conveniently the by-products of the Corporation.

3. Community participation by tobacco growers. The Tobacco and Wine Monopoly Bureau of Taiwan provided a service which assisted farmers to grow high-quality tobacco leaf. The service provided up-to-date know-how, organized mutual-aid groups among the growers, and extended financial subsidies to growers. It was conducted mainly through tobacco growers' associations. Because tobacco farming is limited by numerous factors, it is somewhat more profitable than many other crops. For this reason, it has been considered a special privilege to join the associations and practically all the growers have done so. Programs included cropping information, mutual help, and social-recreational activities for growers and their families.[8]

4. Community participation by banana and citrus growers. The banana growers and the citrus fruit growers have their respective extension services and organizations. The Taiwan Fresh Fruit Production and Marketing

Co-operative Association employed specialists to provide banana growers with technical assistance. To gain efficiency, these specialists have been the example for other agricultural-extension workers, have organized banana growers into small groups, and are conducting their extension service through the groups.

In the same way, the extension workers for citrus fruit growers set up their service.[9] Citrus orchards in Taiwan suffer considerable losses each year from disease and insect damage. Therefore, the most urgent need was for effective controls. A grower's individual efforts could do very little, but joint actions produced effective controls. Because of this experience, citrus growers throughout the province were advised by the agricultural development agencies of the Government to organize themselves into protection teams for joint control projects. All team members were active citrus growers, and all active growers were persuaded to join the teams. Team members were trained and retrained in latest techniques of planting, cultivating, and protecting the citrus groves. They were taught the best ways of harvesting, handling, and marketing. Because the members of each team were trained together, worked at control programs together, and helped each other in all phases of orchard work, it was only natural that socialization developed out of their working relationships.

At the end of 1966 there were 1,004 teams with about 30,000 members. The growers who were young and intellectually more advanced were selected for study groups. Most of these growers had had at least a junior, vocational-agricultural school education. A few were graduates of horticulture departments of colleges of agriculture. Since their knowledge of citrus growing was richer than that of the ordinary growers, they were supposed to be leaders or advisors to the protection teams. They were encouraged to volunteer technical and inspirational assistance to the ordinary growers.

5. Community participation through farmers' organizations.

It seems clear that the agricultural-extension services of the various agencies in Taiwan had had both broad and deep effects upon the people. Whether in business or for fun, the farm people have come into a time when they can no longer escape being involved in some kind of group activity. Today it would be hard to find a farm household which does not belong to at least one of the community organizations.

There is another way of viewing effects of the community organizations and the importance of community participation in the farm people's learning for improvement. In a treatise called A Study of the Results of the Application of Various Agricultural Extension Methods in Taiwan,[10] there is the statement that among 630 farm households 38 per cent got their new agricultural information from personal contacts or advice. Nearly all personal contact, or advice, came from extension personnel of farmers' associations, from the township public offices, the Taiwan Sugar Corporation, the Taiwan Tobacco and Wine Monopoly Bureau, or the Taiwan Food Bureau. About 22 per cent came from the farmers' own primary organizations such as agricultural study groups, home improvement classes, 4-H clubs, sugarcane study groups, tobacco growers' associations, citrus protection teams, and a number of others. Some 25 per cent came from neighbors and friends. The getting of information from one's neighbor or friend can be between two persons only, or it can be an informal evening gathering among several members of the same village, neighborhood, or kinship circle. The three channels together provided for more than 85 per cent of the farm information received by the farm people. As the extension agents came to depend more and more on the farmers' primary organizations for the effective implementation of their programs, the people's community participation became increasingly important.

In an article entitled A Study of the Operation of Small Farms in Taiwan,[11] the authors report that farmers who have up-to-date agricultural information prefer that operational decisions be made by the whole or, at least, most of the family, not by a single individual in authority. Such farmers find it easy to ignore tradition and to make whatever other changes or readjustments will bring about more production and higher income. For instance, when a farmer is able to grow a wider variety of vegetables in different seasons, and when he is able to meet consumer demands and responds to fluctuation or prices, his farm operation will be more profitable than if he dared not reduce the plantings of rice and sweet potato. Farmers who kept themselves informed of the latest agricultural innovations would generally make more efficient use of farm land by multi-cropping and diversification. The more enlightened farmer knows the advantages of deep plowing, close planting, and other labor-absorbing cultivation techniques. By applying more labor, via the use of advanced methods, a farmer would receive greater profits.

Studies[12] were made recently to find out the extent to which farm people participated in agricultural-extension organizations and the results of their participation. The studies discovered that personal

suggestion, recommendation,and encouragement were the chief factors
leading farm people, both adult and youth, into participation. These
suggestions, recommendations, and encouragements came 40 per cent from
the extension agents of the farmers' associations, 36 per cent from
local leaders, chairmen of the study groups, demonstration farmers,
neighbors, friends and family. Members of 4-H clubs had been influenced
by teachers and/or schoolmates. In most cases,these personal contacts
came in various kinds of group relationships and in a social atmosphere.

What had been the motivation for joining an organization?
Seventy-three per cent wished to learn new knowledge and new techniques
and/or prepare for a future occupation. About 19 per cent wanted
teaching materials and teaching instruments from the classes, wanted
more contact with the extension agents or other farmers, or wanted
social prestige and reputation. Only a little over 1 per cent of them
had the idea of getting some financial help or material benefits. These
figures show that the great majority of the farm people had had realistic
and laudable purposes.

For the participating farm people, especially the adult farmers
and farm women, significance of their participation was measured by
the degree of fulfillment of the aims they had had when they joined
the organization. In the study, achievement is rated in four degrees:
very much, some, very little, and none. 'Very much:' more than one-
half of the purpose was achieved; 'some:' less than one-half was
achieved; 'very little:' less than one-quarter was achieved; and
'none:' achievement was zero. The study found that 54 per cent of
the members of the agricultural classes rated their achievement 'very

much.' Less than 50 per cent of the home-improvement classes reached that degree. A little more than one-third of the 4-H club members had reached it. Lumped together, about 46 per cent of all participants rated their achievement 'very much.'

On the other end of the scale were persons who had had no success at all in the realization of their objectives. In the agricultural classes, these accounted for 3 per cent; 4 per cent in the home improvement classes; and 7 per cent among the 4-H club members. Their reasons for failure of achievement were given as follows: 30 per cent in the classes complained that there had been too little contact between themselves and the extension agents. Twenty per cent blamed unsatisfactory scheduling. Another 30 per cent said there had been too much empty formality in the programs. Others said there was no direct relationship between the content of the programs and the practical needs of the local community, and still others cited inadequacy in the extension workers' capability for teaching and guiding.

For members of the home improvement classes, the greatest difficulty was that rural women were so busy most of the time. Meetings, therefore, must be at the right time, but it was always a great problem to find the right arrangement. Consequently, a large number of women could not attend classes or other activities because the time of meetings conflicted with their work.

IV. Participation in the Farmers' Associations

1. The membership. The township farmers' associations were briefly mentioned in the first section of this chapter, but because in the last

ten or fifteen years these associations have affected farm life so much, it is necessary to make some further investigation into their history, structure, and functions.

In 1938, one year after Japan started her ambitious war to conquer the whole of east and southeast Asia and this island was already under Japanese control, the island's farmers were compelled to join the farmers' associations.[13] It has been recorded that in 1940 the total membership in all the associations was 609,817 farmers. With their family members included, they accounted for about one-half of Taiwan's total population at that time. After Taiwan was restored to China following World War II, the associations were thoroughly reorganized in every respect. After reorganization, the associations became truly farmers' organizations. In 1954 there were 340 township farmers' associations and their membership was 589,299. There were two kinds of membership: active members who were persons actually engaged in farming, and associate members who were non-farmers but who lived in the rural areas and had genuine interest in farming and the farm people's well-being. The associations' active membership was 395,087, or 67 per cent, and their associate membership was 194,212, or 33 per cent. By 1958 total membership had increased to 726,681, two-thirds active members and one-third associate members. Associate members enjoyed all the privileges of membership but could not vote in elections or be elected to any office, except that one-third of the supervisors could be elected from among them.

After the reorganization, whether or not every farm household was still required by Government to join the farmers' association had not been clearly stated. In 1958 Government statistics stated the total number of farm households was 808,153 and the associations' members totalled 726,681.

According to customary practice, two or three legally independent families

could actually live together as one household, and they would then be rep-

resented under one name in the farmers' association. If this was the case,

the number of farm households in the membership of the farmers' associations

must have been smaller than that recorded in the census book. This is why

only about 90 per cent of the farm households were members of farmers'

associations in 1958. The ratio between the farm households and the asso-

ciation memberships should, however, be looked at from a more realistic

angle than simply the number of farmers belonging to the association. The

truth is that because of the great number of farm-related functions perform-

by the associations, and the degree and variety of ways in which farming an-

farm life are involved in, or affected by, the associations' activities, no

farm household today can be a going concern without having some relationshi-

with the farmers' associations, and whether or not it holds membership is o

no real concern.

    2. _Farmers' involvement in the associations' activities._ The farmer'-

relationship with the association can be readily seen in reviewing the orga-

zation's functions: marketing, warehousing, processing of farm products f

the members and for Government agencies; procuring, processing, manufacturi-

and distributing of farm requisites; providing agricultural-extension servi-

and providing deposit and credit facilities to members (and to non-members

if special permission is given by the provincial government). Taiwan's far-

now market a variety of farm products through the associations, principally

special vegetables such as onions, Irish potatoes, beans, mushrooms, aspara-

Some farmers also market their pigs and poultry products through the associtions. As agriculture becomes more commercialized, that is, crops being produced entirely or chiefly for the market, the greater will be the farmer's reliance on the associations for marketing. This will be especially important in respect to the increasing export to overseas markets. The important fruits, such as bananas and citrus fruits, are being marketed by the Fresh Fruit Marketing Association.

Ever since their reorganization, the farmers' associations have been charged with the milling of rice for the farmers and for Government agencies. The Food Bureau requires the associations to collect the unhusked rice brought in by farmers as payment for chemical fertilizers and for land being purchased. The associations then mill the grain for the Food Bureau and the Government uses the milled rice as army food and as subsidies to Government employees and teachers in the public schools. In their services of supplying farm needs, the associations are increasingly involved in wholesaling, purchasing, and retailing of insecticides and fungicides and related equipment. As the needs for materials and machines on the farms increase, in relation to the increase of diversification, commercialization, and modernization infarming, the importance and volume of these services will undoubtedly grow very rapidly.

The combined volume of business done by the associations' in marketing, supplying, and processing services is indicated in these cash values.[14]

In 1953 the cash value of the associations' businesses was NT$96,319, 366.82. Of this amount, NT$71,555,428.43, or 74 per cent, represented the value of the association's own businesses of marketing, supplying, and processing, and NT$24,763,938.39, or 26 per cent, was earned by services to members and by services to Government were NT$391,780,449 and NT$67,641,460, respectively. In percentages, if the values in 1953 were 100, those in 1959 were about 377. Considered separately, values of the association's services to members in 1959 were at 548 and values of services to Government were at 273, increases of 448 per cent and 173 per cent, respectively. The significance of the programs of the agricultural-extension service under taken by the township farmers associations have been described in the preceding section of the present chapter. What this indicates is that the associations will surely come to play an even more important role in the modernization of agriculture in Taiwan. They will be the avenue for introduction to, and instruction of, up-to-date farm technology and they will lay the groundwork for building a new, agricultural economy.

The associations' deposit and credit facilities for members have grown rapidly in the first ten years following land reform. In 1952 the farmers' total deposits in the associations' credit division was NT$140,423,000 and the total amount of farm loans made was NT$72,145,000. In 1965 the figures were NT$2,893,995,000 and NT$2,456,785,000, respectively. Deposits increased 1,961 per cent and farm loans rose 3,305 per cent.[15] This rapid growth has been attributed largely to the fast commercialization of agriculture in Taiwan, or development in the marketing of farm products. Actually, the two kinds of growth encourage and build upon each other.

The reason for describing the activities of the farmers' associations at such length is the need to show that farmers in Taiwan have already been deeply involved in, and affected by, the farmers' associations. In this involvement, the associations help make farming progressive and farm life prosperous, and,in return, the farmers give life and power to the associations. This is community participation in its full and democratic meaning.

V. Land Reform and Community Participation

1. <u>Land reform and the new community spirit</u>. More than 62 per cent of the former tenants said it was land reform that aroused community spirit in them, and it was land reform that caused them to foresee the benefits of being members of community organizations. More than 44 per cent claimed that their becoming community-minded was chiefly due to the improvement of their living conditions following land reform. If the improvement of living conditions in these households was,for the most part,attributable to land reform, as has been discovered in the preceding chapter, then the rise of community spirit in these households can also be considered a result of land reform, although an indirect result.

In general, people's having, or not having, a lasting interest in any kind of community organization or group activity depends to a great extent on whether they have a role, and particularly an important role, to play in the organization or activity. About 36 per cent of the former tenants admitted that their satisfying experience in the various organizations was due largely to the fact that they had specific roles and that these roles were, in most cases, more important than those they had had occasionally before. The reason for their having been assigned more important roles was that they had become farm owners. In community organizations owner-farmers' positions are usually higher than those held by tenants.

According to information presented in the preceding sections of this chapter, those farmers who were still tenants at the time of the study conducted themselves much the same as did the former-tenant-now-owners, in respect to community constructions and social-welfare programs, etc. Their households had not acquired owner status, but they had been beneficially affected by land reform. The rent limitation program not only released tenants from the heavy burden of high rental, and so increased their annual income, it also rid them of the feelings of fear, humiliation, and inferiori they had had in relations with their landlords. Since land reform, tenants and landlords have really been standing in equal positions. If this has not as yet been entirely realized in their material possessions, it has been clarified in social and psychological relations. With improved income and bettered social position, and with awareness of a new freedom from fear and humiliation, today's tenant-farmers have morale and ambition equal to those of the owner-farmers. If the former-tenant-now-owner's newly aroused or increased interest in community participation was a product of the land-to-the-tiller program, the current tenant's new interest must have been due to the rent limitation program.

Before land reform, when tenant-farmers were living under miserable con ditions and had acute inferiority complexes, very few of them could hope, or feel the need, to send their children to school. The few households which d educate their children were, in most cases, looked down upon and mistreated. The parents seldom had the courage even to enter the school. They were extremely timid in the presence of a teacher. In the old days, most community affairs were either controlled or dominated by landlords and school teachers the people who were considered gentlemen or gentry. Given the presence of these people, the humble tenants could hardly have any thought of entering the organizations, much less take active parts in them. Land reform changed these conditions considerably. A majority of the school teachers interviewed stated that today the children of both the former tenants and the current tenants are free from abuse and discrimination. Reason? Their parents are no longer timid, down-trodden tenant-cultivators.

The teachers also said that after land reform the new owner-farmers and the current tenants had become at ease and were no longer self-conscious in meeting school teachers. With the large landlords gone from the rural communities, with ordinary landlords having become ordinary owner-farmers, with the school teachers and other intellectuals no longer objects of fear, and with their own desire aroused to be recognized by fellow villagers, it is small wonder that these transformed, small farmers should have become interested and bold in entering community organizations, in taking positions, and in playing their parts.

As has been pointed out previously, in the countryside, even today, one's education or lack of it has, in many cases, great bearing on one's feeling at ease and respected in a community organization. It is true that some people will be shy and timid in group relations whatever their education; nevertheless, it is commonly acknowledged that educated people have the greatest potentiality for important roles, feeling assured, finding enjoyment, and contributing much toward the fulfillment of joint purposes in group activities. At any rate, it is safe to say that education is a prerequisite for spontaneous and satisfying community participation. The influence of education is not limited in the sense that the farmers themselves must be educated; just having their children in school could have about the same effect. There is no question but that many small or tenant-farmers have risen in social status since land reform because of their children's education. It could be very possible that it was this very fact that has made them no longer the grass-seed, ignored, poor-peasant type of farmers.

2. **Land reform and schooling of children.** Land reform has had important effects on the farm people's interest in educating their children as much as possible. The explanation is that, first, land reform transformed most tenants into owners. Those who were still tenants at the time of the study were feeling freer, more respected, more prosperous, and they had the prospect of becoming owners. This was, again, due largely to the effects of rent limitation. Once having gained in status, these newly-transformed tenant-cultivators soon arrived at the decision that their children, if not themselves, must have an education. Without it, they would sooner or later sink back to the old level.

Second, land reform gave the farmers means to improve their living conditions. When living conditions improved, they then found the means, and gained the desire, to send their children to school.

3. **Land reform and agricultural-extension services.** The relationship between land reform and the farm people's community participation has been manifested in the establishment and rapid growth of the numerous farmers' organizations sponsored by the various agricultural-extension agencies. The farmer's chief purpose in accepting extension service organizations is to gain in knowledge and techniques. Improved farming results in improved living conditions. But there is an important question. Do all farmers join the organizations to learn and to seek the new and better things? Do farmers always, regardless of their conditions,

have the desire to learn and, therefore, to attend study groups readily?
No, that is not true. The great majority, at least of peasant farmers, the
hopeless and depressed tenant-farmers, seldom have the desire or incentive
to join such organizations in anticipation of a future improvement in their
work and life. Where a rural township is composed largely of this kind of
farmer, none of those farmers' organizations described in Section III of this
chapter can be active or functional. There are no people to come and make the
organization a going concern. Even if a few people do come, they come blindly;
they come out of forceful persuasion, they come without any clear and definite
objective in mind. Some may even come with selfish ideas of using the organization to gain personal profit. Under such conditions, no community organization can become firmly established, developed, and made capable of fulfilling those functions which it is supposed to perform among and for the farmers.

Now it is quite clear that the farmers must first have optimism, hope,
and faith in the future of both their farming and their lives as a whole
before they can feel interest in new ways or a desire to learn new things.
Secondly, they must be free to make their own decisions on the selection of
crops, cropping systems, cultivation methods, land use, and supplementary
enterprises if they are ever to feel the need or the significance of participating in those organizations which bring the new ways. What good would
it do for a tenant-farmer hopelessly bound by the old, farm-tenancy system
and the traditional, landlord-domination-tenant-submission relationship,
to learn new ways which he cannot put into use, or to produce more and more
when only the least portion of the increase would go to him?

Within the community organizations and activities, there must be men
who have free minds and uninhibited emotions who think deeply, express

themselves genuinely, act sincerely, and learn earnestly. Otherwise, the organization cannot function effectively or reach its objectives. Neither will the members' experience there be meaningful.

According to analyses in Chapter Four and Chapter Five, it was the changes wrought by land reform that led large numbers of tenant-cultivators to become hopeful and optimistic and gave them faith in the future. It was land reform that gave farmers freedom of choice. It was this freedom that encouraged the farmers to look for new knowledge, new techniques, and new ways of living. Given this freedom and encouragement, the farmers voluntarily and enthusiastically joined and supported the instructional programs and other extension-service activities. This should be ample evidence of the existence of a relationship between land reform and the farm people's community participation.

Moreover, the relationship is not accidental, for when the land-reform programs were being implemented, the planners also had in mind the development of the agricultural-extension programs, whereby the changes brought about by land reform could achieve fullest productivity and the benefits therefrom fully and profitably exploited, in order that the whole of agriculture should soon make significant progress.

Finally, let us note this statement:[16]

> The land reform benefited 554,000 (about 75 per cent) of Taiwan's farm families through rent reduction and by acquiring ownership of land they tilled. Before land reform 41 per cent of farm land was operated by tenants. This has been reduced to 16 per cent. Farmers retaining more income, are making land improvements, constructing better houses, buying more equipment. With improved economic and social status, they take greater responsibility in community activities.

Notes

[1]The parents' association is an organization to help the school.

[2]The result of the survey is Rural Progress in Taiwan by E. Stuart Kirby.

[3]"Education in Rural Taiwan," an article contained in Collection of Martin M. C. Yang's Essays (in Chinese), Taipei, 1964.

[4]This section is based on information in (1) Annual Business Report of Taiwan's Farmers' Associations, 1965; (2) A Brief Report on Taiwan's Agricultural Extension Education, 1966; (3) Taiwan Province Agriculture Yearbook, 1965.

[5]The number of demonstration farm households in 1966 has decreased, in comparison with the number of 1960. This shows that the stage of emphasizing result demonstration in agricultural extension has begun to pass, as it has in the United States.

[6]Information is based on articles dealing with the organization and functions of the sugarcane production study classes published in the Taitang Tung-hsun, Volumes 36 and 37, 1965, 1966.

[7]Po-ching Yang, How to Put an Ideal into Practice: Tenth Year Anniversary of the Sugarcane Growers Service Society, 1965, Taiwan.

[8]More information is being gathered and will be added when available.

[9]Circular Message on Citrus Fruits Protection (or Kan Chiu Pao Hee Teng-hsun), No. 1, published by the Hsin-chu District Citrus Fruit Protection Training Center, February, 1967.

[10]Martin M. C. Yang and T. S. Wu, A Study of the Results of the Application of Various Agricultural Extension Means and Methods in Taiwan (In Chinese), 1964.

[11]S. C. Hsieh, T. H. Lee, Y. C. Wang, and Y. L. Teng, A Study of the Operation of the Small Farms in Taiwan in the Taiwan Bank Quarterly, Volume XII No. 3.

[12]T. S. Wu and Martin M. C. Yang, A Study of the Farmers' Reaction to the Agricultural Extension Education; Ching-yung Liu and Martin M. C. Yang, A Study of the Results of Agricultural Extension in Taiwan.

[13]M. H. Kuo, "Farmers Organizations in Taiwan" in the monograph Agricultural Economy in Taiwan (In Chinese), in A Series of the Study of Taiwan, No. 75, April, 1962, published by the Bank of Taiwan.

[14]Ibid., p. 296.

[15]Wei-ming Ho, The Developing of Marketing and the Utilization of Agricultural Resources, pp. 17-18.

[16]E. Stuart Kirby, Rural Progress in Taiwan, p. 27.

Chapter Ten

SOCIAL STRUCTURE AND SOCIAL RELATIONS
AFTER LAND REFORM

I. Traditional Social Structure
   1. The Landlord-as-patriarch and
      Tenant-as-household-dependent
      (Pseudo-kinship) Pattern
   2. The Framework of a Rural Community
   3. Characteristics of the Traditional
      Family
   4. The Traditional Farm Village: An
      Extension of the Traditional Family
   5. The Landlord-tenant Relationship
   6. General Patterns

II. Changes in Social Structure
   1. Family Structure and Family Life
   2. Kinship Relationship
   3. Landlord-tenant Relationship
   4. General Patterns

On the one hand, land reform had transferred some landlords to businesses and industries in the cities while reducing others to ordinary owner-farmers, and, on the other hand, it had lifted the humble and meek tenant-cultivators to the status of landowners with much improvement and respectable living conditions; thus, the social structure and patterns of relationships in rural communities must have been considerably and significantly affected. Importantly, the analyst of change must remember that land reform in Taiwan had not been carried out with violence or destruction but in a peaceful and democratic way. The undertaking was a socio-economic correction based on justice, consideration, compensation for sacrifice, payment for acquisition, and the principle of "live and let live." It was not an overturning, or Fan-shen, carried out with hatred, revenge, and destruction of one by the raging madness of another. It had not created socio-economic upheaval in which landlords as a class were eliminated outright by tenants turned into a mob and possessed by a primitive frenzy. Therefore, if there had been any social change as a result of land reform, it would very probably have been different from the sort of changes aroused in an undemocratic type of land reform. The task of this chapter is to make an investigation into the nature and degree of social change in rural Taiwan following the land reform.

I. Traditional Social Structure

Since changes are differences between things old and things new, or since new conditions arise from old conditions, it is necessary to first show the old conditions before one can say that there has been any change or describe the nature of a change. Hence, a brief review is necessary of the traditional social structure and patterns of relationships in the rural community.

1. The landlord-as-patriarch and tenant-as-household-dependent (pseudo-kinship) pattern. The distinctive feature of rural Taiwan was its characteristic pattern device: landlord-as-patriarch and tenants-as-household-dependents, a pseudo-kinship alliance. In rural communities where there had been no landlords, or the landlord-tenant system was not important, the wealthy families, the rural gentry, substituted for the landlords. In other communi-

ties, the influential clan leaders, or <u>tsu-chang</u>, filled the landlords' place.
In Taiwan the landlord-as-patriarch and tenants-as-household-dependents
relationship was the socio-economic pattern in most farm villages before land
reform. In many such villages, landlords, village gentry, and clan leaders
existed in a combination: The landlords, village gentry, and clan leaders
were the same persons; that is to say, the three statuses appertained to
some individuals all at the same time. In other villages, however, the three
statuses might have applied separately to different persons or households.
It was possible that in some instances several persons, or households, held
the influence or power over village affairs because they were economically
well-to-do and had some sort of education and capability, despite their
being actual land tillers rather than landlords living on farm rents. In
another village, perhaps, all the villagers might have been active farmers
and, generally, on the same economic level. But perhaps some households
happened to be members of the upper (senior) generations of a clan, or of
two or three clans, in the village. Being members of the senior generations,
plus having some kind of personal merits or capability, gave these persons,
or households, status as <u>tsu-chang</u> in the village community.

As in any society, there must be leadership; there must be power
holders or a power center. In communities where no election system existed,
the leadership or power center had to be taken by, or given to, one or more
of the three leader categories: either to any one of them or to several
who held the leadership collectively. It was taken or given with the people's
consensus. In communities where the chief livelihood was the primitive and
individualistic self-sufficient type of agriculture, and where human relations evolved mainly on kinship lines, landlords or comparatively prosperous

owner-farmers, and senior, impressive, capable clan members had been the ideal figures to which the leadership or power naturally went.

Before land reform the farm villages in Taiwan were, in numerous ways, kinship dominant. Being kinship dominant, the traditional feeling, formalities, and even the unifying of kinship, were still apparent and in many cases still strong. Many of the kinship-derived or kinship-sustained institutions and practices were also still there. This was especially true of those communities which were purely Hakha[1] and Hakha-dominated. It was less true of many Min-nan villages. A home economics, extension agent gives this account: The agent was once assigned to a Hakha farm village. She tried to organize in the village a home-improvement class. She was introduced to the official village head,[2] a rather young person, and with his help gathered a group of young and middle-aged farm women at one of the homes. After an inspiring talk by the agent and some exchange of ideas, the group agreed to form a class and settled on an opening date and place of meeting. But when on the opening day the agent arrived in the appointed place, she found that the expected group of women were not present, except for two individuals. The agent was startled and insisted she must know what had happened. Finally, the two women told her the reason. The agent's mistake had been that when she came to the village for the first time, she forgot an important tradition in a Hakha village and failed to make a call on the powerful woman tsu-chang of the community. Without that courtesy call, and without having first informed the tsu-chang of her plans and purposes, the home-improvement class was doomed, for the clan dowager gave word that no woman under her influence was allowed to join such a class. Frightened by this warning, the village women had not the courage to show up on the opening day. The extension worker regretted

her negligence and went to call on the Lao t'ai-t'ai, Old Lady, immediately.

Upon meeting with her, the agent paid her respects and explained the purposes,

importance, and rules of the home-improvement classes. Having been duly re-

spected and fully informed, the tsu-chang quickly passed her order that all

younger women in the village should attend the classes and pay good attention

to the extension worker's instruction.

If the landlords, the wealthy householders, the powerful clan leaders,

or the village gentry, had played the patriarch's roles over the general

populace in the villages, they must also have performed the tasks to enhance

the villagers' well-being, which a real grandfather would have been doing

for his households members. In contrast to the often reported exploitations

and oppressions inflicted upon the small farmers and ordinary villagers by

many landlords, wealthy households, and gentry, there had been many rural

communities which were under protection, guidance, discipline, and benevol-

ence from such persons or households. At one time or another, many a farm

village, or even a rural township, was led out of starvation and perhaps

into community prosperity and security by these good-hearted and community-

minded aristocrats. Even those who at some time had been hard and practiced

exploitation might also have done some good at other times in some ways.

Since the villagers enjoyed their prosperity and security and knew that these

were results of the village leaders' efforts, they felt respect and gratitude

toward their benefactors, much as family members felt respect and gratitude

for their grandfathers or ancestors. Taking into consideration the small

farmer's simple habits and lack of sophistication, one would be inclined to

believe that in the old days, an impoverished peasantry would have felt

completely dependent on its village leaders, much as immature children
are dependent on parents.

2. <u>The framework of a rural community</u>. The physical structure of a
rural community in traditional Taiwan, as in many parts of mainland China,
can be briefly sketched like this: The basic village was a group of between 50 and 200 households[3] whose homes[4] were set closely together in rows,
or in irregular patterns, with lanes, paths, and streets dividing the homes
into separated squares, patches, or clusters. These were physical or visibl
divisions. There were, also, social or invisible divisions. Such divisions
or segregations, were based on kinship lines, or on social and long-standing
family alliances. Some of these divisions coincided with the physical divisions; others did not. A number of households of the same kinship group,
for instance, might cluster in one section, while the families of another
such group were scattered all over the village site. Perhaps ten or a dozen
families might come together chiefly because of the social intercourses goin
on among them and they, in most cases, had their front gates open on the sam
lane or circle. Thus, the two types of division could coincide or they
could cut across each other.

A familiar characteristic of the traditional farm village was a small
number of houses that stood separately at the central part, or in a commanding section, of the village. These were large houses of good quality, with
big courtyards and great front gates. Surrounding these homes were the ordi
ary wood-and-stone houses and the mud-wall-straw-roof huts. In the outstand
ing homes lived the landlords or the rich farm owners. The ordinary, or
small-owner farmers, lived round about them in houses built usually of a

stone foundation, brick and beaten-earth walls, and thatched or tiled roofs. The tenant families were in the mud-and-straw huts.

In northern Taiwan the village's physical pattern is different. Here, a farm village is more an administrative unit than a close aggregation of natural growth. It consists usually of three to five clusters of houses. Such a cluster resembles an American rural neighborhood. It may contain only three or four households or it may have ten to fifteen. The clusters are separated from each other by fields, roads, rivers, or hills. The distance between two clusters varies from several tens of yards to one-half kilometer. It is much more difficult to find the chosen three or five sample households in a northern village than it is in a southern one.

In southern Taiwan, uniting the single, compact farm villages, there are small village-groups. A village-group may include from two to five small and large compact farm villages. For various reasons, but more often by geographical closeness and kinship ties, the two, three, or five villages are drawn together. On the one hand, they may have many kinds of joint activities or cooperative enterprises, such as a primary school, irrigation facilities, and others. On the other hand, they quarrel among themselves, even fight against each other.

Then, in both southern and northern Taiwan, there are rural and urban townships. A rural township is _hsiang_ and an urban township is _chen_ in the Chinese language. A rural township, or _hsiang_, consists of a number of single-farm villages, compact or loose, small village-groups (in the southern section), and a center.[5] The center of a township, whether _hsiang_ or _chen_, is a place in which marketing, manufacturing or handicrafts, commerce, education, communication, medical services, technical services, and politics of the whole township concentrate. There are, of course, many stores, shops, marketplaces, public offices, schools and other buildings. The greatest concentration of population is also in that administrative area and, for this reason, there are a larger number of households in the center than in any of the single villages.

In our discussion, a local or rural community is, in most cases, a rural township. When the term "local politics" is used, it refers to politics within the whole, rural township. Sometimes, under certain circumstances, a single farm village or a small village-group may also be considered a rural or farm community. From a structural-functional point of view, a township-wide rural community would more closely accord with the modern definition of 'community' than would a single-farm village.

Socially, in the invisible framework, a similar configuration existed. The landlords, at least the big, rich landlords, were at the center, were in the commanding positions in the society. They were outstanding in numerous ways. Tenant householders were humble, minute, and as lowly as mud-straw huts. The small-but-owner farmers occupied a position in between, though they also looked upon the landlord with respect and admiration

Upon and within this skeleton, a great complex of relationships and interactions flowed in all directions, smoothly at one time and roughly at another, up in one place and down in another. In their flow, some follow through channels which are comparatively constant and durable, the channels called institutions, social habits or customs. Others change course frequently; still others go on a length of time and then disappear or submerge; later on they may reappear. Grouped together, these relationships result in

social change. No channels of human relations or interactions are unchange-
able. They may remain unchanged for a long time, but not forever. Nor does
any one relationship or interaction change course or appear and disappear
all the time. Also, because the channels or courses through which interactions
flow are paralleling, crossing, uniting, and separating all the time, the
flowing stuffs in the channels come in contact with each other very frequently.
The result of the contacts may be mutual attraction and unification, may be
traveling together hand in hand and in good cooperation; or it may be mutual
repulsion, competition, and fighting for each other's extinction.

According to one school of thought, most of the time, human interactions
have been filled with mutual repulsion, cut-throat competition, struggle for
self-survival, and other destruction. The opposing school contends that
human beings are, by nature, good. Consequently, human interactions differ
from those of animals. Human relationships are characterized by sympathy,
affection, tenderness, and cooperation. The truth, we may venture to say,
most probably lies between the two extremes. Man has most of the natural
impulses and potentialities that animals have. Should he be allowed to, or,
if unfortunately he were able only to, react to the stimulation of natural
impulses or the baser desires, man could have been as 'natural' as the
beasts. But, somehow, man is able to differentiate in terms of his own
interests, what is good only for the moment but destructive afterward, and
what is profitable in the long run and also free from danger or harm. Man
also has the wisdom and willpower to control, and even suppress, the animal
impulses in order to prevent harm, which is an inevitable result of the in-
dulgence of those impulses. Acting positively, he can invent ways and means,
whereby the natural impulses need not be altogether suppressed but may be

appropriately expressed. An appropriate expression is one in which the
impulse is so expressed that it would do no harm but would, instead, make
life more meaningful and enjoyable. The natural development of the human
being would not then be thwarted nor would it become a tropical jungle, a
rampant uncontrolled growth.

The ways and means man uses to control and regulate the expression
and development of his natural impulses and the flow of human interrelationships are, for the majority of the people, 1) his social institutions,
2) the rules established and enforced by the people of means and power in
the society, and 3) the advice and guidance of wise men and leaders. The
terms 'people of means and power' and 'leaders' are to be understood as
corresponding to power structure and functioning leadership rather than to
features of personality.

3. <u>Characteristics of the traditional family.</u> In traditional Taiwan,
as in traditional China, the most important social institution employed to
produce, channel, beautify, and regulate primary human relationships had
been the family and the kinship network. Therefore, there is need here for
a brief review of the traditional family.

For brevity, only important characteristics will be analysed. The
primary characteristic of the family's organization was its compoundness.
By compoundness, we mean that the family was, or had been, composed of two
or more distinct units which could rightfully be considered nuclear families
This does not mean that every family was compound, or that if such a union
existed, it was in existence at all times. But, in general, the traditional
family was a compound family or it had been at one time or another. It

can also be stated that the compound family had been the pattern generally accepted or taken for granted. It was one of the important, traditional social values that a family of prominence ought to be a composite of a number of conjugal units, huge accumulations of material possessions, and all kinds of prestigious social appurtenances and special privileges. Of these three precious things, the first one, multiple conjugal units, was conceded to be of the greatest importance because it was considered the basic condition, or the prime requisite, for the achievement of the others. However, a compound family was not, necessarily, at the same time a big family having numerous people. It is true that any family which consisted of three or more nuclear units could not but be big. But families could have two or three nuclear units and not number more than ten people. Therefore, many of the traditional Chinese families were compound families, but not all compound families were large.

Another characteristic of the traditional family was the everlasting stress upon loyalty and unity among members. This was the spiritual goal toward which all adult members were supposed to devote themselves. Ways of achieving this goal were prescribed, and there were varieties of efforts, rules, organizations or arrangements pertaining to the interrelations among family members. In families where most relationships were smooth, well-managed or organized, and to a certain extent genuine because of some degree of affection for one another, family loyalty and unity were present and keenly felt. This was the base on which family continuity and family prosperity established and grew. At the least, the family was kept united because of these characteristics. A traditional Chinese family included both the living and the deceased members, especially the ancestors. Since the family membership was so inclusive, the interrelations among members were extended to include former members.

There were important reasons for the early Chinese to emphasize family loyalty and unity. First, the nature, structure, and conditions of the early Chinese economy were based on family. It might well be called a family economy. In the countryside, farming was a family business, operated on a family farm, and its products were chiefly for family consumption. In the towns and cities, business activities consisted mainly of handicrafts and commerce in the buying, selling, and transporting of goods which were principally for use in daily living. These enterprises, too, were conducted primarily by, in, and for the family. The traditional farming, handicrafts, and family-operated commerce together built an economy of scarcity. This system dominated life in China for more than twenty centuries, until very recent times. In such circumstances, only by hard work, united efforts, and keeping on good terms with the gods and the family ancestors could a family achieve a living standard barely better than subsistence. It is easy to understand then why family loyalty and family unity were so much stressed.

Second, family loyalty and unity were indispensable to the maintenance of family continuity. Continuity did not mean merely biological reproduction, or a procession of progeny. It was far more than that. The succession encompassed people, material possessions, social values, sentimental feelings, memory of the past, and anticipation of the future. It was an intricate composition, in which family loyalty and unity not only held the elements tightly together but also made it all meaningful. Whenever family members became unconcerned for the family's future and allowed their feeling of belonging to each other to lessen, continuity broke down and lost its meaning.

Third, the early Chinese made little distinction between blood relationship itself and these feelings of loyalty and unity. People of blood relationship simply had to be loyal to each other and united. A group of people who were blood-related but were without loyalty and unity were not a true family, but only a group likely to be plagued by internal struggles.

The fourth characteristic of the traditional Chinese family was the authoritarian management of family affairs by the father, or other member acting in his stead. There is no question but that the administration in a traditional Chinese family was authoritarian. In most families the authoritarianism was benign and benevolent in that the father, or the family head, exercised authority chiefly for the benefit of the family and exercised it with mildness and kindness. Occasionally, of course, authority was used for the user's personal satisfaction, to satisfy his desire for playing with power, to see others subjugated under his rule. There was, however, a peculiar phenomenon in the exercise of authority in most of these traditional Chinese families. When the father was using his authority to make family members behave in accordance with the norm, he nearly always justified his admonition by reference to the ancestors' teachings, conduct, desires or demands, and honors. He said that everyone in the family ought to act according to the ancestors' examples. This was possible only when the members believed in the existence of continuing interrelations between themselves and their ancestors and in the ancestors' spiritual concern for the family's fortunes. It is true that most Chinese people had not seen or felt the existence of the ancestors, but they did accept as reality the presence of a vague and overall ancestral influence. This was enough for them, and they took for granted that the father's words had support from the ancestors. This acceptance, together with the observation that the life and the body of each present family member had come from preceding family members, formed the foundation and superstructure of the cult of ancestor worship, or ancestor veneration. Historically, ancestor worship had a great deal to do with the maintenance of the Chinese family's integration and solidarity.

In a typical traditional Chinese family, authority and service were inseparable. In Ferdinand Toennies' words, "Each authority can be regarded as service and each service as authority." If authority represents rights and service represents duty, then rights and duties are two corresponding aspects of the same thing. If the father, or any family head, had to use authority, it was because authority had the responsibility, as well as the power, to make people behave rightfully and, thus, he enhanced his own position. For in the last analysis, authority was the means by which the family could be served more efficiently or more satisfactorily. On the other hand, service can be regarded as authority. One who can serve people has influence on people. The greater the service, the more the influence. The crystallization of considerable amounts of influence is authority.

The father's authority was especially heavy and extensive in respect to the behavior and affairs of the family. The father paid much more attention to his sons' activities than to the other members. Few mischiefs by a son could pass without the father's notice. When any serious misconduct occurred in the boy's behavior, paternal correction was certain to follow. The first correction was made by admonition. If this failed to produce results, sterner measures were taken. The main point is that judgment on rightness or wrongness was made solely by the father in accordance with his conception of the ancestors' teachings and the community's moral standards. No reason or argument from the son was taken into consideration. The correction was taken with the intent of rescuing a beloved person from potential evil and putting him on the right way to character development. But the carrying out of the correction was always implicitly or explicitly backed by the father's authority. Unless the son was grown up, his father's authority was presently felt and made its impression upon him. This authority not only interfered with, but openly dictated his affairs, such as his marriage, his education, his making friends, his preparation for a career, his cultivating or not cultivating certain living habits, and so on. Whatever his objections or dislikes, the young man had to accept the interference and the dictatorship because the authority was supposedly exercised for his own good and for the good of the family.

A fifth characteristic of the traditional Chinese family was the diffusion or diffusiveness of obligations and rights among the family members. When a relationship was established between two persons, each assumed certain obligations toward the other, and each derived certain rights which he could claim from the other. Among members of a traditional Chinese family, these obligations and rights were not specified or enumerated. Because they were without specification and enumeration, it meant that one was obliged to do anything, everything, and all things and to do it without limit or complaint whenever needed or called upon, for all persons within the family relationship. It meant, for example, that a member could feel that he was entitled to anything and everything that he needs and that the family has. In case he needed help or service, the other members were obliged to give it. This situation was all right as long as all members were united in one common will, a will to make the family as a whole prosper and thrive, and as long as all members were loyal to the family head and the ancestors. But only under these conditions could it be free from these evils: members who took advantage of the situation to fulfill their own selfish purposes by abusing other members' feelings of obligation toward them; members who misused their unlimited rights by inflicting themselves harshly or domineeringly on other members. Should both family unity and family loyalty be missing from the hearts of the members, the absence of any specification and limitation on members' obligations and rights could certainly leave plenty of opportunity for abuses.

The custom of patrimony and male dominance constituted the sixth characteristic of the traditional Chinese family. Male dominance was an outcome of the practice of patrimony. If a family were to be continued through the male line of grandfather, father, son, and grandson, it was only natural that the male members, especially the first-born male, received most of the attention. But there was another reason for male dominance. In a predominantly agricultural society, most of the heavy work and key jobs in making the living were performed by male members. In farm families, especially when farming was done chiefly by human labor and with simple tools, it was a general phenomenon that women voluntarily gave all kinds of priorities and privileges to their men and that mothers depended more upon sons than on daughters. Sisters might not have been much concerned

about their brothers' working capability, but they did have an interest
in young men's strong and handsome bodies, and they threw themselves into
their protection, or into secret adoration for them.

If the patrilineal system had laid the foundation for dominance in the
traditional Chinese family, the womenfolk's affectionate obedience and self-
denial helped greatly to build up the men's feelings of superiority over the
female members. After centuries of assuming there really was inequality
between men and women, the men had simply become used to their dominant position.   The propriety of their making decisions and giving commands was
taken as a matter of course. When there were good things, or favors, or
opportunities to be distributed, that male members had priority and preference was also taken for granted.

A great deal of criticism has been directed at the husband-and-wife
relationship in the traditional Chinese family. It has often been said
that the relationship was entirely irrational and that the husband was
excessively domineering. It was not unknown that a husband took advantage
of his wife's virtuous obedience to abuse her. Actually, however, this
was true only in a relatively small number of unusual cases. In most
normal families, this was not true. The man-and-wife relationship is
always involved in kinships and is reinforced by many kinds of social
forces. Moreover, most couples are able to learn to shape their relationship into one of mutual affirmation by habituating themselves to one another. Habituation involves concession and an effort to adapt oneself to
conditions as they are.

The husband-wife relationship was from the beginning ceremonially
and socially fixed. It was from the beginning a kinship affair. It had

fixed, personal, social, and religious duties and rights. The sexual instinct also played a part but its part was buried by layers of folkways and mores. It was expressed only in terms of continuing the family's line and assuring that the ancestors' tombs or tablets were being well cared for.

4. <u>The traditional farm village: an extension of the traditional family</u>. Understanding the family structure lays the groundwork for understanding the community structure, for in Taiwan, as in mainland China, the community's basic structure was an extension of the traditional family. There were in China farm villages which had resulted from the development of a single family. In other words, all families in the village were members of one descent group, as in <u>Wang Chia T'sun</u>, Village of the Wangs, or in <u>Chang Chia T'sun</u>, Village of the Changs. These were sometimes called clan villages or kinship villages. In these communities, at least when most of the families were prosperous, kinship consciousness was keen and loyalty strong. If any community government was needed, it developed on kinship lines and according to kinship ethics and rules. Their value systems had been passed down from their ancestors. All those characteristics which identified the traditional family appeared again in the collective life of a clan-village community.

In some villages where all families bore the same family name, not all of them had come from the same ancestors. In still other villages, the families had come from different stocks and also borne different surnames. In both types of villages, it was popular practice to use kinship terms in addressing each other. There was a feeling of kinship among the villagers when there was also peace, prosperity, and <u>esprit de corps</u>. The whole village could behave as though it were an extended family. The senior

and capable member, often, also, the richer member, gave direction to community affairs, much like a patriarch in his real kinship group. In regard
to maintaining the society's mores, customs, and social values, and in disciplining the young and caring for the old, such villages functioned very
much as a large and well-organized clan did. Because at most times, under
most conditions, and in outward formalities these non-blood-related groups
arranged themselves and functioned like traditional kinship groups, that
is like the traditional extended family, it seems that there should be no
question but that such village structures could be called pseudo-kinship
relationships.

5. <u>The landlord-tenant relationship</u>. Life as it was carried on in
traditional farm villages had two main aspects, social and economic. Among
the economic activities, production of food and of other daily necessities
was, by far, the most important. The production of food and fiber absorbed
the most expensive and most extensive resources of the farm land. When the
community owned the farm land and practiced the system of assigning land
to tillers at a certain age for cultivation and then taking it back when
the tillers were old, the getting of land was not a serious problem.

When this period was past and land was privately rather than communally
owned, the buying and selling of land and other sorts of land transactions
began. An early effect of private ownership of land and of commerce in
land transactions was to point up the differences between people who had
land and those who did not, and differences between people who had a great
amount of land and people who had only a little. It became evident that
there were a few persons who owned large amounts of land, and large numbers
of persons who had none or only very little. From this situation came the

unfortunate farm-tenancy system: The large numbers of poor peasants had
to rent the land they needed from one of the few big landlords and had to
pay a large part of the farm's produce to the landlord who did nothing in
the actual production except provide the land. As the rate of increase in
population was many times faster than the increase of reclaimed land, chance
for landless tillers to rent a piece of land became fewer and fewer. This
led to two inevitable consequences: one, the complete dependence of the
tenants upon the landlords; and, two, the landlords held virtually complete
control over the tenants. These two conditions together gave rise to the
landlord-as-patriarch and tenant-as-household-dependent socio-economic
relationship. This relationship plus the pseudo-kinship relationship
formed the landlord-as-patriarch and tenant-as-household-dependent pseudo-
kinship social structure of the traditional, rural community in Taiwan.

Portraying the landlord in analogy with a traditional patriarch leads
to a brief analysis of characteristics of landlords as a class and the main
features of their relations with their tenants. The very portrait of the
landlord as a patriarch suggests that he was the head of a big family, not
a tyrant or a despot over a group of slaves. Although a patriarch could
be absolutely authoritarian, harsh, and inconsiderate in treating his household dependents, he could be also benevolent and sympathetic. To a great
extent, both traits had been present in landlord-tenant relations. There
is no need to add that tenants were expected to behave nicely toward landlords, whether sincerely was beside the point. On the other hand, the
landlords, too, were obliged, for various reasons, to be considerate and
kind toward their tenants. There is no truth in rumors that all landlords
were mean people, exploiters, or usurers. Only a few, who lived in remote

places far from the countryside and had nothing in their lives directly related to farming and the farmers' living conditions, were hard and ruthless in the collection of rents, regardless of how genuine and how great the tenants' distresses might be.

That tenants had to be pleasant toward landlords is understandable. But why did the landlords have to be considerate toward the tenants? Notwithstanding the tenant's knowledge of the landlord's power over the land he was cultivating and thereby over his very livelihood and that of his family, many a tenant was expert in playing tricks and cheating his landlord on the rent. He took advantage of the landlord's ignorance of farm conditions and the landlord's lack of knowledge as to the normal amount of produce he could logically expect and was legally entitled to receive. The tenant paid his rent with short measures, inferior products, and substitute materials, and he made false complaints about misfortunes. If he were to depend merely on the exercise of power or legal rights, the landlord would never have been able to solve these problems. Some absentee landlords had used police power, or power from the Government. It might have helped for a moment in crushing the tenant's temporary resistance. In the long run, however, the use of political power was a great mistake, even a tragic one. Therefore, most landlords resorted to softer measures. Softer measures included giving consideration to tenants who had difficulties in getting money for a wedding or other important family affairs, agreeing to a reduction of rent when the crop had been damaged by unavoidable calamities, finding some work or an apprenticeship for the tenant's boy in a shop in the town, generously feeding tenants when they came to deliver the rental payment.

Such favors and generosities were much more effective in minimizing the cheating and clever tricks. There were more constructive advantages too. If the landlord's kindness and thoughtfulness were big enough, the tenant and his family might be won over to a real willingness to help without payment on such special occasions as a wedding, funeral, house-building. On festival days, or in special seasons, various kinds of prized things such as fowl, eggs, fish, fruits, fresh vegetables, were brought by tenants to their landlord as gifts.[6] Above all, the tenant and his family might have come to feel a high respect for, and loyalty to, the landlord. They then would not only have abstained from trying to cheat, but would have done their best to protect their landlord.

The cause of this kind of landlord-tenant relationship was kan-ch'ing.[7] When one person's external action aroused in another person a certain reaction, this feeling is called kan-ch'ing. If the feeling is pleasant, it is good kan-ch'ing; if unpleasant, it is bad kan-ch'ing. Usually kan-ch'ing refers to good feeling. Good actions[8] arouse good feelings. Good feelings give rise to pleasant responses and, thus, two persons have good kan-ch'ing toward each other.

Kan-ch'ing, thus, was a sustaining and strengthening force, much stronger than landlords' legal rights or political power which forced the tenant into weak submission. The tenant, under the weight of great insecurity, knowing that only good kan-ch'ing from the landlord can ensure his use of the farm land year after year, had to do the best he could to cultivate it. Our first thought might be, then, that the landlord should have had less concern for kan-ch'ing, since he was the power figure in the relationship. The fact was, however, that even the wealthiest landlord

needed the tenant's good <u>kan-ch'ing</u> because production could be spurred
and cheating reduced by it. So it was that only by respecting the bounds
of propriety could their relationship be carried on properly.

Bessac has made a very similar observation on this landlord-tenant
relationship in Taiwan.[9] He is convinced that landlords had not been
riding rough-shod over peasants and that a tenant was not the farm serf
described in Tolstoy's stories. The prestige of the landlord, according
to Bessac's observation, did not derive from abusing his tenants but from
being in a position to distribute favors to them, favors such as reducing
rent in a year of crop failure, rent which was vital to the tenant's
existence. A landlord who allowed such flexibility, and did not exploit
his tenants because of his advantageous position, was considered a good
man. Most landlords had been responsive to this ideal, but, of course,
there were gradations in the degree to which any individual lived up to it.

There was still another important reason for the landlord's being
lenient. The rationale undergirding a landlord's high station stood on
the thesis that it had been gained chiefly by hard work and that any
farmer willing to work hard has the hope and possibility of becoming a
landlord, or at least a richer farmer. Most tenants believed that among
their ancestors, there had been landlords; most landlords believed that
their family had at times been very poor, and it really was possible that
a family's status could shift from landlord to tenant within a few generations. Therefore, the landlord family should not be so arrogant as to
look down upon and mistreat tenant families lest a few generations later
their descendants should be the objects of such treatment.

A similar rationale had been uncovered in the village of Taitou, Shantung Province.[10] Bernard Gallin,[11] in his recent case study, states also that the only thing which gave the tenant any security in his tenancy was a good personal relationship or good kan-ch'ing with the landlord. But the good kan-ch'ing could come about only when landlord and tenant lived close enough to have some kind of contact. Contact to a landlord usually meant a paternalistic feeling toward his tenant, and in the tenant a feeling of obligation toward his landlord. The landlord's paternalism was usually expressed in leniency in hard times or similar favors. The tenant fulfilled his extra obligation toward his landlord by giving free labor and gifts. "But such behavior from tenant to landlord depended strictly on their actual relationship so that not all tenants sent gifts or provided help for their landlords."

From the above, one may say that in the old days, if both landlord and tenant had good kan-ch'ing toward each other, their relationship was pleasant and both had security in their mutual dealings. Where there was no kan-ch'ing, or if the kan-ch'ing in each of them was bad, their relationship must have been unpleasant. Knowing these things led all but a few tenants and landlords to make considerable efforts to inspire or cultivate kan-ch'ing in each other.

In one way, this kan-ch'ing-sustained relationship was good, for it rid the landlord of much temptation to use power and be ruthless, and freed the tenant of much resentment, hatred, and the urge to cheat, thus cutting down the number of serious disputes. On the other hand, however, it must have prevented, or at least delayed, establishment of a legal, clear-cut, specific, formally-written and understood farm-lease contract.

Without such a contract, disputes rose immediately whenever <u>kan-ch'ing</u> disappeared. <u>Kan-ch'ing</u> was not something always dependable. In one generation perhaps the landlord and tenant felt good <u>kan-ch'ing</u> for each other and were on good terms; the relationship between the two households was satisfactory, no abusing and no cheating. In the next generation the situation might have totally changed. A new landlord, the old landlord's son, perhaps, was much more demanding than his father had been. He took for granted that everything done by the older tenant would be continued. He thought it all was part of the tenant's obligations. So in case the tenant failed to give the expected free labor or did not present the expected gifts, he thought the tenant was cheating and demanded they be given or the lease would be terminated and the land taken back from the tenant. Perhaps on the other side, the new tenant, son of the old tenant, felt that the landlord was cruel, that the demands went far beyond the limit of his obligation and that he was unable to meet them. Consequently, ill feeling was aroused, and their relationship deteriorated.

In instances where this did occur, it has been observed that, in most cases, the landlord family of a certain generation had been considerate and kind in its relationship to the tenants and the tenants had responded with affection and respect. But later, let us suppose from the third generation, the situation began to degenerate. The landlord's offspring were prodigal sons. They spent money carelessly and lived extravagantly. They required more money, more food stuffs, more labor services. The way to get them was to demand that the tenants pay regularly all that they had been paying, both as regular rents and as gifts. Moreover, the amounts in all categories must be increased. What their ancestors had generously done for the tenants was stopped and forgotten. And, in fact, it was true that in the last few generations, when people's material wants expanded considerably as their standards of living rose, demands of landlords upon tenants became higher and stricter. There was rapid increase in the numbers of landlords who did not hesitate to resort to whatever practices were necessary in order to get the highest possible rents from the tenants. So, there is no contradiction or lack of consistency between what has been said in Section III of Chapter One about the need for land reform in Taiwan or in the preceding paragraphs of this chapter.

6. <u>General patterns.</u> Social structure and social relations in a traditional, rural community in Taiwan were largely similar to those of a traditional family. First emphasis was given to hierarchy or vertical gradation. Horizontal relations received second emphasis. The erection of the hierarchy was based on real or pseudo kinship, on seniority, and on age. These were ascribed factors. Next were achieved factors, achieved by oneself or by cooperation of the household, or by ancestors. Things achieved included land and landed property, wealth, education or capability, cultural sophistication, official honor, impressive and pleasant personality. Some people had a number of these factors, both ascribed and achieved. Others had only the ascribed factors, or only some of the achieved factors. The possession of any one, or any set of these factors, gave the possessor the right, or qualification, to be in a rank higher than that of others. The weight or importance of each factor was different. Consequently, the possession of different factors set people in different ranks. Thus hierarchy, or gradation, was established. Since all of these factors were

value-oriented, that is, a certain trait or a certain condition was considered a rank-making factor because social value had been ascribed to it, persons who possessed these factors were admired and respected by people who did not. Persons who possessed factors which carried the higher values were admired and respected by persons who had factors of lesser values.

Although social change had been slow at most times and, for this reason, the channels of relationship were quite settled in established forms, there was, even so, a constant traffic inside the hierarchy, and it was always a two-way traffic. People were constantly ascending or descending. Those who traveled downward were those who had lost the achieved factors, and it was not easy to keep them. Those who could not keep them had to move down. This had a considerable influence on the manner in which social relations were carried on. In outward bearing, people of low ranks always gave respect to persons of the higher ranks, and, most often, it was genuine respect; but toward some, the respect was pretended, or even mixed with contempt. Most people of high rank were able to restrain themselves from becoming arrogant or looking down upon those below. The proverb warned that when a person reached the top, he should always remember the time when he was down below and so be kind and considerate toward those who though still at the bottom, who might someday be on the top.

II. Changes in Social Structure

In the last fifteen years or so a great many changes have occurred in Taiwan's rural communities. We are concerned here with the new family structure and family life, the decline of the kinship bond, the breakdown of the landlord-tenant relationship, and the new directions of social relations in general.

1. <u>Changes in family structure and family life</u>. In Taiwan an evolutionary type of family change began about fifteen years ago and is still in effect today. In 1962 this writer made a study[12] of the rural family and found evidence which gave proof to the above statement. The following are the significant findings of that study.

a. Changes in the size of the rural family

Because of the limited amount of farm land and for the sake of their children's health and education, most educated and informed people support the idea of having small families. Most rural people have only recently realized the nature and extent of the population problem, or have learned in other contexts of the advantages in having fewer children. This is especially true among the younger generations. The survey showed that most of the 350 family heads interviewed preferred small families to large ones; less than 35 per cent still liked big families.

This implies a decline of the old belief that the more children and grandchildren a family has the greater the blessings which parents and ancestors enjoy, and that having many members means prosperity and social prestige to a family.

Those who prefer small families adduce two important reasons: (1) The economic burden is light because it is easy for a small family to make a living in these days; (2) in small families there are fewer disputes among the members. It is easier to manage the affairs of a small group of kinfolk than to manage the affairs of a big group. Again, we find the arguments contradict traditional ideologies. According to the traditional belief, it was the large families which could produce more and, therefore, make an easier living. It was also an age-long family teaching that the successful family head was the one who could keep a large family in pace and manage its complicated affairs in good order.

Ideals may not always go hand-in-hand with the practicalities of life, and the rural people of Taiwan may already consider the small family to be their ideal. In practice, however, it is the large and medium-sized families that still prevail in the countryside. We found that the medium-sized (about 8 people) and the large families (about 12 people) together accounted for more than 77 per cent of the families covered in the 1962 study.

b. Changes in the structure of the rural family

A majority of the university students who have written term papers on family life in rural Taiwan indicated that far more members of the younger generation prefer a structurally simplified family than prefer the traditional, complicated or extended one. Most of them do not particularly like the modern, conjugal family. It is the single-line, three-generation type that answers their choice. Such a family consists of the grandparents, parents, and unmarried children. There are no uncles, aunts, and cousins living in the house. Our rural survey discovered a similar trend in the farm villages. Of the 350 rural informants, 42 per cent expressed preference for this semi-simplified family, that is, the single-line and three-generation type; but more than 39 per cent liked the modern, conjugal family. Only a little over 17 per cent still felt that the old, extended family was better than the others.

Reasons for favoring a semi-simplified family are as follows: (1) The is so much amiable sentiment and affection between the single-line generations; it is very hard to separate them from each other. (2) The aging, but beloved, grandparents ought to be well taken care of, by living with their immediate descendants. (3) In a semi-simplified family the young children can have affection and care from the grandparents. Such affection and care nourish the youngster emotionally and strengthen his personality. The samples' having given these reasons means that their change in this respect has been selective, not sweeping. Qualities which abide in human nature have not only been served but have also been more appreciated than before. In the change of family structure, also, there is a difference between the ideal and the practicable. Only a small percentage of the informants gave first preference to the traditional extended family; however, over 45 per cent of the 350 are families of this type. The modern, conjugal families account for 33 per cent and the semi-simplified families 21 per cent.

The significant thing is that most people now favor the single-line structure including three or four generations, i.e., a family of grandparent parents, and unmarried grandchildren. If only one of the grandsons is marri and has one or two young children, the family is still ideal, but they certa ly no longer like a family composed of grandparents, married sons and their families, plus married grandsons and their children. The horizontally exter family is most surely passing. As for the modern, conjugal family, it is favored by some of the more progressive young couples. But most still feel that it is a Western product and that, somehow, it is not quite agreeable to the Chinese mentality and sentiment. Their chief concern is about the care and well-being of the aging grandparents.

      c. Changes in the husband-wife relations in the rural family

      Traditionally, the husband-wife relationship was characterized by the husband's dominance and the wife's submissiveness. The most popular ethic in this relationship had been that husband leads and wife follows. In other words, an ideal husband was supposed to be able to take the initiative, to make decisions, and to exercise authority in family affairs. The ideal wife was to be submissive and to follow her husband's leadership willingly. The husband was supposed to be considerate and generous toward his wife, and the wife was expected to be appreciative and tender. But it was frowned upon, or ridiculed, if too much intimacy between the two was seen. In other words, husband and wife were, in the old days, discouraged from exchanging affection and sentiment openly. Traditional Chinese parents would never have agreed with the Hebrew and Christian teaching that a man and woman who were married to each other should make a separate unit of themselves and go away from the parents.

      Such old ideas have gradually declined and changed. The earliest changes were in the marriage customs. According to our survey, today more than 90 per cent of the rural families interviewed hold that a son's or a daughter's marriage should either be initiated by parents and accepted or refused by the involved son or daughter, or be initiated by the son or daughter and approved by the parents. Only a very small number still think that the arrangement should be entirely in the hands of the parents, and the number of families which agree to let their children take full responsibility in handling their matrimonial affairs is still small. However, more than 90 per cent of the samples believed that marriages through free courtship were increasing. About 75 per cent believed that marriage through courtship is better than the traditional type. About 7 per cent of the families see both good points and bad points in the new way of courtship, and 15 per cent feel it is totally bad.

About 93 per cent of those families interviewed believed that in the husband-wife relationship the wife's position has been improved over what it was in earlier times. The improvement is indicated, they say, in the ways of making decisions on family affairs, of disciplining children, and of managing the family's finances. Nearly 85 per cent of the families answered that the wife's words and opinions are solicited, respected, and, in many cases, accepted in planning and making decisions on family affairs. Nearly 80 per cent of the families said that today the wife has much more to say than before regarding the discipline of children and managing the family's finances. Improvement of the wife's position in the family is actually visible in some aspects. Today the husband treats his wife with much more consideration than husbands ever did before. As seen by others: The wife receives more respect and understanding from her husband, more respectful affection, more equality of consideration, more intimacy and sympathy, more friendliness, and more companionship.

These changes can be attributed to a host of factors. The following are the important ones: First, there has been a general enlightenment of the populace. It cannot be specifically pinpointed or is it limited to any particular aspect, but rather, it means that people are better informed, have learned about many new things. In Taiwan today, the people as a whole,

men and women, old and young, people of all statuses and classes, are much
more widely informed than was the case twenty years ago. This general
enlightenment has come from schools, informal social education, agricultural-
extension and home-economics education, youth education (4-H clubs), and increasingly varied social and business contacts between village dwellers and
city folks.

A second important factor is that today's wife has a constructive
and deliberative role in discussing, planning, and managing family affairs.
It is true that she also took part in the old days, but there was a big
difference. In the old days she did it in a passive way; she was too timid,
or too humble, to feel and believe that she was making a contribution of any
significance. Today she knows she is making contributions and that her
contributions are not insignificant. With this confidence, she finds ways
to make more contributions. The husband has changed, too. Formerly he
was quite indifferent about his wife's role in the family's important
business. He knew his wife worked hard, but that did not change his belief
that a woman could do nothing of real importance. Today the husband has
consciously realized his wife's role and the importance of her contributions.
He now admits that, in some respects, he may be more able than she, but in
others, she is the better, and that they are equal.

The chief reason for these changes probably lies in the new way of
planning and conducting the family's farming business which brings us to
a third factor. Traditionally it was the men's job to talk over and
decide what to plant and in what manner to cultivate the farm. But ever
since the agricultural-extension service has been an educational program,
the farmers have been advised to make farming a family business. That

means that the whole family, including father, mother, and grown-up children, should discuss and plan together. It should be done democratically. Everyone, including the mother or wife, is to have the right and opportunity to express himself and exchange ideas and feelings with the others. The final decision should be the decision of the whole group, not just the father's or the son's. In the operation of the farm, too, everyone in the family has a definite and positive role, a share in its success or failure. Many a farm family has adopted a new, operational pattern which combines the enterprises on the farm and the production activities in the home to form one economic unit, or a unified set of enterprise programs. In such families the womenfolk's roles have become more important and more felt by their menfolk.

A fourth factor is the increase in the opportunities for gainful employment for women. With jobs they can be independent of their families, and many young women, usually the unmarried, have left their rural homes to become industrial workers and salesgirls in the city. Many others have gone to cities to be household servants. These girls have learned all the tricks of the trade known to domestic helpers in Western, capitalistic societies. They refuse to accept any of the rules, ethics, and requirements which made a good maid in the old days. Also, every year quite a few rural girls have the good luck to go to secondary schools and junior colleges in the towns and cities. After they finish school very few return to their original homes. Most get married or find office work in the cities. All these opportunities have helped to raise the economic and social importance of women to give them higher positions in the family. The men cannot but make concessions to them.

The fifth factor is the ability of modern women to make themselves more attractive and lovable than before. With the money earned from their own labor and skills, they are able to dress and beautify themselves much better than women in the old days. Beautiful and lovely women can easily win men's affection and secure a husband's concessions.

A sixth factor is, probably, the influence of the people from the Chinese mainland. Most people who came to Taiwan from the mainland after the communists established their regime were of the intellectual class; they had received a good education and lived a modern, democratic family life. The men treated their women with decency and moderation. For this reason, many of the local girls who knew this preferred to marry young men from the mainlanders' families rather than native-reared boys. Partly from fear of being unable to find a wife and partly from admiration in this matter, the local men are taking the mainlanders as examples. Among the mainlanders are also a large number of retired servicemen. Almost all of these men are single and homeless. They are most anxious to marry and settle down, but it is very difficult for them, and those who would succeed must do their best to win the women's hearts and cooperation.

d. Changes in the rural family's parent-children relations

As stated previously, the father-son relationship in many a traditional Chinese family, urban or rural, was characterized by authority and submission, dictatorship and obedience, the father's unreasonable expectation, and the son's excessive tension. Today the situation has changed. In our survey, for instance, more than 67 per cent of the families reported the father-son relationship had become quite intimate. Nearly 27 per cent of the families maintained that the son's attitude is now predominantly one of respect and veneration toward the father. Only about 2 per cent complained that the relationship is still filled with remoteness, fear, or resentment. The survey also discovered that 64 per cent of the families still claimed the father had full authority over his children. That meant he still controlled all the affairs of his children. But about 32 per cent admitted that the father's authority no longer extended over all the affairs of his children, nor did he have entire authority over any of their affairs. Fifty-two per cent of the families still maintained that the nature of the father's authority, and his way of administering his authority, are the same as before; but nearly 39 per cent believed it was no longer the same. The chief difference they saw was that today the authority had limits and was administered with reason and moderation.

As a whole, parents still do have authority over their children but, as said above, it is within limits and with reason and moderation. The reasons underlying the change are much the same as the first four of the six factors described in the section dealing with changes in the husband-and-wife relationships. But it is important to add another reason here: increased education of the young. The young people are, as a rule, far more educated and better informed than were their parents and grandparents. A son who studied, for example, in the vocational-agricultural school and participated in programs sponsored by the agricultural-extension service, soon knew much more about the new ways and ideas than his father knew. After he had had opportunity to apply his new knowledge to improve things on the farm, the family's income increased. When his achievements became known to the neighbors, as they usually did, the son then was not only a favorite in the family but also a leader, an admired person, in the communi-

ty. Naturally, his father would be willing to make concessions to him.
In similar ways, daughters in rural families have won consideration from
their mothers and grandmothers and, therefore, are no longer subject to
absolute parental control. Both the son's and the daughter's achievements
in education and in work help effectively in breaking up the old authoritarian pattern on the one hand and in developing a democratic way of life
on the other.

2. <u>Changes in kinship relationship</u>. Changes in kinship relationships
have not appeared so much in the terms villagers' use to address each other
as in the meaning and functions of kinship. In meaning, kinship today
implies only the knowledge that family A, family B, and family C originated
from the same married couple about 100 years ago. The traditional consciousness of close relationship, of sharing each other's success or failure, helping each other in distress, and of uniting together to defend the common
ancestor's honor and promote intrafamilial welfare, has diminished until it
has almost disappeared.

The change was not due to any lack in affection or family feeling
toward kinsfolk, or to any fear of being labelled as a person depending
on the family relationship. It was due rather to the appearance, since land
reform, of civic organizations and groupings based on special interests,
professional purposes, and educational programs in the farm villages.
These groupings had to cut across kinship lines, and gradually the people
in the groups were drawn together by common interests or similar professional
needs, or just by their being together so much; and they forgot the old
kinship ties.

Formerly child training in orthodox or gentry families stressed teaching and disciplining young folks to have concern for needs and

problems of people of their own kinship groups. It was included in the

performance of memorial ceremonies honoring ancestors on New Year's Day

and on many other special occasions, when young people and adults of all

member families were summoned to the ancestral hall or cemetery to hear

speeches intended to arouse those participating in the ceremonial activities

Both the speeches and the ceremonial activities were meant to generate or

renew the consciousness of blood relationship. If such consciousness were

aroused, people usually became concerned with the needs, problems, and

interests of those with whom they shared kinship. If they had had the means

and morale, kin groups would have held memorial gatherings as often as

custom would permit in a year. Young people of the family were encouraged

and ordered, if necessary, to take active part in the meetings. In the

old days the large and prosperous clans organized and operated a number of

social-welfare and educational programs for their needy or dependent members

both individuals and families. There is no doubt that the young people of

such clans had been well trained and disciplined concerning the needs and

problems of their kinsfolk.

In families of ordinary people such training and discipline took place

in formal or ceremonial visits made to close kin. Such visits allowed the

young people to see the actual needs and problems of poorer kinsfolk.

Young people were usually easily impressed by pathetic sights, and parents

often sent children to take food or other daily necessities to needy

members of the kin group. Sometimes children were sent to help or care

for a distant uncle or aunt who was sick or in other distress. Such

practices were doubtless most effective ways of training the young to a

concern for the needs of other members of the family. Now most of these
activities have been interrupted because so few people still feel the same
warmth of kinship consciousness.

The declining importance of kinship has resulted in the disruption
of the various functions traditionally performed by kinship groups or
kinship organizations. The best-known functions were welfare programs
for the needy members; educational programs for the young people of the clan;
chronicles, records and histories of the kinship group; ceremonials and
memorials, etc. Nearly all such activities have either been taken over by
Government or other public institutions, or are organized and undertaken
on community or interest-group bases, but no longer by kinship groups.

If the real kinship bond had declined or broken down, the pseudo-
kinship relationship had become more a courtesy or formality than a true
feeling. Villagers of old generations complained that the youngsters in
the neighborhood had become very rude, that they no longer respected their
seniors, and that they were greatly different from young people in the old
days. It is probably because of the neglect of this tradition that few
elders still felt a moral obligation to take the trouble to admonish or
advise a village youth, whatever his family, when he was not behaving himself.
Very few of the recognized men of wisdom or capability still freely gave
assistance to the young people, because the latter no longer felt any
kinship-consciousness toward them. In spite of the springing up of modern
civic interest and educational organizations mentioned above, the traditional
unity of the farm village has relaxed in this transitional period; and one
of the factors responsible for the relaxation is the decline of both real
and pseudo-kinship relationships.

3. <u>Changes in landlord-tenant relationship</u>. Enforcement of the farm rent limitation program and the land-to-the-tiller program profoundly changed the traditional pattern of the landlord-tenant relationship. Briefly, rent limitation strained the relationship because the reduction of the rent rate lowered the actual amount of rent paid. The requiring of a written, signed, and registered lease contract between the landlord and the tenant eliminated the illegal, optional, off-the-record practices which made the traditional, landlord-tenant relationship so complicated and irrational. During the life of a formal and written lease contract in which all terms and conditions were clearly specified and defined, and with the elimination of all the favor-laden but irregular practices, the element of <u>kan-ch'ing</u> was no longer needed and, therefore, no longer existed in the relationship. The law did not say that <u>kan-ch'ing</u> was forbidden. If a tenant still wished to have good <u>kan-ch'ing</u> for the landlord and requested the same from him, it was their business. But inasmuch as this was no longer needed, few tenants and few landlords bothered with it. The result of all these changes was that after land reform the landlord-tenant relationship had become simply another cool, legal, business relationship. When the land-to-the-tiller program was carried out, most landlords sold their land, and most tenants became independent owner-farmers. For these landlords and tenants, the landlord-tenant relationship was totally gone. In the following we shall see in the farm people's own words how the landlord-tenant relationship had changed after land reform.

A great many (83.44%) of the 1250 former tenants reported that after rent limitation but before the land-to-the-tiller program, their lease contract was written, signed by both parties, registered with the county government, and all terms were clearly specified. They were asked whether they had felt, in remembering the landlord's earlier kindness, that they should continue to pay the former amount of rent, even though it was higher than the new (37.5%) legal rate. Less than 3 per cent said "yes," and almost 95 per cent said "no." Asked whether they had had the idea that, under protection of the new law, tenants might take action to avenge the wrongs formerly inflicted upon them by the landlords, only a few households (4%) admitted they had thought of it. More than 93 per cent said "no." As for their impression of the landlords' reaction toward rent limitation, only 7 per cent thought that the landlords had tried to terminate lease agreements and take back the land from the tenants. More than 90 per cent of them denied such a thing had occurred.

About kan-ch'ing between landlords and tenants since the reduction of farm rent, more than 86 per cent diplomatically said there had been no change; only 7 per cent admitted lack of friendship. Yet when asked what had been the most serious disputes between landlords and tenants during and after implementation of the rent limitation program, nearly 40 per cent of the households gave answers. To give an answer to this question indicated recognition of the existence of disputes in the landlord-tenant relationship. The frequently mentioned causes of the disputes were the landlords' trying to terminate the lease and take back the land and the tenant's failure, or tardiness, in paying the farm rent.

The current tenants gave similar information. Ninety-two per cent of the 250 households said there was respect and friendship between landlords and tenants before rent limitation, and about 80 per cent said there had been no change in this respect after land reform. About 20 per cent claimed that the relationship had become even more friendly. Less than 8 per cent mentioned deterioration.

In summary, among both former and current tenants, a great majority made the diplomatic statement that there had been no change in the landlord-tenant relationship after the rent limitation and land-to-the-tiller programs. Only a few admitted deterioration. The reason for this avoidance of telling the truth is probably that, in most cases, the landlords and their tenants were living in the same community, in either real or pseudo-kinship relationship, or at least saw each other very often. Therefore, interviewees did not want to say anything which might hurt someone's feelings. Besides, they were the ones who had gained so they could afford to say that nothing bad had happened.

Perhaps for the same reason 82% of the 500, former ordinary-landlord households also denied disputes between themselves and the tenants; only 18 per cent admitted there were disputes. The landlords were asked whether tenants' attitudes had changed toward landlords after land reform. About 50 per cent complained that tenants had become very cool. The other 50 per cent made evasive answers by saying that there had been no change in this matter.

But when asked about their feeling toward the reduction of farm rent, 35 per cent said they had been unhappy and about 44 per cent said "very unhappy." Only 20 per cent said they had not been emotionally disturbed. Most landlords declared at the interview that they had not tried to jeopardize land-reform programs. For instance, 84 per cent said they had not tried to sell the land after farm rent was limited. More than 90 per cent said they had not tried to sell their land privately after they heard of the compulsory purchase that was pending under the land-to-the-tiller program. More than 93 per cent said that they had not used the scheme of dividing an extended household into a number of nuclear families so that more land could be retained. Actually, however, the number of landlords who had tried, under various pretexts, to take back the land from the tenants had become so threatening to the success of rent limitation that the Government had to add more provisions to the original act to prevent the possibility of serious collapse.[13]

The non-farm people's observations on this matter were quite mixed. Seventy-eight per cent of the local community leaders observed that after the rent limitation, tenants paid their farm rents on time and regularly. But 18 per cent said some tenants had failed to pay rent on time, had, in some cases, delayed a very long time. Reasons for the failures or delays were thought to be poor harvests which left the tenant's family without enough to live on, and the tenant's "trying to get away with it." While most of the local leaders said that lease contracts were always written after land reform, 27 per cent testified that there were still some unwritten contracts and that, in those instances, the rent was not as specified in the Rent Limitation Act. The reason for such deviations was that some of the leases were contracted between families which had a kinship relationship or a long-time friendship. Their intent was said to be to do a favor or give help, one family to another.

In regard to kan-ch'ing in the landlord-tenant relationship, 73 per cent of the local leaders remembered that before land reform, tenants had respect for their landlords; 17 per cent said they were friends; only 9 per cent remembered the relationship as cool. What had been the condition after land reform? Most local leaders had to say that the tenant's attitude or feeling toward his former and current landlords had changed from being cool to being unfriendly; 30 per cent believed that they still treated each other in a friendly way, that the tenant still had respect for the landlord. More than one-half admitted that there had been more disputes between land-lords and tenants after land reform, while 45 per cent denied such an observation. The causes of farm-tenancy disputes after land reform were said to be the tenant's failure to pay rent, problems concerning land retained by landlords, the landlord's trying to take back land from tenants, and so on. About one-half of the local leaders admitted that after rent reduction, many landlords tried to terminate leases and take back the land for their own cultivation; the other half denied such a charge. A survey conducted among the people who worked in the local government agencies revealed much similar information.

Mr. Hung-chin Tsai is a younger son of a small-farm tenant. His father and older brothers had the opportunity to purchase about one hectare of paddy land through the land-to-the-tiller program and the family has since been growing in socio-economic status and morale. Hung-chin was supported in his education until he received a master's degree in rural sociology at National Taiwan University. Tsai was the first to study the broad effects of land reform in Taiwan. According to his findings,[14] before land reform most of the people in rural Taiwan had had some interest in farm tenancy, either as landlords or tenants. Those who were strictly owner-farmers or farm laborers were few in numbers. One landlord might have had several, or several tens, of tenants; on extra-large holdings, there were, perhaps, more than a hundred. On the other hand, one tenant might have been cultiva-

ting pieces of land rented from several landlords. This led into landlord-

tenant relationships of considerable multiplicity and complication. In

general, the landlords had had the superior social and economic statuses.

Not a few of them exploited and abused their tenants and their relation-

ships with tenants had been anything but pleasant. However, not all

landlord-tenant relationships were bad. Quite a few landlords had been

kind, considerate, fair, and moderate in their dealings with the tenants.

Thus, the landlord-tenant relationships before land reform can be generally

classified into three types:

First, relationship between resident landlords and their tenant.

Despite their wealth and high social status, most resident landlords were

generous and friendly toward tenants. There was good kan-ch'ing. On

special occasions, such as when the tenant was delivering the rent or on

festival days, the landlord treated the tenant nicely and entertained him

with a good meal. In planting and irrigating seasons the landlord often

went personally to see the tenant to inquire whether there were problems

or urgent needs. When the tenant appealed for emergency assistance, the

appeal was considered and answered. In return, the tenant gave scarce farm

products to the landlord as presents, offered his labor free, or gave other

service for special occasions or events.

Second, relationship between non-resident landlords and tenants.

Non-resident landlords had no direct contact with their tenants. They did

not know them and they did not care about them. There was no kan-ch'ing,

understanding, or sympathy between the two. Rent was collected by the landlords' agents. The agents always tried to collect as much as they could squeeze out. The tenants felt only resentment for the agents and the resentment carried over to the landlords.

Third, relationship between small resident landlords and tenants. Most of the small, resident landlords were farm families in the rural communities and had been for many generations. Their land was accumulated piece by piece through the hard work and frugal living of many past ancestors. Because of labor shortages or other reasons, they themselves were not able to cultivate all the land they owned. A portion of it was rented to poor neighbors or relatives who had extra labor. The landlords and tenants were, in most cases, members of the same kinship group, family friends, or, neighbor on good terms. The relationship between such landlords and tenants had been the best. There was not much difference in their socio-economic level they knew each other's ways in detail, and it was easy to come into common understanding when any problem or dispute came up.

As soon as the Rent Limitation Act was put into practice, the long-established, taken-for-granted landlord-tenant relationship was stirred up and soon suffered a great rupture. Many of the tenants got the idea that the Government was on their side and that the land laws were enacted for their advantage. Armed with such a conviction, they dropped their respectful ways toward landlords. Those who had suffered injustices from their landlords openly assumed hostile attitudes and, in some cases, took action to wreak revenge. Some others quickly forgot the kindness and favors they had received from the landlords.

On the side of the landlords, bitterness and resentment were the consequence of the loss suffered from the rent reduction and from the tenants' returning kindness with extortion. Out of this mutual antagonism rose numerous, serious, tenancy disputes. Fortunately, by this time the Farm Tenancy Committees had been reestablished and considerably strengthened and, consequently, were functioning quite effectively. The greater portion of the disputes were brought to the committees for investigation, concilia-tion, and settlement. Although eventually a dispute was settled in one way or another, any earlier good kan-ch'ing had disappeared forever.

A survey of forty-six former landlord households revealed that more than 30 per cent had, after rent limitation, had serious disputes with their tenants. In recalling these disputes, at a time about fifteen years later, the landlords still showed great bitterness and rage, still expressed wrath about the tenants' change from humility and submission before land reform to arrogance and ingratitude after. They complained that land reform had caused them to lose many kinsfolk and friends who had been their tenants or part-owner farmers.

The former and current tenants were comparatively mild and cautious in words and feelings when talking about their relationships with the land-lords after land reform. Most of them said there had not been significant changes or many disputes. If there had been some, they were not serious disputes. They said that if the lease contracts had been signed and observed exactly in accordance with the provisions of the Act, there should have been no reason for disputes. Without disputes the relationship cannot but be good.

Miss Fu-ying Chien, a graduate of the Department of Agricultural Extension of National Taiwan University and a reporter for Harvest, made case studies of two, former-landlord households. In one of her interviews the ex-landlord said with strong feeling, "The hardest thing for me to swallow is that all those people who before were my tenants now show arroga attitudes toward me as we pass each other on the road. They don't even care to say just a greeting. What a change! Yes, I know, they are now landlowners. They want us all to know they are landowners."[15]

Gallin makes this observation about the new landlord-tenant relationshi in Hsin Hsing Village: "With the tenant's security on the land protected, he no longer had to kowtow to his landlord or attempt to maintain good kan-ch'ing. Today it is common to hear a tenant, formerly courteous to his landlord whether he liked him or not, actually curse him when he comes in his own wagon to collect and load the tenant's land rent. (The tenant formerly delivered the rent to the landlord.)"[16]

4. <u>Changes in general patterns</u>. Any general change in social relatio appeared mostly to have been an alteration of directions, since land reform first emphasis had been shifted from hierarchial relations to egalitarian relations. This new trend may not necessarily have started within the fami al relations, but there should be little objection if we begin the examina tion inside the household. Ever since the farm people became interested in the new technology and enrolled themselves in the various study programs, their sons and daughters made advancements far beyond what was possible for their fathers and mothers. This difference between the two generations has had a profound impact upon the traditional relations between father and son, mother and daughter, parents and children. Because the son's knowledge of farm technology surpasses his father's and he has for this reason made a greater contribution to the improvement of the family's income, he is now on an equal status with his father. In their kinship relationship th

two are still father and son, senior and junior, higher and lower; but in
work experience, in roles played while operating the farm and making plans
for the future of the family, the father no longer treats his son as a
junior, a subordinate, or one to take his orders. In kinship consciousness
and in filial piety the son still has great respect for his father, but in
many practical ways he feels his father is not an authority, or that at
least he himself is not inferior. And, thus, he no longer sets his father
up on high or looks up to him. Instead, he feels they are standing face-
to-face. He still has respect for his father, but he is no longer silent
and uneasy. He shows his thoughts and feelings freely with a pleasant
disposition.

Some fathers, who had been tightly bound by the traditional type of
father-son relationship, found it most difficult to accept this new trend,
but most made the necessary readjustment and took up their sons as equal
partners in farming and gradually, also, in all things concerning the well-
being of the family. People have learned to understand and appreciate the
new ideal of the father-son relationship as one of deep friendship, mutual
understanding, and walking together side-by-side.

The same exposition can be applied to the changed and changing mother-
daughter relationship. It is especially noticeable in families whose
daughters have joined extension programs or home-improvement classes. The
relationship between older and younger brothers had long been egalitarian
in farm households. Starting from five or six years ago a 'farm and home
planning' program has been under promotion by the agricultural-extension
agencies throughout the province. From a rural sociologist's point of
view, the important focus of this program is on having all adult members of

the family around the table, discussing problems,and making plans for the family. It emphasizes the importance of allowing every member equal opportunity and equal obligation to express his ideas and add to the discussion.

Beyond the family, social relations in the farm village have been undergoing the same kind of change. The extension programs and other similar farmers' organizations have all made substantial contributions toward this change. Members of most of these organizations include farmers or farm women of several generations, several land-tenure classes, several age groups, and several social levels. But at meetings and in discussions, all treat each other as fellow members. There is very little distinction or seniority, status,or differences in land tenure. Despite the attention given to differences between owner-farmers and tenants in various circumstances, in these latter-day activities the differences are reduced to a minimum. Today's meetings are arranged entirely differently from the traditional ways. There used to be leaders or dignitaries sitting on a high platform, with the general audience down below. Words and ideas were poured out from on high and dropped down to the floor. Today leaders and audience sit as a panel or in a circle. People look at each other, speak to each other face-to-face. It is truly a shift, a graphic one, from hierarchical to horizontal relationship.

Communication is part and parcel of social relations. Horizontal communication far exceeds vertical communication. Agricultural-extension agencies pass very little information from their high offices in towns and cities down to the farmers in the villages. The effective extension work is done personally in the villages where the farmers or farm women gather.

Agents take part in the gathering as equal fellows. The traditional manner
in which the dignified teacher sits on high and far apart is no longer
effective. Radio programs, television appearances, forum meetings, news-
letters, posters, etc., all emphasize the principles and the techniques of
passing the information horizontally. The results of many information-
diffusion researches show that farmers get most information through their
neighbors, friends, fellow farmers.

Notes

[1]"Hakha" is a collective term of a culturally distinctive group of
people who mainly live in the provinces of Kwangtung, Fukien, Kiangsi,
Kwangsi, and Taiwan. They originally came from north China.

[2]Traditionally, an official village head was a male person implicitly
designated by the village's influential leaders and elected by the common
villager's consensus. He was more the assistant or courier to the village
"boss" than a head. For this reason the official village head was usually
a younger man, without much prestige.

[3]A smaller farm village could have had less than 50 households while
a large one could have more than 200. But a majority of the compact
villages numbered households within the range from 50 to 200.

[4]In farm villages a home consisted of the living quarters, houses
for storage, shelters for livestock, the courtyard, and the enclosing
walls. A gate was built into one of the walls.

[5]Many people call the center of a township 'town.' For this reason
the township center and the township itself are often mixed up. It is
true that many of the township centers in Taiwan today have all the
features or characteristics of a town. But many others still do not. At
any rate, the center, or 'town,' must not be confused with the township
which is the larger geographic area wherein the center or 'town,' is located
A township is an administrative designation for an area which includes
both a center, or a 'town,' and a number of farm villages (in a rural townshi
or hsiang) or a number of urban sections (in an urban township or chen).

[6]The offering of free labor and the presenting of gifts by the tenant
could have developed into evil practices, or practices subject to evil
interpretation as, on the one hand, a form of extortion by the landlords
and, on the other hand, attempts at bribery by tenants who hoped for better
rental plots or other favors at the expense of fellow tenants.

[7]Morton H. Fried, Fabric of Chinese Society: A Study of the Social
Life of A Chinese County Seat.

[8]In this farm-tenancy relationship the tenant's actions which were
good in the eyes of the landlords were the offering of free labor and
gifts on special occasions and the showing of loyalty. The landlord's
good actions, in the eyes of the tenants, were leniency in collection
of rents, help to tenant's children in finding non-farm work, extending
special credits, etc.

[9]Frank B. Bessac, "The Field Research Concerning the Social Consequences of Land Reform in Taiwan" (Manuscript), pp. 36-40.

[10]Martin M. C. Yang, _A Chinese Village: Taitou, Shantung_, p. 132.

[11]Bernard Gallin, _Hsin Hsing, Taiwan: A Chinese Village in Change_, p. 91.

[12]Martin M. C. Yang, "Changes in Family Life in Rural Taiwan."

[13]See Section on 37.5% Farm Rent Limitation Program, Chapter Two.

[14]Hung-chin Tsai, "A Study of the Socio-Economic Effects of Land Reform in Taiwan," pp. 99-105.

[15]Fu-ying Chien, "A Landlord Who Met Failure after Land Reform," pp. 7-8.

[16]Bernard Gallin, _Hsin Hsing, Taiwan: A Chinese Village in Change_, p. 95.

Chapter Eleven

CHANGES IN POWER STRUCTURE AND LEADERSHIP
IN RURAL COMMUNITIES

I. Traditional Power Structure

II. Traditional Community Leadership

III. Changes in Power Structure
1. The Farm People's Interest in
Local Politics
2. Participation in Local Elections
3. New Incumbents in Village and
Township Public Offices
4. New Local Leaders
5. New Leadership Qualifications
6. Changes in Value Concepts

Land reform had also aimed at building and developing a grass-root democracy in rural Taiwan. At least it is reasonable for civic leaders at every level to believe that land reform should have an effect upon politics in the rural communities.[1] In this chapter we shall study changes in power structure and leadership in the rural communities after land reform.

I. The Traditional Power Structure

Power structure is based on status structure. Therefore, before
discussing power structure we should first know the status structure
in a traditional rural community. Yung-teh Chow in a rather sweeping
statement says that traditional Chinese society had two major groups,
the peasantry and the gentry, and that the gentry was differentiated
into two subgroups--the officials and the local gentry.[2] This over-
simplified description is accurate for a traditional county-seat community, but in a traditional rural community there were more than two
status groupings. There were the landlords, and in case there were
no landlords, the richest households in the community took their place.[3]
A second status group consisted of the official village head and his
assistants or lieutenants. A third group included the few persons
who had the reputation of knowing many things, of being capable of
handling controversial matters, of having persuasive personalities,
etc. The village school teacher or teachers and a few other persons
who had some schooling or some self-taught learning, which was somehow
admired by fellow villagers, formed a fourth group. Then there was a
fifth group, the heads of clans, or tsu-chang, whose clans included
only ordinary farm families. Some owner-farmers and tenants who were
recognized as successful in their farming and active in the public affairs
of their own neighborhoods can be considered as a sixth group. Finally,
at the bottom were the large numbers of ordinary peasantry which
included both the small owner-farmers and the ordinary tenants. Further-

more, mention must also be made of the women who enjoyed prestige above all the other women in the community. Even many of the menfolk paid them respect. In status this group of extraordinary women were on a par with some of the men's groups at the middle of the structure. They occupied strategic positions in the power structure and in the process through which the power in community affairs flowed.

Until recently there had been no agent of government, no official, in that basic rural community, the farm village. So there was no comparable status. The so-called official village head, t'sun chang, was a person designated by the first status group mentioned above and 'elected' by consensus of the villagers. Then, in one way or another, the county government or the township public office gave him recognition, and he was, thereafter, subject to summons from the government for official affairs. At the same time he was the front-man for the village's gentry, the first status group. He was the man who administered the gentry's will or effected its plans upon the villagers; it was he who received any kind of insult or physical abuse from government officials and police officers who, as a rule, refrained from offering these compliments to the village gentry directly.

The power structure in a traditional rural community corresponded closely to this description, except that, in numerous cases, the flow of power could be quite erratic. It jumped from one group to another without necessarily having touched the hands of groups between them in the line. It zigzagged instead of following the straight course of established channels. Generally, the power in community public affairs was in the hands of the first status group. These people had the prerogative of initiating a single action or a program, in response to a problem imposed from outside, or in creating a new program for the community welfare. Sooner or later their action became known to the other villagers, who then discussed or grumbled about the matter in private, or in small groups at homes, on street corners or in tea houses, or occasionally at meetings called by the village head upon suggestions from the top authorities. If results of the discussions were favorable, or if there were no serious objections, a final decision was reached by the people who had had initiated the action or program.

Following the decision, plans and details were worked out by a group of people larger in number than the one which initiated the action or program. This meant that more villagers, villagers of the middle status groups, were involved in the creation of work plans. When the work plans were ready, orders for action were issued to the village head and, by him, to his lieutenants. The village head and his lieutenants then distributed responsibilities and work to people in the third and fourth status levels and they, in turn, distributed work to the fifth and sixth groups. No power was formally vested in the hands of the people of the fifth and sixth groups, but they could either be a great help or a great hindrance depending on the way they passed orders down to the general constituency of the community. When people of these groups received proper attention and adequate interpretation of the plans, they lent their influence and persuaded the villagers-in-general to accept the orders and do the work. If they kept silent or showed a negative attitude toward the whole project, however, the villagers might then become seriously discouraged with a given project.

In general, this was the way in which community activities were started and carried out. More often, there was a great deal of deviating and zigzags. In the old days, there was very little, if any, community organization in the sense in which the modern social scientists understand it. The villagers themselves had no conception of an established hierarchy or the administration of public affairs through the framework of the hierarchy. It was the sociologists or social anthropologists who based their schemes on their field observations and worked out a social system.

II. The Traditional Community Leadership

The landlords' group, the first status group in the power structure, played a major role in the leadership of their community. Landlords leadership roles were greatly reinforced by the officials, the representatives of government, who preferred to handle official affairs relating to the community through the wealthy landlords group rather than dealing directly with the common peasants. One reason for this preference was that whether the official business was the levying of a special tax, a demand for a labor force, a suggestion for building a school, etc., the most crucial problems were the raising of local funds and persuading the local populace to comply with the order, demand, or suggestion. It was generally the wealthy landlords who had the power or capability to solve these problems. All that the government's representatives cared about was to have the things done within a specified time limit. How the landlords dealt with the villagers in obtaining the funds or how the labor was distributed was not their problem. In order to have the full cooperation of the landlords, the government's representatives showed them respect and gave them authority.

In the old days, all government officials seemed to have the habit and pleasure of looking down upon or abusing the people who were not officials but rural folks, including the landlords and other people of dignity in the villages. Besides, they always had the evil idea of finding opportunity, while doing business in the villages, to squeeze some money out of those wealthy households. This contradiction between the necessity for showing respect and the habit of condescension and abuse toward the same group of people was solved by having an official village head, or t'sun-chang, in the village's power structure. As pointed out previously, the official village head was a courier, or a front-man, for the landlords. He had a much lower social status. He was, therefore, able to take some humiliation without being too much embarrassed. Thus the government officials could first be polite with the landlords and show them respect, and later get compensation from pouring insulting words upon the village head and his lieutenants. It was, however, also in this way that the village head played his role in the traditional village leadership. His role and those of the landlord or gentry were sometimes mixed and inseparable.

The gentry could not always draw their leadership entirely from the support of government officials. In the old days, the wishes and actions of government officials, were, in one way or another, always positioned against the interests of the general villagers. If the landlords had always acted in favor of the government officials and in conflict with the welfare of the local populace, they would sooner or later have

become enemies of the local community. Their leadership would have had
no real support from the villagers. Locally-popular landlords must have
had the local people's interest in mind and must have done their best to
protect and enhance it. At the same time, they had to use their influence
to persuade the people to comply with the government's reasonable orders.
They acted as interpreters, buffers, and as a bridge between the villagers
and the government. A landlord could not simply be a transmitter, or
worse, a cat's paw of the government. On the other hand, neither could
they be too narrow-minded, caring only about the villagers' interests
and refusing to give help to programs sponsored by the government which
did not give direct and manifest benefit to the local community. In that
case, they would have put the whole village under the wrath of the government officials.

The community status structure was closely interrelated with the
community power structure, and the power structure was closely interrelated with the community leadership. In general, people who had the
highest socio-economic status had the power, and those who had power
were leaders. There were exceptions, however. Some villagers had high
status but did not have power, and some people had power but were not
leaders. Usually people with high status were sought out and given the
power to act in affairs concerning the whole community. With both
status and power, it was easier for them to become leaders than it would
have been with either attribute alone. But it was only easier, not
guaranteed. Even given status and power leadership, they had yet to
win respect to be accepted as true leaders.

Traditionally, the merits which made leaders were: (1) the capability of sensing and interpreting local needs and then formulating programs to meet the needs; (2) the courage, wisdom, and ability to organize people and means for action in defense of the community against any oncoming danger; (3) the capability and fair-mindedness to pacify and arbitrate disputes among community members so they need not resort to legal machinery for settlement; (4) being informed and concerned about such community problems as famine, poverty, and epidemics and being able to devise measures to prevent or solve them; (5) good judgment and persuasiveness in setting out norms and ideals for members of the community; (6) knowledge and training necessary for properly conducting family rituals, community ceremonies, and religious services.

The persons in status groups higher than ordinary villagers were all considered leaders in the community. They were leaders on different levels and had different characteristics. But whether they were real and durable leaders depended entirely on their having some, or all, of the characteristics noted above. Usually no one leader would have all of them. But each leader had to have one, two, or several qualifications. The usual situation was that any one person had one or two meritorious qualities and performed one or two functions well. When people in the several status groups, in combination, had all the merits and were able to offer someone skilled for each function, the community had good leadership. Sometimes, however, there were only a few persons with limited capabilities. Then there was one-sided, unbalanced, or incomplete leadership. Sometimes, also, in a deteriorating community there was no person who had adequate merits to enable him to lead the community activities. It is hard to say whether it had been a lack of leadership that caused the community deterioration, or vice versa.

In spite of the statement that persons in the upper status groups might not necessarily have been community leaders, it is, nevertheless, a fact that it was these people who had greater potentialities and more opportunities to acquire the needed merits. For instance, members of the landlord, or other well-to-do, households had the opportunity and means to acquire education, knowledge, and wide information, and they had the cultural heritage with which the first kind of leadership qualification could be cultivated and developed. To make workable proposals and to take action on them to solve community problems required the backing of financial and human forces. Without such backing the proposals usually attracted no heed, and action was never taken. This had been a very old assumption; unfortunate tradition had grown. The unfortunate tradition was that many of the families of means and high status failed to produce persons of education, wisdom, and capability. Yet the community blindly followed the old tradition and granted its positions of leadership to members of those families. Communities were slow in putting aside tradition and granting recognition to persons who had the leadership qualifications but were not members of those patrician families or of high status groups.

III. Changes in the Power Structure

With all the changes in the family system and in kinship relationships, the disappearance of the landlords' superior social and economic status, the increase of the owner-farmers' and tenants' interest in community affairs, plus the introduction of political election procedures to the farm villages, it seems that the traditional power structure would have had to face drastic changes. If so, how great were these changes? First let us examine the farm people's political interest after land reform.

1. <u>The farm people's interest in local politics</u>. Of the 1250 former tenants, only 10 per cent said they had been interested in local politics before land reform; 90 per cent said they had had no interest. Ten years after land reform the number of households interested in local politics had increased to 31 per cent, but those which had not become interested still accounted for 68 per cent. Of the 250 current tenants, in the ten years after land reform 25 per cent said they had become interested in local politics and about 74 per cent said they had not. Among the 250 original owners, interest was somewhat higher than in the other groups. Those which had some interest in local politics at the time of the interview accounted for about 35 per cent which was 10 per cent higher than among the current tenants and 5 per cent higher than among the former tenants. In terms of percentage of households interested in local politics, the three categories of farm households should be rearranged in this order: original owners, 35 per cent; former tenants, 31 per cent; current tenants, 25 per cent. The interval in instance was 5 per cent.

Investigation was made to find out whether the small farmers had become interested and concerned about what was going on in the nation and the world and in what the national and local governments were doing. Our findings were as follows:

About 22 per cent of the former tenants did become interested in national and world affairs after land reform, and this new interest had much to do with their new outlook in farming. Asked whether they had any suggestions to give to the Government in regard to national and local reconstruction or developmental policies and programs, only a few gave answers but the answers were interesting. They suggested there should be means whereby farm people could be adequately informed of national and world events in order that they may have a stronger and more responsible voice in public affairs; that agricultural education be strengthened still further; that prices of farm products be raised; that the Government assist and educate farmers in marketing farm produce and purchasing farm supplies; that the cost of living be stabilized.

The current tenants, by more than 30 per cent, said that after land reform they became more concerned about national and local government. They were, however, unable to make any suggestions as what the Government ought to do to enhance the well-being of farm people. But 71 per cent gave approval to the nation's program to consolidate fragmented farm lands.

More than 45 per cent of the original-owner farmers said they had, after land reform, begun to pay more attention to the Government's policies and undertakings. Another 50 per cent began to pay some attention, but not too much. To the question as to what specific help they would like to have from the Government, they gave several answers: The Government agencies ought to help and guide unemployed farm people into new jobs or occupations; the Government ought to help in repairing and building country roads; public loans should be made to farmers who wished to

carry out land-improvement projects; prices of farm products should be
raised; land taxes should be lowered; more schools should be built; the
exchange ratio between rice and fertilizer should be adjusted and corrected; more waterworks and irrigation facilities should be built; programs for control of plant diseases and pests should be strengthened; the
efforts to fight against poverty should be increased; interest rates on
farm-production loans should be cut; the security force, or peace-keeping
force in the countryside should be increased. A majority of these farmers
also supported the farmland consolidation program.

In contrast, 70 per cent of the 575 former landlord households said
they had become either less interested or had felt no interest at all in
the community's local politics since land reform. Only 25 per cent said
they were as interested as before. The non-farm people's observations on
this were different. Most (86%) of the Government employees, for instance,
said that the former tenants had shown new interest in local politics after
land reform. These households also believed that the current tenants and
hired laborers had become more interested than before. But most Government employees agreed that the landlords really had lost interest in local
politics. Observations of the local community leaders were: More than 46
per cent thought that after becoming owner-farmers, the former tenants had
developed an interest in local politics; and 23 per cent said they had become more interested than before land reform.

Tsai's study[4] reveals that after land reform, the farm people as a
whole, including the former landlords, had become more attentive toward
political affairs such as administrative orders, declarations of national
and local policy, and proclamations of reconstruction and reform programs.

This change was due largely to the land reform and its various side-effects. It had affected the farm people's life so much that most of them had been made to realize that they could no longer be indifferent toward political changes and political movements if they were to obtain the benefits and avoid the hurts. But those whose earlier interest had increased were those who had been most intimately affected by the land-reform programs, people like the landlords and the tenants. Tsai also reports that 35 per cent of the former landlords had not, because of land reform, changed or diminished their interest in political affairs, and 48 per cent had actually become more interested than before. Only 17 per cent had said that their interest had dropped. More than 75 per cent of the former tenants had become more concerned with national and local politics after land reform. Less than 20 per cent said they had made no change in this respect. But they did not specify whether 'no change' meant continuation of interest or disinterest.

Among the people who had some interest in politics, there were differences in the depth, breadth, and meaningfulness of their interest. Some people might have been interested in politics long ago. But in most cases the interest had been shallow, limited, and without much understanding and appreciation. The land reform had apparently led a large number of people in each category of farm households to become quite seriously concerned with the politics of their communities. Their concerns were more purposeful and perceptive. In other words, more plain farmers became informed of, and actively involved in, the community's public affairs.

Some former landlords had privately confided to Tsai that after land reform they could no longer exercise direct leadership in the community because their wealthy-landlord status or traditional-gentry status. But many of the

were unwilling to voluntarily give up the role, or, in other words, they did
not give it up without a struggle. Soon they found that leadership could be
kept through political efforts. This meant that if a former landlord should
run for public office and be elected, he then would become a political figure
in the local community. Generally, the country people still have high respect
for a political personage whether they like him or not. It is somewhat like
the pre-land reform feelings of tenants for their landlords; whether they
liked them or not, they respected them. This wish to keep their traditional
role in community leadership was an important reason for some of the former
landlords' interest in local politics.[5] In Miss Chien's report, "A Landlord
Met Failure after Land Reform," the chief cause of this former landlord's
failure was that he spent a major portion of the proceeds from the sale of his
shares of corporation stocks on running for election as a county magistrate.
He lost the election and his money was gone. This landlord's statement about
why he was interested in the election serves as a good illustration of Tsai's
confidential information:

> I had been thinking. Since a great part of my property
> and wealth are gone, it seemed very likely that the local
> people would no longer respect me. They would no longer
> feel I had prestige and so would not offer me their loyal-
> ty any more. Instead they would look down upon me and
> ridicule me. Should I accept all this as a predetermined
> fate? No, I should not. On the contrary, I would run for
> public office. If I could be elected to the office of the
> county magistrate all the prestige and leadership would be
> restored and kept for me. And it so happened that the
> program of self-government in townships and counties through-
> out the Province had just been officially proclaimed. It
> was my opportunity. So, I became very much interested in
> politics. I not only participated in the election once,
> but several times. But alas! I met failure every time. [6]

In this connection Tsai has another piece of confidential information.
He was told that the political standings of former, big landlords could be

classified into two opposite extremes. At one extreme stood all those
who tried to keep and multiply their former power and positions by identi-
fying themselves with, or submitting themselves to, the current political
authorities or the ruling party. These people had wholeheartedly supported
the present Government and its party by offering their loyalty and means,
and by complying with all legislation and all programs instituted by the
Government. As their reward many gained political favor and appointive
positions at all levels.

At the opposite extreme were those who did not want to support the
Government and the ruling party. But neither did they want to give up
power and position. These people also resorted to political means to
get what they wanted, but instead of going over to the Government and its
party, they turned in an opposite direction. They worked hard to create
something like an opposition party. They identified themselves as cham-
pions of the political feelings and interests of those groups which had
a grudge or a complaint against the authorities. When they felt more or
less assured of the needed support, they stood for election to all kinds
of public offices. Many of them succeeded. Tsai has live illustrations
of both extremes but is obliged not to disclose their identity.[7]

In summary, after land reform, there was a general increase of interest in political affairs, especially in local politics. The increase
was largest among owner-farmers due either to their own ambition or to
other people's persuasions. Many former landlords, especially the big
ones, had also felt much concern for public affairs of their local community. More of them had been concerned about the safekeeping of power and
position or of increasing these through political involvement. A few

had wished only to make greater contributions to the community in some kind of political capacity. Only those who had left the community, physically or emotionally or both, and were attending to new businesses in the cities had lost interest entirely in the politics of their original societies.

2. Participation in local elections. About 96 per cent of the 1250 former tenants told the interviewers that when there was an election, all family members who had the right to vote went to the polls. About 80 per cent of the households whose members voted in each election said their doing so was out of their own interest. A little more than 20 per cent admitted it was due to persuasion. Had the people of these households themselves run for public office in the election? Yes, but not many; only 7 per cent of them said their people had run, and 92 per cent said "no." Of those who had run, a small percentage did so before land reform, but 80 per cent had done so after. Also, of those who had run, 90 per cent were elected. The prime reason for such success had been their having had the trust of the people in general. The second reason was their being known to be active in public-welfare activities; and the third, their having good public relations, that is, good relations with the local people. Reasons which they felt were of less importance were good credit, great wealth, integrity, etc. A small percentage reported that they had helped others to run for office. A few of them did so before land reform, but a majority gave such help after they had become owner-farmers and their living conditions improved.

Of the current tenants, less than 8 per cent reported running for public office; 92 per cent never had run. Of those who did run, more than 84 per cent were elected. The reasons for their election were having been active in public-welfare activities and having good public relations. A few of these households had also been invited to help others in their races.

About 24 per cent of the original owners had taken part as candidates in elections; 75 per cent had not. Of those who did run, about 94 per cent met success. About 18 per cent of these households had received requests for help in elections.

On this point the former landlords again showed their modesty. According to their reports to the interviewers, only 16 per cent of them had run for public office in the ten years after land reform, and the other 83 per cent had had no interest in doing that. The number of them who had helped others to run, also, was about 15 or 16 per cent. Most of them refused their help. With the 75 large landlords, it was somewhat different. In the ten years after land reform, more than 21 per cent of them said they themselves had been in the running, and about 30 per cent had helped others to run.

The public-office seekers in both groups of former landlords were asked about the purposes behind their political efforts and aspirations. This is what interviewers were told: their purposes were to serve the local people; to provide the local community the needed social-welfare undertakings; to put rural development projects into practice; to end disputes and antagonisms among contending factions in the community; to improve social conditions of the community; to open new opportunities for the development of businesses; to find a solution for critical water shortages; to gratify the local people's support; to prepare for running for the office of representatives in the county assembly.

In Yen-tien Chang's case study[8] there is information showing the farm people's voting participation in the election of village head, township mayor, hsien magistrate, township representative, hsien representative, and provincial representative, before and after land reform, first for the year 1948 and then the year 1965. This information is greatly different from that revealed in our survey. Their participation was computed for each of the three categories and as an average of the three. Thus, in 1948, in the election of village head, the voter participation of the owner-farmers was 42.2 per cent; of the part-owner farmers, 38.5 per cent; of the tenant farmers, 42.9 per cent; and the average, 41.8 per cent. In 1965 the four figures were 77.7, 76.9, 78.6, and 77.7. The increase in each case was 84.12, 99.74, 83.22, and 85.89. In the 1948 election of township mayor, the voter participation of the three classes of farmers was 32.5, 42.3, 17.9, and 31.8 was the average. In 1965 the figures were 81.9, 84.6, 82.1, and 82.3. The increase in each case was 152.00, 100.00, 358.66, and 158.80. In the election of hsien magistrate, the voter participation percentages were, in 1948, 38.0, 50.0, 32.1, and 38.6; in 1965, 80.1, 92.3, 67.9, and 80.0; the increase in each, 111.00, 84.60, 115.00, 107.00.

In the election of township representative: 1948, 21.7, 26.9, 21.4, 22.3; 1965, 49.4, 53.9, 50.0, 50.0; the increase, 127.65, 100.00, 133.60, 124.20. In the election of hsien representative: 1948, 41.6, 46.2, 28.6, 40.5; 1965, 81.3, 84.6, 67.9, 80.0; the increase, 95.43,

83.12, 137.41, 97.53. In the election of provincial representative: 1948, 38.6, 42.3, 25.0, 37.3; 1965, 81.9, 88.5, 64.3, 80.5; the increase, 112.18, 109.22, 157.2, 115.81. In summary, all these figures are put in a table as follows:

Voter Participation by Percentages

	Village Head			Township Mayor			Hsien Magistrate		
	1948	1965	Change	1948	1965	Change	1948	1965	Change
Owner Farmer	42.2	77.7	84.12	32.5	81.9	152.0	38.0	80.1	111.0
Part-Owner Farmer	38.5	76.9	99.74	42.3	84.6	100.0	50.0	92.3	84.6
Tenant	42.9	78.6	83.22	17.9	82.1	358.7	32.1	67.9	115.0
Average	41.8	77.7	85.89	31.8	82.3	158.8	38.6	80.0	107.0

	Township Representative			Hsien Representative			Provincial Representative		
	1948	1965	Change	1948	1965	Change	1948	1965	Change
Owner Farmer	21.7	49.4	127.7	41.6	81.3	95.4	38.6	81.9	112.2
Part-Owner Farmer	26.9	53.9	100.0	46.2	84.6	83.1	42.3	88.5	109.2
Tenant	21.4	50.0	133.6	28.6	67.9	137.4	25.0	64.3	157.2
Average	22.3	50.0	124.2	40.5	80.0	97.5	37.3	80.5	115.8

According to these statistics, ten years after land reform, the farm people of every tenure class had become very much interested in the participation in local politics. It is interesting to note that the increase in percentage of voter participation among farm people had been especially large in the elections of township mayor, township representative, and provincial representative. Next largest was in

the election of <u>hsien</u> magistrate. The reason for this was probably
that in the eyes of the general populace, the township mayoralty and
the township representative are the offices holding most of the direct
political power and civic influence upon local people and affairs. A
person in either of these offices has great opportunity to manipulate
public opinion and make decisions concerning community problems. Having great influence on public opinion and decision-making are the things
today's people yearn to have. They envy and respect people who have them.

Greater power and greater influence on more people and larger businesses, however, can be had only by one who has put himself into a top
position in provincial government. But the Provincial Governor is still
appointed by the National Government, or by the President; he is not
elected by the people. The provincial government's department heads and
other chief personnel are also appointees. Only the provincial representatives, the members of the Provincial Assembly, are elected by the
people. As a result, the competition for these positions has been extremely keen. A great many former big landlords, wealthy citizens, influential chieftains, partisan leaders, patriarchs of powerful clans, aspire
to get into this office. Those who have tried for it have usually made
tremendous efforts to persuade the people to elect them.

The <u>hsien</u> magistrate's office is also considered desirable, except
that informed people know that a <u>hsien</u> magistrate has a heavy burden of
work with little, or no, real and independent power. The magistrate is
virtually a courier for the provincial government, a transmitter of
communications between the provincial government and the township public
offices. From a realistic point of view, the rewards of being a <u>hsien</u>

magistrate are not only much less than those of the office of provincial
representative, but it also ranks second to the township bosses.

3. <u>New incumbents in village and township public offices</u>. We may
well wonder whether from among the farmers themselves, greater numbers
were in public office or in community leadership. First, to repeat
what has already been recorded in a previous paragraph, more than 7 per
cent of the former tenants said that they had taken part in races for
community offices and in nearly all cases had done so after becoming
owner-farmers through land reform. Of those who had run, only 9 per
cent failed to be elected.

A similar percentage of the 250 current tenant-farmers had actually
run for public positions and usually these candidates were elected. Of
the 250 original owner-farmers, 24 per cent had been in the running, and
more than 93 per cent won election.

According to reports of the 100, local, community leaders, of the
52 village heads who served a first term, about 39 per cent were original
owners; more than 44 per cent, landlords; 15 per cent, men of commerce;
and less than 2 per cent, new owner-farmers. There were 58 second-term
village heads among whom about 40 per cent were original owners; about
23 per cent were men of commerce; about 35 per cent were landlords; and
less than 4 per cent were new owners. In their third term there were
59 village heads of whom 46 per cent were original owners, 27 per cent
were landlords, 20 per cent were men of commerce, and 7 per cent were
new owners. In their fourth term were 67 village heads. Of these,
63 per cent were original owners, 22 per cent were business people,
less than 8 per cent were landlords, and less than 8 per cent were new

owners. The number of village heads serving at the time of the study was
61. Of these, more than 67 per cent were original owners, 18 per cent were
business people, more than 8 per cent were new owners, and about 7 per cent
were landlords.

The above statistics show that in the early days, most village heads
were landlords and owner farmers; next came business people, and only a
very few of the tenant-farmers and new owners had gained this position.
In Taiwan, a village head, even in the old days, had real power and prestige.
Villagers respected him. Therefore, in most of the cases, he had to be a
landlord or an owner-farmer. A tenant was not deemed qualified for such a
position. In recent years because land reform had taken away many of the
landlords' erstwhile qualifications, the number of village heads of landlord
status decreased considerably, whereas the number of village heads from
among original and new owner-farmers increased very much.

Following is a report on 'who's who' among township representatives.
Of those in their fourth terms, more than 23 per cent were landlords; 41
per cent owner-farmers; more than 28 per cent new owner-farmers; and more
than 7 per cent business people. Of the fifth-term representatives, landlords accounted for 21 per cent; owner-farmers more than 37 per cent; new
owner-farmers 36 per cent; business people less than 6 per cent. In the
sixth term, the percentages were 18, 42, 35, and 5; of the seventh term,
they were 20, 48, 32 and 0. Overall, there were 14 per cent landlords,
33 per cent owner-farmers, 25 per cent new owners and 28 per cent business
people. Business people were considerably more numerous among the township representatives than in other offices.

One hundred local government employees were interviewed about their views of the importance of farm people in local politics. More than 29 per cent believed that landlords were of first importance; 53 per cent believed they were of second importance; 18 per cent put them in the third position. Among owner-farmers, both original and new, more than 65 per cent thought they were of first importance, a little over 30 per cent gave them second importance, and less than 5 per cent agreed they were of third importance. Only 8 per cent of the appraisers gave first importance to tenant-farmers. About 19 per cent said second, but more than 73 per cent rated them the third.

In the formerly-cited Second Socio-Economic Survey of Rural Taiwan, there is information regarding local politics at the township level. Statistics compiled from the Survey show that in the year of 1959, when the survey was conducted, 10 (55%) of 18 township chiefs were farmers. Only 3 were landlords; the others were owner-farmers. The statistics also show that practically all township chiefs had roots in farming, rural commerce, or professional occupations in the localities where they were serving. A great deal of authority was vested in the hands of the township general secretary. In township politics the general secretary was second only to the township chief in importance. The survey revealed that a majority of the township secretaries were local people from familie engaged in farming.

The township assembly of people's representatives was important in township politics. The 18 townships together had, in 1958, 493 assembly-men. Over one-half were farmers and another 23 per cent came from familie engaged in farm-related local businesses. The township assembly holds the power which can either support the township public office in community improvement programs, or hinder it from doing the things which need to be done. If most of the representatives are farmers or are in farm-related business, the farm people are then in a strategic position in the township's new power structure.

At the township level, besides the public office and the assembly, the farm-tenancy committee is a body politic of considerable importance. The committee's chief function is to arbitrate disputes between landlords and tenants. The committee is made up of 11 members: 2 landlords, 2 owner-farmers, 5 tenant-cultivators (members of each tenure group are chosen from among representatives elected by farmers of their own agrarian status), the township chief who serves as chairman of the committee, and the official in charge of land affairs who serves as secretary to the committee. In 1959 farmers occupied most seats on the committees. There was rather keen competition in all townships for seats on the committees, which meant that committee members and the committee itself enjoyed social prestige and wielded political influence on affairs of the township.

Each of the 18 townships had an arbitration committee. This agency provides villagers an opportunity for a fair settlement of disputes short of, or prior to, court suits which are usually too expensive for the villagers to attempt. The number of members on such a committee varies from 5 to 9 and more than 72 per cent of the members on the 18 township arbitration committees were people other than farmers. Individually, however, the committees differed considerably in their number of farmer members. In the township of Yuan-chang, about 86 per cent were farmers in 1958. In Hsinpu-chen and Chishan-chen also, the majority of members were farmers. An

arbitration committee's influence or importance is indicated by the number
and nature of cases of disputes handled. In the year 1958 the 18 township arbitration committees handled a total of 1,035 cases. On the average
a committee had 57.5 cases in a twelve-month period. In nature, practical
all the cases were concerned with the payment of debts or fulfilling of
financial obligations, with property rights, matrimonial relations, inheri
ance, adoption, and kinship relationships.

The township farmers' association is not a Government agency, but is
deeply involved in local politics. Because it is a business organization
of real importance, influencing the work and lives of nearly all farm peop
as well as many others in the rural towns, its directors, supervisors, and
general manager usually had a considerable amount of power or influence in
the local community. For this reason, people take seriously the elections
for farmers' association directors and supervisors and the appointment of
the general manager. There is often keen competition for these offices.
Members of the association meet in their respective village, small-agricul
tural units to elect representatives to the association's annual meeting i
which is vested the control of the township's farmers' association. A boa
of directors, usually 11 to 15 members, and a board of supervisors of 3 or
5 members, are elected by the representatives from among themselves. A
general manager, employed by the board of directors, is responsible for
managing the association's affairs according to decisions and policies mad
by the board of directors. The association's first organizational law spe
cified that at least two-thirds of the directors must be from among owner-
farmers, tenant-farmers and farmhands; not more than one-third could be fr
among graduates of agricultural schools and workers on Government farms.

In 1957 the ratio was changed to 85 per cent owner-farmers, 13 per cent tenant-farmers, and others 2 per cent. The ratio in land tenure status of supervisors was, in 1957, 63 per cent owner-farmers; 11 per cent tenant-farmers; 24 per cent associate members; others, 2 per cent.

According to the 1965 Annual Report of Farmers' Associations in Taiwan,[9] there were in 1964, 21,499 township farmers' association membership representatives, of whom 87 per cent were owner-farmers; about 10 per cent were tenant-cultivators; and about 4 per cent were farmhands. There were 4,037 directors, of whom 88 per cent were owner-farmers; about 10 per cent were tenant-cultivators; and 2 per cent were farmhands. There were 1,153 supervisors, of whom 74 per cent were owner-farmers; about 16 per cent were associate members of non-farm people; about 8 per cent were tenant-cultivators; and 2 per cent were farmhands. There were 5,000 small-agricultural-unit leaders, of whom about 86 per cent were owner-farmers; about 10 per cent were tenant-cultivators; and 3 per cent were farmhands.

In summary, the land reform, the practice of local self-government, the introduction of a democratic election system in townships and villages, the increase of education among the ordinary farm people, general improvement in rural conditions, together all have profoundly changed the power structure and leadership in the rural communities. The land reform removed most of the large landlords from rural communities and into businesses or politics. Some did stay in rural towns but changed their occupations. Small landlords had, in most cases, become real owner-farmers. The land reform had converted many tenants into owner or part-owner-farmers. Thus, the group of original owners was greatly enhanced in both number and character by these new members. The popularization of both formal and informal education brought self-respect and self-confidence to the small farmers who formerly had lacked it, so that they either desired a leadership role or were, at least, no longer afraid of being in a leader's position. If, however, most of the small farmers still had to toil all the time with all their energy to make a bare living, as they did before, they would, even now, have been unable to give any time or energy to community affairs. Therefore, significant improvement in the farm people's living conditions has been another big factor ushering the owner-farmers and some of the better-off tenants into village and township public office.

4. Another line of new local leaders. There is another kind of rural leaders who have often been neglected by researchers whose studies on rural leadership have followed chiefly political or administrative routes. This leadership includes the chairmen and secretaries of the farm study groups, home-improvement classes, sugarcane-study groups, demonstration or model farmers, local 4-H club leaders, heads of tobacco-production improvement societies, chairmen and secretaries of the banana growers' associations, leaders of citrus fruit protection teams, and the principal personnel of several other farm organizations. These people are nearly always volunteers. They are leaders who receive no material rewards, get no publicity, and seldom are remembered or mentioned by dignitaries. However, they play very important parts in the improvement of rural conditions in general and, in particular, in the development of a modern, advan agriculture.

There had been such volunteer and unknown leaders in the traditional days. The more capable, more experienced, and more respected men and women who remained ordinary farmers and farm women in village neighborhood were good examples. There is, however, a great difference between such leaders in the traditional days and those today. Formerly such leaders came out of unplanned, unheralded, unselfish service and only after many years of work experience were they recognized by neighbors. Then they gave service and leadership in haphazard ways. In most cases, their influence and advice were on matters not directly related to production or improvement of either family or community living conditions, but rather on things of a moral nature. They had few opportunities to serve because life was, by and large, stabilized and ran in established courses.

Today's local volunteers work under very different conditions. First, they are deliberately and systematically recruited. After being invited to leadership, they are given well-planned training in all the necessary functions of dynamic group leaders. They become leaders and actually serve in on-going programs. They have well-organized work plans to follow and a defined focus to give direction to their leadership roles. Therefore, today's volunteer is much more efficient, effective, and productive than was the traditional neighborhood leader. Further, there are hundreds of thousands of volunteer leaders in rural communities throughout Taiwan today, and the great majority of them are farm people living in the villages. Only a small percentage might not be bona fide farmers, but rather, people in occupations directly related to farming and to life in the farm villages.

5. _New leadership qualifications_. To hold and use political power, one must be in a position of leadership. We have examined how, after land reform, many original and new owners and a moderate percentage of new tenants and farmhands entered leadership positions and how former landlords had tried through politics to safeguard their places of leadership. It is now time

to see whether there had been any changes in the factors or characteristics

which made people public leaders. If there had been changes, what were

the new qualifications?

The 100, local community leaders interviewed in the summer of 1964

said that election to leadership was due to these factors: enthusiasm in

public-welfare activities; sincerity and integrity in social relations; a

sense of responsibility; capability in handling public affairs; having wea

Business people in the rural towns were comparatively better informed

concerning the things which made people local leaders. When asked to name

some of the factors and to rate them by degree of importance, they express

opinions as follows:

They mentioned wealth, education, good conduct, status, capability, a

interest in public affairs as factors. In regard to the period before lan

reform, about 63 per cent rated wealth as of first importance; about 14 pe

cent gave it second importance; and less than 8 per cent gave it third pla

For the period after land reform, 45 per cent gave it first importance; 17

per cent second importance; and 14 per cent third importance. The ratings

show that after land reform, almost 20 per cent fewer people considered

wealth the most important factor in making people local leaders. More peo

listed it as second or third in importance.

As for education, about 18 per cent said that before land reform, it

was of first importance; 25 per cent said second; and 32 per cent said thi

After land reform, more than 30 per cent gave it first importance; 18 per

cent second; and 33 per cent third. After land reform education became

more important in people's minds. Ratings on good conduct are, for the

period before land reform, 14 per cent, 30, and 23. After land reform the percentages were 10, 25, and 7. This factor lost a great deal of weight after land reform.

Position or status as a leadership-making factor had also lost some importance. For the period before land reform the ratings were 2, 19, and 11; after land reform they were 9, 19, and 17.

Capability was rated first by about 4 per cent, second by 8 per cent, and third by 19 per cent in the period before land reform. Afterward ratings were 5, 14, and 17. People paid more attention to this factor after land reform, but only as a factor of second or third importance. Very few people considered interest in public affairs to be a factor of any importance either before or after land reform.

In the report of the Second Socio-Economic Survey of Rural Taiwan, statistics concerning rural leadership in 18 townships show that over 80 per cent of the rural leaders in 1959 were graduates of elementary or secondary schools, or of special (vocational) training institutions; a little more than 19 per cent had higher education; and only less than 1 per cent had no schooling at all. This information seemed to indicate that education was an important factor for becoming a local leader. An inquiry similar to the one conducted in our study was made among the then local leaders. Almost 90 per cent emphasized first a willingness to serve the public. This was very different from the result in our study. Sixty-seven per cent of those queried agreed that wealth was an important factor. Next in popularity were particular virtues mentioned by 55 per cent; great influence in the local community, membership in a prosperous and large clan, and belonging to a political party each got 33 per cent.[10]

Gallin quotes several residents of Hsin Hsing Village as saying, "The office of village mayor must be filled by a person who is not bound to his fields or to other work to support his family. He must have interes in village affairs and enough money to meet the expenses of the traditional functions of the office. He must be able to entertain any public officials or police visiting the village; he must have enough education and social acumen to carry on successfully the necessary relationships with villagers as well as outsiders with whom he is in frequent contact as village head."[11] Gallin also notes that "respect for a man is not based entirely on his wealth and power" in Hsin Hsing Village.[12]

Perhaps one should make a differentiation between leadership qualifications in accordance with the two types of rural leaders. Qualifications for leaders in the community's public offices must be different from those which made farmers the local volunteer leaders. It seems safe to say that qualifications for the second type of leaders should be: above average knowledge and successful experience in farming or other particular fields; a willingness to help fellow villagers; ability to organize groups and conduct meetings; a pleasant personality. This second kind of leadership would not require much wealth or position.

6. <u>Changes in value concepts.</u> No person can be really accepted and respected as a leader if his character and personality are in question. This is especially true in a community where the inhabitants are closely related and under each other's strong influence. Because character and personality have much to do with the social values of the local people, it is necessary to examine the leadership qualifications in the context of the community's value concepts.

One definite difference is that land was no longer the object of
highest value. Farming was still the chief livelihood in the farm villages
and land was still valuable, but, now, something else can take its place;
it can be given up for something desired more. Specifically, since land
reform more people have been investing money in things other than land;
some sold their lawfully-retained farm land and then added the proceeds
to their business capital. Surely this meant that the development or
expansion of a successful business was more valued than was the keeping
and use of the land. This is quite different from the old practice of
using any available profit to buy more land. This change had, of course,
been, in part, the result of land reform, for the limits on rent made
ownership of land no longer as profitable as before and the land-to-the-
tiller program gave the land owners fair warning that such reform measures
could happen again and that there is no more the old-fashioned security
in land ownership. Then, in the years after land reform, developing
industries and businesses are seen by every one in every place. Many
people have become rich through business or have earned a living better
than they had from toiling on a small farm. Although it is true there have
also been losses and bankruptcies in business, there are failures and risks
in farming and in land investments too. Most of the younger people in the
former-landlord households and in quite a few of the ordinary farm families
have struggled for an education. After they got it, they refused to return
to farming or other livelihoods tied to land. They went into numerous
kinds of non-farm businesses and were successful. In the minds of these
people, certainly, land was no longer the most valuable thing in their lives.

The philosophy behind this change, in the minds of the new farmers, the farmers whose farming has been much commercialized, and the sons of farmers, holds that farming is not a way of living but a means whereby a living is to be earned. Farmers operate a farm very much as a business man operates a shop. The operation has an objective and that is to earn a living. One can earn a living either by operating a farm or by operating a shop, depending upon which gives a better result. Thus, the operation of a farm and the operation of a shop are exchangeable; one can take the place of the other. The main need in the shop operation is for machinery, and the main need in the farm operation is for land. To say that the farm operation can be given up in favor of a shop operation means that the land can be sold to buy machinery. Thus, the value of land is comparable to the value of machinery. It is no longer the most valuable thing.

Another change in social values was related to the traditional virtue of suffering greatest hardship and living in utmost austerity, which has been losing ground in the last decade or so. Many old, conservative people shook their heads in lamentation when they saw this new general trend. But most younger people have acquired a so-called 'dare to spend money' attitude. This new attitude means, according to Bessac[13], that farmers nowadays dare to spend money on farm improvement. No longer is every family so careful about spending even a penny, in order to save every dollar. The dollar was saved, but the farm was left depleted. In addition, 'to dare to spend money' related to the fact that heads of households have given in to the demands of other members and, as incomes have risen, have bought more luxury or comfort goods such as better clothing, electric fans, radios, or bicycles. To most of the young villagers, it really means that one now may

defy one's elders in matters of custom, and such actions require the spending of money.

Accompanying the new 'to dare to spend money' attitude is the new concept that while one ought to work to earn an honest living, one does not
have to work as hard as a slave. When there is work to be done, one works
in accordance with his capability and capacity. When there is no work, one
can amuse oneself or take a rest. One does not have to keep on working
just to satisfy the traditional teaching that one ought to work all the
time and endure the greatest hardship. Though one should not waste his
money, one may spend the money he has earned in a proper and useful way.
There is no need to save the money if there are no means of reinvestment.
It is ridiculous to live in utmost austerity when one has the means to improve his living conditions.

These two changes in value concepts meant that the people no longer
sought for leadership qualifications solely among landlord or land-bound
personalities. The ability and willingness to endure hardship and frugality
are also no longer the criteria most esteemed for evaluating neighborhood
leaders. On the contrary, success in business and community-mindedness are
criteria for today's community leaders. In the village it is the farmers
who dare to spend money for the new technology, farm improvement and the
expansion of their farming, who are more admired and respected, and who
are being elected to posts of leadership.

Notes

[1]Specifically, it is hoped that the traditional pattern and essence of the village and township governments may change from an oligopolitic (or panchayati system in India) to a majority-participation-politic.

[2]Yung-teh Chow, Social Mobility in China, p. 47.

[3]Martin M. C. Yang, A Chinese Village: Taitou, Shantung, p. 132.

[4]Hung-chin Tsai, "A Study of the Socio-Economic Effects of Land Reform in Taiwan," pp. 148-153.

[5]In complying with the landlords' request, Tsai has not included this information in his writing.

[6]Fu-ying Chien, "A Landlord Who Met Failure after Land Reform," pp. 3-

[7]Tsai gave this piece of information and the piece mentioned previously (see footnote 5 of this chapter) to the writer in a letter which supplements his master's degree thesis.

[8]Yen-tien Chang, A Case Study on the Impact of Land Reform on Economic and Social Progress in Taiwan.

[9]Annual Business Report of Taiwan's Farmers' Associations, pp. 4-5.

[10]Martin M. C. Yang, A Preliminary Report on the Result of the Second Socio-Economic Survey of Rural Taiwan, p. 14.

[11]Bernard Gallin, Hsin Hsing, Taiwan: A Chinese Village in Change, p. 116.

[12]Ibid, p. 117.

[13]Frank B. Bessac's manuscript, p. 42.

Chapter Twelve

LAND REFORM AND MODERNIZATION OF RURAL LIFE

I. A Recapitulation

II. Modernization

III. Dynamics of Modernization

IV. Characteristics of the New Farmers
    1. Learning and Adopting New Farm Technology
    2. Desire for Education
    3. Productivity
    4. Thought Before Action
    5. Better Planning and Management
    6. Joins Organizations
    7. Broader Perception

V. Other Factors for Modernization
    1. Practical Progress
    2. Social Factors
    3. Industrialization and Urbanization

VI. Modernization of Agriculture
    1. Freedom from Ignorance and Superstition
    2. Freedom from Traditions
    3. Freedom from Fear of Natural Calamities
    4. Freedom from Scarcity of Farm Credits
    5. Positive Features of a Modernized Agriculture

I. A Recapitulation

It has been indicated in these chapters that land reform in Taiwan
has eliminated the injustices of the traditional land tenure and farm-
tenancy systems to a great extent. It has made possible and guaranteed

that the cultivators own the land they cultivate. For the time being,
those who must cultivate land owned by others will get a fair share of
what they have produced. This, too, is provided by law. As a result
of these provisions, the income of farm households has been moderately,
or even greatly, boosted.

Of even greater importance is the revolutionary agrarian change
that has freed the tenant from the bondage and heavy burden inherent in
the traditional landlord-tenant relationship. Although the Chinese
tenant-cultivator had never been as oppressed as Europe's farm serf of
the Middle Ages, his hardship and humility were, nevertheless, sad
enough to qualify him as one of the poor creatures of the world. Land
reform either completely extinguished the landlord-tenant relationship,
as occurred in the land-to-the-tiller program, or made significant guarantees against unsatisfactory practices by the new, farm-lease contracts.
The farmer's actual gain in terms of land acquired, or farm rent saved,
might not have been so very attractive, but his new feeling of being free,
his status as an owner-farmer, and his consciousness of now being the
social and legal equal of his former landlord --- all worked to raise
the morale of the peasants.

Lifted morale generated happiness, hope, and optimism in the farmers'
hearts. These intangibles created the spirit, the power, and the magic
by which bodies and machines could be set in motion.

Optimistic attitude, hopeful outlook, and higher social status joined
forces with tangibles such as land ownership, increased income, saved rent,
and greater security in lease contracts to make the new owner-farmers and
the newly-independent tenant-cultivators enthusiastic and productive farmers

What is even more significant, however, is the new nature of farming and the new agricultural mentality. The new farming is for commercial purposes rather than for the purpose of home consumption. It is varied, progressive, innovative and offers the young people a new kind of challenge equal in its demands to the vitality of their modern educations.

Significant improvements in plant science, animal husbandry, farm technology, and other related fields have been primary factors in changing Taiwan's agriculture after land reform. The increase in profits from farm production and supplementary enterprises brought improvements in living conditions both in material abundance and in non-material and cultural advancements.

One of the ancient Chinese sages said, "Only when people have adequate food and clothing will they begin to be concerned with social relations among their fellow citizens and be conscious of being respected or looked down upon by others." This statement is still true today. For after the farm people had enjoyed improved living conditions for some years, they began to become increasingly involved in civic and social life. Their appreciation of this aspect of life broadened and deepened. In the latter part of the ten-year period after land reform, the Taiwan farmers began entering a large number of primary and secondary community organizations, most of which have defined and positive functions such as participating in agricultural or economic development, education, political reconstruction, personality building, and self-expression.

The extinction of the landlord-tenant relationship, the eradication of improper practices by the new lease contracts, the changing nature of agriculture, the rise of the farm people's socio-economic status and the growing participation of farm people in community affairs have, together, greatly affected the social structure and social relations in farm villages and rural towns. In the process of developing, the new structure tends toward a composition of only one or two levels with numerous sub-groups, each having particular interests or functions. These groups are linked together by cooperation and joint action. Thus, the new structure is no longer chiefly hierarchical; rather, it is egalitarian.

These social changes have, as a matter of course, profoundly changed the power structure in farm villages and rural towns. The village oligarchy is being displaced by a new structure in which a majority of the local populace participate either directly, or indirectly, through modern, democratic election procedures. Leadership in the new power structure can generally be classified into two types: 1) the elected political or administrative leaders, and 2) the leaders in local civic and professional, or special-interest, organizations.

When all these changes are integrated, they form a totally new picture of Taiwan's farm community. The process of integrating these changes may be called the modernization of rural life in Taiwan. This last chapter will sum up the changes, elaborate more fully on the nature and the processes of this modernization, and attempt to deal with the question, "Is land reform a precondition for the modernization of the rural life?"

II. Modernization

Modernization means that people in a community intentionally or unintentionally break away from their old traditions and adopt new thinking, new things, and new practices in their daily life and work. It means

shifting away from undesirable old ways and things to desirable new ways
and things. Things must be desired, because if they are merely new but
not wanted by most of the people, they will not be adopted. There would
be no modernization.

Modernization can be thought of as cultural change. Cultural change
may be revolutionary at one time and evolutionary at another. Most times,
it is evolutionary. Modernization, or the action toward it, may start
overnight in some specific, limited area. But it will take a long time,
numerous pain with many setbacks and reintegrations before a new cultural
complex evolves. In this sense, modernization is a process brought about
as social and cultural change.

Modernization is a continuous taking on of the new and giving up of
the old. There comes a time when most people see that old ways and things
have been supplanted by new ways and things and that a new culture complex
has appeared; it is said that they then have a modern society. In this
sense, modernization is a concrete configuration formed by a set or sets
of things which are new in comparison with those in the past. These two
concepts are not separate or independent from each other. For modernization is a process of change, and a modernized society, or a new culture
complex, is the result of the process of change as seen at a given time.

For example, in an old city, a new building is constructed to take
the place of an old, uncomfortable, and collapsing house; bumpy, dusty,
muddy, and crooked land is rebuilt into a straight, level, solid street
paved with asphalt. This is the beginning of the process of modernization,
the beginning of change from old to new. If the new buildings and the
new street are accepted by most of the dwellers of the city, more new

buildings and new streets will soon be built. New buildings and new
streets soon give rise to other changes. People's minds and behavior
begin to change too. It is possible that in one or two decades most
things in the city, especially material things, will have changed.
Then, the total effect will be a new city. The whole process of change,
from its beginning to the time when people see a new city, is modernization.

There are numerous other concepts of modernization, for modernization
has often been the subject of endless arguments.[1] Among the most controversial concepts are Westernization, industrialization, and democratization.

People from most of the oriental countries are apt to equate modernization with Westernization. This is because most things new and wanted in
oriental countries originally came from, and were later made in imitation
of, the West. From about the nineteenth century cultures of the Western
countries came into favor among oriental peoples. From the beginning of
the twentieth century the oriental peoples started to include Western
things in their life and work. They then learned from the West the knowledge and techniques to make those things themselves in imitation of the
West. Western things took the place of old, traditional things in the
oriental countries where, as a result, new societies and new cultures have
arisen which are similar to those of the West. And so it is that **modernization and** Westernization are synonymous in some people's minds.

The regretful consequence of mistaking Westernization for modernization
is that some people of those countries which were formerly subjugated and
exploited by Western powers and Western cultures have developed a resentment of everything Western. Yet the social and economic changes, the real
modernization of their societies, have led toward Western things. There-

fore, they feel they must say that if this is modernization, they do not want it.

The reason for considering modernization as synonymous with industrialization is also obvious. Most new things of the twentieth century have been the products of industries. Many other things which are not direct products of industries are closely related, or it has been industry which gave rise to them. Furthermore, practically every one of the new civilizations has industries and industrial patterns as one of its chief features. If there has been any significant change in economics, the change must inevitably have come from development of industries. No wonder it is so easy for people to mistake industrialization for modernization.

Some people dislike industrialization or a civilization predominantly industrial and criticize it as too mechanical, too mundane, too lacking in humanity. They are critical of modernization because they identify modernization with industrialization.

Thinking of modernization as democratization is also understandable. Most of the Western countries which have developed new civilizations in the nineteenth and twentieth centuries have taken democracy as their chief political system. Autocracy, oligarchy, and other traditional political systems have been supplanted. Democracy was the most popular type of government in new countries and new cultures until recently when socialism or communism have become great political experiments. In many ways, democracy is closely related to Western cultures and industrial development. Since both Westernization and industrialization have been mistaken for modernization, democratization, too, would, quite naturally, be considered as one aspect of modernization.

Neither Westernization nor industrialization nor democratization is modernization, however. For, as previously stated, modernization is a process of cultural and social change. The results of the process may be the main features of Western civilizations. It is possible, however, that they may not. They may not be exactly the Western things; they may be simply new things; and they may have made the culture, the life, and the work of a community new.

But since most things made in Western countries or in Western patterns are liked by a great majority of the people of the developing countries, the modernization of such countries will tend to be Western. Since most of the world's economic changes and developments are moving toward industrialization, modernization for the developing countries will also have to be predominantly industrial. Only the trend to democratization is, to some extent, avoidable. In many countries modernization in its governmental aspect is not, or may not be, leading toward democracy.

Some people prefer the concept of 'development' to 'modernization.' While the idea and the term 'development' are popular and widely used by people who are in charge of national or international public affairs, 'modernization' as a summing up of all social and cultural change and the characteristics and manner of the change, and as a way to see change in one total configuration or integration, has its own merits or advantages. In the concept of 'development' things must grow, expand, and enlarge. In 'modernization' the essential and universal point is change, numerous kinds of change. If there is no change, there is no modernization. But change may not necessarily move toward expansion or enlargement. In change there are often developments, but not every change is

necessarily a development. For instance, the modernization of men's
dress in certain oriental countries has been a change from traditional
dress to a Western type of dress. In this change, or modernization,
there seems to have been no development. The current concept of
'development' is often used in reference to economic development,
while 'modernization' in this study means change of a total culture.

III. The Dynamics of Modernization

We have used as an example the first building and the first paving in
asphalt as the very beginning of modernization in an old city. But this is
not to say that modernization can be originated in so simple a manner. To
set in motion the modernization of a society or a culture something is needed
which is not only new and widely liked by the people but also has power or
great appeal. In other words, there must be something dynamic to start the
modernization process and keep it moving. While in process, it again needs
dynamics to broaden its scope or dimensions so that all aspects of a society
or culture will be involved in the change.

The above concept may be called the dynamic of modernization. Our
discussion of the modernization of rural life in Taiwan will be chiefly
within this frame of reference. Generally speaking, urban modernization
was started by the industrial revolution. It is known how the industrial
revolution in Europe and North America gave rise to, or set in motion,
numerous forces for change in the civilization. Later on, the industrial
revolution performed the same functions wherever it spread. It is also
to be noted here, but expounded later, that the industrial revolution was
started by change in technology.

In analogy, rural modernization in numerous European countries was begun by land reform. In other words, it was a revolutionary land reform that set in motion the modernization of the rural life of those countries. If land reform were to be able to touch off modernization in these countries, it had to be revolutionary. This meant it had to be a thorough reform, one which did away with all poor practices and irrational principles in tenure and tenancy systems. It was not necessary to have war and killing.

A revolutionary land reform is characterized by the appearance of new freedoms and new vitality as it liberates the hitherto oppressed tenants and peasant farmers from economic oppression, psychological depression, and traditional bondage while simultaneously generating in these newly-liberated land-tillers motivations and energy to improve their work and present living conditions and build for a more prosperous and peaceful life in the future.

The information that has been presented and analysed in this book makes it quite clear that the land reform in Taiwan had been a revolutionary land reform. As we now proceed, we shall first see how the land reform performed its first set of functions, that is, how it contributed to new freedoms.

In the first place, land reform changed the traditional landlord-tenant land tenure into a land-to-the-tiller farm system. This change had freed tenant-cultivators from the domination of landlords and made them independent owner-farmers. The old landlord-tenant relationship had not been all bad, and the ownership of a small piece of land could hardly make any great appeal on the grounds of realistic benefits; but as an incentive, the new freedom, independence, and social status bestowed by land reform did give the new owner-farmers and the new tenant-cultivators hope, together with the prospect that it might be possible from then on to be part of an agriculture of advancement and a life of prosperity. This hope and prospect served as the starting point from which further steps were taken.

The land reform had, secondly, changed the landlord-as-patriarch and tenants-as-household-dependents pseudo-kinship structure to an association of independent, free-willed, individual cultivators who grew to be highly sophisticated farmers. The serious disadvantage of the old structure was that people in such a society accepted everything as it came. They were born into certain statuses, certain families, certain jobs, and certain ways of behavior. If they accepted their fates, most people did not have to do much thinking, did not have to develop their own interests or make choices. If they did work hard and made a struggle, their work and the struggle were according to a traditional pattern and within already de-fined limits. For example, many farmers did work hard and put up battles against natural elements and man-made hinderances; but in the end, when the hard work and hard struggle were done, nothing had changed, and there still was nothing more than the same, age-old, subsistence agriculture. In this kind of agriculture the only goal was that the farmer and his family should be able to exist; nothing more was in the plan.

The preceding two points signify that freedom makes for progress, whereas control and bondage result in stagnation. In traditional societies, control was exercised by the long-established ways in which men worked and lived. People followed traditions as a matter of course. Very little resistance or rebellion ever arose because most of the people were never conscious of the control. If there was agrarian rebellion, it was waged against those who held the authority and had acted to oppress them, or they rose up simply to grab food for survival. They had no thought of rebelling against tradition and the accustomed type of farming. Thus, with or without agrarian rebellion, the rural life as a whole, and farming in particular, for a long time remained the same; there was no change or progress.

Modern controls are instituted and exercised chiefly through central planning. Especially in the areas of economic development, whether in industries, commerce or agriculture, central planning is the key. Central planning means governmental planning, hence Government control. The establishment of a business, its production, marketing, consumption, export, import, all must be controlled by Government. The actors perform exactly according to the Government's minute plans.

Central planning may have different objectives in different countries or societies. The objective may be to build up a military-power state, which can be done only at the expense of the welfare of the general populace; it may be to favor privileged classes so that they may enjoy a full measure of material comforts; or it may be to raise the economic conditions of the masses. But regardless of what the objectives may be, the result of central planning and governmental control is the same in every country-- absence of progress in every aspect of the ordinary man's life. Yet, from the beginning of this century, collectivism has become the dominant view. Intellectuals in nearly every country take for granted that a modern economy should be conducted by centralized control and on five-year or four-year plans.

Milton Friedman made such a statement after his observation tours in Europe and Asia:

Wherever we found any large element of individual freedom, some beauty in the ordinary life of the ordinary man, some measure of real progress in the material comforts at his disposal, and a live hope of further progress in the future--there we also found that the private market was the main device being used to organize economic activity. Wherever the private market was largely suppressed and the state undertook to control in detail the economic activities of its citizens (wherever, that is, detailed central economic planning reigned)--there the ordinary man was in political fetters, had a low standard of living, and was largely bereft of any conception of controlling his own destiny.[2]

The main theme of Friedman's writing is that economic progress can be made only in freedom from detailed or strict state control and that detailed central planning would certainly curtail the initiative and efforts of the people and prevent any real economic development. In fact, not only would planned political fetters kill progress at its beginning, the bondage of obstructive traditions or social institutions could and did actually have the same deadening effect. This Friedman also knows because he says, "In Japan there was a thorough dismantling. of the feudal structure, a vast extension of social and economic opportunity, rapid economic growth, and widespread improvement in the lot of the ordinary man."[3] Whereas "In India there was much lip service to the elimination of caste barriers yet shockingly little actual progress"[4] has been made.

The land reform in Taiwan thoroughly eliminated the evils of the landlord-tenant relationship and freed the rural people from the bondage of most of those traditions which discouraged change and slowed progress. At the same time, the government authorities and a majority of the intellectuals had not been quite convinced of the advantages of modern collectivism or central planning. They left plenty of room for the individual farmers and the individual business people to make their own plans and decisions.[5] As has been pointed out in Chapters X and XI, the recent changes effected in the social and political structures and public leadership by the land reform and its derived influences have created conditions which make the establishment of any detailed governmental control impossible.

Thirdly, the land reform paved the way by which the traditional farming-as-a-living culture changed to a farming-as-a-business culture. The actual change has started and is gaining momentum among farm families and in some special types of farming. For instance, the big banana growers may not particularly enjoy cultivating and harvesting bananas, but they are glad that this special type of farming earns them extra-large amounts of money which makes their lives materially more comfortable, more nearly matching the living standard and pattern of well-to-do city people. This means that these farmers' daily living is gradually becoming separated from their farming. In their minds there are two different sets of thoughts. One set is concerned with farming and the other set is concerned with the family's living. The differences and the distance between the two are becoming wider and wider as farming becomes more and more a business.

In a farming-as-a-living culture, farmers were apt to follow the traditional pattern. Few people ever thought about the matter; fewer had any desire to change it; and still fewer had the courage to make any significant effort for change. The premise was that one was born into a certain kind of living; if one was born into farming, then farming was his living; the ways and type of farming had been established by his ancestors and had become tradition; an easy and safe way of working and living was to follow tradition. Things which change most slowly are things which form the content and the pattern of a people's living, and things which change most rapidly and readily are things which figure in the operation of a business. These facts explain why there had been few changes when farming was a living and many changes when it was operated as a business.

IV. Characteristics of the New Farmers

The result of these basic changes was the birth of a new type of farmer in Taiwan. The characteristics of the new farmer are as follows:

1. Learning and adopting new farm technology. The new farmer is willing and anxious to learn and adopt new technology. At first, farmers were chiefly interested in learning for the sake of increased farm production which, in turn, promised increased resources for home consumption. This was indicated by the fact that in the agricultural-extension services of the several agencies, the farm advisors have been important in numbers and in tasks performed; that the most successful study programs have been the horticulture classes and the tobacco classes; and that from the beginning to the present many people have considered agricultural extension as nothing but giving the farmers farm-production advice.

The interest in production technology was followed by interest in handling and processing harvested products. The Taiwan farmers now sell more and more of their farm products; they raise many more cash crops and livestock for domestic and overseas markets; they know that products for the markets and especially the overseas markets must be handled carefully and according to internationally-standardized methods; and they have also learned that products such as citrus fruits can be marketed more profitably and conveniently if they are first processed. For these reasons, the agricultural-extension workers have recently begun to teach farmers the latest methods of handling and processing farm products.

With increased income farmers' interest in improving their living conditions grew and expressed itself chiefly in their homes and family life. This is why the home-improvement classes which started several years ago are still gaining wider and wider participation. The farmers' willingness and anxiety to learn gave incentive for the invention or discovery of new technology and subsequent frequent changes of technology.

All these factors together have formed one of the important bases for rural progress in general and agricultural advancement in particular.

2. Desire for education. Practically all of the new farmers and their families now wish to have formal or general education and to have as much as they can obtain. They observe the people who have made great successes in professional fields and in civic activities, and they envy people who have a great deal of education. Social status is built on education, and the more education, the better the opportunities for status. The new farmer has cultivated in himself an ambition to get ahead, or at least a desire to be as good as others. He has learned that education is essential for the realization of this ambition.

3. Productivity. Education, when it is adequate in amount and in quality, has the power of enabling the farmer to be alert and adaptable amid ever-changing ideas, techniques, life attitudes, social and economic trends,organizations, and institutional functions. Farmers with these qualities are generally more productive than those who can work only according to established rules and methods. Therefore, productivity is the third characteristic of the new farmer in Taiwan.

4. <u>Thought before action</u>. The new farmer must think before he acts. Because he has broken away from traditions and does not follow the practices laid down by his ancestors, the old ways no longer have the power to bind him. A great advantage in thinking before acting is the opportunity of making comparisons between successful farming and unsuccessful farming, seeing the causes of success and causes of failure while there is a chance to make corrections. Progress will come only to the farmer who can and does make corrections.

When the advantages of thinking before acting have been covered and appreciated, the farmer's personal thinking soon leads to family thinking and to thinking among men in the neighborhood. In the tradition-bound farm household, it has been very difficult to persuade parents and grown-up children to adopt the newly started "Home-and-Farm-One-Unit-Management-Planning" program.[6] These families have not yet been freed from the traditional inhibition of the junior members and women in the presence of the family head, especially the patrician father. But in families whose sons and daughters have attended study groups and whose parents have become so enlightened as to let their children have free voices in family affairs, the family meetings have been very effectively and profitably conducted.

Deliberations among men or women in the neighborhood have become increasingly frequent and influential in the villagers' daily life, for all but a few have become willing to speak out vigorously and exchange ideas. Many of the ordinary farmers have learned to make speeches which are coherent and valuable concerning the results of shared ideas among men of the neighborhood.

It has also been said that in the first few years immediately after land reform, the farmers' thinking was, in general, rough, fragmentary and shallow.[7] At the time when this study took place their thinking had deepened, become systematic, rational, and even refined. Their explanation of events and problems showed considerable advancement in logical thinking. This, too, must have been a result of freedom from the bondage of traditions, of training received from participating in agricultural-extension programs, as well as their own ever-increasing farm experience.

5. Better planning and management. The new farmer does much more planning nowadays than before, and there is an important reason for it. The new farmer owns his land and is free to use it as he chooses, but the amount of land is very limited. His is a very small farm. He must use it wisely or he may endanger the living of his family.

Besides, many new income-producing crops have been introduced to Taiwan in the last decade. New varieties of important crops and livestock have been bred and put in use. New cropping systems, new cultivation methods, new ways of combining several crops or several enterprises into one composite operation, all require the farmer and his family to plan as comprehensively and as carefully as they can. It has to be so before any success can be moderately assured.

The new farmer must understand his nation's economic problems, too. In Taiwan, even in ordinary times, there are a number of crops competing with sugarcane. When the international market in sugar is depressed, farmers would like to plant any crop but sugarcane. But sugar production must be kept going, or the economy of free China would be in great danger. Therefore, the extension workers of the Taiwan Sugar Corporation do their best to keep the farmers in the business of growing cane. It is not enough that the extension workers teach the growers the technical know-how; it is of more importance nowadays to convince them that in the long run, in the total picture of the farm-and-home operation, and specifically in localities where irrigation facilities are not adequate, to keep sugar-cane in a three-year or five-year crop-rotation system is still profitable. The task of convincing them requires a lot of figuring and planning.

It is no wonder then that the farm advisors have begun to shift from teaching know-how to teaching planning and management. Extension education as a whole has begun emphasizing planning, management, evaluation, market-ing, and other considerations in agricultural economics. The previously-mentioned "Home-and-Farm-One-Unit-Management-Planning" program has soon become known to, and appreciated by, numerous farm households, and it is now being extended in several tens of rural townships.

6. _Joins organizations._ The new farmer has learned since land reform to join community organizations and to make realistic use of them. In the old days the farmer also joined some organizations, but his joining was usually in name only or in a negative sense and with a negative attitude, except for a few neighborhood or kinship circles. In the recent years, however, there has been a rapid increase in the number of farmers who take their participation in the farmers' association and its affiliated organi-zations seriously. The chief reason for this change could be that the farmers' associations now perform functions which are closely and vitally involved in the farm people's work and lives. Most farmers now do business with the associations almost daily.

So far, the farmers in Taiwan have joined these organizations chiefly for realistic purposes. They wish to receive all the farm-related and farm-home-related services performed by the organization. They join the various classes because they really learn from them. Social life and recreation are the by-products of the group activities. Another important point is that the participants go voluntarily, of their own interest or choice. Most of the organizations are formed around one or two professional or special interests. If there was persuasion, it has come from the extension workers and was given in the belief that the participation is vital to the family's progress. Their persuasion is not backed by force or bribery. Up to this time, none of the organizations is partisan or politically oriented. In the farmers' associations, farm-and-home classes, fresh fruit marketing cooperatives, etc., no partisan indoctrination or political conversion is being undertaken. The participants show no interest in such things.[8] Finally, the farmers' organizations have not as yet become too numerous, but vigilance must be taken early enough so that the mistake of being over-organized will not be repeated.

7. <u>Broader perception</u>. The new farmer has a much broader awareness, so broad that the likes and dislikes in food consumption of the city people and of people abroad are included in his thinking. Obviously, this is a result of the commercialization of Taiwan's agriculture in recent years. Formerly farmers occasionally sold small amounts of farm produce to dealers in the nearby towns or to collectors who came to the villages, but few ever knew to whom and where their produce eventually went. There-

fore, they had no idea about the people who consumed or made use of their products.

Now the farmers are selling some of their produce all the time and in large quantities for markets at home and abroad. Consumers in the large cities and in foreign countries have all become highly selective in regard to the products' quality, sanitation, grading, packing, beauty, and convenience of handling. The grocery dealers and the people in the farm-produce, marketing organizations have all learned the consumers' likes and dislikes. These people themselves have no time to take care of all these things in order to meet the consumers' demands. They instruct the farmers that when their products are transported to the warehouses of the marketing organizations, they should be prepared in full accordance with national and international standards. At the farm-and-home classes, special crop-study classes, and other agricultural-extension programs, such instructions are repeatedly discussed and demonstrated. The discussions are concerned with the likes and dislikes of consumers in the big cities and in other countries, the city people's and the foreign people's ways of living, their cultures, their histories, etc. Thus, the Taiwan farmers have become national and international-minded. It is in their own interest that they have become so.

In addition, in the last ten years Taiwan has been sending farm-cultivation, demonstration teams to a number of countries in Africa and Southeast Asian countries. Most team members are ordinary, successful farmers. Only the two or three leaders in a team are chosen from among agricultural school graduates. The farmers who have been members on these teams and served two, three, or more years in foreign countries, upon their returning home, must have been effective forces for enlightening other farmers about international affairs and cultures that are different from their own.

African countries which have really been convinced that the farming business in Taiwan is the right kind for them have sent groups of trainees to Taiwan. These trainees have often been brought out to the fields where they worked side by side with the ordinary farmers. These programs also have made considerable contribution to the broadening of the farmers' vision and mind.

V. Other Factors for Modernization

When a large percentage of farmers have the characteristics mentioned above, it means that the people and the inner forces necessary for modernizing rural life are available. Next, the outward conditions should be readied which are the facilities and implements with which the desires and programs of modernization can be put into effect. There must also be supplementary elements by which the newly-made changes can be kept up and expanded. So far as Taiwan is concerned, the land reform had been a precondition for the birth of those factors, facilities, and implements.

1. _Practical progress._ The important outward factors are, of course, the improvements which the Taiwan farmers have achieved in the ten or fifteen years since land reform. Details of the improvements have been treated in Chapters Seven and Eight. Improvements in the farm people's living conditions are largely the result of the increase of production on the farm and in supplementary enterprises. It has been clearly shown

that the increases were stimulated and facilitated by the results of land reform which not only redistributed and rearranged the chief means of farm production but gave farmers incentive to use their means more efficiently and more intelligently. The major portion of the increased production should be attributed to the farmers' new efficiency and intelligence. Improved housing, clothing, health care, and food consumption had been directly, or indirectly, influenced by land reform.

2. Social factors. Modernization has its social aspects and social modernization in rural Taiwan is tied to changes in the various community organizations. Such changes have been enumerated and discussed in Chapters Nine, Ten, and Eleven. Characteristically, most of the changes have been the shift away from landlord or village-gentry domination toward general participation. It can also be said that it has been a change from traditional oligarchy toward modern democracy. It is, however, not necessarily the Western type of democracy.

Another important point in this regard is that the new rural organizations differ from the traditional ones in that the traditional organizations played negative and regulatory roles in the farm people's life, whereas, the new organizations were established chiefly to promote the public welfare and productive activity among the farmers. Briefly, the new community organizations can be divided into two categories: public-administration organizations and farmers' voluntary associations. Organizations of the first category are political and those of the second category are educational. These new organizations have already considerably modernized the social and civic life of rural Taiwan.

In the new community organizations, especially those of the second
category, the participation was widely spread among the farmers in general;
it was not limited to a small, special group. The participation was positive. Every member had a role to play. At meetings everyone was encourage
to speak, to express his own ideas and feelings, to involve himself in grou
actions; and the ideas and actions were all, in some way, related to the
participant's daily life and work. In such organizations the social relations were more egalitarian than hierarchical. Arrangements and connectior
were made between persons and persons, ideas and ideas, things and things,
and between the right kind of persons and the right kind of things. It was
a most intricate, delicate, yet systematic, functioning framework. Within
this framework, each man's free will, voluntary energy, and genuine inspira
tion constituted the 'blood,' the spirit, and the moving power with which
the organization functioned to accomplish whatever was needed for the fulfillment of the rural life, for either individual or community. Not all
the new community organizations were filled with such inspirations or functioned in such a way, but, to a great extent, the successful ones could
exemplify what has been described.

    3. <u>Industrialization and urbanization</u>. Industrialization and urbani-
zation were the other two factors which had a great deal to do with the
modernization of the rural life. Because they were outside of farming and
the rural communities, they should be thought of as supplementary factors.
At any rate, if there had not been these forces, modernization of the rural
life might not have been able to get started or the process might have been
extremely slow. The reasoning is very obvious. It was because of the deve

opment of the textile industry that great quantities and great varieties of
fabric could have become available to city people and then to rural people
at reasonable prices. It was the availability of abundant, high-quality,
and low-priced materials, in conjunction with the farm people's increased
income, that had hastened the modernization of the rural people's clothing. Likewise, it was the development of cement, brick, and glass manufacturing that made it possible for so many farm households to build
new houses or to remodel old ones. The availability of electric light
and power in the farm villages and rural towns, or to say it more specifically, the rural-electrification program had made one of the greatest
contributions to the modernization of Taiwan's rural life. The chief
reasons for the fast expansion of the program were the farmers' great
demand for it and the quick development of the power plants.

One could now find in practically every farm home electric lights,
electric fans, and electric radios. In an increasingly large number of
rural homes, there were also electric cookers, irons, phonographs,
refrigerators, etc. All these things signaled modernization in the
rural homes. But the reason the farmers could afford to have these things
was that the prices were within their financial capability, and this
was possible because all these appliances were manufactured by industries
recently developed in Taiwan.

Up to the time of this study, the industries which had developed in
Taiwan during the last ten or fifteen years and had had great influence
on the modernization of rural Taiwan were: textiles, cement, electricity,
electrical appliances, glass, lumber, rubber and plastics, bicycles and

motorcycles, improved farm implements, garden tractors, metal articles, and new home-furniture manufacturing. For the modernization of country roads, oil refineries made a great contribution by supplying asphalt.

In modernizing rural life, the industries had not only supplied the material articles and facilities, they had also contributed to the change of family life, to the reshaping of the rural household's economy, and to the change of many rural youth's mentality or attitudes. Young people from farm villages found work in industry. After a length of time on the job, they acquired many new ideas, new manners, and new interests or tastes. They brought these back to the farm villages, and changes in the old traditions got underway. Changes in ideas always serve as the driving power for material changes.

Urbanization helped rural modernization in Taiwan in two ways. The material things which made up the specialties of the city life, the surface appearance of urbanization, attracted the rural people. They bought and used these things in their homes too. As a result, there was modernization in the rural life. In the old days city life and objects and technology almost always stayed within the city limits. City people had no inclination to take what they had to the countryside, and few rural people made an attempt to adopt the city people's way of life. So the city ways and the city things stayed in the cities. In the modern times urbanization has expansion as part of its nature, continuous and vigorous expansion. The first targets of this expansion are the rural towns and the farm villages situated on main transportation and communication lines. Once a rural town or a strategic village is reached or invaded by forces of urbanization, change is initiated and the process of modernization begins.

In summary, it seems safe to say that rural Taiwan is well on its way to modernization. Its people had the desire and the psychological preparation for modernization. To a considerable extent they had the objective factors or conditions which were needed for the implementation of the desire and programs of modernization. In addition, growing industrialization and urbanization made it impossible for rural life not to be modernized.

VI. Modernization of Agriculture

However, since the chief livelihood in the rural districts was still predominantly agriculture, the rural people's life and work were still so closely related to this business that there should be no question that unless Taiwan's agriculture had also been significantly and manifestly modernized, the modernization of rural life as a whole would have been halted.

1. Freedom from ignorance and superstition. There are numerous indicators whereby the modernization of Taiwan's agriculture can be discerned and gauged. One indicator is in the amount and kind of freedom farmers had been able to enjoy in the planning and operation of their farming business. There was freedom from ignorance and superstition, superstitions which were results of the farmers' ignorance. If the agriculture was to make significant progress toward modernization, the farmers themselves would have to be educated first.

Because of the relatively high effectiveness of the agricultural-extension education and the widespread general enlightenment among the great masses through mass communication, farmers in Taiwan have begun to enjoy considerable advances toward this freedom although there is still room for improvement.

2. <u>Freedom from traditions and old experiences</u>. The second kind of freedom is freedom from the bondage of traditions and grandfather's experiences. Farmers in the old days were inclined to farm according to tradition and the experiences of their grandfathers because in their mind this was the safest way. In Taiwan, because of the effectiveness of agricultural-extension programs and because of the manifest advantages of the innovations, older farmers had become less sure about merits of traditions and past experiences. The young sons and daughters had simply put those things aside and acted in accordance with what they had seen or learned in classes and at demonstration farms, from reading farm magazines, and through other information-diffusion channels. It is interesting to note that in many farm households, the educated sons and daughters had begun to have voices stronger than those of their parents in planning and operating the family's affairs.

3. <u>Freedom from fear of natural calamities</u>. Third, there began to be some relief from the old, constant dependency on the kindness of nature and fear of her harshness which had made agriculture a business of considerable risks. When there was threat of drought, storm or flood, the farmers could only spread their hands, for they were completely at the mercy of the elements. This kind of agriculture was primitive. In advanced agriculture farmers can do a great deal to control natural calamities, that is, to prevent damage or to minimize it. It is most important of course, to free the farm from the threat of the calamity insofar as possible.

For example, there was a considerable area of dry and hilly land between the counties of Taoyuan, Hsinchu, and Miaoli in the northern part of Taiwan. Until four years ago agriculture in this territory was very poor. Rainfall was very scarce, and no water resource for irrigation was available. Because the land was poor in productivity, living conditions of the farm people in this area had been miserable. An outsider was struck by the extreme poverty in every farm village and the people's apathy. Then, four years ago, the renowned Shishmen Dam was completed and irrigation canals were built into these districts. The dry and hilly land immediately changed to irrigated fields where water is always available when needed. The agriculture drastically changed within less than two years, and one now finds a much different farm picture from that which existed four years ago. The farm people, no longer apathetic, now have strong interest in improving their conditions. The Shishmen Dam, a man-made irrigation facility, gave the farmers freedom from the threat of calamity which in this case was drought.

In the past fifteen or so years Taiwan has done a great deal in building and repairing irrigation facilities and water resources in the dry areas. A new irrigation method was adopted which minimizes waste of water and irrigates more hectares with the same amount of water. The repairing of river banks, the removing of sandbars from river beds, and many kinds of soil conservation projects have helped to prevent or reduce the damage from floods.

Then, as mentioned before, Taiwan had, in the years after land reform, made considerable progress in the control of crop and livestock diseases and pests. This progress had included more effective methods, more effective and cheaper insecticides and fungicides, and better instruments for applying the chemicals.

4. <u>Freedom from scarcity of farm credits</u>. Fourth, there is now freedom from the scarcity of capital and operational funds. When agriculture was in its subsistence stages, the farmer and his family dug or plowed the field with their own labor. Some of them might have an animal to help. They had a few simple tools which might have lasted a number of years. The seeds were saved from the last harvest. Their fertilizers, if any, were homemade compost of animal manures, night-soils, and whatever refuse they could gather. All weeding, cultivation, and irrigation, if any, were also done by the farmer and his family. Occasionally they might have been aided by neighbors or relatives in one way or another. The harvesting was a joint effort among several neighbors working from one family's farm to another's. When the meager crops were gathered inside the home, that year's farming was accomplished. The next year and the next and the next, the same actions were repeated in the same manner. This kind of farming needed very little in the way of capital.

After agriculture entered a more advanced stage, the picture changed. The field to be plowed must be well prepared with improved plows and strong draft animals or power-driven machines. The farm needs to be improved almost every year with fertilizer or productivity-sustaining materials. The seed will be changed at every planting and the new seed will have been produced and certified by authorized, special seed farms. The farmer has to buy at a time not too far away from planting. The planting, cultivation, and all other work of the farm will be done with improved and complicated tools or machines operated by people who have the skill or experience, and they must be constantly repaired and renewed. Operating the mechanized tools requires fuel, oil, electricity, etc. To protect the crops and livestock from diseases and pests, the farmer needs still more expensive materials and tools and skillful labor. Then the harvesting and the handling for market of what has been harvested also needs special implements, special labor, and special transport.

The purpose in mentioning these things is to emphasize the fact that when agriculture is at an advanced stage, there is great need for capital and operational funds. When such funds are available and adequate, the agriculture can be kept at the advanced stage and the advancement may go farther. When such funds are not available or are available only in limited amounts, the agriculture will either be unable to enter an advanced stage or will decline.

In Taiwan such funds have been available. For instance, the latest statistics on farm credits[9] tell us that in 1964 the aggregate amount of farm loans was NT$28,315 million (100%) of which 406 million (1.5%) were long-term loans for the purchase of farms or other durable capital goods; 2,783 million (9.8%) were middle-term loans chiefly for important farm implements or machinery; and 25,126 (88.7%) million were short-term loans mainly for operational funds. In the same year outstanding farm loans totalled NT$5844 million (100%) of which 1,242 million (21.3%) were long-term loans; 1,402 (24.0%) were middle-term loans; and 3,200 million (54.7%) were short-term loans.

A report from JCRR says that in 1966, 237 township farmers' associations made farm loans totaling NT$255 million. More than 77 per cent of these loans were spent on farm equipment. The rest were used as operational funds.[10]

Agencies which provided the farm loans were of three main types: The first type included agencies which specialized in the handling of farm credits, such as the Taiwan Land Bank, the Taiwan Cooperative Bank, and the credit divisions of the farmers' associations. The second type of agency was the commercial bank which made farm loans as a side-line. The third type included such government organizations as JCRR, the Provincial Food Bureau, the Buying and Selling Bureau, the Wine and Tobacco Monopoly Bureau, the Taiwan Sugar Corporation, and the Sugarcane Growers Service Society.

Because farmers are still constantly crying for farm loans, the availability of farm capital and operational funds in Taiwan evidently is still far from adequate. Consequently, a great deal of the potential for modernization of agriculture must have been held back because many of the things which the farmers had wished to do could not be done. This situation might have been greatly improved since 1964 because after 1965 the new owner-farmers no longer needed to put aside the large amount of money for land purchase, and this amount would certainly have been shifted to farm capital and operational funds.

5. <u>Positive features of a modernized agriculture.</u> All the above were freedoms in a negative sense, in that farmers had been freed in varying degrees from those shortcomings or evils. But advanced and modernized agriculture must have positive features and first, it must have an advancing technology.

In the most primitive technology, man worked with his hands and with one or two very simple, primitive tools. In the temperate and cold zones, he worked all day long in order to produce enough for a very simple living.

Later on, people discovered the use of draft animals and a quite sophisticated wooden plow with an iron share. Men were no longer slaves of the
land but masters of the work animals and the plow. Still later, mechanized
farm implements and power-driven machines arrived and the farmer became
master of the machine. Up to this day, in one way, this last stage represents the highest advancement of farm technology. Agriculture that has
this high level of technology is highly-modernized agriculture.

Second, any cultivation method or farm tool which can save the
farmer and his family more time, energy, and cost is considered better
or more advanced than that which cannot accomplish these purposes. This
is another way to measure the advancement of agricultural technology.
The use of method A, for example, cost 100 dollars and made a product worth
500 dollars. Later on method B appeared. The use of method B cost 70
dollars and made a product which was also worth 500 dollars. This was a
technological advancement. Still later on there was method C. The use
of method C cost 120 dollars, but it made a product worth 700 dollars.
Although the cost of method C was larger than that of either A or B,
the net profit from method C was much greater. For this reason, many
people hold that this second kind of technological advance is better than
the first kind, because the second represents a further refinement in
agricultural progress.

Another point is that, in general, people are apt to give most
attention to the improvement of production technique. They are less
likely to think of advancements in harvesting, handling, processing, and
marketing. But in a country where the agriculture is really at the
highest known stage of advancement, production technology is no longer

so important. It is techniques which made the farm products more marketable and helps them to command higher prices from both domestic and overseas consumers, that win customers away from like products supplied by producers using less advanced marketing technology. The produce displays in the supermarkets of the United States of America and in many of the European food markets, when compared with those commodities exhibited in food markets in the less developed countries, give validating support to the above statement.

In Taiwan the advancement of agricultural technology had been uneven up to the time this study was made. One could find all stages of technology, from the first primitive stage to the last power-driven-machine stage. In the mostly poor and backward hills, there were farmers who still did the farm work chiefly by hand and with very simple wooden or bamboo tools. But in the agriculturally rich areas, garden tractors and electrically-operated machines were used by quite a few farm households and the number has been increasing with great speed. Personal observations proved that in a few areas in the western-central parts of Taiwan, the numbers of tractors and the numbers of water buffaloes were about equal to each other. The general impression was that tractors were overtaking the buffaloes. Looking at the picture as a whole, the farm-implement aspect of Taiwan's agricultural technology was then at the mid-point on the route to advancement.

In other aspects the emphasis was still largely on changes which would save time, energy, and cost rather than on changes which might increase the cost but also increase production so much that the final profit would be much greater. It is also true that until very recently, improvements had been made mostly in farm production techniques, and to lesser degrees in methods and facilities for better harvesting, handling, processing, and marketing. But ever since such products as bananas, citrus fruits, pineapples, mushrooms, asparagus, found large markets overseas, attention has been increasingly given to the improvement of methods and techniques of harvesting, handling, processing, and marketing these crops. Shippers of these products made strong appeals to agricultural-extension workers and to the producers themselves to seek fast and effective advancements in techniques for such purposes.

Professor Yi-tao Wang[11] of National Taiwan University divides agricultural techniques into two categories. One category includes techniques which deal directly with the agriculture itself such as techniques of breeding new crop seeds and new livestock varieties, methods of cultivation and feeding, methods of applying fertilizers, methods of controlling insects and diseases, etc. The second category consists of techniques of an engineering nature, such as farm implements, and land improvement. In addition, there are also techniques of farm management, such as general agricultural survey, the keeping of farm records, the basic agricultural survey.

In the last fifteen years Taiwan has made great progress in seed improvements. Numerous improved breeds have been developed in the important crops. There has also been manifest success in the improvement of hog breeds. In cultivation methods there has been significant progress in intercropping, intra-cropping, crop rotation, irrigation, deep plowing, straight-row-dense-planting, application of fertilizers, insect and disease control, etc. The amount of chemical fertilizer applied per hectare of paddy rice increased more than 99 per cent in a twelve-year period from 1952 to 1964. In farm implements we find that in the five years from 1960 to 1965 the number of power-driven sprayers increased 1,316 per cent; water pumps, 283 per cent; tractors, 169 per cent. Professor Wang in his study reached a similar conclusion, that the improvement or advancement in agricultural technology in Taiwan had been chiefly in those things which were used to increase crop or livestock production.

In land improvement Taiwan has started a significant project called Land Consolidation. A pilot project was first run in 1960 in one of the rich farm areas of central Taiwan. When the result was pronounced a success by both the Government and the farmers involved, the whole project was ready for extension. From then on, it has been one of the important farm policies and programs being undertaken by the Government. The principal ideas underlying this project are as follows:[12]

Because of the traditional land tenure, cultivation methods, and inheritance system, the farm land in Taiwan had through many generations become extremely fragmented. Each piece of land was exceedingly small and in shape, very odd or irregular. In many cases the land farmed by one household was separated in a number of pieces which were scattered over several localities. The distance between the farmer's house and a piece of his land could be as great as several li.[13] If it was paddy field, the same irrigation and drainage ditches served many of the pieces; and since they were not separated, the farmer had to extend the ditch to a distant piece of his land across a number of pieces which usually belonged to other families. Consequently, there was much waste of water, and irrigation disputes rose with great frequency between families. The arrangement of farm roads or paths was even more irrational. They were extremely narrow and crooked. It was very difficult to transport loads to or from the fields, yet these numerous roads and paths occupied a considerable amount of the precious land. This had been the traditional picture of Taiwan's farm land familiar to everyone who had been in the countryside. When the farm economy was chiefly one of self-sufficiency, and the agricultural technology was limited to human labor and primitive hand tools, this situation was perhaps not a great disadvantage. In recent days, however, agriculture has become commercialized and the technology has entered the age of mechanization. The old situation has become a great hindrance and obstacle in the way of Taiwan's agricultural advancement.

Land Consolidation is designed to remove the hindrances. Consolidation really includes two main steps of which the first is consolidation, and the second is redivision. The authority must first persuade a group of farm households whose pieces of farm land are in the same area to agree to pool all the pieces together. This is consolidation. Then a committee under the direction of the Government appoints land and other experts to draw up the blueprint of a geographical graph. The boundaries of this graph match, more or less, those of the original area. The total land within the boundaries of the graph is redivided into regularly-shaped and rationally-sized blocks, square or oblong. Farm roads are so arranged that every block can be reached without crossing over another block. The roads must be wide enough for the passage of modern farm machinery and motor vehicles. Irrigation ditches

and drainage facilities are arranged according to the same principle so
that water can get in and get out, directly from and to, the ditches.

After the blueprint has been worked out and everyone involved has
put his signature on it, actual consolidation, redivision, and the
building of roads and water routes take place. When all these are done,
the farmers get their new farms. The block or blocks which a farm
household receives correspond, more or less, to the total amount it
originally owned. If it receives more, the household will agree to
pay for the extra portion according to a price already fixed. If
it receives less, it should get the appropriate compensation.

The merits of the consolidated and redivided farms are that the
size of the new farm is suitable for the use of animal-drawn implements
and power-driven machines; the farmer no longer has to walk back and
forth between a number of widely-scattered pieces of land and, thus,
it could save a great deal of his time and labor; farm management is
more efficient; there are no more difficulties in transportation on
the farm and the former waste of irrigation water will be eliminated;
because of the elimination of many of the old roads, some land has
been saved for the cultivation of crops and, thus, it increases the
total production of the whole farm area.

According to a recent report,[14] the Land Bureau of Taiwan announced
that the Government has made up a plan to accomplish in ten years the
consolidation of 240,000 hectares of the farm land. In the past five years
consolidation of 60,000 hectares has been completed. It is hoped that
by 1977 the farm land of the whole province will have been consolidated.

The second positive feature of an advanced or modernized agriculture is the farmers' capability of making comprehensive and intelligent plans for their farm operation, of making decisions on specialization or diversification, of making best use of the family's farm labor when and if it is available, of making profitable change-over from one kind of enterprise to another, of applying those appropriate principles developed by the agricultural economists, and of making the best and the largest cash gain on a small farm--the most highly-intensified operation.

Comprehensive and scientific planning is a very important feature in advanced agriculture. Reasons for its importance have been elaborated in previous sections of this chapter. Either specialization or diversification can be a feature of the highly advanced agriculture. No primitive or less-developed agriculture is capable of being highly specialized of profitably diversified. Only the highly-advanced, large and rich farms have the needed qualifications. Diversification takes a great deal of calculation, integration, and knowledge of a great number of crops or enterprises to make it a success. In general, the use of much farm labor signifies backwardness of a society's agriculture. In particular cases, however, large amounts of farm labor can be used to produce big profits, as when the farm is too small for mechanized large farm implements but there are good markets for a number of truck-farm products. Large amounts of family farm labor can, to a considerable extent, replace capital and operational funds. The family may be able to produce the finest of products for overseas markets and make good profits. Backward farmers can only plant crops which have been planted through

many generations. When there is great need for change, they dare not
make it because they fear failure. In advanced agriculture, farmers can
make quick and timely changes to avoid big losses and to catch new opportunities. To sum it all up, the total objective was to make the best and
greatest use of the small farm so that it could produce the largest profit.
One could find all these features in Taiwan's agriculture, but they were
present in differing degrees.

In conclusion then, what had been the relationship between Taiwan's
agricultural advancement or modernization and the land reform? Professor
Wang attributes the advancement to a number of factors, such as the
increase of population, the increase of national income, the development
of transportation and communication, the universalization of education,
the financial and technical aids from the United States of America, the
four-year agricultural development plans, functions performed by farmers'
organizations, the availability of farm credits, the development of overseas farm products markets, and the advancement of agricultural technology.
In regard to effects of the land reform, Wang says:

> Due to completion of the land reform the percentage of owner farm-
> ers increased tremendously and the number of tenant cultivators
> decreased relatively. As a result, the distribution of farm land
> has been greatly corrected and the farm tenancy became rational.
> The greatest effects on the farmers have been the lifting of their
> morale, the transfer of land ownership, and the security of the
> farm lease right. Through the farm rent limitation act the tenant
> cultivators can now get a larger share of the results of their
> labor. Under all these effects the farmers have become deeply
> interested in the improvement of the farming business. They are
> doing the best to increase the farm equipments and the operational
> funds. In one word, since land reform the new owner farmers and
> the new tenant cultivators all increased considerably the input of
> funds and labor in the farm operation. The degree of intensifica-
> tion has raised a great deal.[15]

This is a fair statement. Land reform gave the farmers incentive and a base whereby they started to improve their farming. The improvement has been so extensive that their living conditions in general and the conditions in specific areas have undergone progressive changes. These changes made the land tillers interested in education in general and in learning new and better farm technology in particular. Because of their new morale, their higher social status, their improved living conditions, and their possession of education, the new farmers have also become enthusiastic about community participation and taking part in various civic organizations. As a result, the social structure, power structure, and public leadership in the farm villages and rural townships have experienced significant changes, or changes there have begun. Furthermore, due to the effectiveness of the agricultural-extension education, the mass communication media, the expanded marketing of farm products, and other inspirational and mind-broadening factors, a majority of the younger farmers have acquired characteristics which qualify them as people of a modern world. Thus, the rural life in Taiwan is on the way to modernization.

Notes

[1] In the academic year 1966-67, the senior specialists of the Institute of Advanced Projects of the Center for Cultural and Technical Interchange Between East and West adopted "Modernization" as the subject for discussion at their seminars. Arguments regarding its meaning or definition and its different concepts lasted more than ten sessions. Participation was wide and the atmosphere extremely enthusiastic. Sociologists and cultural anthropologists were apt to treat the subject academically or scholarly, whereas people from developing countries were likely to be caught by concepts such as Westernization, industrialization, democratization, etc.

[2] Milton Friedman, The Easy Chair: Myths That Keep People Hungry, Harper's Magazine, April, 1967, p. 16.

[3] Ibid., p. 22.

[4] Ibid., p. 22.

[5] Taiwan has also made and implemented several four-year plans of economic development. In agriculture the chief efforts have been directed to the increase of per-unit production of important crops through the improvement of technology and aids from the Government. Only the chemical fertilizer and the price of rice are now under Government control. This control is retained to encourage farmers to grow rice to assure the adequacy of food of the whole population and to see that the

price of such a basic commodity does not fluctuate so much as to threaten

the Province's economy. In industries the Government efforts have also

been directed more to assistance than restriction.

[6]A new agricultural economics-program was initiated experimentally in

Taiwan by Professor Arthur Peterson of Washington State University in

cooperation with the agricultural economics departments of National Taiwan

University, Provincial Chunghsing University and five township farmers

associations, with some financial assistance from the Agricultural Devel-

opment Council, New York. The experiment was started in 1962 and expan-

ded into a program which is now being promoted in several counties. It

is in the joint charge of the Provincial Government's Department of

Agriculture and Forestry; the farmers program is that the adult members

of a farm family should hold family meetings at which the family's home

economics and farm operations are discussed as one economic unit and all

family members are encouraged to express ideas, suggestions and experience,

and to make joint decisions. In the management of home and farm, every

member is assigned a specific role and fulfills specific obligations.

The family meetings are to be held as frequently as the need arises to

review and evaluate the operation.

[7]According to persons of JCRR who had been in charge of the First

Socio-Economic Survey of Rural Taiwan in 1953, the local leaders of the

rural communities showed this kind of thought at the township forums.

The situation changed greatly in 1959 and was still better in 1964.

[8]The person who has first responsibility for the organization and

promotion of sugarcane classes is a member of the ruling party and an

official in the Sugar Corporation. The Kuomintang doxology is read at the opening of each class meeting. As pointed out previously, the party

man and the reading of the doxology play no more important role at the

meeting and the enrollers simply ignore this part. However, any attempt

to turn a farm-study group into a partisan organization will eventually

defeat all its purposes, including the party's objective. The party

authority ought to take warning from the utter failure of the Communists

in this respect.

[9] Yi-tao Wang, "Agricultural Development in Taiwan." (Chinese) in
The Taiwan Land Finance Quarterly, Vol. III, No. 4, December, 1966, pp. 12-13

[10] The Central Daily News, February 8, 1967.

[11] Yi-tao Wang, "Agricultural Development in Taiwan," pp. 14-18.

[12] "Land Consolidation in Taiwan" by Yi-tao Wang and Chi-lien Hwang, in
The Taiwan Land Finance Quarterly, Vol. III, Nos. 2 and 3, June and September, 1966.

[13] This li is a geographical distance unit. Approximately 3.3 li equal
1 mile.

[14] The Central Daily News, February 16, 1967.

[15] Yi-tao Wang, "Agricultural Development in Taiwan," p. 10.

BIBLIOGRAPHY

The Agrarian Reform Law of the People's Republic of China; together with
    Other Relevant Documents. Peking: Foreign Languages Press, 1950.

Arneson, B. E. The Democratic Monarchies of Scandinavia. 2nd ed. New York:
    D. Van-Nostrand Co., 1949.

Bessac, Frank B. "The Field Research Concerning the Social Consequences of
    the Land Reform in Taiwan." Manuscript, University of Montana, 1965.

Chang, Yen-tien. A Case Study on the Impact of Land Reform on Economic and
    Social Progress in Taiwan. Taipei: 1965.

Chien, Fu-ying. "A Landlord Who Met Failure after Land Reform." Manuscript
    in Chinese, 1966.

Chow, Yung-teh. Social Mobility in China. New York: Atherton Press, 1966.

Danstrup, John. A History of Denmark. Lindberg: Copenhagen Wivel, 1948.

Denmark Politics and Government, 1849-1866. In Danish, 1959.

Dore, R. P. Land Reform in Japan. 1959.

Flores, Edmundo. Land Reform in the Alliance for Progress. Princeton:
    Center of International Studies, Woodrow Wilson School of Public and
    International Affairs, Princeton University Press, 1963.

Fried, Morton H. Fabric of Chinese Society: A Study of the Social Life of
    A Chinese County Seat. New York: Praeger, 1953.

Friedman, Milton. "The Easy Chair: Myths that Keep People Hungry."
    Harper's Magazine. April, 1967.

Fuma, Elias H. Twenty-six Centuries of Agrarian Reform: A Comparative
    Analysis. Berkeley: University of California Press, 1965.

Galalla, Sead M. Land Reform in Relation to Social Development in Egypt.
    1962.

552

Gallin, Bernard. Hsin Hsing, Taiwan: A Chinese Village in Change. University of California Press, 1966.

Grad, Andrew Jonah. Problems of Agrarian Reform in Japan. New York: International Secretariat, Institute of Pacific Relations, 1945.

Ho, Wei-ming. The Developing of Marketing and the Utilization of Agricultural Resources. Manuscript in Chinese, Taipei: Joint Commission of Rural Reconstruction, November, 1966.

Howe, F. C. Denmark: The Cooperative Way. New York: Coward-McCann Inc., 1937.

Hsieh, S. C.; Lee, T. H.; Wang, Y. C., and Teng, Y. L. A Study of the Operation of the Small Farms in Taiwan. In the Taiwan Bank Quarterly. Vol. XII, No. 3.

Joint Commission of Rural Reconstruction. JCRR General Report X. Taipei: 1959.

Kirby, E. Stuart. Rural Progress in Taiwan. Taipei: Joint Commission of Rural Reconstruction, 1960.

Klein, Sidney. The Pattern of Land Tenure Reform in East Asia after World War II. New York: Bookman Associates, 1958.

Kuo, M. H. Farmers' Associations and Their Contributions toward Agricultural and Rural Development in Taiwan. Bangkok: FAO Regional Office for Asia and the Far East, 1963.

Lauwerys, J. A., ed. Scandinavian Democracy. Development of Democratic Thought and Institutions in Denmark, Norway, and Sweden. Published by the Danish Institute (det Danske Selskab), the Norwegian Office of Cultural Relations, and the Swedish Institute, in cooperation with the American Scandinavian Foundation. Copenhagen: 1958.

Liu, Ching-yung and Yang, Martin M. C. A Study of the Results of Agricultural Extension in Taiwan. Taipei: Department of Agricultural Extension, National Taiwan University, 1964.

Lu, Nien-tsing. An Analysis of Farm Family Economy of Owner Operations under the Land-to-the-Tiller Program in Taiwan. Taipei: Research Institute of the Land Bank of Taiwan, 1966.

Mannich, Peter. Living Democracy in Denmark. Toronto: Ryerson Press, 1952.

Mitchell, C. Clyde. Land Reform in Asia: A Case Study Prepared for the NPA Agricultural Committee on National Policy. Washington National Planning Association, 1952.

Mitrany, David. The Land and the Peasant in Rumania: The War and Agrarian Reform (1917-1921). London: H. Milford Oxford University Press; New Haven: Yale University Press, 1930.

National Government of the Republic of China. The Land Law. (The Land Law that was promulgated on June 4, 1930; enforced, March, 1936; and amended, April 29, 1946.)

Neale, Walter C. Economic Change in Rural India: Land Tenure and Reform in Uttar Pradesh, 1800-1955. New Haven: Yale University Press, 1962.

Nelson, Lowrey. Land Reform in Italy. Washington: National Planning Association, 1956.

Rowntree, Benjamin Seebohn. Land and Labour: Lessons from Belgium. London: Macmillan and Co., 1910.

Royal Institute of International Affairs. Agrarian Reform in Latin America. Oxford: Oxford University Press, 1962.

Semon, Sir Ernest D. The Smaller Democracies. London: V. Gollanez Ltd., 1939.

Senior, Clarence Olson. Land Reform and Democracy. Gainsville: University of Florida Press, 1958.

Singh, Baljit. Next Step in Village India, A Study of Land Reform and Group Dynamics. Asia Publishing House, 1961.

Smith, Thomas Carlyle. The Agrarian Origins of Modern Japan. Stanford: Stanford University Press, 1959.

Socio-Economic Research Division (Planning Commission). Seminar on Land Reforms, Proceedings, and Papers. SER Publication, Seminar Series No. 1. New Delhi: 1966.

Taiwan Provincial Farmers' Association. The Accomplishment of Agricultural Extension Education Work in Taiwan during 1958. Taichung: 1959.

Taiwan Provincial Government. Regulations Governing the Lease of Private Farm Lands in Taiwan Province. Taipei: 1949.

-----. Taiwan Province Agriculture Yearbook. Taipei: 1965.

-----. Annual Business Report of Taiwan's Farmers' Associations. Taipei: 1965.

Taiwan Sugar Corporation. "Observation Tour on Sugarcane Experiment Farm Testing the High Production Varieties." Taiwan Sugar Corporation Information Bulletin. Vol. 36, No. 18, 1966.

554

-----. "Observation Tour on Farmer Heng Hsien-wu's F152 Sugarcane Farm."
Taiwan Sugar Corporation Information Bulletin. Vol. 36, No. 18, 1966.

-----. A Report on the Organization of Sugarcane Production Study Classes.
1966.

-----. "The Organization and Functions of the Sugarcane Production Study
Classes." Taiwan Sugar Corporation Information Bulletin. Vols. 36
and 37, 1966.

Tang, Hui-sun. Land Reform in Free China. Taipei: Joint Commission of
Rural Reconstruction, 1955.

Teng, Tsu-jui. The Outstanding Success of Agrarian Reform Movement in China
1st ed. Peking: Foreign Languages Press, 1954.

Teng, Yi, ed. Facts about the Implementation of the Land-to-the-Tiller
Program in Taiwan. 1955.

Tsai, Hung-chin. "A Study of the Socio-Economic Effects of Land Reform in
Taiwan." Master's thesis in Chinese, Graduate Institute of Rural Socic
Economic Studies, National Taiwan University, 1965.

Udenrigsministeriet Denmark. Copenhagen: Danish Statistical Department, 19

United Nations. Department of Economic and Social Affairs. Progress in Lar
Reform. Third Report. New York: 1962.

Wang, Yi-tao. "Agricultural Development in Taiwan." The Taiwan Land Finan
Quarterly. Vol. III, Nos. 2 and 3, June and September, 1966.

Wang, Yi-tao and Hwang, Chi-lien. "Land Consolidation in Taiwan." The Tai
Land Finance Quarterly. Vol. III, Nos. 2 and 3, June and September, 19

Warriner, Doreen. Land Reform in the Middle East; A Study of Egypt, Syria
Iraq. 2nd ed. London, New York: Royal Institute of International
Affairs, 1962.

Weld, William Ernest. Agrarian Reform in Yugoslavia, Romania, and Czecho-
slovakia; Changes in Land Tenure in Foreign Countries. New York: 19

Westergaard, Harold Ludwig. Economic Development in Denmark before and dur
World War I. Oxford: The Clarendon Press, 1922.

Wu, Tseng-shieh. A Study on the Diffusion of Agricultural Information.
Department of Agricultural Extension, National Taiwan University, 1964.

Yang, Martin M. C. A Chinese Village: Taitou, Shantung. New York: Columb
University Press, 1945.

-----. A Preliminary Report on the Result of the Second Socio-Economic Survey of Rural Taiwan. Department of Agricultural Economics, National Taiwan University, 1960.

-----. "Changes in Family Life in Rural Taiwan." Journal of the China Society. Vol. III, 1965.

-----. "Changes in Agricultural Technology Affecting the Rural Community." Unpublished manuscript in Chinese, National Taiwan University, 1965.

ACKNOWLEDGMENTS

This study was made possible by a grant from the Agricultural
Development Council, Inc., formerly the Council on Economic and Cultural
Affairs Inc., in New York. The awarding of the grant was due largely to
the intrinsic merits of, and the call for, such a study. But it was due
also to the favorable recommendations given by Dr. A. B. Lewis, the
Council's associate in agricultural economics for the Far East region,
and by Dr. William H. Sewell, professor of Sociology of the University
of Wisconsin, who had come to Taiwan with Dr. Lewis to obtain first-hand
information regarding the need and feasibility of such a study. The two
scholars together reviewed the proposed outlines of the study and made
many valuable suggestions. Another person who gave support to my
application for financial assistance from the Council was Professor
Arthur W. Peterson of Washington State University, who was then visiting
professor of agricultural economics at National Taiwan University. He
himself had made several field studies about Taiwan's agricultural
economy in the years from 1962 to 1964; and he participated in the
discussions in the planning stage of this study. Other scholars who
gave help in one way or another at this stage were Dr. Jack C. Ferver,
agricultural extension advisor from Michigan State University to
National Taiwan University, and Dr. A. T. Mosher, then executive
director of the Agricultural Development Council.

Regarding the content or the important topics of the study and the kinds of people upon whom the study was going to be made--the population from whom the necessary data were to be gathered--I received good suggestions from the aforementioned Dr. Lewis, Professor Sewell, and Professor Peterson; and also from Professors Y. T. Wang and T. T. Chang of the Department of Agricultural Economics of National Taiwan University. My colleagues Mr. Ching-yung Liu and Mr. Heng-chin Tsai, in the Department of Agricultural Extension, NTU, also offered useful ideas and information. I consulted with the late Dr. Hui-sen Tang, who played a very important part in the designing and implementation of the land reform in Taiwan, and with Mr. Wen-chia Wang, professor and chairman of the Department of Land Administration of Provincial Chung-hsing University.

The preparation of the various questionnaires for interviewing the samples of the ten kinds of people and the carrying out of the field interview of the more than three thousand samples had been exacting tasks. In the performing of these tasks, help came from a group of thirty-five splendid young people. Five of them served as field-interview team leaders, whose responsibilities were to supervise the interviewers while they were doing the interview in the field and to keep up their morale whenever depression appeared. They were Messrs. Ching-yung Liu, Heng-chin Tsai, Yung-chang Lee, Tsong-shien Wu, and Tien-seng Wang; four of them were faculty members of the Department of Agricultural Extension. The thirty interviewers were largely senior or junior students of the same department. They all endured tremendous amounts of the summer heat and the hardship of traveling across the rough countryside and the steep hills and of finding the sample families not in a mood for interviewing or not cooperative. To them--listed alphabetically in the following--I wish to extend my deep appreciation: Cheng-nan Chang, Hui-hsing Chen, Kuo-hui Chen, Cheng-nan Chien, Fu-ying Chien, Chao-hsing Chuang, Chao-shih Chung, Shun-liang Heng, An-tien Hsieh, Yee-ho Hsu, Ming-tu Li, Wu-nan Li, Cheng-heng Liao, Cheng-tseng Lin, Chien-yee Lin, Min-hsing Lin, Tsu-hui Lin, Chia-chin Liu, Hsiu-nan Lu, Chun-lin Pan, Ching-hsin Shih, Wen-lung Tai, Chun-nan Tsai, Chih-huang Tuan, Chi-chi Wang, Chang-fu Wang, Min-sheng Wu, Hsin-kao Yeh, and Fu-sung Yen.

The big field interview, or the collection of data from the more than three thousand samples of the ten categories of people, was satisfactorily accomplished in the middle of August, 1964. The processing of the field data, the gathering of additional information from existing literature, and the undertaking of a number of case studies were being done in a ten-month period immediately following the field survey. Messrs. Ching-yung Liu, Heng-chin Tsai, and Tien-seng Wang continued to give their assistance in supervising the data processing as well as in locating materials dealing with the results of, and the people's reaction toward, the land reform. Those who did the processing of the field data were Miss Ya-min Ho and Messrs. Ching-nan Li and Wan-tsun Lu.

The processing of the field data and the collection of additional materials from other sources were all finished at the end of July, 1965.

The writing of a report--which I was to do--on the results of the study should have been started immediately after the completion of these tasks. But I was so preoccupied by teaching, research, and administrative responsibilities in the Department of Agricultural Extension that I found it difficult to find any one day to do any serious writing. I started to write and then stopped it a number of times.

It was about this time that I received a proposal from the Institute of Advanced Projects of the Center for Cultural and Technical Interchange between East and West in Honolulu, Hawaii, suggesting that, if interested, I may accept a grant from the East-West Center and go there to do any research project that I might have in mind and to participate in seminars that are to be conducted for the purpose of cultural and technical interchange between East and West. I accepted the invitation and went to Honolulu at the beginning of September, 1966. The East-West Center authorities, especially Dr. Minoru Shinoda, director of the Institute of Advanced Projects, were so kind that they allowed me to do nothing but write a manuscript entitled "Socio-Economic Results of Land Reform in Taiwan"--which took the place of the report on the results of the aforementioned study. I used ten months, which meant my whole term at the East-West Center, to finish the writing. Needless to say, I was able to complete the last but most important phase of the study by the invitation and the grant from the East-West Center.

When the writing was in its preparatory stage I kept thinking that it cannot and should not be merely a report on many itemized

facts; but rather that it must tell a story or stories about how the land reform was started and carried out and how the reductions had been for the tenant-farmers, the landlords, and people in other walks of life; and that this story should reveal (1) whether the rural life as a whole has been significantly affected by the land reform and (2) how the other factors or forces worked together or upon the effects of the land reform in changing the conditions of rural Taiwan. To accomplish such purpose or purposes, the scope of the writing had to be expanded considerably and the kinds and amount of materials and data had to be increased immensely.

About the scope of the writing, I decided to write a medium-sized book instead of a report. I prepared a detailed tentative outline and distributed it among my colleagues of the Senior Specialists Program, of the Institute of Advanced Projects, and among about a dozen professors of the University of Hawaii. Many of them responded kindly and gave me valuable comments and suggestions. Special mention is due Professors Perry F. Philipp, Heing Spielmann, and Joseph T. Keeler, who are all of the Department of Agricultural Economics of the University of Hawaii. Professor Philipp's suggestions were so valuable and important that they made me re-write the whole outline, with a totally changed organization of the materials. Dr. Spielmann and Dr. Keeler each made a number of suggestions that certain additional topics and discussions be included in the writing. The senior specialists of the Institute of Advanced Projects had specially arranged a seminar at which they discussed the land reform in Taiwan and offered comments about the content of the proposed book. There were responses also from people in Taiwan; special gratitude is due Professor Wen-chia Wang because several of his suggestions helped to add to the total content, the lack of which would have constituted a serious shortcoming to this book.

In the task of collecting more information and materials, significant help came from Messrs. Ching-ying Lin and Heng-chin Tsai. The two either jointly or separately collected and sent me a number of books, bulletins, monographs, and pamphlets. Without this help, the completion of the writing might have had to be considerably delayed. Here, too, Professor Wen-chia Wang also sent me three of the books that I needed very badly.

When four chapters of the first draft of the manuscript were finished, forty copies of them were mailed to scholars and specialists on land reform, in different places over the world, to solicit comments and criticisms. This purpose was fulfilled--comments, criticisms, information, and encouragement came in from various persons. I was especially grateful to Dr. A. B. Lewis, whose letter has been used as a footnote in the manuscript. Sincere comments also came from three Indian scholars whose names are Dr. C. H. Shah, leader of agricultural economics of the University of Bombay; Dr. Shah, a senior member of an agricultural economics research institute in India; and Dr. M. B. Desai, head of the Department of Agricultural Economics, University of Borada, India.

While I was preparing the writing of chapters eleven and twelve, I sent a list of ideas and topics to Messrs. Hunter H. C. Chiang, Ta-

chou Hung, Li-chin Ma, Ching-yung Liu, and Heng-chin Tsai, of the Department of Agricultural Extension of National Taiwan University, for discussion and collection of materials. They gave me the results of their discussions, which were very useful, and sent me most of the references I asked for; Mr. Ma wrote me a special letter expressing his own ideas on each of the points on the list.

I wrote the manuscript in English, which is not my native tongue. Upon my request, the East-West Center kindly engaged Mrs. Grace Merrits, a student counselor of the University of Hawaii, to correct and polish my English. I am grateful to both for this help.

This acknowledgment cannot be complete without the mention of the good services given by Mrs. Hazel O. Tatsuno, Mrs. Arline Uyeunten, and other members of the staff of the Senior Specialists Program. These ladies did all the typing, mimeographing, and mailing of the first draft and of the edited copy of the manuscript. They also took care, on my behalf, of all the details pertaining to the writing of the book. My morale was kept high by their sweetness and kindness.

Martin M. C. Yang